Africa Bible Commentary Series

General Editors

Old Testament
Dr Nupanga Weanzana

New Testament
Dr Samuel Ngewa

Advisors

Tokunboh Adeyemo, Solomon Andria, Issiaka Coulibaly,
Tewoldemedhin Habtu, Samuel Ngewa, Yusufu Turaki

Africa Bible Commentary Series

1 & 2 TIMOTHY AND TITUS

Samuel Ngewa

© 2009 Samuel Ngewa

Published 2009 by HippoBooks, an imprint of ACTS and Langham Publishing.

Africa Christian Textbooks (ACTS), TCNN, PMB 2020, Bukuru 930008, Plateau State, Nigeria. www.actsnigeria.org

Langham Publishing, PO Box 296, Carlisle, Cumbria, CA3 9WZ, UK
www.langhampublishing.org

ISBNs:
978-1-78641-265-2 Print
978-1-78368-663-6 ePub
978-1-78368-665-0 PDF

Samuel Ngewa has asserted his right under the Copyright, Designs and Patents Act, 1988 to be identified as the Author of this work.

All rights reserved. No part of this publication may be reproduced, stored in a retrieval system or transmitted, in any form or by any means, electronic, mechanical, photocopying, recording or otherwise, without the prior written permission of the publisher or the Copyright Licensing Agency.

All Scripture quotations, unless otherwise indicated, are taken from the Holy Bible: Today's New International Version™. TNIV®. Copyright © 2001, 2005 by International Bible Society®. All rights reserved worldwide.

British Library Cataloguing-in-Publication Data
A catalogue record for this book is available from the British Library

ISBN: 978-1-78641-265-2

Cover Design: projectluz.com

Cover Design: To a Tee Ltd, www.2at.com

The publishers of this book actively support theological dialogue and an author's right to publish but do not necessarily endorse the views and opinions set forth here or in works referenced within this publication, nor guarantee technical and grammatical correctness. The publishers do not accept any responsibility or liability to persons or property as a consequence of the reading, use or interpretation of its published content.

Dedication

This book is dedicated to all the pastors and Bible teachers whom the Lord has provided me with an opportunity to train for service in the kingdom of God. All those who call me Mwalimu (Teacher) are a blessing to my heart, beginning with the students I taught at Mukaa Bible School, and continuing with the students at Ukamba Bible College, Scott Theological College and now at the Nairobi Evangelical Graduate School of Theology. May the Lord bless his people through each of us as we use this book to understand, preach and teach The Book better.

CONTENTS

Introduction to the Africa Bible Commentary Series xvii
Foreword to 1 & 2 Timothy and Titus............. xix
Acknowledgements.................................. xxi
Abbreviations..xxii

Introduction to the Pastoral Epistles.............. 1

1 TIMOTHY

Unit 1 1 Timothy 1:1–2
Making Contact 7
    The Author... 8
    The Recipient 9
    The Greeting.. 10

Unit 2 1 Timothy 1:3–7
Timothy's Mission.................................... 12
    The Push.. 12
    The Place 13
    The Job Description 14
    The Goal.. 15
    A Case in Point....................................... 16

Unit 3 1 Timothy 1:8–11
The Proper Use of the Law 19
    Nature of God's Law.................................. 19

Who Needs the Law 20

Unit 4   1 Timothy 1:12–14

Paul's Personal Reflection 24
    Paul's Present 25
    Paul's Past. 26

Unit 5   1 Timothy 1:15–20

The Unchangeable Truth 29
    The Nature of Truth 30
    Paul's Response to the Truth. 30
    The Response Required. 33
    Deviators from the Truth 35

Unit 6   1 Timothy 2:1–8

Paul's Call to Prayer 38
    Components of Prayer. 39
    Who to Pray For 40
    What to Pray For. 41
    Who We Pray To. 42
    What Makes Prayer Possible 43
    Paul's Role 45
    How to Pray 47

Unit 7   1 Timothy 2:9–15

Women and Godliness 49
    Clothing 50
    Authority 51
    Childbearing. 55
    Contemporary Application 56

Unit 8   1 Timothy 3:1–7

Overseers, Pastors and Teaching Elders 59
    The Role of an Overseer 60
    Qualifications of an Overseer. 60

Unit 9   1 Timothy 3:8–13

The Role of a Deacon 71
    Qualifications of Deacons 72
    Appointment of Deacons................................. 74
    The Reward for Good Service 74
    Women Deacons... 76
    Concluding Observations 77

Unit 10   1 Timothy 3:14–16

Paul's Reason for Writing 79
    Practical Reasons for Writing........................... 80
    Theological Reason 82

Unit 11   1 Timothy 4:1–5

Gathering Storms 85
    What To Expect 86
    Why Some Will Fall....................................... 87
    Refuting False Teachings................................ 88

Unit 12   1 Timothy 4:6–16

Timothy's Role 93
    Summary.. 94
    Details... 96

Unit 13   1 Timothy 5:1–2

People Management 107
    Relating to Older Men 107
    Relating to Younger Men 108
    Relating to Older Women............................... 109
    Relating to Younger Women........................... 109

Unit 14   1 Timothy 5:3–16

Relating to People in Need 111
    Who Qualifies for Support? 112
    Who Doesn't Qualify for Support?.................... 114
    Meeting Needs Today.................................... 121

  CASE STUDY – Practical Care for Widows 124

Unit 15 — 1 Timothy 5:17–23

Relating to Church Elders ... 125
- Honour Elders ... 126
- Be Wary of Accusations ... 128
- Rebuke Sin Publicly ... 129
- Avoid Favouritism ... 130
- Don't Rush Things ... 132
- Live a Life above Reproach ... 133

CASE STUDY – A Leader's Social Skills ... 136

Unit 16 — 1 Timothy 5:24–25

Sin and Good Deeds ... 136
- Obvious and Hidden Sin ... 137
- Obvious and Hidden Good Deeds ... 138

Unit 17 — 1 Timothy 6:1–2a

Masters and Slaves ... 141
- Slavery in the New Testament World ... 142
- Relating to Masters in General ... 144
- Relating to Christian Masters ... 145
- Conclusion ... 146

Unit 18 — 1 Timothy 6:2b–12

Sound Doctrine and Godliness ... 147
- Teach These Things ... 148
- Definition of Sound Teaching ... 148
- Character of False Teachers ... 149
- Contentment ... 151
- Timothy's Role ... 156

Unit 19 — 1 Timothy 6:13–21

Concluding Charge ... 161
- Witnesses to the Charge ... 161
- The Substance of the Charge ... 162
- Prayer ... 165

2 TIMOTHY

Introduction to 2 Timothy 169

Unit 1   2 Timothy 1:1–3

Making Contact 171
    Author 171
    Recipient... 172
    Greetings 172
    Paul's Attitude to Timothy 173
  CASE STUDY – Relationships Between Pastors 175

Unit 2   2 Timothy 1:3–7

Words of Encouragement 177
    Models of Love and Service................ 177
    Timothy's Faith.................................. 179
    A Challenge 180
    Meeting the Challenge 182
  CASE STUDY – Children and Faith 185

Unit 3   2 Timothy 1:8–10

A Call to Suffering............................... 187
    A Call for Courage 188
    God's Call.. 190
    Our Saviour 192

Unit 4   2 Timothy 1:11–18

The Example of Paul 196
    Paul's Model of Ministry.................... 196
    Paul's Model of Suffering 197
    An Example of Suffering 199
    Prayer for the Dead?.......................... 201
    Timothy's Ministry 202

| Unit 5 | 2 Timothy 2:1–7 |

Endurance in Suffering 206
- The Power behind Endurance 207
- The Fruit of Endurance 208
- Models of Endurance 210
- The Overall Lesson 215

| Unit 6 | 2 Timothy 2:8–13 |

Encouragement in Suffering 217
- Remember Jesus Christ 218
- Remember Paul's Example 220
- The Unchangeable Promise 222
- Remember! 227

| Unit 7 | 2 Timothy 2:14–16, 22 |

Ministry to Others and Our Personal Lives 228
- Ministry to Others 228
- Personal Qualities 231

| Unit 8 | 2 Timothy 2:17–21 |

Honour or Dishonour? 240
- Who Not to Imitate 240
- What to Trust 242
- God's Grading System 245
- On the Honour Roll 247

| Unit 9 | 2 Timothy 2:23–26 |

The Marks of a Good Leader 249
- Not Quarrelsome 249
- Kind to Everyone 251
- Able to Teach 251
- Not Resentful 252
- Gently Instructing Opponents 252

Contents   xiii

Unit 10   2 Timothy 3:1–5a

Characteristics of the Last Days 257
The Challenge Ahead 258
Characteristics of the Last Days 258
Characteristics of People in the Last Days 259

Unit 11   2 Timothy 3:5b–9

People to Avoid 269
Stay Away from Evil People 270
Five Reasons to Stay Away from Them 271

Unit 12   2 Timothy 3:10–17

Words of Wisdom 278
Paul's Example 279
Expect Persecution 282
Timothy's Responsibility 283
Timothy's Roots in Scripture 285

Unit 13   2 Timothy 4:1–2, 5

Paul's Final Charge to Timothy 290
Divine Witnesses 290
The Basis for the Charge 292
The Content of the Charge 293

Unit 14   2 Timothy 4:3–4, 6–8

Problems and Rewards 299
The Urgency of the Charge 300
Paul's Example 302
Paul's Reward 304

Unit 15   2 Timothy 4:9–22

Concluding Matters 307
Paul's Final Instructions 307
The Lord's Faithfulness 312
Confidence in the Lord 315
Parting Words 317

TITUS

Introduction to Titus 323

Unit 1 Titus 1:1–4

Establishing Contact 325
    The Author 326
    The Method of the Author 331
    The Recipient 333
    Greeting 334

Unit 2 Titus 1:5–9

Establishing the Church at Crete 336
    Taking Time to Finish the Work 336
    Appointing Elders 338

Unit 3 Titus 1:10–16

Uprooting Error 345
    Silence Those in Error 345
    Rebuke Them Sharply 347
    The Urgency 349
    The Goal 353

Unit 4 Titus 2:1–6, 9–10

Doctrine and Life 358
    The Importance of Sound Doctrine 359
    Older Men 360
    Older Women 362
    Younger Women 365
    Younger Men 368
    Slaves 369
    To Sum Up 373

Unit 5	Titus 2:7–8, 11–15

Promoting Sound Doctrine 376
Titus' Responsibility 377
Grace and Sound Doctrine 382

CASE STUDY – Working Together for Change 389

Unit 6	Titus 3:1–11

Our Past, Present and Future Lives 391
Remind the People 392
The Basis for the Charge 397

Unit 7	Titus 3:12–15

Concluding Matters 405
Stress This 405
Avoid That 407
Final Instructions 410
Greetings and Prayer 413

NOTES

1 Timothy 417
2 Timothy 439
Titus 457

BIBLIOGRAPHY 465

INTRODUCTION TO THE AFRICA BIBLE COMMENTARY SERIES

The church of Christ in Africa rejoiced at the launch of the *Africa Bible Commentary (ABC)* in 2006. This one-volume commentary was unique in being a product of African soil. Seventy African scholars representing many countries and denominations contributed commentaries on each of the sixty-six books of the Bible as well as articles on various themes of relevance to the African context.

But even as the *ABC* was being released, the ABC Board was looking ahead. A one-volume commentary does not provide enough space to deal with many important issues. Thus was born the Africa Bible Commentary Series.

This series provides more depth of study, width of explanation, and variety of application than was possible in the *ABC*. The contributors are Anglophone or Francophone African scholars, all of whom adhere to the statement of faith of the Association of Evangelicals in Africa.

Besides the African authorship, there are a number of other features that make this commentary series distinctive. First, each commentary is divided into preaching units to help pastors develop a series of sermons on that particular book of the Bible. The main text deals with issues that could come up in such a series, while more complex academic issues relating to the original languages and academic controversies are discussed in the comprehensive endnotes. Each unit ends with questions that can be used to stimulate discussion of the themes in that unit. Each book in the series also contains a number of case studies and brief articles expanding on the practical application of points mentioned in the text.

It is hoped that this combination of features will make these books valuable to pastors, students, and small group Bible study leaders, as well as to ordinary Christians who are interested in getting a fuller understanding of God's Word.

The Africa Bible Commentary Series will be published under the HippoBooks imprint, named in honour of the great African theologian Augustine of Hippo. This imprint is owned by a consortium of African publishers from across the continent (currently WordAlive in Kenya, ACTS in Nigeria and Step in Ghana). The aim is to ensure that the series will be widely available in Africa. In the West, the books will be distributed by Zondervan.

The general editor for the New Testament series is Dr. Samuel Ngewa of the Nairobi Evangelical Graduate School of Theology (NEGST), Kenya, while the editor for the Old Testament series is Dr. Nupanga Weanzana of Bangui Evangelical School of Theology (BEST), in Bangui, Central African Republic.

The Africa Bible Commentary Series is based on Today's New English Version (TNIV). Its main goal is to relate the best biblical scholarship to the African context. This is no easy task. May the Lord bless the work of our hands and use it to strengthen his church in Africa. May our words also bring insight and encouragement to our fellow-believers around the world.

Samuel Ngewa
Easter 2009

FOREWORD TO 1 & 2 TIMOTHY AND TITUS

We will long remember the launch of the *Africa Bible Commentary* in Nairobi in July 2006. The symbolism of that impressive ceremony crowned five years of arduous work by seventy theologians, all sons and daughters of Africa. Pastors, students and preachers at last had access to a resource that would expound the Word of God in words that were intelligible to Africa. We can say without too much exaggeration that armed with this one-volume commentary the African reader will be able to grasp the essential message of the gospel from Genesis to Revelation.

But there is a need to go further, to dig deeper into the Word in order to arrive at a fuller and more precise understanding of God's revelation. Thus was born the idea of producing a series of Bible commentaries, dealing with each book of the Bible in far greater detail. True there are already many such commentaries, but almost all of them were produced in the West and use a vocabulary and categories that are alien to African readers. It can even be said that these commentaries are among the most difficult books for Africans to read. The Africa Bible Commentary Series will be like many of these commentaries in terms of its spirit of loyalty to the text and faithfulness to God's revelation, but it will place a high premium on readability and on applications to the spiritual life of Africa. It will not be content merely to explain concepts but will focus on the relevance of those concepts for the life of the church.

I thus salute the publication of this first commentary in the Africa Bible Commentary Series. My colleague, Prof. Samuel Ngewa, chose to begin with a commentary on 1 and 2 Timothy and Titus. This choice was deliberate. The church faces many problems in Africa. It is numerically large but spiritually weak. This is often because those in leadership have not received sufficient nourishment. This commentary will help church leaders to examine themselves in the light of Scripture and to lead the people of God in a way that conforms to Scripture.

There is a Malagasy proverb *Ny biby tsy misy lohany tsy mandeha*, meaning "an animal without a head isn't going anywhere". Feeding the head, the leaders of the church, will enable the body of the church to live and grow.

One of the distinctive features of this series of commentaries is the emphasis they place on applications in the context of our churches in Africa. In other words, they are informed by the belief that listening to or reading the Word should always lead to obedience and to putting what one has read into practice.

I would like to express my sincere congratulations to Prof. Ngewa for the way he has written this commentary, for his deep knowledge of the texts and the context, the illustrations drawn from African life which help to illuminate the text, and for his mastery of the ongoing debates between scholars. He gently states his positions with firmness and clarity. He invites his readers to move beyond the debates, which are often technical, and instead to focus on the essential message of each passage and to allow themselves to be affected by it. He presents his ideas, or rather the ideas in the text, as in a sermon, which is appropriate given that these are the Pastoral Epistles. Bravo Prof. Ngewa!

Solomon Andriatsimialomananarivo
Prof. of Theology and Pastor
Abidjan, Côte d'Ivoire
April 2009

ACKNOWLEDGEMENTS

As this work goes to press, I praise God for planting in me the desire to contribute to my fellow pastors by writing about three major subjects: the central figure of salvation who truly saves, the shepherds of the flock who truly know their work, and a defence of the gospel that truly balances firmness and love. The first subject was addressed in *The Gospel of John: A Commentary for Pastors, Preachers and Teachers*, the second is addressed in this commentary, and the third will be the topic of my commentary on Galatians.

I started work on a commentary on the Pastoral Epistles several years ago. When I mentioned this to Pieter Kwant, the director of Langham Literature, he invited me to send my material to him. There the race began. I am grateful to Pieter for all his encouragement as we moved ahead to turn my writing into this book.

Pieter's first action was to bring Isobel Stevenson onto the scene. Isobel is a copy editor of high reputation. She has looked at every section of this work, at times with the thoroughness that most people dedicate only to their own work. She pushed me to express my ideas in a way that my readers would most easily understand. It is because I had such an editor stand alongside me that this work is what it is.

Along the way, the Lord also brought Paul Karaimu and Debbie Head to the team, and their contributions, too, have been tremendous. I thank God for all these editors and for their help in making me think more relevantly all the time.

ABBREVIATIONS

Books of the Bible

Old Testament

Gen, Exod, Lev, Num, Deut, Josh, Judg, Ruth, 1–2 Sam, 1–2 Kgs, 1–2 Chr, Ezra, Neh, Esth, Job, Ps/Pss, Prov, Eccl, Song, Isa, Jer, Lam, Ezek, Dan, Hos, Joel, Amos, Obad, Jonah, Mic, Nah, Hab, Zeph, Hag, Zech, Mal

New Testament

Matt, Mark, Luke, John, Acts, Rom, 1–2 Cor, Gal, Eph, Phil, Col, 1–2 Thess, 1–2 Tim, Titus, Phlm, Heb, Jas, 1–2 Pet, 1–2–3 John, Jude, Rev

Translations of the Bible

Abbreviation	Translation
ESV	English Standard Version
HCSB	Holman Christian Standard Bible
KJV	King James Version
Message	The Message
NASB	New American Standard Bible
NEB	New English Bible
NIV	New International Version
NKJV	New King James Version
NRSV	New Revised Standard Version
RSV	Revised Standard Version
TNIV	Today's New International Version

INTRODUCTION TO THE PASTORAL EPISTLES

Mutua was enjoying playing soccer with a friend. But suddenly the game was interrupted by his sister's call: "Mutua, you are to come and wash the dishes!" Mutua looked at her: "Who said so?" His sister replied, "Mummy". Mutua continued to play for another fifteen minutes before he slowly walked home to find out what dishes needed to be washed.

Was Mutua a bad boy? Perhaps not. He had probably learned that his mother's words did not carry as much authority as his father's. If daddy had told him to do something, he would have to obey immediately. For mummy, fifteen minutes later was all right.

Like Mutua, we all attach importance to a statement in proportion to who has said it. That is why it matters who wrote the books in the Bible. Whether we admit it or not, the importance we attach to their message is proportional to our perception of the importance and credibility of the writer. Thus this study of 1 and 2 Timothy and Titus (known collectively as the Pastoral Epistles) has to begin with a discussion of who wrote them.[1]

The traditional position, which is supported by the opening verse of each of these books, is that these letters were written by the Apostle Paul. However, not all scholars agree with this position.[2] Some think that these letters were written by some later believer who used Paul's name.[3] Still others argue that what we have contains fragments of letters written by Paul, but that most of the content was composed by someone else.[4]

The arguments put forward by those who oppose Paul's authorship fall into four main groups:

- *Historical or biographical arguments.* Some of the events mentioned in the Pastoral Epistles are very difficult to fit into the account of Paul's ministry in the book of Acts. Paul speaks of leaving Titus in Crete to organize the church there (Titus 1:5), but Acts does not mention any visit to Crete.[5] It is also difficult to fit in the journey to Macedonia that is mentioned in 1 Timothy 1:3.[6] The imprisonment mentioned in 2 Timothy does not seem to be the same as that mentioned in Acts 23–26 or in Acts 28.[7] However, these problems only discredit Pauline authorship if we assume that the book of Acts deals with all of Paul's life up to the time of his death. But the book makes no such claim. Given that Agrippa and Festus considered Paul innocent of the charges against him (Acts 26:32), it is likely that he was eventually released from his imprisonment in Rome. He could then have embarked on the missionary journeys referred to in the Pastoral Epistles.

- *Linguistic argument.* The words and style of writing in the Pastoral Epistles are very different from those in Paul's other writings. The letters contain words that are not used in any of his other letters and omit words that are often used there. Some scholars thus insist that these letters cannot have been written by Paul.[8] This argument is a strong one. But it is quite possible that Paul changed his vocabulary and his style of writing to suit the new circumstances these churches were facing. It is also possible that he dictated his thoughts to a scribe, called an amanuensis, and that the style of these letters is influenced by the person doing the actual writing. Some have suggested that Luke may have been Paul's amanuensis.

- *Doctrinal or theological argument.* The Pastoral Epistles do not mention some of Paul's key teachings in his other letters, such as salvation by faith, believers' union with Christ, and the role of the Holy Spirit.[9] Some argue that this proves that Paul cannot be the author. This argument, however, raises the question of why Paul would need to repeat these things to Timothy and Titus, two of his key assistants who had worked alongside him and must often have heard him teach on these topics. Furthermore, in the Pastoral Epistles he is addressing a new situation, and we would expect him to deal with different issues and to express his theology in different terms.

- *Ecclesiological argument.* Some argue that the church in Paul's day was not as structured as the one we meet in the Pastoral Epistles and would not have had bishops, elders and deacons. Thus these epistles must have been written some time after Paul's death.[10] But this argument ignores the evidence that Paul took an active interest in the ways churches were organized. In Acts 14:23 he appoints elders and in Acts 20:17, 28 he meets with the elders of the church in Ephesus. Moreover the type of organization referred to in the Pastoral Epistles is very similar to that adopted at Qumran and in Jewish synagogues. It would thus have been familiar to Paul.[11] Moreover, the problems with false teaching in the churches for which Timothy and Titus were responsible may have necessitated organization and strict discipline.

While the arguments against Pauline authorship do raise real questions, there are plausible answers to each of them. We do not need to reject the traditional understanding that Paul was the author of the Pastoral Epistles. Thus in this commentary I will be working from the traditional belief that Paul's imprisonment in Acts 28 ended in his release and that his ministry extended at least four years after this imprisonment. He probably wrote 1 Timothy and Titus some time between ad 63 and 67. Then he was re-arrested, and during this final imprisonment he wrote 2 Timothy, which was his last testament before his execution in ad 67 or 68.

1 TIMOTHY

UNIT 1
1 TIMOTHY 1:1–2

MAKING CONTACT

Africans have often been accused of wasting time. While this may sometimes be true, there is at least one area in which it is more a misunderstanding than a correct evaluation. Traditionally, when an African adult visited a neighbour to borrow something like salt or a burning piece of charcoal to start a fire, it was considered impolite to make the request as soon as one arrived. Instead, there would first be general conversation about how the day was going, how the crops were doing that year, and so on. If neither of the two was in a hurry, this general talk could continue for an hour or more – at times to the point that the borrower forgot what he or she had come for. The conversation established such a strong relationship that when the request was finally made, it was seldom refused. The general conversation was not manipulation of the other person but maintenance of a relationship based on friendship and willingness to share.

Unfortunately, this practice is seldom followed today. Our rushed lives are characterized by individualism. Greetings, when exchanged at all, are quick and casual. Heart-to-heart sharing has been pushed out of our lives. Instead of living in relationships we live by ourselves, and when crises come we find we are all alone. We need to relearn the importance of making and maintaining relationships.

The Apostle Paul lived in a culture that knew the importance of relationships, and so he includes greetings before addressing the issues he wants to write about. He begins almost all his letters by identifying himself and those he is writing to, and greeting them pleasantly. When he does not include a greeting, as in the letter to the Galatians, it is a sure sign that there is a serious problem that needs to be addressed immediately. There is no such problem with those to whom he is writing the Pastoral Epistles, and so all three of them begin with his name, the name of the recipient, and a greeting.

The Author

As discussed in the Introduction, there is some debate about the authorship of the Pastoral Epistles. In this commentary, we will accept the assertion that the author of 1 Timothy is *Paul* (1:1). The book of Acts and his other letters tell us a good deal about Paul, both as a person and as an apostle. He was originally known as Saul, and came from the Jewish tribe of Benjamin (Phil 3:5).[12] He had been a zealous persecutor of the church before his conversion (Acts 8:1–3).

Paul describes himself as *an apostle of Christ Jesus*, that is, as someone who has been sent on a mission by Christ Jesus. He describes himself in the same way in all his letters, except those addressed to situations in which there are no major problems (specifically, Philippians, 1 & 2 Thessalonians and Philemon).

The role of an "apostle" (a Greek word) is closely related to the role of the person the Jews referred to as a *shaliach*.[13] A shaliach was sent out to faithfully represent the person who sent him. His actions were backed by their authority and he was authorized to respond to different situations in terms of what he knew of their likes and wishes. The title thus combined authority and faithful service. Paul sees himself as working in this way in relation to Christ.

In the Bible, the term "apostle" is used specifically to refer to the twelve men whom Jesus himself appointed to preach and lay the foundation for his church (Mark 3:14 niv). Paul qualified as an apostle like these men because he received the same commission from Jesus when he encountered him on the road to Damascus (Acts 9; see also 1 Cor 9:1; 2 Cor 12:11–12). He was recognized as an apostle by the Jerusalem Council (Gal 2:1–10).

In a looser sense, people like Barnabas, Apollos, Silas and Timothy are also sometimes called apostles because they, too, were preaching and founding churches (see Acts 14:14; 1 Cor 4:6, 9; 1 Thess 1:1; 2:6–7).[14] This usage has led some African preachers to call themselves apostles, and to claim that they have the same authority as Christ's original apostles. Such preachers sometimes forget that the role of a shaliach was not just to speak with authority but also to act in the same way as the one who sent him. Christ laid aside his glory (Phil 2:5–8), washed his disciples' feet (John 13:3–5) and laid down his life for those he came to save (John 10:11; Gal 1:4). Those who claim to be apostles need to be reminded that they cannot claim to speak with authority unless their lives demonstrate the utmost self-sacrifice for the flock.[15]

Paul insists that he is an apostle *by the command of God our Saviour and of Christ Jesus our hope*. In his other letters, Paul often speaks of himself as being an apostle "by the will of God" (e.g. 1 Cor 1:1; 2 Cor 1:1). Here, however, he uses the word "command" in order to stress that he has received an order that must be obeyed. He is not speaking on his own initiative but has been given a commission that he must carry out. He is like a soldier delivering a message given to him by his commanders – and in Paul's case, these commanders are none other than God and Christ Jesus. Thus his message in this letter is backed by God's authority.

It may seem odd that Paul stresses his authority when he is writing to his close friend and faithful colleague. But this was not just a personal letter; it would also be read to the congregation. By stressing his own authority, Paul was strengthening Timothy's position in Ephesus and supporting the authority of his teaching.

The Recipient

This letter is addressed to *Timothy* (1:2). The name Timothy is formed from two Greek words: *timao*, which means "I honour", and *theos*, which means "God". Thus, Timothy means "one who honours God" or "one whom God honours".

Timothy is first mentioned in Acts 16:1–3, when he became Paul's companion on his second missionary journey. Thereafter, he is frequently mentioned in Paul's letters.[16] Paul here refers to him as his *true son*. The word translated "true" is the one that would normally be used to refer to a legitimate child, born to parents married to each other. Paul uses it to show that Timothy is a genuine convert, a true believer who has proved his faithfulness as he has been mentored by Paul. The words *in the faith* indicate that this is the sphere in which his faithfulness has been proved.

The Greeting

In many situations where we would say "hello" in English or "habari" in Swahili, people in the Greek-speaking world of Paul's day would say *chairein*. Paul liked to Christianize this greeting by punning on the word and replacing *chairein* (greetings) with *charis* (*grace*). He would then add the common Jewish greeting, "shalom" or *peace* (which is similar to the greeting "salaam" used by some people in Africa, who greet each other with "salaam alaikum". Paul used this combined greeting in most of his letters.[17]

In 1 Timothy and 2 Timothy, however, he adds a third item to his greeting: *mercy*. Ephesus was not the easiest of churches to pastor, and Paul may have "sensed that Timothy needed this nuance of God's favour because he felt himself in special difficulty and needed not only a strength and enabling but also sympathy, tenderness, and comfort".[18]

The greeting expresses Paul's prayer that Timothy will know God's grace, that is, his favour on undeserving sinners and his special encouragement of believers. He is also praying that Timothy will know God's mercy, that is, his compassion and pity. Finally, he is praying that Timothy will know God's peace, that is, that his heart and mind will be satisfied with the Lord's goodness and daily protection.

The blessings Paul prays for would make Timothy a very successful minister, but this does not stop Paul from praying that he will receive them. Paul is not like some African leaders who are afraid that their disciples' success will overshadow their own. For example, I have known cases where a church leader has asked for the transfer of a junior worker who is so successful that he or she is attracting praise. Paul was not like that. He would be happy for Timothy's ministry to demonstrate the fullest extent of the blessing that comes from both *God the Father and Christ Jesus our Lord*. Paul specifies this dual source of blessing in all his writings except Colossians 1:2, where he only mentions "God our Father".

Questions for Discussion

1. Any nation or church is only as great as its next generation. If it does not prepare them for leadership, that nation or church will die with the current generation. Yet we often see the generation in power or in leadership guarding their glory to the point of undermining the next generation. Reflecting on this and on Paul's relationship with Timothy, what lessons can we learn for our nations and churches?

2. How can we apply the principles identified in the discussion of Question 1 to our own church when it comes to relationships between older and younger believers, long-time church members and newer members of the same church, and a senior pastor and a newly employed assistant?

3. An apostle was called to exercise authority and model faithful service. We are called to follow the apostles' example (1 Cor 4:16–17). If you are a church leader, reflect on how you model your behaviour on that of the apostles. If you are a church member, do you see the right blend of authority and service in your church leaders? Discuss what you have experienced without condemnation or self-justification, remembering that our goal is to grow together into a greater degree of Christ-likeness.

UNIT 2
1 TIMOTHY 1:3–7

TIMOTHY'S MISSION

One of the most widely read books at the beginning of this century was Rick Warren's *The Purpose-Driven Life*.[19] People reading it in public places reported that those next to them would often ask what it was about. The words "purpose-driven" caught people's attention, for even non-Christians long to find a life of purpose and meaning.

When we discover what we are meant to do in life, daily tasks become purposeful and life acquires a new sense of mission. In 1 Timothy 1:3–7, Paul spells out Timothy's mission in order to make sure he understands the task he is meant to accomplish and his role as leader of the church in Ephesus. If Timothy fails, it will not be because he did not know what he was supposed to do.

Paul had been with Timothy in Ephesus, but had left him there when he went on to Macedonia (1:3). Before leaving, he had given him instructions about what to do. But Paul may have feared that with all the other life challenges and emotions surrounding his departure, Timothy would not remember everything he had been told, or that he would be nervous about implementing it. So Paul writes to him to remind him of his mission.

The Push

Timothy was still a young man (4:12) and he may have been hesitant about taking responsibility for the church in Ephesus, with its many problems. So Paul *urged* (1:3) him to do so. He did not merely politely request that Timothy consider taking on this task. (Elsewhere, he speaks even more strongly to Titus, saying, "I directed you" – Titus 1:5). This reminder of Paul's urging reassures Timothy that his mentor is confident that he will be equal to the task.

The Place

The church for which Timothy was responsible was based in Ephesus (1:3), the principal city of the Roman province of Asia Minor. It was a religious centre and the site of a famous temple of Artemis (known as Diana by the Romans). She was the goddess of hunting, the wild and fertility. This temple dated back to 550 bc and was one of the seven wonders of the ancient world.

Paul first visited Ephesus briefly as he journeyed from Corinth to Caesarea along with Aquila and Priscilla, whom he had met in Corinth (Acts 18:2, 18–19). He may have started the church there and then left his companions to care for it.[20] Paul's second and last visit to the city is recorded in Acts 19 and lasted at least two years and three months (Acts 19:8–10; 20:31).

The strategic importance of a great city like Ephesus in Paul's mission to the whole province of Asia Minor and the surrounding regions may have led him to attach particular importance to the well-being of the church there. That may explain why he asked such a close friend as Timothy to remain there.

We may need to use a similar strategy to Paul when thinking about our churches in Africa. Just as Paul chose one of his best assistants to serve in the Ephesian church and gave him every possible moral and emotional support, so we may need to place our best pastors in urban churches and to keep them in our prayers. Such pastors may be ministering to government ministers, permanent secretaries, the directors of various institutions, judges, and others who occupy all kinds of influential offices. Even the ordinary members of urban churches will be influential when they visit the rural areas from which they came.

Pastors may sometimes be attracted to urban churches because the salary may be higher than in many rural areas. But they should never accept such a pastorate without an awareness of the awesome responsibility that serving there imposes. We as church members should remember to uphold urban pastors in our prayers, for their good ministry will trickle down to all corners of the African society.

The Job Description

Timothy is to *command* certain people in the church in Ephesus to stop doing something. The verb is the one a Greek commander would use when issuing orders to his subordinates.[21] As Paul's representative, Timothy can speak with Paul's authority. He must not hesitate to exercise that authority. The problems he has to deal with are so serious that they must be confronted, and cannot be addressed by negotiation.

Timothy is to issue two orders to *certain persons*, that is, to a specific group in the church. First, they *are not to teach false doctrines*. The word translated as "false" carries the idea of "a different kind" in the Greek.[22] Some people were teaching ideas that were very different from the true gospel that Paul and Timothy preached. Second, they must not *devote themselves to myths and endless genealogies*. Someone who is devoted to something is highly committed to it. These people were not merely passing on information; they were actively promoting their ideas.

Scholars are not absolutely certain what Paul means when he talks of "myths and endless genealogies". There are three main possibilities:

- Gnostic teachings about the relationship between a benevolent Supreme Being and the supposedly evil material world. The "endless genealogies" are then the genealogies of the spirits, or *aeons*, that supposedly emanated from this Supreme Being.[23] Those who accept this interpretation point out that the asceticism recommended by the false teachers (1 Tim 4:3) fits with the gnostic teaching that material things are evil. The false teaching about the resurrection (2 Tim 2:18) also seems to have gnostic leanings.

- Jewish stories about the Old Testament patriarchs. These are not the stories included in the Bible, but other legends that had accumulated around them. The "endless genealogies" would be efforts to construct or maintain detailed Jewish family trees. In support of this interpretation, it can be pointed out that the false teachers want to be "teachers of the law" (1:7), which would probably be the Jewish law.

- A mixture of gnostic and Jewish teachings. This is the most likely possibility.

But whatever the case, these teachers are preoccupied with speculation about issues that are neither important nor useful to the cause of the gospel. Their ideas are a threat to the church and contrary to the gospel. Devotion to such ideas serves only to *promote controversial speculations* (1:4). People are being encouraged to play with and argue about ideas purely for the purpose of mental stimulation, not because they actually want to find answers to real problems. Such controversies are pointless. They do nothing to advance *God's work*, that is, his plan of redemption through Jesus Christ, *which is by faith* (1:4). Neither human speculation of the kind favoured by the gnostics, nor debates about ancestry and arcane details of the Jewish law have any effect on the past, the present or the future of God's plan of redemption. Redemption comes only by faith.[24]

We see a variant of this problem when pastors use their pulpit to promote some political party. This is not to say that pastors should not teach that God hates corruption, injustice, crime, and marginalization. When those are the issues, politics and biblical teaching go together. When, however, preachers use their position to support the political party or candidate they favour, what they are preaching is their personal opinion and is not calculated to help their listeners grow more like Christ-like in their attitudes and in their responses to daily challenges. Instead, some members of the congregation will turn their ears off and there will be political controversies within the congregation. Paul would insist that pastors should focus on the issues that unite us and make us grow in God's grace.

The Goal

Timothy is not called to issue this command just to establish his authority or to root out error. His ultimate goal must be to promote *love, which comes from a pure heart and a good conscience and a sincere faith* (1:5). Whereas 1:3–4 focused on the negative aspects of Timothy's task, here Paul stresses the positive side. Others may "promote controversial speculations"; Timothy is to promote love. Stopping the spread of error is only the start of his assignment.

The type of love that Timothy is to promote is *agape* love, the unselfish, self-giving love that Paul talks about in 1 Corinthians 13. Such love is not selfish and does not count the cost but takes pride in what is achieved for the glory of God and the good of his people.

Love must come from the heart. Today, we think of the heart as the seat of emotions, but in Paul's day it was the centre of thoughts as well. Those whose hearts are "pure" will not have divided loyalties, but will love God wholeheartedly and love their neighbours as themselves (Luke 10:27). Their love will have no limits. In Paul's case, his love extends not only to Timothy and those who support him but also to those who oppose him.

Another characteristic of this love is that it comes from "a good conscience". It must be comfortable in the presence of "the inner judge that accuses us when we have done wrong and approves us when we have done right".[25] Someone with a good conscience does not live with a sense of guilt. Of course, some people feel no guilt because their consciences have been branded or seared by a carefree or rebellious attitude (1 Tim 4:2). But Paul is not speaking about such people. He is speaking of the conscience of someone who is responsive to God and seeks to live a godly life.

The final element in this love is "sincere faith", that is, faith that is free of hypocrisy and pretence.

The false teachers create controversy that hampers the work of God; by contrast, those who have the type of love described here promote his work. Thus such love is the goal of Paul, Timothy and everyone else who joins them in serving God.

A Case in Point

Some people at Ephesus have not pursued love but have *departed from* it. The Greek verb carries the sense of "failing to aim at something" or "failing to strike something". These men have failed to strike the right path and so have lost their way. They have replaced meaningful activity with *meaningless talk* (1:6).

As an example of how they have lost their way, Paul speaks of their desire to become teachers of the law (1:7). There is nothing wrong with such a desire – indeed, it is honourable. But these people want to teach the law without obeying it. They are not prepared to pay the price that Paul has paid for preaching the gospel by staying true to it. As a result, all that they have to offer is "meaningless talk" because they do not really understand what they assert dogmatically (1:7). The emptiness of their teaching is even more apparent when it is contrasted with God's truth as revealed in Paul's apostolic teaching.

We still suffer from meaningless talk in some of our churches today. There are some preachers who evaluate the success of sermons by whether they made people laugh and enjoy themselves. While there is nothing wrong with making people laugh, a sermon that only entertains and does not lead the listeners to ask themselves what areas they should grow in has not achieved its true purpose. That purpose is to build people up in their relationship with Christ.

Questions for Discussion

1. African life once involved a routine of waking, taking the animals out to graze, bringing them home, talking around the fire, and going to sleep. Today our routines have changed: we wake, go to the office, return home, watch TV, and go to bed. Is that all there is to our lives? To what extent are Christians in Africa modelling how to live everyday life with a purpose, plan and goal, knowing that the ultimate judge is Christ their Saviour?

2. Africans traditionally used stories to teach lessons. Even today, a story is often remembered better than a sermon. Can you remember a story with a moral lesson that you were told by a grandparent or parent or some other mentor? What was the story and what was the lesson behind it? How would you react if your pastor used a story like this instead of a sermon on Sunday? Are there some dangers to watch out for when using stories? If so, what are some of them?

3. In every African society, there was a procedure through which a boy was initiated into manhood and a girl to womanhood. The procedure often involved hardships and risks, which some welcomed

and others dreaded. Have you ever been in a position where you were facing an experience you dreaded and someone came alongside you to encourage you, saying something like, "You can do it"? Did you ultimately find satisfaction and success in the very thing you were afraid of trying? Share what someone said or did to encourage you, or what you have done to encourage someone else. Then think about specific ways in which we as African believers need to encourage each other to venture out for the kingdom of God. How does Paul serve as a model here?

UNIT 3
1 TIMOTHY 1:8–11

THE PROPER USE OF THE LAW

My wife and I have three wonderful daughters: Mwende, Katee and Ndinda. When they were twenty, nineteen and seventeen years of age, a time came when I would have to be away from my family for close to a year. In preparing my daughters for my absence we talked about many things, including how they should treat their mother and relate to each other. They were horrified when I said that I would give them a list of rules. I assured them that they would be good rules. "But there are no good rules!" Ndinda responded.

When the time came to present them with my list of rules, they found that I had written down only one: "Since you were young, your mother and I have done our best to teach you values that we believe will be a blessing to you. Be guided by them, and all will be well." Six years later, our daughters continue to live by the positive values we taught them.

My children are not perfect. Like all of us, they have needed guidance at various times in their lives to help them find and keep on the right path. But Ndinda's assessment was right: they did not need rules because they were already determined to do what was right. This is much the same point that Paul makes in 1 Timothy 1:8–11 as he discusses the good and bad use of the law.

Nature of God's Law

Paul begins by telling us that the character of the law remains the same regardless of how one uses it. Ndinda thought that there were no good rules, but Paul knows that God's law is, by nature, *good* (1:8a). He is so certain of this that he says *We know*, implying that all his readers will agree. If so, why does he bother to make this point? The reason is that he does not want his position to be misunderstood. He has just said that those who want to be teachers of the law are engaged in meaningless talk (1:6–7). Their talk is not meaningless because the law is bad but because they are using it wrongly. That is why he adds the words *if one uses it properly* to his statement that the law is good (1:8b). The law is the law, but that is all it is. It must be used in ways that conform to its nature and purpose. It is not the basis for speculation (1:4) or for salvation (Rom 3:20).

Who Needs the Law

The next question that arises is, who does the law apply to? Paul begins his answer to this question by pointing out who it does *not* apply to. It is *not* made *for the righteous* (1:9a). Those who are righteous already appreciate the place of the law in God's purpose and live by it. The Holy Spirit leads them in ways that correspond to the demands of the law. There is no need to lay down laws for such people. Their way of life already fulfils the law's requirements.

The law is, however, needed by those who are walking on the path of unrighteousness. They need rules to guide or correct them. In 1:9–10 Paul gives fourteen examples of the type of person the law applies to. His list includes many behaviours that are specifically forbidden in the Ten Commandments:

- *Lawbreakers* and *rebels* reject all laws, both God's and those of the society they live in. They are criminals who dismiss all laws as no more than human rules. In Africa, they would be the ones who carelessly dismiss traditional taboos like the prohibition on marrying a close relative.

- *The ungodly and sinful* acknowledge that some laws come from God, but still choose to ignore them. While it is possible for us to challenge some taboos that are not found in God's word, such as the rules forbidding women to eat certain parts of animals, these people deliberately ignore what the Scripture has to say about murder, lying, and sleeping with someone else's spouse.

- *The unholy and irreligious* live thoroughly secular lives and treat spiritual matters with contempt. They are quite comfortable ignoring both society's taboos and God-given commands because this has become part of their character.
- *Those who kill their fathers or mothers* are not just those who kill them physically but also those who harm their parents by refusing to show them respect. By not honouring their parents, such people are breaking the fifth commandment (Exod 20:12).
- *Murderers* are those who kill men or, more specifically husbands (the Greek word Paul uses here refers specifically to men).[26] This should not be taken to mean that it does not matter if it is a woman who is killed! Paul focuses on the man because in his time killing the breadwinner was equivalent to killing the entire family. Murder is forbidden in the sixth commandment (Exod 20:13).
- *The sexually immoral* engage in fornication and adultery. The word pornography is derived from the Greek word *pornoi*, which is used here. Such people are violating the seventh commandment (Exod 20:14).
- *Those practicing homosexuality* have "abandoned natural relationships" and burn with lust for people of the same gender (Rom 1:27). By engaging in sex outside marriage they, too, are violating the seventh commandment.
- *Slave traders* rob their victims of their liberty and also of their dignity and human worth. They are breaking the eighth commandment, "You shall not steal" (Exod 20:15).
- *Liars* tell lies without the slightest shame and violate the ninth commandment, "You shall not give false testimony against your neighbour" (Exod 20:16).
- *Perjurers* lie even when they have sworn a solemn oath to tell the truth. They are breaking the third commandment, for they are misusing God's name when they use it to make promises they have no intention of keeping (Exod 20:7). They also break the ninth commandment against giving false testimony.

Paul ends this section with *and whatever else is contrary to the sound doctrine* (1:10). His list is meant only to provide examples, not to cover all possible categories.

It is striking that Paul moves directly from talking about categories of people who are unrighteous to talking about vices, that is, unrighteous acts. He does not differentiate between the sinner and the sin because every sin involves someone doing or not doing something. Thus when we say that God hates sin but loves the sinner, we do not mean that the sinner who continues sinning enjoys God's love. Those who refuse to repent will experience God's wrath (Rom 1:24, 26, 28). However, God's arms are open to any sinner who chooses to return to him (Luke 15:20). The close relationship between an action and the person doing the action also means that anyone whose deliberate act leads to someone's death, whether by sorcery or by passing on HIV/AIDS, is equivalent to a murderer.

Paul contrasts these behaviours with "sound doctrine". The word translated as "sound" could also be translated as "whole" or "healthy". The same Greek word lies behind our modern word "hygiene". A life that is based on the gospel is whole and healthy and needs no treatment by the law, but a life that is morally disordered is diseased and needs the medicine of the law.

Teaching that is sound is in accordance with *the gospel concerning the glory of the blessed God* (1:10b–11). This phrase could also be translated as "the glorious gospel" (niv), in which case the gospel itself is being described as glorious. However, it seems more likely that Paul is saying that whereas the law reveals human sinfulness, the gospel reveals God's glory in the form of his power, majesty, compassion, wisdom and love.[27]

The fact that God is "blessed" is also part of his glory. He remains blessed regardless of whether his creation acknowledges him. This glorious and blessed God is the source of the gospel that has been entrusted to Paul.

Questions for Discussion

1. What is the relationship between freedom and laws? Traditional African societies accepted the principle that "you do not question your chief's instructions; you simply obey them". Following independence, some African presidents wanted their nations to accept the same principle. As we now move toward more democratic governments, what principles should guide us? For example, how do we balance the principle of love for others in what we do with the principle of truth in what we say? Is it possible to misinterpret freedom of action, freedom of speech, and freedom of association as meaning that there is no law at all?

2. Some Western church leaders have taken a mild view on the issue of homosexuality whereas most African church leaders hold that it is sin. As you examine this passage, do you see good basis for the position of the African church leadership?

3. Paul was entrusted with the gospel in his time, and we carry that same responsibility in our time. What personal qualities do trustees need to have to carry out their task faithfully? What challenges do we face as trustees of the Good News in Africa today? How do the gospel and the law relate to the twenty-first century with its emphasis on personal freedom?

UNIT 4
1 TIMOTHY 1:12–14

PAUL'S PERSONAL REFLECTION

When we make time for personal reflection, we discover something about who we are. Unfortunately, we do not do this often enough. This was true even of a godly man like King David. His psalms reveal him as a man who did take time to think about his own life and emotions and to examine himself to make sure that he was walking in God's ways and obeying his commands (1 Kgs 3:14b). But in one particular period of his life, he seems to have missed a lot about himself. That was the time when he fell into an adulterous relationship with Bathsheba, Uriah's wife. When she fell pregnant, David desperately tried to cover up his sin. When all other methods failed, he had Uriah murdered on the battlefield. Then David brought Bathsheba to his house and she became his wife (2 Sam 11).

David's reflection in those days probably focused on what others would think about him if they learned what he had done, and not on what God thought about it. Once he had engineered the successful cover-up, he probably avoided opportunities to reflect. He may even have been successful in doing this – until Nathan confronted him. Forced to face up to his crime, David confessed his sin (2 Sam 12:1–13). Psalm 51 records David's prayer for forgiveness and shows the insight he gained as he reflected on who he was and what he had done.

Reflection is an essential element in spiritual renewal. As Psalm 51 shows, times of reflection not only enable us to recognize the awfulness of our sins, they also open our eyes to the Lord's love, mercy and forgiveness. No matter how ashamed we become of what we see in ourselves, God is able to forgive us and give us strength to move forward. Regular reflection makes us more effective servants of Christ. If we do not pause to reflect, we may merely be keeping up an appearance of righteousness that may fool ourselves and others, but does not fool God.

In 1 Timothy 1:12–14, Paul gives us a glimpse of his own reflections on his present and past life. His words may be sparked by his memory of how it was that he came to be trusted with the message of the gospel (1:11).[28]

Paul's Present

Paul's view of himself is based on what Christ has done for him, and thus he begins his reflection with the words, *I thank Christ Jesus our Lord* (1:12a). He honours Christ who has made him all that he is. There are three aspects to what Jesus has done for him: Christ has strengthened him, considered him faithful, and taken him into his service.[29]

When he speaks of Christ *who has given me strength*, Paul is not speaking of being strengthened to do his daily work. He is thinking of his experience on the Damascus road which was "his initial call to the ministry and the gifts he received that enabled him to perform his apostolic tasks".[30] Paul does not tell us how this strengthening took place, but it is possible that what he has in mind is his movement from "life under the law" to "life under grace" (Rom 6:14; 1 Cor 9:20). While the law killed Paul, the mercy of Christ brought newness of life, which is equivalent to "being strengthened" (Rom 7:11–13).

The basic sentence structure of 1:11 is *I thank Christ ... that he considered me trustworthy*. This is the main reason for Paul's gratitude; the rest of the sentence is made up of subordinate clauses. He seems to be saying that Christ first considered him trustworthy, and then went to work on him to strengthen him and put him to work.[31]

Being considered trustworthy means the same as being found faithful. Note that Paul is not here speaking about his human qualifications; rather, he is expressing his amazement that God saw him as trustworthy. From God's perspective, Paul was regarded as faithful on the basis of what Christ has done for him and in him and what God foresaw would be Paul's response to it. From Paul's perspective, God's trust in him is an amazing act of grace for which he thanks God.

God's purpose in working in Paul was to make him a servant of Christ by *appointing me to his service* (1:12). The Greek word translated "service" in this verse is *diakonia*. It is made up from two other Greek words: *dia* (through) and *konis* (dust). It suggests moving so fast to carry out a duty that one leaves in a cloud of dust!

The English word "deacon" comes from the same root. In the New Testament, the term is used to refer both to an administrative position and to anyone who has any kind of official position in the church. The latter meaning is what is intended in this verse. Paul is both an apostle and a deacon in the service of Christ. In the same way, every believer who holds firmly to the truth of God and walks with God in faith is a minister for Christ. The gifts and assignments may differ, but the goal of the ministry is the same – to glorify God and enhance his kingdom.

Paul is acutely aware that he does not deserve anything he has received and that his ministry is a privilege. He was *shown mercy* (1:13b) – and mercy is not something anyone has a right to expect. Mercy is only shown when we deserve punishment.

The reason he was shown mercy was because *the grace of our Lord* was poured on him (1:14). This grace turned Paul's life of unbelief into a life of faith, and his life of violence into a life of love. His faith went far beyond the simple conviction that God would provide his next meal. It was a life-transforming faith. The love he came to know was an unselfishness *agape* love.

The faith and love that Paul received are found *in Christ Jesus*. Thus these gifts are found wherever Christ is. They are present in lives that he has changed and in the community in which he is allowed to govern. And they are not in short supply. Paul says that this grace has been *poured out on me abundantly*. The word could even be translated "superabundantly". This grace was more than Paul could exhaust. It overwhelmed him and overflowed to others.

Paul's Past

To indicate how little he deserved God's mercy and grace, Paul reminds his readers that he had previously been *a blasphemer and a persecutor and a violent man* (1:13b; see also Acts 8:3; 9:1–2; 26:9–11). The word translated "blasphemer" literally means "someone who injures with words". Paul had spoken evil of Christ; yet Christ had not responded in anger, but had instead called him to be his servant. Christ responded to the verbal injuries with mercy and grace. What an example of forgiving love!

The only reason Paul can think of to explain God's showing such goodness to him is that he had *acted in ignorance and unbelief* (1:13b).[32] He had not deliberately rejected grace. He simply did not know any better! He thought that his zeal was furthering God's work. When giving the law, God had announced that he would accept repentance for unintentional sins but not for defiant sins, which are those sins that someone refuses to repent of even after being confronted about them by others. Such defiant sins would be punished by the community or by the Lord (Num 15:27–31). With Christ's coming, the pattern changed. He set the example for Christian ministry by insisting that he had come "to seek and to save what was lost" (Luke 19:10). We are to work to save even the worst of sinners, just as God saved Paul on the way to Damascus (Acts 9:1–20). However, we should never take God's grace for granted, particularly after we have had a "Damascus" experience of our own (Heb 10:26–31).

Paul is not denying responsibility for his own actions when he says that they were done in unbelief. Rather, he is trying to stress God's mercy and grace in moving him from the sphere of unbelief into the sphere of faith in which he now lives. What he deserved was judgment. What he received was mercy.

As we listen to Paul reflect on what he once was, what he now is, and how the change came about, we can understand why he exclaims, "I thank Christ Jesus our Lord" (1:12). These words do not simply express a general attitude of thankfulness; they are his spontaneous response to his reflection on what Christ has done for him.[33]

Questions for Discussion

1. In Africa, some people are considered so bad that even Christians celebrate when they are shot by police or burned by their fellow villagers. Had the young Paul lived in our day, Christians would probably have celebrated his death. But Paul's testimony is that

God extended his mercy to him and turned the worst enemy of the gospel into the greatest soldier for it. No one is beyond change. So what should be our attitude when the police shoot criminals who are not shooting at them, or when people are burned to death by their neighbours for such crimes as stealing maize, goats or cattle?

2. During the East African Revival between the 1930s and 1960s, it was common for converts to publicly confess the details of their past sins and express appreciation for God's grace that changed them. It came to be felt that the worse one had been before conversion, the sweeter one's testimony, which led to a tendency to exaggerate one's sinfulness, or even to make up additional sins to confess! How does what Paul does compare with that practice? Do you think that truthful open confession like that practised during the revival enhances the holiness of God's people? Should we or should we not be encouraging such confession today? Give reasons for your answer.

UNIT 5
1 TIMOTHY 1:15–20

THE UNCHANGEABLE TRUTH

On September 2, 2004, a headline in Kenya's *East African Standard* newspaper read: "The News Is Real This Time Round". Three Kenyan hostages held in Iraq for 42 days had finally been released. Many had feared that they would never be released or that they had been killed.

A month before, on August 2, a government minister had announced that the three had been released, only for the country to find out that what he said was not true. Newspaper headlines quickly went from "Relief as Hostages Are Freed"[34] to "Minister Under Fire over Hostage Hoax".[35] It turned out the minister had spoken on the basis of information that had not been verified and that turned out to be false.

Have you ever been in a similar situation? Have you passed on information that you thought was true only to find out that it was not? In 1 Timothy 1:15–20 Paul tells us about a truth in which we can have absolute confidence. He describes what he has to say as *a trustworthy saying* (1:15a). He uses the same expression four more times in the Pastoral Epistles (1 Tim 3:1; 4:9; 2 Tim 2:11; Titus 3:8) to stress that what he is going to say, or has just said, will remain true under all circumstances. It is an unchangeable fact. It will remain true no matter what society thinks or critics say. Paul accepted this truth. So must Timothy, and so must all others who want to be in the right. This truth *deserves full acceptance*.

The Nature of Truth

What is this unchangeable truth in which Paul has so much confidence? It is that *Christ Jesus came into the world to save sinners* (1:15). Every word in this statement is significant.

The first words give the name of the one of whom Paul is speaking. He is referred to as both "Christ" and "Jesus" to emphasize different aspects of his work. The title "Christ" is the Greek version of the Jewish title "Messiah". This title is given to someone who has been anointed and appointed to his office by God. The name "Jesus" is a variant on the Jewish name "Joshua", which means "Yahweh saves" (Matt 1:21). Together, the two names make the point that this person is someone God has appointed for the mission of saving others.

The past tense "came" is used because Paul is speaking of Christ's incarnation, the date appointed by God when he entered the world as a baby born to a virgin mother (Gal 4:4).[36] The description of him as having come "into the world" is an indication that he came from somewhere else. His origin is in heaven (John 6:38).

The reason he came was "to save". Paul does not elaborate on how this saving was accomplished, for he assumes that Timothy, who has been his companion for many years, already knows this. Other New Testament writings make it clear that Jesus accomplished this goal by dying in the place of sinners (Matt 20:28; Mark 10:45; Luke 19:10).

The word here translated as "sinners" is a very inclusive one and derives from a verb which means "to miss the mark".[37] The image is of someone shooting at a target, which in this case is God's righteousness. The shot goes wide and lands somewhere else. And we all shoot wide. None of us manages to hit the target, that is, to meet the standard of God's righteousness (Rom 3:23; 10:3). God's plan of salvation is to bring us back on target. That is the mission on which Jesus Christ came. This is the truth of which Paul is absolutely certain.

Paul's Response to the Truth

The word "sinners" turns Paul's thought inwards towards himself, and then outwards towards the God who devised this wonderful plan of salvation.

Paul's view of himself

Christ came to save sinners – and Paul unhesitatingly identifies himself as the worst of all those Christ came to save. He does not say this simply because he persecuted Christians (and through them, their Lord) in the past. Instead, he uses the present tense, *I am the worst* (1:15b).[38] He is constantly aware of how often he misses the mark in his own life. The closer we get to God, the more we realize his holiness and our own sinfulness.

But the focus here is not solely on Paul's self-awareness; rather it is on the mercy Christ showed him on the road to Damascus (see comments on 1:12–14). That experience turned the once proud, Christ-blaspheming Pharisee into a humble, Christ-serving apostle. He is convinced that the reason he was forgiven was to demonstrate Christ's *immense patience*. Paul had trained as a rabbi, and so he uses a rabbinic rule of argument called "from the greater to the less".[39] If God forgave a great sinner (Paul), then he will surely also forgive lesser sinners, provided they meet the one condition for salvation – faith.

The condition for salvation is faith. Salvation is *for those who would believe in him and receive eternal life* (1:16). Paul believed and was saved, and so must every other sinner who wants to receive Christ's saving grace. It is true that earlier Paul had acted in ignorance and unbelief (1:13), but when Christ revealed himself to him, Paul responded with faith. The people in Ephesus need to make the same response. They cannot plead the excuse of ignorance, for in 1:15 Paul clearly summarized what it is they need to believe. Unless they respond to the truth in his "trustworthy saying" with faith, they cannot receive eternal life.

Eternal life means far more than just a long life; it means a life that is lived in Christ. The number one blessing it gives is God's presence. We need to stress this point because in many African countries preachers emphasize the material blessings God gives us rather than the fact that God is with us no matter what we may be going through (2 Cor 12:9–10). Because eternal life is more a matter of quality than of quantity, we can already begin to enjoy it here on earth, although we will only know all its fullness in the future.

Paul's view of God

Earlier Paul had burst out in thanks to God (1:12), and now he again bursts out in praise, ascribing honour and glory to God. Two things stand out in this verse: the kind of God this honour and glory go to, and the duration for which this honour is to be paid.

Paul uses four descriptors for God. He is the *King eternal, immortal, invisible, the only God* (1:17).[40] The reference to him as the "King eternal" probably sprang to Paul's mind because he has just been speaking of God's gift of "eternal life" to those who believe (1:16). The Greek literally means "the King of the ages" and makes the point that God rules all ages past, the present age, and the ages to come. Similarly, in some African traditions the Supreme Being is described as the "Ancient of Days", meaning that on the first day of creation, God was there already.[41] One never asks where God came from, for his age has no limit. He was, is and will be.

The description of God as "immortal" focuses on the fact that God will never ever cease to be. He has been, is, and will always be. What a contrast with us mere mortals, whose lives are as evanescent as the morning mist (Jas 5:14)! The central African proverb, "God never dies, only men do"[42] corresponds well with this biblical truth.

God is "invisible", beyond the reach of humans. Africans have long known this.[43] They saw God in what he did (for example, in sending or withholding rain), and tried to deduce his nature from his actions (for example, the gift of rain means that he is loving, and his withholding of rain means that he hates and punishes sin). God told Moses that no one can see him as he is, in his essence, and live (Exod 33:20). However, God does sometimes choose to reveal himself. In the Old Testament, he did this in what are known as theophanies (Exod 3:1–6; Isa 6:1–5). In the New Testament, he reveals himself to us in the incarnate Christ. But in all cases, God is the one who initiates his revelation of himself to humans.

Finally, Paul speaks of "the only God", a strong assertion of monotheism. People may speak of many other gods, but there is no other who deserves the title. This is the area in which there is the greatest divergence between the African and the Christian concepts of God. Some African people groups were traditionally inclined to be monotheistic while others were explicitly polytheistic, but no group was free of belief in other beings, especially ancestors, who obscured people's perception of God. They did this by suggesting that God was too distant or too majestic to be bothered about daily matters. So instead of worshipping God, people would pour out a libation to the ancestors. Some in Africa still seek help from the ancestors and spirit powers whenever there is crisis because they have failed to grasp the full truth that there is only one God, who is to be honoured and glorified *for ever and ever*. The Greek literally means "into the ages of ages". There is no time limit to his reign.

Paul concludes this hymn of praise with *Amen,* a Hebrew word that means "let it be so" (Num 5:22; Deut 27:15–26). It is as if he is underlining what he has said in order to emphasize how much he wants to praise God. He does the same in the two other short hymns of praise to God (doxologies) in these letters to Timothy (1 Tim 6:16; 2 Tim 4:18).

The Response Required

Once again addressing Timothy as *my son*, Paul says, *I am giving you this command* (1:18a) – but what command does he mean? Is he speaking of the earlier command to stay in Ephesus and teach the church there (1:3, 5)? Some commentators think so.[44] Others argue that Timothy is being instructed to *fight the battle well* (1:18b).[45] There is also a third possibility that relates the command to the "trustworthy saying" in 1:15. This interpretation focuses on the fact that the "command" in 1:3 refers to maintaining sound doctrine and the godly character that goes with it. Then 1:15 sets out what constitutes sound doctrine: "Christ Jesus came into the world to save sinners". By saying that this truth "deserves full acceptance", Paul is indirectly issuing a command. He is telling Timothy that this is the truth that he is to uphold.[46] It is the basis for godliness.

The tniv translation is weak when it says that Paul is "giving" Timothy this instruction. The Greek word has a meaning that is closer to "entrust", as in the nrsv translation (see also 2 Tim 2:2).[47] It has the idea of handing over something very valuable that the recipient must keep safe. Today, the same word would be used for depositing a large sum of money in a bank account. A similar word would have been used in traditional Africa to describe a dying witchdoctor passing on his or her powers to a relative. Those who have been entrusted with these powers fear that if they do not maintain them, they will be punished by the spirit of their predecessor. Thus some of them are violently opposed to any suggestion that they should become Christians. They have been entrusted with something they regard as very precious, and they must guard it. If these heirs of witchcraft are this committed to preserving powers that do not produce life, how much more should we as Christians guard the gospel, which is the power of God, providing salvation (Rom 1:16).

Paul is not giving Timothy a new assignment. This assignment is part and parcel of his ministry, for it is *in keeping with the prophecies once made about you*.[48] These prophecies may have been made when Timothy was assigned his task in Ephesus.[49] Or they may have been made at the time of his ordination to ministry in general, assuming that he was ordained in the same way as Paul in Acts 13:1–2. At Paul's ordination, the leaders of the church laid hands on him and Barnabas. Something similar had probably been done for Timothy (4:14; 2 Tim 1:6).[50] There is no way of knowing exactly what Paul is referring to here, but it is clear that some type of prophesy led to, or accompanied, Timothy's involvement in ministry.

Paul reminds Timothy of these prophecies in order to encourage him. As he often does, he uses a military metaphor, telling him that *by recalling them you may fight the battle well* (1:18).[51] While engaged in this battle, Timothy is to be *holding on to faith and a good conscience* (1:19). Paul similarly linked doctrine and morality in 1:5, and he will do so again in 3:9. The doctrine Timothy is to fight to protect is set out in the "trustworthy saying" in 1:15. He faces not only an intellectual fight as he teaches this truth to others but also spiritual warfare as he rebukes those who are in error (1:3–4).

The danger of such warfare is that it may lead to arrogance and pride as one defends the truth, so that one becomes a bully. We sometimes see this happen when church leaders are so focused on church discipline that they ignore the suffering of the one under discipline. In the process of defending truth, they throw love out of the window. This is not how God deals with his children! God may cast out his child (in the sense of withdrawing his blessings from that person), but he does so only for a moment to help the person recognize his or her sin. The moment that person confesses and turns back to God, God stretches out his hand to them. Yet some who exercise discipline on God's behalf want the sinner to continue to suffer a little longer. Such an attitude serves their personal interests and not God's. God comes in the moment the door is opened (Rev 3:20).

The way to avoid falling into a bullying spirit is to allow the doctrine one is teaching to have the same impact on one's own life that it had on Paul – it reminded him of his own sinfulness (1:16). The awareness of what Christ has done for us will enable us to model the love "which comes from a pure heart and a good conscience and a sincere faith" (1:5) and to manifest the fruit of the Spirit (Gal 5:22). No matter how hard the battle, we must make sure that our conscience, our inner judge, is pure and is not accusing us.

Deviators from the Truth

When we ignore our consciences and allow them to become deadened, we risk shipwreck of our faith. This was what had happened to *Hymenaeus and Alexander* (1:20a). These specific men may be mentioned because they had been leading others astray. Someone called Hymenaeus is later mentioned as one of those teaching that "the resurrection has already taken place" (2 Tim 2:17–18). Alexander may be the metalworker mentioned in 2 Timothy 4:14 as having done "a great deal of harm" to Paul. He may or may not be the same person mentioned in Acts 19:33.[52] Beyond this, not much is known about these men. What is important about them is that they are examples of what Timothy should never let happen to him.

The interconnection between doctrine and ethics, theology and behaviour, is striking. Once we allow our consciences to become damaged, we can very easily find ourselves holding very strange beliefs without being at all bothered by them. It becomes easy to believe in false teachings without being aware that we are destroying our faith.[53]

This point is somewhat obscured by the niv translation, which reads "some have rejected these", implying that these persons have rejected both the faith and a good conscience. The tniv (and nasb) translation is closer to the original Greek, *holding on to faith and a good conscience, which some have rejected.* In the Greek, the "which" is singular, indicating that only one thing was being rejected.[54]

Paul has a strong response to those who have shipwrecked their faith: he has *handed* them *over to Satan* (1:20b). In the battle between truth and error, there are only two kingdoms: the kingdom of God (in which the church exists) and the kingdom of Satan, which God has permitted to exist for a limited time. Excommunication (which is what Paul is probably speaking about here) meant that the person was excluded from the church, and was thus returned to the kingdom of Satan. For Hymenaeus and Alexander, excommunication was meant to discipline them by teaching them not to make false statements about God and his plan of redemption.[55]

Paul had recommended that the Corinthian church apply the same punishment to a church member who was practising incest (1 Cor 5:5). It seems that the Corinthians may have got carried away in their excitement at exercising discipline, for in 2 Corinthians 2:5–11 Paul has to remind them that once discipline had achieved its goal, it is to be lifted.

Questions for Discussion

1. In many parts of Africa, traditional healers or witchdoctors play a key role in the community. Witnessing to them is among the hardest part of an evangelist's work. In some circles, therefore, they are written off. Evangelists only visit the homes of their neighbours, and hope that one day something will happen to make the witchdoctor turn to God. Yet many witchdoctors view themselves as working in partnership with God, rather than against him. It might even be that if Paul had lived in African society, he would have described himself as "the traditional healer of traditional healers"! He had been deeply rooted in his traditional faith, but when he was turned around by the power he could not resist, he became an outstanding example of God's power at work to change lives. If God could do this for Paul, what should our attitude be towards those in our communities who are difficult to witness to? How should we act towards them? What

has been your own experience with people who were hard to reach in your community?

2. Truth was not always an important factor in the work of traditional healers in Africa. What was important was not what the healer believed but what the one needing help could be persuaded to believe. If a client believed that holding a piece of feather or jumping up and down seven times could heal him or her, then that might be prescribed. Or someone might be told that they were being bewitched by "the neighbour across the river", without the healer knowing anything except that there was such a neighbour because the client had described his home. Yet the client would leave feeling that issues had been satisfactorily diagnosed and treated. The end was seen as justifying the means. How is this different from how Paul tells Timothy to conduct his ministry, that is, "holding on to faith and a good conscience"?

3. In most African churches, someone who has been excommunicated cannot take communion, have a church wedding, or even sing in the choir. The length of the period of excommunication is sometimes determined on a sliding scale, depending on the type of sin the person has committed. But should someone remain excommunicated after he or she has sincerely repented, as far as we can tell? What are the merits and demerits of focusing on the kind of sin committed and not on the attitude of the sinner towards what has been done? Can you think of specific cases within your own church that relate to this issue? Be careful that you do not break the principle of confidentiality if you choose to mention them. In what ways is Paul's description of himself as "the worst of sinners" an example for us?

UNIT 6
1 TIMOTHY 2:1–8

PAUL'S CALL TO PRAYER

One of the most beautiful prayers in the Bible is found in Genesis 18:22–33. It is beautiful, in part, because it is unselfish. Abraham was praying fervently on behalf of his nephew, Lot, even though Lot had not treated him well and had chosen the best land for himself (Gen 13:5–12). It is also beautiful because it demonstrates God's patience, as he allows Abraham to bargain with him, changing his request six times as he pleads for the cities of Sodom and Gomorrah. Abraham was well aware that he had no right to expect God to answer his prayer, but God graciously listened to him. Even though God could not find even ten righteous people in these cities, he delayed his judgment, giving Lot and his family time to escape (Gen 19:15, 29). Unfortunately, not all of them used this opportunity (Gen 19:14; 19:26).

Abraham's prayer was powerful and effective. But is it a model for how we should pray today? Should we still be praying for cities and their leaders? If so, what should we pray for them? And where do our responsibilities end and those of others begin? These questions were important in Paul's day, and they are still important for us today. We can learn a lot from Paul's instructions to Timothy and the Ephesians.

Paul obviously considered this a matter of prime importance. The opening chapter of this letter was intended to encourage Timothy to carry out his task as a leader. Now, Paul gets down to some details of church life, and the first topic he raises is prayer. Prayer is urgent and important. Without prayer, worship is not complete and the church is in danger of becoming just another community group.

Components of Prayer

Speaking of the "components" of prayer may make it sound as if prayer can be assembled using a toolkit. This is not the case. Nevertheless, it can be helpful to consider the elements that go into prayer. One common approach is to use the acronym ACTS, which stands for adoration, confession, thanksgiving, and supplication. While Paul would not have known of this acronym, there are similar elements in the list he gives us in 1 Timothy 2:1:

- *Petitions* acknowledge that we need help.[56] In this sense, they can be linked to the idea of confession in the ACTS acronym.
- *Prayers* is a general term, which includes all the components of prayer mentioned in the ACTS acronym, in this verse, and elsewhere. It embraces everything that communicates our devotion to God. In the Bible, this word is never used for any communication directed to a person but only for communication directed to God.[57]
- *Intercession* has the idea of someone or some group speaking to a superior on behalf of someone else. Three parties are involved in such a prayer: God, the person in need, and the person or persons who are praying for them.[58] In the ACTS model, supplication is equivalent to intercession.
- *Thanksgiving* brings balance to our approach to God. We should not only tell him of our own needs and the needs of others, but we should also thank him for what he has done. Kelly describes such prayers as "blessing and thanksgiving to God for all his goodness, from the creation of the world to the sending of his Son to suffer, die, and rise again for man's salvation".[59] Even if we may not have something specific to thank God for each time we pray, we can still thank him for his creation, which we enjoy all the time, and for the privilege of being among those he has redeemed. These are grounds for the adoration identified in the ACTS acronym.

Paul's list does not cover all possible components of prayer. He is not attempting to that. What he is doing is emphasizing the importance of prayer.[60]

Who to Pray For

When we pray for people, we are wishing them well. And the people for whom we wish things to be well are often related to us in some way. We see this in the secular world when politicians favour their families and those from their own people group. Our response is often to accuse these politicians of favouritism and discrimination against outsiders. But are we guilty of the same thing when we pray? Paul seems to imply that this was a problem in the church at Ephesus. A sense of exclusiveness may have led to some discrimination in the sense that the believers were reluctant to pray for certain people. Although we have no evidence to support this theory, it would explain why Paul here places such stress on praying *for everyone* (2:1) and carries on to emphasize that God desires *all people to be saved* (2:4), and that Christ gave himself *as a ransom for all people* (2:6).[61]

Kings are a subset of the "everyone" for whom prayers should be offered. Paul does not have specific kings in mind, but rather is speaking of those who are in leadership positions, whether they lead an empire, a country, a province or a city.[62] They need to be prayed for not just as individuals but in terms of the office they hold.[63]

It is worth remembering that when Paul wrote this letter, the Roman Empire was led by Nero, an emperor who persecuted Christians. Paul knew his record and could understand why Christians might be reluctant to pray for him. Nevertheless, prayers must be offered for him and for his successors. They may be oppressive rulers, but their administration may still benefit some people, and even living under a bad ruler is better than living in a state of anarchy. Christians need to pray that such rulers will be led to govern according to God's will. How can they be expected to carry out their duties properly if no one is praying that they will have the wisdom to govern well?

Prayer does not guarantee us a good leader, for God in his mysterious dealing with us may still allow bad rulers like Pharaoh (Exod 6:1–12:30) and Nero. But lack of prayer for our leaders takes us one step closer to (or a step deeper into) bad rule.

Prayer for our rulers also does not mean that we endorse everything they do or see them as above criticism. We should always remember that the ultimate ruler is God himself, and that his rule balances love and justice for all. Human rulers are his agents (Rom 13:1–5), and if they deviate from his path of truth and righteousness, they are not serving him faithfully. When we pray for such rulers, we do not ask the Lord to bless and prosper them, but rather ask the Lord to work in their hearts to help them recognize the wrongs that they are committing or permitting. We may even pray for God to remove an evil ruler. It is also not wrong for Christians to be involved in an active political campaign to remove a corrupt ruler from office, even while praying for God to speak to that ruler.

Nor is it enough to pray only for the king or president. Christians are also to pray for all those who govern under and on behalf of the ruler. Just as the "all men" at the start of this list included everyone, so "all those in authority" leaves out no one who has a position of power. In the African context, this includes everyone from the village elder who has to resolve a boundary dispute between neighbours to the president whose decisions affect the entire nation. Regardless of the scope of a person's authority, they need our prayers if we are to enjoy just and righteous government.

What to Pray For

The ultimate purpose of our prayer for those in authority is to enable us to *live peaceful and quiet lives*. Some have suggested that "peaceful" means "free from outward disturbance", and that "quiet" means "free from trouble within" or "inner peace". But we do not have enough evidence to support this distinction.[64] It seems more likely that "peaceful and quiet" are complementary terms, which together mean "freedom from war, from rebellion and from anything which would disturb the peace of the realm".[65]

When the surroundings are peaceful, it is easier to live *in all godliness*.[66] Here "godliness" is equivalent to "piety". This word lacks the theological richness of terms like justification and sanctification, which Paul uses elsewhere when talking about life in Christ. But he may have chosen to use it here because it was a term the false teachers were using. Paul does not want to cede it to them, for it is a term that is broad enough to cover both our relationship with God and our relationship with others. As Barclay notes, a godly person does not forget "the reverence due to

God ... the rights due to others ... and the respect due to self.[67] We can recognize the importance of all three of these dimensions if we think about the many African leaders who attend church and claim to show "the reverence due to God". But when it comes to running the country, many of them "ignore the rights due to others", that is, the rights of the very people they are meant to lead. Their details of their personal lives also reveal a lack of self-respect, and lead others to lose respect for their office.

While it is easy to identify this error in others, it is more challenging to identify it in ourselves. We need to constantly ask ourselves: Do we truly love God? Is serving others more important than serving our own interests? Are we maintaining our personal dignity in all areas of life, including our behaviour and speech? Can our lives be described as godly?

The term coupled with "godliness" in 2:2 is translated as *holiness* in the tniv, but would be better translated "dignity", as in the nasb. It indicates lives that are lived honourably and taken seriously, rather than being carelessly wasted.

Who We Pray To

The reason we should pray for all men is because it *is good*[68] *and pleases God our Saviour*,[69] who is the one to whom our prayers are addressed (2:3). Paul then adds further information about the character of this Saviour: he *wants all people to be saved* (2:3, 4). It would be easy to take this verse as offering hope of universal salvation. But to do so is to misinterpret Paul. The Greek word translated "wants" does not mean that this is God's perfect will, which cannot be thwarted. Rather, Paul uses a word that indicates only God's general purpose for humanity – he offers salvation to all. To put it another way, Paul is not saying that God wills "to save all people", but that he wills that "all be saved".[70] The difference may be illustrated using an everyday example. Weddings and funerals in Africa are open to anyone who wants to attend. No one is turned away because they are not holding an invitation. Everyone who arrives is welcome, and there are no hurt feelings if someone does not arrive (unless, of course, that someone has an important role to play, like the best man). In the same way, everyone is invited to enjoy God's salvation. All who come will be welcomed, but God's purpose will not be frustrated if some people choose not to be saved.[71]

Being saved is described as equivalent to coming *to a knowledge of the truth* (2:4; see also 2 Tim 2:25; 3:7; Titus 1:1).[72] Some amount of knowledge has to precede saving faith. But mere head knowledge, mental acquaintance with certain facts, does not bring about salvation. The knowledge that Paul is speaking of here needs to be appreciated and accepted.[73] In this sense, coming to a knowledge of the truth is equivalent to being converted.

But how much of the truth does one have to know in order to be saved? Is Paul referring to the whole of God's revelation, a complete set of doctrines? This seems unlikely. Those who have not begun the journey of salvation need to know just enough truth to start on the journey. For example, when preaching in a market place, we would not present a full systematic theology. Instead, we might start by pointing to the Supreme God whom almost all African people groups acknowledge. Then we should identify this God as the Father of the Lord Jesus Christ whom God sent to offer his life as a sacrifice for our sins. Finally, we might explain how one exercises faith in this Jesus so as to have fellowship with God. This is all the truth one needs to know in order to be saved. It is the truth Paul summarized in his "trustworthy saying" (1:15) and expanded on in 2:5–6. In order to be saved, one needs to know only enough of the truth to recognize one's own sin, Christ's work of atonement, and his role as a mediator between us and God (2:5).

However, once people have begun to walk the path of salvation, they need to learn more of the deeper teachings of the gospel about such things as the work of the Holy Spirit in our lives, prayer, and the like.

What Makes Prayer Possible

Paul begins the next section with the word "for" because he is answering an implied question: How is it possible to pray for everyone and to extend the offer of salvation to all? The reason that Paul gives is that there is only *one God*, who is the God of all (2:5a). He has ruled that everyone must approach him in the same way, through the *one mediator between God and human beings*.

A mediator is someone who acts as a go-between when for some reason people cannot talk to each other directly. For example, a young man may want to marry a certain young woman, but his family may sense that her family would not welcome this request. So the family finds a mediator, someone who is a friend of both families, who can act as a bridge upon which each party walks to reach the other. The same process takes place when a village elder is asked to help settle a land dispute between two neighbours. The one asked to act as mediator needs to have a full understanding of each party's position and to be able to represent both parties in any negotiations.

Christ is qualified to act as a mediator because he understands both God and us. Paul has already spoken of Christ's divine origins (1:15), but now he emphasizes the other side of the coin as he speaks of *Christ Jesus, himself human* (2:5b).[74] As a human man, Jesus could act on our behalf too. He is thus eminently qualified to act as a mediator.

But this mediator between God and humanity is more than merely a go-between. He committed himself to bringing about the reconciliation of these two parties by giving *himself as a ransom*[75] *for all people* (2:6a). The word "ransom" reminds us of the sad practice of kidnapping people and holding them until those who love them pay a large sum for their release. The "ransom" is the sum paid to win the release of the prisoner.[76] We were prisoners, and Christ offered himself as the payment to set us free.[77] If our freedom requires such a price, people must be of great value to God. No wonder we need to pray for "all people to be saved" (2:4).

Speaking of Christ's giving himself as a ransom for many, Paul says, *This has now been witnessed to at the proper time* (2:6b).[78] The phrase "at the proper time" conveys the idea that this was the time when the circumstances were just right, and also the idea that God controls the circumstances in which this testimony would be given. But to whom was it given? There are three possible answers.

- Christ's work is a general testimony to the existence of God's plan of salvation, which has finally been fulfilled. All the preparations in terms of the forerunners of Christ and the prophecies about him have culminated in his coming into the world to save sinners.[79]

- Everyone: Christ's offering of himself is a testimony to humankind.[80] Men and women should see what he has done and be moved by it.
- The Ephesian church: Christ's paying of a ransom testifies to the value of human beings in God's eyes and is thus a testimony to them about the importance of their praying for everyone.[81]

Although all three possibilities are plausible, the second seems the most likely. The testimony was probably intended to be heard by everyone. Christ's redemption of us is a testimony to how much God loves every man and woman. Given this understanding, it is unnecessary to argue about whether this testimony was given in the past on the cross, in the present when Paul is preaching, or in the future when Christ returns (see 1 Tim 6:14–15).[82] The testimony is given at all these times, and excludes none of them.

Similarly, it is not necessary to argue about whether the witness is solely about Christ's being a ransom "for all people" (2:6a),[83] or whether it also includes the words about Christ as a mediator in 2:5,[84] or covers all the content of 1:4–6a.[85] It is best to focus on the general truth on which all agree: God cares about human beings.

Paul's Role

This testimony is the reason God called Paul – *for this purpose I was appointed a herald and an apostle* (2:7a).[86] He was appointed to this position for the specific purpose of proclaiming Christ's role as mediator between God and humanity. The passive voice makes it clear that he did not appoint himself to the task but was called to it (see 1:12).

Paul's role as a proclaimer is evident from the word translated "herald".[87] Heralds proclaim a message that someone else gives them. It is not their own message. The key qualification for being a herald is having a loud voice and being prepared to deliver exactly the same message you were given.[88] In Africa today we see someone acting as a herald when a provincial commissioner or governor reads a speech written by the president to people gathered in different locations. Once the exact words of the speech have been read, the reader may decide to emphasize some particular points in it. But whatever is said must be consistent with the message from the head of state. Paul saw his duties as a herald in the same light. It was his duty to announce what the Lord had stated. Sometimes he might need to explain some point in more detail, but whatever he said had to be consistent with the message he had been told to proclaim.

Besides being a herald, Paul is also an apostle – a position with more authority than is usually enjoyed by a herald, who merely carries out a task.[89] As an apostle, he had been given the task of teaching the Gentiles about the mystery of salvation (2:7c).[90]

Paul's stress on the fact that his mission is to *the Gentiles* may be intended to convey a message to any Jews among the believers in Ephesus. These Jewish believers might have tended to be exclusivist, and Paul is gently reminding them that the gospel was open to everyone, including non-Jews. He made the same point when he emphasized the importance of praying for everyone (2:1).

Paul describes himself as *a true and faithful teacher of the Gentiles*. The niv translates these words as "a teacher of the true faith to the Gentiles", while the nasb and nkjv adopt a more literal translation, "a teacher of the Gentiles in faith and truth". The different translations show that these words can be interpreted in more than one way. They can be read as saying that what Paul preached was only faith and truth.[91] Or they may be read as saying that Paul himself was faithful and truthful as he proclaimed his message. Or they can be seen as a Greek expression which would be interpreted as "the true faith", as opposed to the false teachings that Timothy was to oppose.[92]

After introducing himself as a herald and an apostle, Paul suddenly interjects *I am telling the truth, I am not lying* (2:7b). He makes this point both positively and negatively[93] – but what is it that he needs to confirm so strongly? Is it the statement that he has just made about his office, or is it the statement that follows in which he says that his mission is to teach faith and truth to the Gentiles? And why does he need to say this to his close friend Timothy?

The answer to the last question is that Paul is not speaking only to Timothy but also to the members of the church in Ephesus who will have this letter read to them. Some of them may have needed this strong reminder that Paul was an apostle. Others, who may have been Jews and tempted to regard themselves as in the inner circle of the faith, may have needed to be reminded that Paul's mission to Gentiles was "proof of God's will to save all men, and therefore of the obligation to pray for them all".[94] Paul is telling them that their message of exclusiveness was not only "counter to the Saviour's desires (2:4) and the mediator's death (2:6), but also contradicted the core of Paul's divinely appointed ministry".[95]

How to Pray

Paul concludes by giving instructions on practical details in regard to prayer (2:8). He begins these instructions with the word translated *I want*, which expresses an "authoritative desire" or "command".[96]

The instruction is directed specifically to men as opposed to women. Some have interpreted this as meaning that Paul is forbidding women praying in public worship. But Paul did not forbid this in Corinth (1 Cor 11:5). It may be that special circumstances in the Ephesian church led him to take a different position there (see commentary on 2:9–13).

But, some will argue, Paul speaks of *the men everywhere*, that is, wherever there is a worshipping group.[97] Yet it can equally be argued that what Paul means is "in every place where believers gather in and around Ephesus", for the believers met in house churches.[98] Given the whole context of Paul's writing, it makes sense to limit this command to Ephesus but to seek to apply the general principle on which Paul is operating to all churches in all times.

The men who pray should be *lifting up holy hands*. This was the standard posture when praying at that time. As Kelly says, "The most general attitude for prayer in antiquity, for pagans, Jews and Christians alike, was to stand with hands outstretched and uplifted, the palm turned upwards."[99] What is distinctive here is that the lifted hands are to be holy. The one praying should have an attitude that is acceptable to God. The Jews recognized this and would symbolically wash their hands before praying. But Paul is not here concerned about any ritual cleansing but with the heart and the spirit. He gives two examples of what a holy attitude involves. First, one must be *without anger*. Anger precludes forgiveness, and without forgiveness God does not answer prayer (Matt 6:12). Second, one must not be *disputing* or encouraging dissent. This attitude was important given the arguments that were likely to have arisen because of the problems in the Ephesian church.[100]

Worship that is not combined with relationships that honour the gospel is no more than a ritual and does not draw people to God. We must forgive and settle all disputes before we can truly worship and honour God. This is Paul's call to the church in Ephesus.

Questions for Discussion

1. Some years ago, a certain African leader was killing many people in Uganda and creating havoc all over East Africa. At a meeting of pastors and other church leaders, I was asked whether there is a place for such a person in our prayers. Most of those present felt that the answer was "No!" But on reflection, many of us began to see that we needed to pray even for him. What in this passage communicates that prayer for others goes beyond the way we feel about them? How does this point relate to current leaders of nations, churches, institutions, families and so on for whom we may not have warm feelings?

2. Paul says that his ministry is characterized by faith and truth, implying that his goal is to promote saving faith in the Lord Jesus Christ in a manner in which he is true to God (as a faithful servant), to others around him (without pretence), and to himself (maintaining a clear conscience). Do ministers of the gospel today have a similar focus? In light of your answer, do you have any recommendations about the training pastors receive today?

UNIT 7
1 TIMOTHY 2:9–15

WOMEN AND GODLINESS

Over the past century, women's issues have drawn increasing attention. Now the United Nations even supports the annual celebration of International Women's Day on 8 March. This day is often used as an opportunity to speak out against violence against women. Speakers will argue that because women have been treated as inferior to men, they have sometimes been denied their full humanity. Many are raped, forced into marriages they do not want, and infected with HIV/AIDS. There is thus a call for women to be empowered and for their interests to be protected.

This call needs to be heard by Christians. We, too, need to examine our cultural attitudes towards women and evaluate them in the light of what the Bible says. As we do this, we need to remember that we are all influenced by the presuppositions we absorbed as we were growing up. Thus, to give one example, those who come from cultures where a woman has no say in the family will find it difficult to accept women speaking out in the church the family attends.

But cultures change. In recent years, men have become more accepting of women having a say in how things are run. Moreover, men have been challenged by discovering that some women can sometimes do things even better than men. So what does God wants to do with and through women in twenty-first century Africa?

As we seek to answer this question, we must take care that we are neither culture-bound (hanging onto the past), nor culture-led (simply changing with the times). We must be guided by the teaching of Scripture expressed in passages such as 1 Timothy 2:9–15.

Clothing

Paul introduces his discussion of women with the words *I also want the women*. The "also" has sparked much discussion. Some argue that it is linked to the instruction addressed to men in 2:8. There Paul said "I want men" to pray in this way, and here in 2:9 he is giving directions for how women should pray.[101] The message of the verse is then that "men will pray aloud with outward gesture; women will also pray, but with care not to draw attention to themselves"[102]

Others argue that it is not necessary to restrict the meaning in this way. They say that the "also" simply indicates that whereas in 2:8 Paul was addressing men, he now turns to address women. This instruction is simply the second item in the list of Paul's "wants".[103]

But this is not the end of the controversy. There is also debate about whether Paul is talking only about how women should dress during public worship,[104] or whether he is speaking about their dress in general.[105] This debate can only be resolved by looking at the context of the instruction.

Paul's main concern in 1 Timothy is to encourage behaviour that will promote the Christian faith and not hinder it. He exhorts men to have "holy hands" when they pray (2:8) because he knows that hypocrisy, a mismatch between our character and our words, hinders God's work. Given this focus on character, it seems likely that Paul is telling the Christian women in Ephesus to wear clothing that reflects the godliness in their lives. Such godliness should be displayed at all times, not merely in worship services.

So how should Christian women dress? Paul's first requirement is that the clothing should be "respectable" (esv) or "proper" (nasb).[106] It should not send the wrong message about their morals or lifestyle. Paul then expands on this description, saying that they should dress *with decency*, or as the esv puts it, with "modesty".[107] In other words, they should not display more of their bodies than is culturally appropriate. Finally, they are to dress with "propriety", or as the esv translates it, with "self-control".[108] Someone who is self-controlled in how they dress will neither be a slave to fashion, nor go to the opposite extreme and completely neglect their clothing.

Having laid down this principle, Paul proceeds to give a specific application of it that applies to the women in Ephesus. For women there, dressing with modesty and self-control meant they should not show off *elaborate hairstyles or gold or pearls or expensive clothes* (2:9). The words translated "elaborate hairstyles" literally mean "braided hair", as in the niv. Paul is not speaking against going to the hairdresser or braiding one's hair. He is simply saying that it should not be done in contexts where it would constitute excessive ornamentation – or in a context where the time spent doing the braiding is at the expense of time spent doing good deeds. Such deeds are far more important than fashionable clothing *for women who profess to worship God* (2:10).

Paul is not saying that Christian women should never dress well. He is simply setting priorities. Inner character is far more important than outward appearance. What one wears should be *appropriate*, never out of keeping with one's character.[109]

The general principle that Paul lays down will apply differently in different cultures and at different economic levels. But Christian women in every culture need to determine what type of clothing is modest and discreet, remembering that the highest goal of any believer is to glorify God.

Authority

1 Timothy 2:11–15 is a passage about which there are strong disagreements. So it is helpful to deal with what it meant for Timothy and those at Ephesus first, before we look at its significance and application today.

Interpretations of the meaning of this passage fall into two main groups: the historical or traditional view and the progressive view. Those who adopt the historical view insist that women should never serve as pastors, elders and overseers in the church. Those who adopt the progressive position say that women's ministry should not be limited. Every student of Scripture needs to examine both views and form their own opinion about what Paul is teaching.

Paul begins by saying *a woman should learn* (2:11a). Scholars debate whether the different ways Paul introduces his instructions indicate that they have different levels of authority. Does the imperative, "a woman should learn" represent a firmer instruction than the "I want" in 2:8, and is this different from the prohibition "I do not permit" in 2:12?[110] The answer seems to be that all of these expressions should be given equal weight. They are simply different ways of expressing Paul's opinions, shaped by the Holy Spirit and carrying apostolic authority, about what type of behaviour will bring honour to God in Ephesus.

Paul's specific instructions

Paul's first instruction is that a woman should learn *in quietness and full submission* (2:11). But what exactly does the Greek word translated "quietness" mean?[111] It can be translated as "in silence" (kjv) or as "quietly" (nasb). Silence is not the same as quietness, and thus the different translations have different implications for what women may or may not do.

Similarly, when women are told to learn in "full submission", we inevitably ask, in submission to whom? While Paul is clearly calling on women to acknowledge some authority over them, he does not specify what authority. The possibilities suggested by commentators include men in general, their husbands, the congregation, social norms, sound teaching and the teachers or overseers in the church.

It becomes easier to identify whose authority Paul is likely to be referring to if we focus on Paul's reason for writing his two letters to Timothy. His main purpose was to encourage soundness in belief and character in the church in Ephesus. Timothy was to teach these to others who would be capable of passing on his instruction (2 Tim 2:2). Given this focus, it seems likely that the women were being asked to submit to the teachers and overseers in the church at Ephesus, and to their sound teaching.

This interpretation fits in well with Paul's second instruction, *I do not permit a woman to teach or to assume authority over a man; she must be quiet* (2:12). Some argue that the "I" in "I do not permit" indicates that Paul is here giving his own opinion rather than making an authoritative statement. But it seems more probable that Paul is here speaking as an apostle and making an authoritative pronouncement on what behaviour will contribute positively to the building of the Kingdom of God.

But this gives rise to a further question: Does this ruling apply to the kingdom of God at all times? The verb is in the present tense, which could either be used to express a universal truth or could be translated "I am not permitting", implying that this ruling applied only to the circumstances prevailing in the Ephesian church at that time.

There is also debate about what exactly Paul meant when he spoke of "a woman". Did he possibly mean one particular woman who was in authority over one particular man? Or is he using a generic singular, so that "a woman" represents all women? If so, does he mean all the Ephesian women who had been led astray by false teachers? Or all the women in Ephesus? Or all the Christian women of his day? Or all Christian women throughout the centuries?

Assuming we can resolve the question of which women are being referred to, we run into another problem. Who were women not permitted to teach? Was it anyone at all, men in general, their husbands or the overseers? Given Paul's general concern with order in public worship, the overseers seem the most likely candidates. The women are not to assert that they already know everything and can teach others. They must allow the overseers to teach and correct them.

Once we have resolved the problem of whom the women were not to teach, we run into the problem of what it was they were not to teach. The options include that they were not to spread erroneous teaching, not to teach the truth of the gospel, or not to teach anything at all, including the truth of the gospel. In the context of this letter, is seems most likely that what they are not to teach is the gospel. Linking this with the point above, Paul seems to be telling the women to allow the overseers to teach them the truth of the gospel and not vice versa.

Paul not only says that he does not allow women to teach, he also says that he does not allow them "to assume authority over a man". The Greek word used here may refer to exercising authority in a neutral sense, or it may mean the negative exercise of authority, which could be described as "domineering", or even "instigating violence".[112] If the context here is public worship and Paul's first instruction is that the women are to allow the overseers to teach them, it seems likely that Paul is here thinking of negative aspects of authority.[113] It seems that some women were refusing to be taught by the church leaders, claiming that they knew better.

If this interpretation is correct, then this passage also tells us how much authority Paul accorded a teacher of the gospel. In today's terms, such a person might even be thought of as being dictatorial – not in terms of their attitude to others, but in terms of their insistence on the truthfulness of what they are passing on. The truth was a deposit that had been entrusted to Paul, who had passed it on to Timothy, who was to entrust it to others. This truth must be passed on accurately, and thus those to whom it is entrusted are endowed with great authority. Women were told to leave this authority in the hands of men, specifically the men appointed as teachers over the congregation. Instead of seeking to teach, the women were called upon to be "quiet" (see comment on 2:12).

Today, the truths that Paul and Timothy taught have been preserved for us in the New Testament, and it is this book which is our authority. However, this change does not mean that we no longer need to respect the authority of those who proclaim its message.

Basis for Paul's instructions

Paul gives two reasons for asking women to leave it to men, particularly those men who are overseers, to teach and exercise authority, namely, *Adam was formed first, then Eve* (2:13) and *Adam was not the one deceived; it was the woman who was deceived and became a sinner* (2:14).[114]

Paul's argument goes back to the account of creation and the fall in Genesis 2 and 3. God created Adam before he created Eve. Eve was also the one who first fell for the serpent's deception. In saying that she thus "became a sinner", Paul is not denying that Adam also fell into sin. To do so would go against his own teaching in Romans 5:12–14, where he stresses that everyone is a sinner because Adam sinned. Paul's point here is that Satan deliberately set out to deceive Eve, and that she listened to him and disobeyed God (Gen 3:13). Her disobedience had lasting results in that it transformed her into a sinner.[115]

Thus far everything is clear. But the problems arise when we ask what point Paul is making when he stresses that Adam was created first. Is he saying that men are natural leaders?[116] It is difficult to prove that men have some special God-given talent for leadership. It is also undeniable that some women have more leadership qualities than some men. Thus it seems likely that Paul is not talking about the ability to lead or about one sex being superior to the other. If this was what he meant, he is contradicting his own words about our equality in Christ (Gal 3:28).

It seems more likely that he is talking about the men being the leaders because God has put them in that position for the sake of order in the family and in larger groups, such as the church. His focus is on good order, not on ability. In the Ephesian situation, Paul is telling women to let men (overseers) be the teachers and exercise authority over them (and not vice versa) because that is the order God established from the very beginning.

When Paul mentions Eve's being the first to sin, he is using this example to make the point that what happened in Eden is also happening in Ephesus. For some reason, the women were being easier prey for the false teachers. The ringleaders in spreading the false teachings were men (1:3). Like the serpent in Genesis 3, they were the deceivers. Many of the Christian women in Ephesus were in the ranks of the deceived (2 Tim 3:6–7). Paul is telling the women there: "Do you see what is happening among you? It's the same thing that happened to Eve. So let the overseers teach you." He is asking them to allow the male overseers to be their teachers. If they do this, fewer of them will fall prey to false teachers and the effects of the false teachings will be reduced.

Childbearing

What are the women in Ephesus to do if they are not to teach in the church? Paul answers this question by addressing the nobility of the role of women and its benefits for salvation. He says *women will be saved through childbearing – if they continue in faith, love and holiness with propriety* (2:15).

The word "women" is not present in the original Greek, which simply reads "she shall be saved". The "she" here must be Eve, the results of whose disobedience are still present with us. But why does Paul, writing in the first century ad, use the future tense when talking about Eve?[117] It seems that he is thinking of Eve as more than just Adam's wife. He sees her as representative of all the women in Ephesus, many of whom were being deceived by the false teachers. This may be why Paul does not use the name Eve in 2:14, but instead speaks of "the woman".

But what does Paul mean when he speaks of women being "saved through childbearing"? If we take this as referring to spiritual salvation, then Paul is offering a form of salvation by works. But in letters like the one to the Galatians, he vehemently opposes any such notion and insists that salvation is by grace alone.

Does Paul then mean that believing women will be kept safe during childbirth? In Genesis 3:15, Eve's punishment included suffering during childbirth. Is Paul saying that this curse will be lifted for women who meet the conditions given (if they continue in faith, love and holiness with propriety)? This is an attractive option – but it is not true to human experience. Many devout Christian women have died in childbirth.

Other commentators have read these words as implying that woman will be saved through the birth of the Messiah, a descendant of Eve through many generations of mothers (Matt 2:18–25; Luke 3:23–37). But why would Paul use a future tense when speaking about Jesus' birth to Mary, an event that had happened some sixty years before Paul wrote to Timothy?

The best solution to this problem seems to be to interpret the verb not as "saved" but as "preserved", as in the nasb translation.[118] Paul is applying the saying, "an idle mind is the devil's workshop." If women occupy themselves with childbearing and the challenges that go with it, they will be able to avoid the error some women in Ephesus have fallen into. But busyness alone is no guarantee of preservation from error. It needs to go hand in hand with a decision to practice the virtues of "faith and love and sanctity with self-restraint" (nasb). Paul is teaching the women in Ephesus how to stay away from trouble by keeping busy and living Christian lives.

Contemporary Application

How are we to apply 1 Timothy 2:9–15 today? Are Paul's instructions about the role of women intended for the church in all ages? Or are they intended only for the church in Ephesus? The answer seems to be that this passage gives universal principles that apply in all ages, but that these principles have specific local applications.
- The universal principle about dressing is that a Christian woman should not allow the way she dresses to give others a bad impression of the faith. However, what specific elements of her dress will give a bad impression is culturally determined. For example, in some areas

it may be unacceptable for a woman to wear trousers, whereas in other areas this might not cause any comment. Thus many African women dress differently when visiting their rural homes than they do in the city, or dress differently at home than they do when attending church. They know that others will judge their morals by their clothing. Some women may need to be reminded of this when it comes to how much of themselves they choose to expose in public.

- The universal principle on authority is that God has established a chain of command so that his people will live orderly lives. This chain of command gives the leadership position to men. However, the ways in which this principle is applied are culturally determined. In Ephesus, the particular question was about who should teach and who should not. The instruction that women should not teach is not the universal principle but the specific application. In different cultural settings, the principle will have different applications. This point becomes clear when we remember that many African men were taught by a female teacher at some point in their schooling. The fact that mattered was not her gender but whether she was a good teacher. We are clearly living in a different era from Paul and Timothy. It would therefore be wrong for us to apply Paul's instruction literally. If a woman can train a man to do mathematics, what a joy it should be to see her show a man the way of salvation! Of course, a woman pastor has to show wisdom as she teaches. There are still some men in Africa who would be turned off if she were to assert herself too strongly and unnecessarily. Her behaviour must not defeat the goal of Christian ministry, which is to nurture all to become like Christ.

- The universal principle about childbearing is that there is more than enough work for everyone to do. Paul must not be misread as saying that every woman must give birth. He is speaking in terms of the common pattern in his day whereby almost all women were married and had children. Today, some women have other occupations. What is important is not the specific job that a man or women does, but the fact that any job is honourable if done as to the Lord. Thus a woman who stays at home to care for her children is doing as honourable a job as the man who works as a pastor. This is a truth we do not want to lose in Africa, for a society is only as strong as its families. But whatever task we have been assigned, working hard at it will help to keep us from error if we combine our devotion to our job with devotion to virtue.

Questions for Discussion

Before tackling the questions below, you should take plenty of time to study this difficult passage and to discuss it with others so that you can understand how Paul's instructions to the believers in Ephesus relate to us today.

1. We are living in an age when many people are very aware of fashion trends. What kind of clothing would you describe as modest, decent and showing self-control in twenty-first century Africa? Do not focus solely on women's dress; also consider what style of dress is appropriate for Christian men.

2. African traditional culture has not encouraged women to speak with any degree of authority in the presence of men. The same attitude has been evident in the church. At one time, it was even debated whether a woman could teach a Bible class; now the debate is about whether she should hold a pastoral role in the church. Given that both men and women have been given spiritual gifts, have women in ministry been treated unfairly in Africa? How does a correct interpretation of this passage help change that? Are you aware of efforts that have been made to correct this problem within your denomination and church.

UNIT 8
1 TIMOTHY 3:1–7

OVERSEERS, PASTORS AND TEACHING ELDERS

In November 2004, my wife and I were eager to hear the verdict in an American murder trial that had lasted for several months. A young man was accused of killing his pregnant wife. All the evidence against him was circumstantial, and it seemed to us that his guilt could not be proven beyond reasonable doubt. Our hearts had gone out to all the parties involved. We had prayed for the Lord's comfort for the murdered woman's parents; for peace of mind and courage for the young man's parents as they wrestled with the idea that their beloved son might be a murderer; for the young man himself, that he would repent of any evil he might have done.

Shortly after 1:00 p.m., the verdict was read. The jury found him guilty of first-degree murder for killing his wife and of second-degree murder for killing her unborn baby. He faced the death penalty. I turned to my wife, and said, "He is going to die because he was unfaithful to his wife."

In the course of the trial it had come out that the young man had been involved in an affair with a twenty-nine-year-old woman. Some of his most private words to her had been taped and were played by the prosecution for all the world to hear. In North America, unfaithfulness to a spouse is not a crime that merits death. But the evidence that the young man was an adulterer and a liar led many people, including the jurors, to conclude that he was probably also a murderer, and had a marked influence on the outcome of the trial. His character led to his condemnation, even though all the other evidence of his involvement in the crime was circumstantial.

It truly does matter what kind of persons we are! People will judge the truth of statements made by us or about us on the basis of what they know about us. This is the point that Paul makes to the leaders of the church in Ephesus. He has already reminded the ordinary men and women in the church of how they should live, and now he turns to the leaders. They are the guardians of the gospel and their character will influence how others view the Christian faith.

The Role of an Overseer

The first type of leader Paul mentions is the *overseer* (1:1). This word is singular, not plural, and is translated as "bishop" in the kjv. Consequently some people think that the church in Ephesus had a hierarchy, with a bishop who had authority over a number of elders, who in turn were superior to deacons.[119] But the singular here seems to be generic, referring to the whole category and not to an individual. In fact, the titles of overseer and elder seem to have been used interchangeably (Titus 1:5–7). For example, in 1 Timothy 3, there is no mention of elders, and the office of an overseer is presented as directly above that of a deacon. It seems that in the hierarchy of the early church, an overseer was the same as a teaching elder (see Acts 6:1–4). Elders are mentioned in 1 Timothy 5:17, where they appear to be the same as the overseers mentioned in 3:2. The title "elder" emphasized someone's age and maturity, whereas the title "overseer" focused attention on the office he held.

Paul has no doubt that the office of an overseer is a noble one (3:1b). In fact, he is so certain of this point that he emphasizes it by introducing it with the words *here is a trustworthy saying* (3:1a).[120] Anyone who seeks such a position *desires a noble task*. Such a desire is good because of the important role an overseer plays in the church.

Qualifications of an Overseer

It is one thing to desire an honourable position; it is another thing to qualify for it. Paul thus turns to the qualities that an overseer should have. The most important one is that he must be *above reproach* (3:2a).[121] This requirement can be seen as summarizing all the other requirements. The same pattern of first making a general statement and then giving specific details is evident in 2:1–2, where Paul first urges prayers for "all men" and then goes on to mention "kings" and "those in authority" as specific objects for prayer.

Someone who is "above reproach" is "not open to attack" and lives a life that is "not open to censure".[122] The overseer should have "no obvious defect of character or conduct, in his past or present life, which the malicious, whether within or without the church, can exploit to his discredit".[123]

Although overseers' lives must not leave any loophole for criticism, this does not mean that they must be totally free from both internal and visible sin. If this were the requirement, then no one in Ephesus or anywhere else would qualify, for the New Testament explicitly states that we all sin (1 John 1:10). Nor must the overseers be hypocrites, disguising their own sinfulness. Rather than being show-offs who parade their righteousness, they must have solid character and must deserve their reputation.

Just as the list of people to be prayed for in 2:1–2 was not exhaustive, so the list of virtues given here does not cover every possible requirement for an overseer. Paul is simply listing some examples of the types of virtues required, probably focusing on those which mattered most in the Ephesian situation.

Husband of one wife

The fact that being *faithful to his wife* is the first item in Paul's list may indicate the importance Paul attached to this requirement. A similar requirement is given for deacons in 3:12 and for elders in Titus 1:6. There is, however, debate about what exactly Paul meant, for the phrase could also be translated as "the husband of but one wife" (niv). The following possibilities have been suggested:[124]

- An overseer must not be a bachelor. He must be married. This interpretation focuses on the need for maturity. However, it is unlikely for several reasons, one of which is that it would disqualify Paul and Timothy, for they were not married.
- An overseer must not have been married more than once, for any reason, including:

  a) *Divorce*. Divorce was very easy in Paul's day, and this may explain why someone who had been divorced and remarried might be excluded from the office of an overseer.

  b) *Death of a first wife*. Remarriage after one's first wife died may have been taken as a sign of weakness, and thus one who was "above reproach" would not have remarried. This attitude is suggested by the reference to widows who have "had but one husband" (alternative translation of 1 Tim 5:9 – see commentary). Paul may be suggesting that they should be satisfied with one marriage, and not seek a second one.

  c) *Polygamy*. While some assert that polygamy was common at the time when Paul wrote these letters, others deny this.[125]
- An overseer must not be divorced. This interpretation would also exclude any man who has married a divorced woman.[126]
- An overseer must be faithful to his wife. This interpretation is based on a literal translation of the Greek as "a one-woman man".[127] One of the strengths of this position is that it focuses on the character of the person at the time he is appointed to office. If someone's behaviour towards his wife is not chaste and mature, he is not qualified to be an overseer or deacon.

The church in Africa has generally interpreted this verse as meaning that a pastor must be married and may not be polygamous. The result has been that many mature people of good character have been denied ordination till they are married. At the same time, many who were polygamous when they came to faith have been denied the full exercise of their gifts. If, however, we accept the last of the possible interpretations presented above, and understand that Paul was focusing more on the person's moral integrity than on their marital status, every believer's gifts would be utilized fully. What Paul is saying is that those overseers who are married (as most of them are) must be faithful, and that those who are not married must display purity of character.

Temperate

Someone who is *temperate* is not a heavy drinker. But Paul addresses the issue of drunkenness in 3:3, and thus his focus here is unlikely to be on the amount of wine or beer consumed. He is probably using the word metaphorically, in which case it means that the overseer must be "clear-headed, self-possessed, sound in judgement and not an extremist".[128] The same word is used in 1 Timothy 3:11 for deacons' wives (or deaconesses) and in Titus 2:2 for older men.

Self-controlled

Someone who is *self-controlled* is also of "sound mind, discreet, prudent, … chaste or having complete control over sensual desires".[129] Such people are level-headed when making decisions or, as Aristotle put it, they desire "the right things in the right way and at the right time".[130] The same quality is required of elders (Titus 1:8) and of older men (Titus 2:2). It is equivalent to "discreet" in 1 Timothy 2:9 (nasb).

Respectable

Someone who is *respectable* is someone whose outward behaviour is in harmony with their inner being, and who is dignified, decent, orderly and honest. The word describes someone "whose life is beautiful and in whose character all things are harmoniously integrated".[131] This virtue is closely associated with self-control. The same word is used in 1 Timothy 2:9, where it is translated as "modestly" in relation to women's clothing.

Hospitable

Someone who is *hospitable* keeps an open house, but this house is simply the outward manifestation of an open heart. The house to which others are invited does not have to be a palace and the entertainment offered to guests does not have to be lavish. The person's attitude is far more important than their material circumstances. Hospitality is also expected to characterize Christians in general (Rom 12:13; Heb 13:2; 1 Pet 4:9; 3 John 5) as well as specific groups like widows (1 Tim 5:10). Overseers and elders have a particular responsibility to set a good example to other believers in this respect (see also Titus 1:8). A hospitable overseer spreads a spirit of hospitality, so that hospitality is also offered by the members of the congregation.

In New Testament times, hospitality was needed by messengers who travelled from church to church, wandering teachers and preachers, needy members of the church, and slaves who had no homes of their own.[132] Even today, when the need arises and a preacher of the word comes our way, giving him or her food and accommodation as he or she passes through makes us partners in his or her work. But such service does not exhaust the opportunities for hospitality in Africa! Until HIV and AIDS have been controlled or a cure is found, there will be a constant need to provide hospitality to children whose parents have died. We may care for these children under our own roof, or we may help an uncle, aunt, grandparent or some other relative to care for them. Another option is to sponsor one or two children in an orphanage, rather than allowing such homes to rely entirely on overseas help. Street children, too, call for our hospitality. While some of them may have chosen to run away from adequate homes, there are many who are the destitute children of single parents who desperately need a helping hand.

The question in Africa is not where can I be involved but what should I be involved in? May the Lord grant that each African believer will do the best he or she can to extend the hand of hospitality, in a planned and continuing manner, to at least one person in need.

Able to teach

Overseers should be skilled teachers. They need to know the truths of the gospel and must have the skill to pass them on to others. This characteristic is the one that particularly distinguishes them from deacons, who are not necessarily called *to teach*.

We gain a better understanding of overseers' duties as teachers from passages such as 2 Timothy 2:24–26 and Titus 1:9. They are to be loyal to the apostolic teaching, ready to instruct the congregation, and alert to refute any error that arises.[133] To be able to carry out these tasks, overseers need "knowledge of both mind and heart" in order to lead their people "into a deeper experience of God" and to know how to respond to error.[134] They must be "qualified by education and moral power to impart sound Christian teaching in opposition to many false teachers".[135]

Good teachers will relate what they teach to their hearers' lives just as older people in traditional settings used to do when they told stories with a moral point that was relevant to their hearers. Our goal must be to teach the whole counsel of God, but as we do so we need to help others to cross the bridge from the content of the passage taught to what it means in their everyday lives.

Most congregations in Africa are now taught by trained pastors, but at times an untrained elder has to serve as a leader until such time as there is a trained pastor. Such an elder must be able to accurately handle the word of God, must be a reader, and must be open to improving his or her knowledge through seminars and conferences. If teaching ministry is neglected there will be no spiritual growth among the believers.

Not given to drunkenness

An overseer must not overindulge in wine. Paul's repetition of this command in 1 Timothy 3:8 and Titus 1:7 suggests that *drunkenness* was a problem in Ephesus and in Crete, where Titus served. If so, that may explain why Timothy had decided to abstain totally from wine (1 Tim 5:23). Some of us would agree with him and argue that Christians should not drink at all, but that is not the point being made here. Paul is warning against being drunk, which would have been seen as a vice and a disgrace in Ephesian society.[136]

More can be learned about Paul's attitude to wine from his instruction to Timothy in 1 Timothy 5:23.

Not violent

The words translated here and in Titus 1:7 as *not violent* literally means, "not a giver of blows".[137] This phrase may be linked to the preceding warning against drunkenness, in which case Paul is saying that an overseer must not become belligerent when drinking. Sometimes those who have indulged in alcohol physically abuse people they think have offended them. However, given that candidates for the position of overseer must not be given to drunkenness, this link appears unlikely.

The presence of the word *but* after the words "not violent" suggests that this characteristic should be linked to gentleness, the characteristic that follows it, not the one that precedes it. Paul is probably warning against appointing the sort of impatient person who might be tempted to treat "irresponsible or recalcitrant members of his flock" roughly.[138] This qualification can also be linked with the later requirement regarding an overseer's home life. Any one who uses violence on his wife or children is automatically disqualified from church leadership. Yet despite this, I am sometimes asked whether it is wrong for a pastor to beat his wife. Someone who does this should not even be a pastor! Pastors and all those in leadership positions in the church should model loving consideration for all, including their own families.

Gentle

Those who are *gentle* are gracious, patient and considerate, as the translation of the same word in Titus 3:2 indicates.[139] They do not lose their tempers when others cause them frustration. The Greek philosopher Aristotle described gentle people as not insisting on every detail of their legal rights but instead being prepared to take individual circumstances into account.[140] Such people are prepared to listen to those who disagree with them.[141] They do not hold grudges, but are willing to forgive. They seek to apply the spirit of the law, rather than the letter of the law. It may be that Africa is plagued by so many warring groups (even within the church) because we have chosen leaders who are self-asserting rather than gentle when dealing with others. The church leader is called upon to model a life that will result in living in peace with all persons (Heb 12:14).

A gentle leader is prepared to make sacrifices for the sake of the kingdom of God. He or she will not get into a lengthy legal dispute with a neighbour about a yard or two of land, but will recognize that such a dispute will drive the neighbour away from the church, and not draw them to Christ. At the same time, as Paul made clear in his instructions to Timothy, the leader will be prepared to stand up for the fundamental truths of the gospel.

Not quarrelsome

We can get a better idea of what not being *quarrelsome* means by looking at how it is translated in different versions of the Bible. The nasb translates it as "peaceable", the kjv as "not a brawler", and The Message as "not thin-skinned". Overall, a person with this quality is not inclined to fight. Relating this to the preceding quality of gentleness, Ellicott says that the peaceable person is the one "who is not aggressive ... or pugnacious, who does not contend"; by contrast, the gentle person, "goes further, and is not only passively non-contentious, but actively considerate and forbearing, waiving even just legal redress".[142]

Not a lover of money

Some people are prepared to do anything to make money. They will lie, cheat, engage in unethical business dealings and take bribes. Overseers should not be like that. They should be well aware that there are values that are far more important than any amount of money.[143] Paul repeats the prohibition on loving money in his list of the qualifications for deacons in 1 Timothy 3:8 and for elders in Titus 1:7.

Unfortunately, some African church leaders fail to meet this standard. Some of them even become very wealthy by stressing that God blesses us to the degree we give to him. If the leader is persuasive, money pours in – some of it from persons who are not even making ends meet. This situation has led to the saying that one of the quickest ways to get rich is to found a church. But no true pastor will allow the amount of money he or she will earn to be the sole factor in determining whether to found or move to another new church.

Manages his own family well

In 3:4–5, Paul not only states a quality an overseer must have, that is, *he must manage his own family well*, but also gives an example to illustrate what he means by it, and then gives a reason why it is important that an overseer model good parenting.

The word translated as "family" in the tniv is a Greek word that referred to a household. The household in New Testament times was broader than the immediate family and included servants and relatives. However, the emphasis on children in the example which follows suggests that Paul is focusing on the family as composed of a husband/father, wife/mother, and children. It would also include any other children who are under the overseer's care. In Africa today, many families include children who were not born into the family but who have come into it because their birth parents died of AIDS or in some other disaster. Such children are also members of the household.

Paul illustrates what it means to manage a family well by saying that the overseer must *see that his children obey him, and he must do so in a manner worthy of full respect* (3:4). Parents then faced similar problems to those we face when raising our children!

How should we apply this requirement in our churches today? Given the translation of this phrase in the niv as "see that his children obey him with proper respect", should pastors be expected to resign if some of their children rebel?[144] It seems that this requirement must be understood in conjunction with the clear teaching of Scripture that everyone, including pastors' children, has to decide whether to accept or reject the truths they have been taught. Looked at this way, the focus is not so much on what the children have chosen as on what their father and mother have done. Will those around say, "in spite of all their parents' nurturing and teaching, the children have chosen to disobey", or will they say, "no wonder the children are not obedient to the word" since there has clearly been a lack of teaching. The general principle set out in Proverbs 22:6 indicates that we can expect that in the majority of cases where teaching has been done well, it will bear fruit in the children's lives. But even a child who has been taught well can rebel.

Although Paul elsewhere exhorts wives to submit to their husbands (Col 3:18), he does not mention their obedience here. This may not have been an issue in Ephesus. Moreover, it is likely that anyone appointed as an overseer will have a wife who supports his management of the home and his ministry.

The reason why one's home life is relevant when seeking any leadership position (see also 1 Tim 3:12 and Titus 1:6) is that those who can lead their own families well demonstrate managerial ability that they can also use in the church family. Those who are unable to perform well in the smaller sphere are not qualified to perform similar duties in the larger sphere of the church.

The juxtaposition of the verbs *manage* and *take care of* in 3:5 gives a clue to the type of management that Paul has in mind. As pointed out in relation to the requirement that overseers not be violent, overseers are not to be the type of people who rule as dictators, beating and terrorizing the members of their household. Parents who emphasize punishment with little attention to nurture fail the child and the community. Their children learn only that when they are caught doing wrong, they are punished. Rather, overseers are to care for and protect their families and exercise loving leadership, nurturing the good in the child, as well as punishing what is bad.[145] Children raised in this way will learn to do what is right not from fear of punishment but because they recognize it as promoting their own good. A church led by someone with this attitude will be characterized by loving concern for all the members.

Not a recent convert

Using a gardening metaphor, Paul insists that an overseer should not be "newly planted". What he means is that an overseer should not be a new believer but should be someone with deeply rooted faith. Paul does not mention this requirement when he compiles his similar list for Titus, possibly because the church in Crete was still so young that there was no one in it who was not *a recent convert*. But the church in Ephesus had been in existence for at least ten years by the time Paul wrote this letter, and so this instruction was realistic for them.[146]

One good reason for insisting that overseers were not recent converts was that Gentile converts needed time to learn more about the faith they had accepted, including its ethical content. Jewish converts would also have needed time to move away from the legalism they had known and accept the freedom that comes with grace. But these were not the main reasons that Paul mentioned: he said that the reason for this requirement was that a new believer may easily *become conceited* if appointed to such an important office *and fall under the same judgment as the devil* (3:6).

Commentators are not certain exactly what is meant by the last part of that phrase. They suggest three main possibilities:

- The pride of new converts will eventually cause them to receive the same condemnation that the devil received. In other words, their pride will lead to their being expelled from God's presence, just as the devil was expelled from heaven when he became proud and rebelled against God.[147]
- The pride of new converts will provide an opportunity for the devil to attack them and accuse them.[148]
- The pride of new converts will lay them open to attack by "one of those people to be found in every community, whose delight is to find fault with the demeanour and conduct of anyone professing a

strict rule of life". In this interpretation, the Greek word *diabolos* is given its literal translation as "slanderer", and the one doing the slandering is assumed to be another human being.[149]

Good reputation with outsiders

In the Pastoral Epistles, overseers are shown to have three spheres of responsibility: the family, the church in which they serve, and the world (society in general). An overseer must be a successful leader in all three spheres and must enjoy "the respect of others in the day-to-day business of life".[150]

The church is surrounded by a non-believing society that watches everything it does. Overseers with a bad reputation are a stumbling block to the gospel, for they will give outsiders a negative image of the church and its leaders (3:7). The outsiders will then be unwilling to listen to the message of the gospel proclaimed by the overseer, and the devil will rejoice that another Christian leader has fallen into his trap.[151] We must never forget that the devil is a hunter who will use any means to catch his prey and hinder the Lord's work.

At almost every mission station in Africa you can find someone who, over the years, has strongly resisted coming to saving faith in the Lord Jesus Christ. When asked why, they often say something to the effect that they have not seen Christianity demonstrated by the people of the mission station. Unfortunately, the same observation can be made about many churches. It underlines the importance of earning the respect of those outside the church by living what we preach – love, fairness, and righteousness.

Questions for Discussion

1. Which of the required qualities for a leader would it be easiest for you to meet? Which would you find more difficult?
2. Is the leadership of the church in Africa above reproach? Drawing on your own observations and experience, identify examples of behaviour that meets the requirements for Christian leaders and behaviour that falls below the standards.
3. What role can you and your church play to correct the problems you have identified?

UNIT 9
1 TIMOTHY 3:8–13

THE ROLE OF A DEACON

Many African homesteads include at least two buildings – a larger one referred to as the main house, and a smaller one serving as a kitchen. The main house is where members of the family eat and sleep, watch television, listen to the radio, hold family meetings, and so on. It is decorated with things like family pictures and is where flowers are placed on the table. The smaller building that contains the kitchen receives far less attention. It has only one main function: meal preparation. Yet, the kitchen is just as important as the main house. If the food that comes from the kitchen is contaminated, it will cause serious problems for everyone in the main house.

The main house and the kitchen may have different functions but they were built for the same purpose – to provide for the needs of the family. The same may be said of the different leadership positions in the church. Some leaders focus on the spiritual nurture of believers while others focus on providing for their material needs. But all of them are united by their shared desire to build the kingdom of God.

In New Testament times, spiritual nurture and teaching was done by elders or overseers, while deacons made sure that the other needs of the church and its members were met (Acts 6). Today, the terms elder and deacon are often used as if they are interchangeable. But what is important is not the term we use but that all the needs of believers and the ministry are met.

The qualifications that Paul presents at this point in the letter apply to the people whose primary duty is the general welfare of the church and its members. Paul discusses what qualifies someone to be a deacon, how deacons should be appointed, and the rewards of serving well.

Qualifications of Deacons

Six of the eight qualities required of a deacon are almost identical with the requirements for overseers.[152] The only two that are not found in the overseers' list are *sincere* (3:8) and *keeping hold of the deep truths of the faith* (3:9). The qualifications are so similar because Paul's focus is not on the duties associated with each office but on the character of the person holding the office. All church workers should be expected to be of generally similar character, with only a few special characteristics directly associated with particular offices.

The comments on the qualities expected of deacons will be brief because most of these qualities have already been dealt with in the previous unit.

- *Worthy of respect* is similar to the requirement that an overseer be "respectable".[153] The word can also mean "noble", "worthy", "esteemed" and "serious".[154] Kelly describes it as "an adjective which covers at once inward temper and outward bearing".[155]

- *Sincere* could be more literally translated "not double-tongued". Sincere people do not say "one thing to one person and a different thing to the next person".[156] They are not gossips.[157] Barclay comments, "In going from house to house, and in dealing with those who needed charity, deacons had to be completely straight. Again and again, they would be tempted to evade issues by a little timely hypocrisy and smooth speaking. But those who would do the work of the Christian church must be honest and direct."[158]

- *Not indulging in much wine* is related to the requirement that an overseer is "not given to drunkenness". The Greek word translated "indulging" has the meaning of "occupying oneself with something to the point of addiction". The same term is used to refer to the false teachers' preoccupation with "myths and endless genealogies" (1 Tim 1:4), to those who "will abandon the faith and follow deceiving spirits" (1 Tim 4:1), and in the instructions to Timothy to devote himself to the Scriptures (1 Tim 4:13).

- *Not pursuing dishonest gain* is closely related to the requirement that an overseer must not love money, but probably goes beyond it.[159] It may refer simply to how a deacon earns a living, making the point that it must be done in an ethical way and not involve any questionable dealings. In practical terms, this means that a deacon who is a business person must not hoard items until prices increase in order to get double profit, or hike fares on taxis or buses because it is a holiday and people are desperate for transport. The person who meets this qualification is the one who offers fair and honest service to others. But Paul is probably referring to more than just honesty at work, for the deacons' responsibilities to the church also involved taking care of church finances and distributing alms to the poor. They would thus have been exposed to the temptation to use the church's money to feather their own nests.[160] Paul's point is that deacons need to be above "making money on the side with no questions asked".[161]

- *Keeping hold of the deep truths of the faith with a clear conscience* is not paralleled by any requirement for overseers, which is strange as we would expect it to apply to them above all. Paul may have assumed that this knowledge of the faith could be taken for granted in those appointed as overseers. When it comes to deacons, some may be tempted to assume that matters of faith are less important because deacons' work involves practical rather than spiritual matters. Paul stresses that this is not the case. Deacons must also be committed to the "deep truths of the faith",[162] that is, they must not only have the faith that makes them believers, but must also demonstrate an ongoing commitment to sound doctrine.[163] They must hold this faith "with a clear conscience", that is, with no pretence, but with sincerity that is backed up by holy living.[164]

- *Must be faithful to his wife* is the same requirement as for overseers (3:2).

- *Must manage his children and his household well.* This corresponds to the requirement that an overseer "must manage his own family well and see that his children obey him, and he must do so in a manner worthy of full respect" (3:4).

Appointment of Deacons

Before anyone can serve as a deacon, *they must first be tested* (3:10). The nasb gives a slightly more accurate translation of the original Greek when it says, "these men must also first be tested". The "also" in this translation suggests that just as the overseer had to pass certain tests before being appointed, so did the deacon.[165] Once again, Paul is emphasizing that deacons are not exempt from scrutiny just because they deal mainly with practical matters.

The question that arises is, how were they tested? Some commentators suggest that they had to pass some sort of formal examination, at which "the candidate's background, reputation, and adherence to the mystery of the gospel would be checked".[166] This test would probably have been followed by some type of probation period before a deacon was confirmed in the office. Those who take this position argue that the problems in Ephesus would have made such a test essential. Timothy and the overseer (if one had already been appointed) would have been the examiners.

Others, however, argue that the testing "does not refer to any formal examination of the candidates for deaconate, either by Timothy or the officers of the church, so much as to the general verdict of the community concerning their life and conversation".[167] We know that from the very early days, the character of those appointed to serve in the church was carefully scrutinized (Acts 6:1–6). The parallel between 3:7a and 3:10b also suggests that the test was simply determining that the candidates had a good reputation in the community.[168]

The requirement that there be *nothing against them* is better translated as "if they are beyond reproach", as in the nasb. This means "blameless" or "irreproachable"[169] and is synonymous with the "above reproach" that summarized the list of qualities of overseers in 3:2.

The Reward for Good Service

Paul gives deacons an incentive to carry out their responsibilities when he speaks of the reward for *those who have served well* (3:13).[170] The tense of the verb indicates that the reward is not given before the service is done, nor necessarily while it is being done, but only after it has been done.[171] Service always precedes reward.

Church officials quite often express their discontent about what is termed "lack of recognition". (They tend to do this far more often than they encourage each other to give the best possible service.) Unfortunately, the complaints are sometimes self-serving, with leaders demanding a reward despite giving poor service. Paul's principle is that those who serve well will be rewarded well and vice versa.

The reward for good service is not financial but rather *an excellent standing*, a phrase that reminds us of the "noble task" in 3:1. The Greek word translated "standing" means "step" or "position", and can also be used figuratively to mean advancement in one's career or a rise in status. Paul may thus be speaking of a promotion, with a deacon who has served well being promoted to an overseer.[172] Or he may mean that such deacons will grow closer to God or that their service will result in their developing a strong bond with the godly leader who is the overseer. Yet another possible meaning, and one that is widely supported by commentators, is that the deacon's influence, usefulness and opportunities within the community will grow. Deacons may not be very well known when they are first appointed, but as they serve faithfully, trust grows, and with greater trust comes greater influence.[173]

The second reward for faithful service is *great assurance in their faith in Christ Jesus*. The word translated "assurance" can also mean "confidence". The sphere in which they experience this confidence is "in their faith", and the one in whom they have faith is "Christ Jesus". But before whom do they experience this confidence? Is it before God, so that, as Barrett says, "The good deacon has not only a good standing with men, but a free and confident approach to God"?[174] Or is this confidence before other people? Mounce says, "The meaning here is that deacons who serve well will be bold in their faith and have courage to express what they believe."[175] Or is it actually a combination of both these views, so that as Kelly says, faithful deacons "will be conscious of an increasing boldness in proclaiming the gospel and of an ever-deepening confidence in their approach to God".[176]

"Faith", as used here, seems to be primarily the deacon's personal trust in Christ, rather than the body of truth that was referred to in 3:9, although, as Hultgren says, "they gain a sense of certainty in the truth of the Christian faith".[177] The deacon's personal faith in Christ is the basis for this confidence. It is not self-confidence. It is an assurance that does not lose sight of God's grace, which enables them to serve. Deacons do not lose sight of what Christ has done in and for them.

Women Deacons

In the niv translation of 3:11, Paul speaks of "their wives". But the word "their" has been added by the translators. And the word translated "wives" could equally well be translated as *women*. There has thus been considerable debate about whom exactly Paul is talking about. Some commentators assume, like the niv translators, that Paul is talking about deacons' wives.[178] Others argue that there were women who served as deaconesses.[179] While it is impossible to be dogmatic on the point, the fact that "their" is omitted and the lack of corresponding instructions for elders' wives provides grounds for assuming that Paul is talking about a group of women leaders, equivalent to deaconesses. That the existence of such a group is within the spirit of the New Testament's teaching is evident from Paul's description of Phoebe as a "deacon" in Romans 16:1 (see niv footnote and nrsv). The primary meaning of the Greek word from which "deacon" derives is "service". It is used for Mary's service (*diakoneo*) to Jesus in John 12:2. That is why translations such as the niv and nasb can refer to Phoebe in Romans 16:1 as a "servant" rather than as a "deacon". It is possible that one key responsibility of female deacons was to make sure that the general needs of female believers were met.

Paul lists four qualifications for these women:

- *Worthy of respect.* This is identical to the requirement for deacons discussed in the commentary on 3:8.
- *Not malicious talkers.* This corresponds to the requirement that deacons must be sincere, or "not double-tongued" (nasb) in 3:8. The Greek word translated as "malicious" is actually *diabolos*, which is often used to refer to the devil. But in the Pastoral Epistles, it refers to humans on at least three occasions (1 Tim 3:11; 2 Tim 3:3; Titus 2:3). By using it, Paul is making the point that those who spread gossip or speak evil of others are actually doing the devil's work,

for the devil delights in making malicious accusations and causing trouble between people.
- *Temperate*. In general terms, this qualification corresponds to the requirement that overseers and deacons should not drink to excess (3:3, 8).[180] However, it also suggests that the woman should be both "temperate in her use of alcohol and clear-minded in her judgements".[181]
- *Trustworthy in everything*. She is to be the type of person who is faithful in everything she does.[182]

Concluding Observations

When Paul writes to Timothy about matters of leadership, he does not focus on what a leader should be doing but on the leader's character. When both the teachers of the word (elders) and the managers meeting everyday needs (deacons and deaconesses) maintain consistency between what is taught and how general business is run, the enemy has no room for an attack on the gospel. In fact, the false teacher is silenced or at least made very ineffective.

Yet the leaders' duties probably did affect Paul's choice of which particular qualities to mention for each group, for the characteristics Paul mentions are in many ways the opposite of those displayed by the false leaders Timothy was to oppose. Whereas the deacons (and, by implication, the overseers) are to have a clear understanding of "the deep truths of the faith" (3:9), the false teachers were spreading "false doctrines" (1:3). The false teachers enjoyed controversy (1:4), but true leaders are not to be quarrelsome (3:3). The false teachers saw godliness as means of financial gain (6:5b), but leaders are not to be lovers of money (3:3b). The false teachers were wreckers of their consciences (1:19b), but leaders are to have clear consciences (3:9b). In compiling his list of characteristics, Paul is not writing to correct faults in the church leaders but rather to encourage them to continue on the right course in order to avoid becoming like the false teachers.

In sum, regardless of whether one is serving God's church as an overseer, a deacon, or a deaconess (or a deacon's wife), one's life must support and not detract from the cause of the gospel.

Questions for Discussion

1. A man looking for a wife might be told, "Women from that homestead make good wives". Or he might be warned against looking for a wife in a different homestead: "Don't marry a woman from there; they are not good wives". A woman might be given similar advice about a man. The reputation of the homestead was based on how people there had been seen to behave. In the same way, the reputation of the Christian church is affected by the behaviour of overseers, deacons and members. What qualities of the church of Christ in Africa would lead an outsider to give it a positive evaluation? What qualities could result in a negative evaluation? What qualities do you think would attract others to come to the church?

2. When Africans offered a traditional sacrifice, the animal offered not only had to be healthy but also had to come from the herd of someone with a good reputation. The elder asked to make the offering also had to be more than just an old man, he had to be someone who was recognized as living in a way that was pleasing to the traditional gods. In what specific ways do you see the same principles being applied in Paul's list of the qualities required of church leaders? Has the church in Africa today taken these principles seriously when choosing its leaders? Take time to discuss each response to this question, and draw on examples from your own experiences or observation.

3. List ten things you think Paul would include in this list if he was writing to the pastors and deacons in your church today. Beside each item in your list, indicate how it is related to what Paul says to Timothy (and the Ephesians) in this passage. (For example, "The married pastor should take his or her spouse along when doing pastoral visitation" – based on Paul's instruction that an overseer should be above reproach.)

UNIT 10
1 TIMOTHY 3:14–16

PAUL'S REASON FOR WRITING

A tree is made up of the roots, trunk, and the branches from which the leaves sprout. The roots anchor the tree and absorb water and minerals from the soil. These nutrients are then drawn up into the trunk, the central part of the tree, and from there they are distributed to the branches and leaves, which use them to manufacture food for the entire tree. The food then returns to the trunk and flows through it to nourish the roots. While the trunk neither absorbs raw materials nor manufactures food, it provides an essential link between all the other parts, binding them together as one tree.

If we were to think of 1 Timothy as a tree, then 1 Timothy 3:14–16 would be the trunk, uniting the discussion on prayer and ministry in chapters 2 and 3 with Paul's practical instructions on how to deal with false teaching and other matters in chapters 4 to 6. These three verses give the reason why Paul has taken the time to send Timothy the advice given in the earlier chapters and serve as the basis for the advice he will give in the rest of the letter.[183]

Paul introduces the section with the words, *I am writing you these instructions* (3:14). But which specific instructions is he referring to? Is he thinking about what he has been saying about public worship and church leaders?[184] Or of all that he says in the letter up to 4:1–5?[185] Or of the whole letter, including "the conduct of individual Christians, the qualifications required in ministers, and sound doctrine in contrast to the doctrine of false teachers"?[186] This last option is the most likely.[187]

The "you" to whom Paul is writing is Timothy. However, because these letters were only semi-private, the congregation was also free to read them and benefit from the instructions. They, too, would be interested in the practical and theological reasons Paul gives for writing the letter.

Practical Reasons for Writing

When it came to the practical reasons for writing this letter, Paul has both short-term and long-term goals.

Short-term goal

We may wonder why Paul bothers to write to Timothy, seeing that he is "hoping to come to you before long" (3:14 nasb). Is this letter merely giving basic information that Paul will expand on when he arrives, or are these instructions to be followed in preparation for Paul's arrival? Both of these interpretations are possible, but it seems more likely that the tniv captures Paul's meaning with its translation: *although I hope to come to you soon*.[188] Paul plans to visit Timothy, but he cannot be certain that these plans will work out. God is in charge of his life, and his plans for Paul may be different from Paul's own plans. Meanwhile, Timothy is dealing with important issues, some of which urgently need attention. So Paul sits down to write this letter so that if he is delayed, Timothy will know what to do (3:15). Given the importance of the issues, Paul is happy to take the time to write down everything he wants to say to him face to face. No matter what happens to Paul, Timothy will have received the complete message.

Long-term goal

Paul's ultimate goal in writing this letter is to inform Timothy and the members of the church in Ephesus how people ought to conduct themselves in God's *household* (3:15a).[189] The Greek word translated "household" in the tniv can also be rendered "house". If the latter is used, the focus is on the place, whereas "household" focuses on the people who live in the house. Given Paul's focus on people throughout this letter, and his mention of the management of "one's family" (3:5, 12), "household" fits the context best. He is speaking of how to behave when in the "fellowship of believing men and women, united in a common allegiance to Christ and in worship together".[190]

It is important to know how to behave because this is no ordinary household; it is "God's household".[191] It belongs to him. He is the head, every believer is a member, and every member has been given a task to do. But the word "God's" does not only indicate that it is his possession, it also indicates that this household is identified with him. So it must act in a way that upholds his honour and promotes the kingdom of God. After all, the church is "God's chosen instrument for proclaiming to men the saving truth of the revelation of the God-man, Jesus Christ".[192]

Paul's next words, *which is the church* (3:15b) make it clear that we are right to identify this household with the church. The word translated "church" is *ekklesia*, which means "called out". The church is made up of those whom God has called out from the world to be his people, representing him and promoting godliness. And he has given this task to small local churches, not simply to the universal church.[193] Every congregation is to behave in a way that promotes the kingdom of God.

Faced with this awesome task, it is encouraging to remember that the owner of this church is *the living God*.[194] The church may appear weak, but there is tremendous power behind it. This God is no mere idol like the statue of Artemis (Diana) that was worshipped in the great temple in Ephesus (Acts 19:21–27). Paul stresses this point again in 1 Timothy 4:10. It is something that needs to be heard and remembered by faithful believers and communicated to the idol worshippers around them. The living God is the one who sustains his church.[195]

Some commentators point out that this message also needs to be heard by the false teachers in Ephesus. The living God watches over his church, from which he expects honour, commitment and faithfulness. He will not stand by and watch while harm is done to it, but will "discipline those who damage his house (see 2 Tim 4:1)".[196] While this point is true, the focus of 3:15 is on God's abiding providence as a Father watching over his household.

Paul has described the Christian community he is writing to as "God's household" and "the church of the living God". Now he adds a third description: *the pillar and foundation of the truth*.[197]

In Paul's day, the roofs of buildings like the temple of Artemis in Ephesus were supported by beautiful pillars. This leads Barclay to suggest that the function of the church as a pillar is to display the beauty of the truth.¹⁹⁸ But in 1 Timothy Paul is not focusing solely on truth that is beautiful and that needs to be shown in order to attract others, but also on truth that is unchangeable and that needs to be upheld. He is saying that the church provides the needed structure for the unchangeable gospel to be passed on from one generation to the next.

While it is fairly easy to understand what Paul means when he speaks of a pillar, there is far less certainty about what he means by the second term, which is variously translated as "foundation" (tniv), "support" (nasb), "ground" (kjv), "buttress" (esv) and "bulwark" (nrsv). Some of these translations suggest that the church is the firm ground on which the truth stands, while others suggest that the church's function is to support the truth and prevent it from being distorted. The second of these interpretations is the one supported by many commentaries which speak of the church as the "stay", "protector" and "fortress" of the truth.¹⁹⁹ This interpretation seems to fit the Ephesian context best. In modern terms, we might speak of the church as being a watchman guarding the truth.

Theological Reason

Paul also has a theological reason for writing to Timothy. He wants to restate the basic truths which the false teachers were denying. Thus in 3:16 he links the church's role as guardian of truth with the truth about the nature and person of Christ (his pre-existence, his incarnation and his exaltation) to bring this section of his letter to a climactic conclusion.

Paul prefaces this theological statement with the comment that what he is about to say is *beyond all question* (3:16a). He is stressing that these are not his own ideas but the "unanimous conviction of Christians", accepted "without controversy" (nkjv).²⁰⁰ The false teachers may have been trying to undermine these truths, but Paul insists that the church as the pillar of the truth must stand firm on these points.

To emphasize the extent to which these truths are accepted, Paul does not present them in his own words but instead quotes part of a hymn or a creed (that is, a statement of faith) that the believers in Ephesus would have known.²⁰¹ (We know that these words must be a quotation because the sentence starts abruptly with "He" without any indication of who this "he" is).²⁰²

Each line in this creed starts with a verb in the past tense, which emphasizes that the action referred to is a historical fact – this was what happened. The verb is also in the passive voice, which communicates that these actions were done to Jesus and were not things he did on his own.[203] The six lines communicate six truths about Christ:[204]

- *He appeared in a body:* The verb "he appeared" (literally, "was manifested") implies that Christ existed in another form before he took on a human body and was born of the Virgin Mary. Although this line can be read as applying to all of Christ's life, the focus is probably on the time when he entered our world as a human being.[205]
- *He was vindicated by the Spirit:* The word translated "vindicated" has various meanings, but the one intended here is probably to "make free or pure".[206] Christ was made pure by the Spirit in the sense that he was conceived by the power of the Holy Spirit, and so did not inherit our sinful nature when he became human. Unlike us, he was free of original sin.
- *He was seen by angels:* Angels were involved in the events surrounding Christ's birth, both protecting him (Matt 1:20–24; 2:13, 19) and proclaiming his coming with songs of praise (Luke 2:8–13).
- *He was preached among the nations:* Jesus' disciples went out to many nations, preaching that the Kingdom of God was open to anyone who believed in Jesus and acknowledged him as Lord.
- *Believed on in the world:* As the disciples proclaimed the good news of the Kingdom revealed in the person of Christ, many came to believe in him.
- *Taken up in glory:* After his resurrection, Christ ascended to heaven (Acts 1:10–14).

Surprisingly, the creed does not even mention Christ's death – possibly because this was part of his incarnate life and was a fact that no one in Ephesus disputed.

Together, the truths expressed in the creed represent *the mystery from which true godliness springs.* Here, the word "mystery" does not have its modern meaning of something that is impossible to understand but rather refers to "God's redemptive plan which has been kept secret from all ages but has now been revealed".[207] This revealed plan of God is the core of the message of salvation that is summarized in the creed Paul quotes.

Paul describes this mystery as the "mystery of godliness" (niv) because in the Pastoral Epistles godliness involves both belief and conduct.[208] Belief in the truths expressed in the creed is an essential part of godly living.

Questions for Discussion

1. Africans often do not make a will until they are about to die. The result is that when illness or death comes suddenly, there may be confusion about what they intended to say or the survivors may have to rely on the word of whoever was with the dying person. Given that Christians are to set an example for others, what principle does Paul demonstrate here when he writes to Timothy concerning matters he may possibly be able to discuss with him later? What are the pros and cons of applying this principle in Africa? Should every member of a family know what is their parents' will long before death comes?

2. Many mainline denominations in Africa recite what is known as the Apostles' Creed. However, many African independent churches do not recite this, in part because they do not want to follow the same pattern of worship as the other churches. If you were to be asked to draw up a creed for African churches, which five Bible truths would you give the greatest priority, and why?

UNIT 11
1 TIMOTHY 4:1–5

GATHERING STORMS

When winds begin to blow around an area of low atmospheric pressure over the ocean, they pick up water and gain strength. Within a day or two, a cyclone (or hurricane) can form with winds blowing harder than 125 kilometres an hour (75 miles an hour). As the storm moves over the ocean, it endangers all ships in its path. As it approaches land, the powerful waves it generates wreak havoc on the shore. Torrential rains cause flooding and mudslides, while strong winds tear trees and structures apart. Calm returns only once the storm has moved inland, away from the environment that created it.

One of the most famous hurricanes in recent years was Hurricane Katrina, which devastated New Orleans in 2005. But many storms have also hit Africa. Mozambique was hit hard by Cyclone Eline in 2000 and, seven years to the day later, by Cyclone Favio in 2007. When cyclones Elita and Gafilo hit Madagascar in early 2004, more than a hundred people were killed and thousands were left homeless.

When such a storm approaches, people are helpless. All they can do is run inland to escape the storm, or try to find shelter and pray until it has passed. No one except God can deflect the storm from its path or lessen its force.

There are many similarities between false teaching and cyclones. Both build up gradually from seemingly small origins, both are nurtured or ended by the surrounding conditions, and both unleash powerful destructive forces that are beyond human control. We need to keep a wary eye open if we are not to be caught unprepared.

A doctrinal deviation often begins with a minor theological argument that gradually grows to become a destructive, heretical teaching. Or it may begin as a comment made during a lecture that is later developed and publicized through an academic article. Eventually, it may be defended in a book, and the new heresy may take the world by storm.

But there is one difference between a cyclone and a heresy. We can do nothing to avert a cyclone. But we can do something to prevent ourselves and the church of Christ in Africa from slipping into heresy. So in 1 Timothy chapter 4, Paul warns Timothy about approaching storms and gives him instructions on the type of ministry he will need to exercise to help those he serves survive them.

What To Expect

Those who are familiar with the climate of the area in which they live are not surprised when hurricanes or cyclones are predicted. They know that such storms occur in certain seasons. Similarly, Timothy is not to be surprised when some people fall away from the faith. Their fall away has been foreseen by the Holy Spirit, who *clearly says* that this is going to happen (4:1). This was true in Timothy's time and it is true in our day also. It is something the church must expect and prepare for till the second coming of Christ. At certain times, the storm may be stronger, but there will always be storms.

The verb translated "says" is in the present tense.[209] Some commentators say that this indicated that the Holy Spirit is revealing this truth to Paul as he is writing his letter to Timothy. Others say that Paul is using the present tense to refer to a truth the Spirit has revealed on several occasions, some in the Old Testament (Dan 12:1) and more in the New Testament (Mark 13:22; Acts 20:29–30; 2 Thess 2:3, 11–23; 2 Pet 2:1–3; 3:3–4; 1 John 2:18; 4:1; Jude 18). Still others say that Paul is speaking about some specific revelation he received in the past that is true when he writes to Timothy and at all other times. We have no way of knowing which possibility is correct, or even whether Timothy and the believers in Ephesus would have known of all the other New Testament prophecies, for not all of the New Testament had been written or widely distributed at the time Paul was writing. But although we may not be sure of exactly when the Spirit said this, the message itself is perfectly clear.

The troubles the Spirit is predicting will take place *in later times*, which could also be translated as "in the last times".[210] For Paul and other New Testament writers, these times began with the founding of the church when the Holy Spirit came at Pentecost. They cover the entire period from Pentecost until Christ returns, which is the next major event in God's plan for the world.

The specific trouble that is to be anticipated is that *some will abandon the faith* (4:1b).[211] The nasb translates this as "fall away from the faith". They will fall from a high point and end up at a low point. Such people will not necessarily claim to have left the Christian faith, but their personal beliefs will differ from the accepted body of beliefs that make up the Christian faith.

Why Some Will Fall

The route to this abandonment of the faith will begin with paying attention to *deceiving spirits* (4:1b). The New Testament's understanding of the spiritual world is similar to that of traditional Africa. Africans recognized that there are good spirits who seek the good of humankind and evil spirits who seek to harm us. The New Testament refers to the good spirits who work for God as angels and the evil spirits who seek to frustrate God's purpose as demons. In Ephesus, these invisible servants of Satan are leading the attack on the church through propagating *things taught by demons*. It seems unlikely that Paul is here describing the false teachers he referred to in 1:4 as "demons". What he is saying is that the teaching they are spreading in the church does not come from God but from Satan, whom demons serve.[212] Satan orchestrates the work of spreading the false teaching that causes some to fall from faith.

Satan is described in Scripture as the father of lies (John 8:44). It is thus no surprise that those who are influenced by him and become his tools to spread his teaching can be characterized as *hypocritical liars* (4:2).[213] Such people put on a false face and conceal the truth about who they are. They know full well that what they are teaching is not in accordance with the faith, but they claim that it is, and pretend to tell the truth while deliberately misleading others. They are like the con men who prey on unsuspecting people who come from rural areas to buy spare parts for a car. The friendly con man claims to be able to take them to a place where they can get good parts cheaply, and the trusting buyers follow him. Sometimes they are assaulted and robbed on the way; at others times, they are cheated by being sold old, defective parts that have been cleaned and repackaged as if they were new. Should a buyer try to return the useless part, he will find that the people who sold it to him have moved to a new location.

Satan and his team use the same type of trick to rob us of the truth of the gospel. Satan presents himself as a helpful friend, or an "angel of light" (2 Cor 11:14), but he is actually a schemer (Eph 6:11). He will, for example, assure believers that the old ways are far more powerful than this new way of faith in Christ. He is so successful in misleading them that some witchdoctors boast that their clients include equal numbers of Christians and non-Christians. Just as someone buying spare parts needs to be alert to the wiles of the con men, so believers need to be alert to the wiles of the devil.

The consciences of those who deliberately set out to deceive others in this way *have been seared as with a hot iron* (4:2b). In many parts of Africa, cattle are branded with a hot iron so that it is clear who owns them. These teachers carry Satan's brand on their consciences, indicating that they belong to someone other than the God the believers belong to.[214]

Searing can also be interpreted figuratively as implying that their conscience, their inner judge, has been burnt so badly that it no longer functions. However, in the present context Paul seems to be focusing on who they belong to, and not on their level of insight. The teachers know what they are doing. They are disobedient rather than ignorant.

The actions of the false teachers reflect what they have already become. What they promote comes from, and is in conformity to, the desires of Satan or his agents. The church needs to be alert to defend itself against such attacks.

Refuting False Teachings

The false teachers were forbidding people to marry and telling them not to eat certain foods (4:3). It is not clear where this teaching came from, but a number of ideas of the time could have played into it. For example, there was the dualism that taught that the spirit is good and matter evil. Consequently anything spiritual was seen as good, while anything material, including anything involving the body, was seen as evil.[215] This would explain the false teachers' disapproval of the physical relationship involved in marriage, as well as their restrictions on what one ate, for food is also a material substance. The dietary restrictions may also have come from the type of legalism that demanded strict adherence to the rules set out in Leviticus 11:1–47.[216]

It is possible that the teachers came to advocate this lifestyle because they had heard the correct teaching that we have been raised with Christ and need to start living new lives (Gal 6:15; Col 3:1). However, they had expanded on this truth, and may have been telling believers that since God was restoring the new earth, they should "attempt to act the life of the resurrection paradise by following the model given in Genesis 1 and 2".[217] In other words, they taught that believers should be like Adam and Eve, living without formal marriage and eating only plant foods, not meat (Gen 1:29).[218]

We see a similar pattern at work in Africa. Teachers begin with a point that is true, but move beyond it to make false claims. For example, some of the truths we find in the Bible were already known to African Traditional Religion. We saw that when we looked at Paul's comments on the nature of God. It is also true that Africa has needed to throw off its bondage to colonial powers and assert its own identity. However, these two truths are taken too far when some scholars argue that all the truths of the Jewish faith were already known in African Traditional Religion, and that this religion is all Africa needs.

Paul reminds Timothy that it is not our duty to make up truths that suit the political and philosophical context of our times. If we did this, all truth would be relative. What we are called to do is to pass the teachings of Christ and his apostles on to the next generation. To do this, we need to make sure that our teaching is effective and relevant. Thus we may choose to use our traditional beliefs as contact points to help people understand the truth of Christ, but we may not use them as substitutes for it. The church must grasp this important principle if it is to be assured that what it leaves behind for the next generation is an effective and life-saving gospel.

Paul does not explain why the false teacher's prohibition of marriage is wrong, possibly because he has already spoken positively about marriage in 1 Timothy 2:15 and 3:2, 12 in relation to the marriages of overseers and deacons. He also actively encourages young widows to marry (1 Tim 5:14). He clearly sees marriage as a divine institution that should not be forbidden.

Paul's attitude to food is different from his attitude to marriage. Rather than arguing about what Christians should or should not eat, he insists that we should be guided by the law of love: "Christian love should inspire abstinence not because the food as such is unclean but in order to help the weak brother."[219] When writing to the Christians in Rome, Paul insisted that believers should not judge one another on the basis of what they eat (Rom 14:13–23). He said that all food is clean, but that it is wrong for someone to eat what causes someone else to stumble in their faith (Rom 14:20). It was the same principle of loving each other and not causing someone else to stumble that led the Jerusalem Council to include some points on what not to eat in their directions to Gentile believers (Acts 15:29).

The situation that Timothy was facing in Ephesus went beyond merely judging others as less spiritual based on what they ate. Some teachers were actually setting up rules about eating certain foods. Such teaching implied that the way of godliness was the way of law. This false teaching had to be checked.

Paul gives two reasons why it is wrong to reject certain foods. His starting point is God's intention in creation. God wants what he has created to be enjoyed. So Paul speaks of *foods, which God created* (4:3) and insists that *everything God created is good, and nothing is to be rejected* (4:4). The goodness of creation is clear from Genesis 1:4, 10, 12, 18, 21, 25, 31, which ends by summarizing God's work of creation as "very good". God created food, and so food is inherently good.

Paul's teaching that all food is good is in line with Jesus' teaching that food does not make a person unclean (Mark 7:15, 19) and with Peter's vision in Joppa (Acts 10:9–16). It is also consistent with his own teaching on the subject in his other letters (Rom 14:2–3; 1 Cor 8:7–13; 10:23–33). Barclay sums up this position well: "True Christians do not serve God by enslaving himself with rules and regulations and insulting his creation; they serve him by gratefully accepting his good gifts and remembering that this is a world where God made all things well and by never forgetting to share God's gifts with others."[220]

Paul's other reason for arguing that those who believe and know the truth (Christians) should not reject food is that any food can be *consecrated by ... prayer* (4:5). Nothing is to be rejected provided it is *received with thanksgiving* (4:4b).[221]

Many Christians say grace, offering a prayer of thanksgiving before eating food.[222] Some speak as if this thanksgiving has a magical property to it: "The very fact that we thank God for it makes a thing sacred. Not even the demons can touch it when it has been touched by the Spirit of God."[223] This approach fits with the African traditional belief that a word said by a powerful person or an object set aside by a person in contact with the spiritual world possesses magical power. However, the scriptural position is that all things are at the disposal of our God, to use as he pleases. Food blessed in prayer will not necessarily be untouchable by demons. God may choose to allow Satan and his agents access to it. The power is not in the thing blessed but in the God who does the blessing. When God uses an object to achieve his purpose (for example, Paul's handkerchiefs and aprons – Acts 19:12) it would be a mistake to confuse his use of the object with the power the thing itself has. It has power only as long as God chooses to use it for a particular purpose.

Our prayer of gratitude, therefore, does not make the food good. All it does is confirm the goodness that the food already has. Kelly rightly insists that Paul's "sentence does not claim that an additional sanctification, over and above its intrinsic goodness as God's creature, is imparted to food by saying grace. What it states is that the grace sets the food in its true perspective and in that way enables us to regard it as sacred."[224]

Our food is consecrated not only by prayer but also by *the word of God* (4:5). What does this mean? Some say that it is a reference to the account of creation in Genesis 1, where God's creative word produced all that exists, including the food for which we give thanks.[225] Others interpret it as a reference to the verses from Scriptures that formed part of Jewish prayers at mealtimes.[226] Still others relate it to the gospel message, with its insistence that our acceptance by God is not based on works, such as what we eat or do not eat.[227] While it is not possible to be dogmatic on this point, it makes good sense to see the word of God here as Scripture read at the table. Acknowledging that God made food for our use and thanking him for providing it is all that is needed to fulfil all righteousness in matters of food – so long as the food is rightly acquired, does not cause anyone to stumble, and it is good for our health.

God made food good, and our prayer of gratitude confirms its goodness. Like the false teachers, we will fall into error if we deviate from holding firmly to God's declared intention and fail to receive what he gives us with gratitude.

Questions for Discussion

1. Some African people groups may refuse to eat a particular animal because there is believed to be some relationship between that animal and their clan. For example, one group refuse to eat rabbit. Long ago, a rabbit distracted a snake that was about to strike at one of the fathers of the clan, and so it was decreed that the rabbit was the saviour of the clan and should never be eaten. A Christian member of that clan has eaten a rabbit, and has been called before the judging council of the clan. You have been asked to speak before the council. What principles could you draw from this passage to guide you on what to say?

2. This passage shows that it is important to arrest an error (a wrong or misleading statement) before it becomes heresy (a wrong or misleading teaching). What should be our response when we hear politicians who seek to unite people making statements like "all roads lead to Rome"? Is it acceptable for Christian politicians to say things like this when seeking to attract the votes from people of all walks of life? Are there principles that can help us to distinguish which statements we should challenge and which we should leave unchallenged?

UNIT 12
1 TIMOTHY 4:6–16

TIMOTHY'S ROLE

There is an old story about a treasure that would belong to the person who could follow instructions without being distracted. The instructions were very simple: "Follow that ball as it rolls along, and no matter what you hear, do not look behind you." Soon someone set out to find the treasure. He followed the ball along a long and lonely road, lined by stones. All of a sudden, he heard a voice behind him: "Where do you think you're going"? The shock of hearing a voice made him turn – and immediately he became a stone, like the other stones that lined the road. A second person then tried to reach the treasure. He remembered the instruction about not looking back, and ignored the voice asking where he was going. Then he heard a second voice: "Look at you! How can you think you'll ever find the treasure!" He was shaken, but managed to ignore that voice too. But when he heard a third voice saying, "Slit his throat!", he whirled round, ready to defend himself. Immediately, he became another stone lining the road.

A third person wanted to find the treasure. He was given the same instructions as the first two, but he thought about them carefully. He knew that he could easily be distracted by what he heard, and so he decided to take precautions to prevent himself from hearing. Carefully he stuffed his ears with cotton, until he could hear nothing. Then he set off down the long and lonely road, following the ball. The stones spoke to him and called out threats, but he could not hear them. He followed the ball without turning until he reached the treasure.

My father used to tell me this story because he wanted me to learn the lessons it teaches. The first is that if I want to achieve anything, I must think and plan how I am going to do it. The second is that to achieve my goal I have to turn a deaf ear to all distractions. These are the same lessons that Paul is teaching Timothy in this section of the letter. Timothy has a gift and a goal, namely, building the work of Christ at Ephesus. There are many people and things who want to distract him from that goal, for they serve a different master. So Timothy is given instructions about what he needs to do in order to achieve his goal. The same principles apply to us as we pursue our goals in the course of our daily activities as individuals, within our families, and in Christian service.

Paul tells Timothy to do certain specific things as an individual believer and as part of his ministry of counteracting the negative effects of the false teachers. As he has done before, Paul begins with a summary statement (4:6), which he then expands on in the verses that follow.

Summary

Timothy will demonstrate that he is a *good minister* by pointing out certain truths to the members of the church in Ephesus.[228] The verb used here, translated as "point out", indicates that this must be done with humility. Timothy must not "dogmatically and pugnaciously lay down the law". Teachers "must act rather as if they were reminding people of what they already knew or suggesting to them, not that they should learn from them, but that they should discover from their own hearts what is right".[229] This same attitude of humility is also evident in the description of those Timothy is speaking to as his *brothers*, a term which conveys the idea that he and all the others in the Christian community are member of one family – the family of God. They are all brothers and sisters, with God as their Father. The principle laid down here is true at all times. The most successful and effective pastor, teacher, counsellor and leader is the one who appreciates what those ministered to have already attained. Those who think that they know it all while everyone else knows nothing become dictators who cannot move others towards godliness.

Within this family of God, Timothy is not only a brother but a *minister*, or servant, *of Christ Jesus*. The word translated "minister" is *diakonos*, the same word translated as "deacon" in 3:8. Here the focus is on the duty to serve, and not on any office. The same idea is found in 1:12, where Paul thanks Christ for appointing him to "his service". Both Paul and Timothy are serving the same master. The false teachers may follow "things taught by demons" (4:1), but Timothy serves Christ.[230] Acknowledging Christ as our master helps us to keep things in perspective. No matter how elevated our position within our church or society, we are only servants of a higher commander.

Paul's use of the future tense when he says *"you will be* a good minister" does not mean that Timothy is not already a good minister. It simply indicates that this will be an ongoing and unchanging fact as he faithfully carries out the task he has been assigned.[231]

Paul is not specific about exactly what Timothy is supposed to be pointing out, for he refers to it in general terms as *these things*. People have debated whether he is speaking of the message of the whole letter,[232] or only about a particular part of it, for example, what has just been said about food and marriage[233] or the instructions on worship and church administration in 2:1 to 4:5.[234] My own position is that Paul means Timothy to communicate all the points he discusses in the whole letter, including all that he has to say about the law, salvation and ministry in the church.

Timothy's service is tied to his having been *nourished* or "brought up" (niv) in the faith. The words may make us think that Paul is here speaking of Timothy's training by his mother when he was a child (2 Tim 1:5), or what he learned from Paul, his mentor. But Paul knows that a pastor does not serve well on the basis of past knowledge. Timothy needs to be living the truths of the faith day by day and continuing to grow spiritually. So Paul uses a present tense verb to show that the bringing up is still carrying on. The nasb translation captures the meaning with its translation, "constantly nourished".[235] As Timothy serves as a good minister, he himself will be growing in the faith. He is not to be a mere theorizer, offering others spiritual food that he does not eat himself. He is to live and to judge himself by the standard of the doctrine he proclaims.

Timothy will get the nourishment he needs from *the truths of the faith* and from *the good teaching* he has followed. These two ideas are very closely related. It seems likely that the first refers to the complete message of the gospel, whereas the "teaching" involves teaching about specific aspects of that message.[236]

Timothy has followed the "truths of the faith" and "good teaching" and has allowed them to nourish and shape him.[237] Paul is thus not telling him about things he does not know, but is reminding him of the importance of what he already knows so that he can continue to serve well.

Sadly, many pastors in Africa fail to advance in knowledge and reflection from where they left off when they graduated from college or Bible school. Some may go for years without ever reading a new book, even for their own personal spiritual enrichment. In some cases, this may be because they cannot afford to buy a book. However, those who pour out what they know but have no source of fresh knowledge will sooner or later find that they have run dry. We should thus thank God for the Pastors' Book Sets distributed by SIM, for the one-volume *Africa Bible Commentary*, and now for this Africa Bible Commentary Series.

Church leaders run the same risk when they only attend seminars and conferences as speakers and leave as soon as possible after their own session. They may claim to be too busy to attend the full conference, but this is the path to dryness.

Paul reminds Timothy of the need to grow in knowledge and be refreshed constantly. The pastor must not only renew his or her spiritual vigour daily but must also keep growing in the knowledge and practice of the word he or she is called to proclaim.

Details

Now Paul moves on to talk about specific personal and ministerial challenges Timothy faced as the leader of the church in Ephesus. He offers some specific instructions on how to deal with these issues.

Avoid silly stories

Paul begins by encouraging Timothy to *have nothing to do with godless*[238] *myths and old wives' tales* (4:7a). He is not to listen to them or to repeat them himself. He is not even to enter into arguments about them. The best way to handle such stories is to ignore them.

It seems that the stories Paul has in mind were not folk tales that teach a moral lesson but stories that are godless in the sense that they have nothing to do with holy living, and in fact may even be "radically ...

opposed to the holy".[239] While some ideas may need to be discussed or refuted with arguments, these tales are merely silly,[240] or as the nasb says, "fit only for old women". Paul is being sarcastic.[241] Old women who sat around gossiping and swapping stories were stereotypically assumed to be very gullible, ready to believe anything. Today, urban legends and other stories proliferate in many groups. But Paul's principle still stands: a pastor should not get side-tracked into dealing with silly stories.

In applying the principle to our times, we also need to think in terms of peace, ethics and priorities. Pursuing peace should keep us from frivolous speech. Whether engaging in a political debate, delivering a rebuke or encouraging others, we should always be sure that what we have to say is based on solid facts. Ethical considerations should lead us to avoid stories that are ungodly or merely meant to damage someone's reputation. The principle of priority should encourage us not to neglect the building of the kingdom of God by wasting our time on worthless stories. However, Paul is not saying that a pastor must never relax and even laugh with others. Some African pastors try to make everyone around them speak only about spiritual matters. But pastors need to take some time to relax and socialize with others, talking about everyday issues. Doing this will make them more approachable, so that people will be more at ease when approaching them for help on spiritual matters. Pastors should never forget that although they teach about spiritual things, they also live here on earth.

Value godliness

Instead of sitting around listening to godless "old wives' tales", Timothy should be in training like an athlete, exercising regularly as he actively pursues his goal of being *godly* (4:7b). As someone living in Ephesus, he would have been familiar with the dedication with which athletes prepared for competitions, for the city had a number of gymnasia.

Paul stresses this metaphor even more in the next verse, where he contrasts the benefits of physical and spiritual training. He admits that *physical training is of some value* (4:8).[242] But its usefulness is limited to a few areas, primarily involving bodily health. *Godliness*, by contrast, *has value for all things*. It benefits both body and soul. And its benefits are not limited to this life, but are also to be experienced in *the life to come*.[243] This does not mean that a pastor should never belong to a soccer team or take part in some sport. A fit and healthy body also glorifies God and may be part of the pastor's testimony. Paul is simply saying that godliness is worth more than physical fitness; he's not saying that it should replace it.

Paul's words here leave no doubt that the blessings of salvation are for us as whole people, body and soul, present and future. He underscores this point using a phrase he has already used twice in this letter: *This is a trustworthy saying* (4:9; see also 1:15; 3:1).[244]

Paul also makes it clear that he is not calling Timothy to a discipline he does not practise himself, for he says *that is why we labour and strive* (4.10a). The "that" is most likely the trustworthy saying about the benefits of godliness. The "we" probably includes at least Paul and Timothy, although it may also include Paul's other co-workers and the other apostles. Here Paul also demonstrates a key principle of successful leadership, namely that both the leader and the led should be working side by side. By doing this the leader not only motivates those following him but also provides them with a model of how to do something. Armchair leadership builds no one up and does not result in effective ministry. This principle applies at all levels of ministry. A bishop or senior pastor must still be involved in soul winning while providing leadership. A pastor must not simply direct things from his office but must be out there doing things with the people. Those who train pastors should not stay at home while expecting their students to go out and conduct field ministry. By ministering alongside their students, teachers will be preparing them to be faithful pastors and teachers.

Paul does not minimize the effort that training in godliness requires. He first describes it as "labour", using a verb that might be used to describe a farmer working "energetically, to the point of weariness".[245] Many African readers know from experience how hard farming is. Months before the rains come, the land has to be tilled (often with no more than a hoe or fork), and manure dug into it to fertilize the soil. When the rains come, seeds have to be planted, and when those seeds germinate the soil has to be kept clear of weeds until the crop is ready for harvest. This is hard work!

Paul's second verb, "strive", again reminds his readers of athletes, for the word can mean to "fight, struggle, or engage in a contest".[246]

Both "labour" and "strive" are in the present continuous tense, showing that this is an ongoing struggle. But the struggle is worth it given the nature of the God Paul and Timothy serve and in whom they have put their hope:[247] he is both *the living God* and *the Saviour of all people* (4:10).

This is the second time in this letter that Paul speaks of God as "the living God" (see comments on 3:15). Because God is alive, the promise referred to in 4:8 will be kept. Because God is alive, we his servants can keep in touch with him on a daily basis. And because God is alive, we can confidently proclaim his message of salvation to others, knowing that he is the "saviour of all people".

But what does it mean to say that God is the "saviour of all people"? Does it mean, as some argue, that everyone will be saved in the end? That position is not supported by the rest of Scripture, or even by the rest of this verse, for it ends with *especially of those who believe*. This clause could also be translated as "to be precise, believers". The point that Paul is making is that God is the saviour of all those who believe.

Other commentators have pointed out that God's salvation is freely offered to all, including both Jews and Gentiles, and that God's general care extends to all people. But believers are in a special relationship to him that is not shared by unbelievers.

Command and teach

Paul next instructs Timothy to keep commanding and teaching *these things*, that is, the truths Paul has been teaching (4:11). Both *command* and *teach* relate to conveying information, but in different ways. The difference may relate to the audience Timothy is addressing, the method of communication he uses, or the content he wants to communicate.

- *Audience.* Timothy must command the false teachers, ordering them to stop teaching (see 1:3). By contrast, faithful followers need gentle teaching to build up their knowledge of true doctrine.
- *Method.* Any good teacher will use more than one approach when teaching a group of students. Timothy will find that it is not enough simply to condemn an error or command people to accept a truth. A better way to teach people and refute error is to present the positive truth which corrects the error.[248]

- *Content.* What Timothy is to teach is what God has done and the theory about how one should live, whereas what he is to command is what his listeners should be doing, that is, the practical application of the theory.[249]

Timothy was probably already teaching in Ephesus, but he may not have been commanding as he should: "It is likely that because of a natural diffidence, Timothy was not sufficiently assured of his authority in the church, lacked self-confidence and needed an impetus to his faith".[250] So Paul is here giving him a word of encouragement. He can assert himself as leader knowing he has Paul's full support.

Paul models what he means here as he both commands and instructs Timothy. If only senior leaders in our churches would be as careful to encourage and support their younger colleagues, not crushing them but encouraging them to assert their authority wisely!

Don't be intimidated

The elderly were respected in ancient societies, whereas commands and teaching given by a younger person might be dismissed. So Paul tells Timothy that he is to not let anyone look down on him merely because he is young (*neotetos* – 4:11). When we read this, we need to remember that the word *neotetos* could be used to describe anyone who could be called up for military service, which in practice meant anyone up to the age of forty.[251] Given what we know of Timothy's life, we can estimate that by the time this letter was written he was probably in his thirties.[252] Yet in comparison to Paul and some of the older members of the church in Ephesus, he was a young man.

Although this instruction is directed to Timothy, Paul was well aware that this letter would be shared with the Ephesian congregation. He is indirectly reminding them that they should not look down on his representative, even if they regard him as a young man.

Most new graduates from Bible schools and colleges in Africa are young in comparison to some of those they serve. Yet in general most church members, including the elderly, respect their pastors – as long as the young pastors also show respect for them and for their life experiences. When a pastor fails to show respect for those in the congregation, there will be a flood of criticisms of the pastor and stress will be laid on the fact that he or she is a young person.

Timothy is to do what he does in such a way that he commands respect regardless of his age. The same challenge applies to all young pastors in Africa. But no matter how well they conduct themselves, they may encounter problems. Satan is actively working to harm God's kingdom, and even a pastor who serves very faithfully may come under attack. At such times, the call is to stand firm, confident in the companionship of the Chief Shepherd, Jesus Christ (1 Pet 5:4). There should be no fear.

Set a good example

Timothy's life must be characterized by such maturity in Christ that he is an example to those who are older than him and might despise him (4:12a). This command is introduced with the word *but* to bring out the contrast between his age, which might bring disrespect, and his behaviour, which will bring him honour. He is not merely to be a model *for the believers* as the tniv has it, but is to be, as the nasb says, an example "of those who believe" – showing what a real Christian looks like.[253]

Not content just to tell Timothy that he should be an example in general, Paul lists five specific areas in which he should show maturity: speech, conduct, love, faith and purity (4:12b).[254] The first two elements (his speech and conduct) relate to Timothy's public ministry, while the final three (love, faith, and maturity) relate to his personal life, but will inevitably be reflected in his public life.[255]

- *Speech* refers to Timothy's "day to day conversation, including both personal conversation and public teaching".[256] He must watch what he says at all times. Like him, we pastors in Africa must guard our tongues. For example, when we are travelling in a bus or taxi, the people around us often talk freely about many things. A pastor can join in the casual conversation, but must never forget God's perspective on what is said. Nothing that is said should damage another person's reputation. Nor should a pastor use the pulpit as the place to get back at an opponent. A pastor's words should instead be a source of blessing and encouragement to all.
- *Conduct* refers to the way Timothy lives and his general behaviour. We should not act in ways that bring into question our fitness to

be God's servants. For example, a certain pastor became involved in a bitter land dispute. When some believers tried to speak to him about his conduct, his response was "in matters to do with my land, do not bring Christianity into it!" There were areas of his life in which he was not prepared to conform to the teachings of the Bible. He was failing to set an example of how believers should conduct themselves. A believer, and especially a Christian leader, must subject every aspect of life, including family life, business life and political life, to the scrutiny of Scripture.

- *Love* must include love for God and for others. Without love for God, *agape* love, the type of love that is not conditional on other's behaviour, is impossible. The Bible also teaches that our love for others is a reflection of our love for God (1 John 4:20). Thus if we refuse to love the members of some ethnic or political group, we are actually failing to love God. Even when members of that group have been cruel to us, we are called to promote peace and love and not to increase tensions and make the fighting more intense. This will not always be easy to do. We need to recognize that ethnic identity is a reality of life, but that the gospel calls us to a love that binds us together in our diversity. Christians do not cease to be Jews or Gentiles, or Yoruba, Kikuyu, Sukuma, Akan, Mende, Dinka, Zulu and so on – but Christian love should bind us all together.

- *Faith* has to do with Timothy's personal trust in God. However, it can also be translated "faithfulness" or "trustworthiness", which brings out the idea that Timothy must be someone others can rely on.[257] These two qualities are closely linked. Those who have faith that God will provide for all their needs will be able to fight the temptation to divert funds for personal matters. Lacking such faith, some pastors have taken funds that were supposed to be spent on a specific project and have instead used them to paying their children's school fees. They may intend to repay the money to the fund, but when they fail to do so it has negative effect on their ministry because they are not perceived as faithful. Consequently donors will also feel a need to specify how every cent they give is to be spent, and may attempt to exercise too much control in order to prevent abuses. Similarly, pastors who have faith in God will trust him when it comes to planning their careers. This does not mean that the pastors will not work hard and think ahead, but it does mean that they will be satisfied with what God provides, rather than constantly scheming to improve their situation. Pastors should be models of faith and of faithfulness; the type of people who can be trusted with anything.

- *Purity* conveys the idea of a sinless life, and includes things like innocence and integrity of heart and purity in actions and thought.[258] Pastors are called to live lives that please him who sees the hidden things of the heart and mind. At the end of the day, each one of us knows best how we stand before God.

To sum up, Timothy's example is to show other believers what it means to love God and other people, to be faithful both in God's eyes and in the judgment of other people, and to be pure in thought and actions.[259] Someone who lives like this shows a spiritual maturity that makes questions of age irrelevant.

Those of us whom the Lord has placed in strategic places in his work in Africa are the Timothies of our day. We must set the example of godliness for our societies. If most pastors in Africa were to set such an example, and believers were to follow their example, the continent would be far ahead of where it is in maintaining godliness in all walks of life.

Read, preach and teach

Timothy is to devote himself to *the public reading of Scripture, to preaching and to teaching* (4:13). All of these activities were key parts of public worship. Although there is considerable overlap in meaning between "preaching" and "teaching", it seems that the preaching is directed to the emotions of the hearers and the practical application of some passages in Scripture, whereas "teaching" is more directed to their minds, and may be more like a lecture.[260]

Our church services usually include time for worship, reading of the word, prayer and preaching. The worship provides a time to turn our hearts towards God; the reading of the Bible provides a time to hear from God; the time of prayer is an opportunity to tell God that we are dependent on him; and the preaching is an opportunity for a servant of God to expound God's word and help us apply it. Being devoted to these means that each of them must be done well – there is no place for rushed, last-minute preparations. Every detail of the service must be carefully prepared and thought through.

When it comes to preaching, many sermons appeal to the emotions, calling on people to change their behaviour or remain faithful to the right course. But the teaching part of preaching should not be neglected. Believers need to gain knowledge of what the Bible says about different matters. If they are deeply rooted in the word, they will be able to stand firm when false teachings are presented to them. Pastors should thus also be leading church members to spend time in Bible study.

Do not neglect your gift

Timothy had received some *spiritual gift* (4:14 nasb). We are told it came to him through a prophetic message when elders laid their hands on him (4:14b; see also comments on 1:18). The warning suggests that Timothy may well have been neglecting it. Although we are not told what this specific gift is, the context suggests that Paul may be referring to Timothy's hesitance to exercise his full authority as the leader of the Ephesian church. It also reinforces the preceding instruction relating to his public ministry of reading, preaching and teaching.

When students apply for admission to theological institutions in Africa, they are usually asked to give a statement about their call to ministry. While at the institution, they are asked to give words of testimony. It is very important that students not neglect their call and their testimony. They should never let the joke about seminaries being cemeteries apply to them. Their studies must go hand in hand with personal devotion. They must sharpen and put to use the special gifts that God has given each of them. As they do this, they will grow in maturity and Christ-likeness (Eph 4:11–12).

Be diligent

Timothy is not to take a relaxed approach to carrying out his responsibilities, but is to work hard to make sure that they are done properly (4:15). The *matters* Paul refers to may be the message of the whole letter, but it is more likely that he is referring to the immediately preceding instructions about living an exemplary life and leading in public worship. Others will be watching Timothy's behaviour and will take note of his growth in his own life and as a teacher. Seeing this, they will no longer look down on him but will respect him and emulate him.

Sloppiness is alien to the kingdom of God. God is constantly at work, and we should be like him. We should not be the type of people who go to work determined to do the minimum necessary to remain on the payroll. That is not the Christian way. The principle for the Christian is "Whatever you do, work at it with all your heart" (Col 3:23). One reason our African roads are in such terrible condition is that those assigned to repair them only work as long as someone is watching them. Service in many public offices is slow not because the office is understaffed but because the employees work at the speed of a chameleon! There are many Christians in Africa. If we were to show what diligence really means, it could make a great difference to our entire continent.

Be alert

Paul concludes his instructions by telling Timothy to watch his *life and doctrine closely* (4:16). He must not comfortably assume that what he is doing and teaching is correct, because it is very easy to drift slowly away from what is right. Timothy must thus regularly check that he is still on the right path, persevering in living and proclaiming the truths of the faith.

Today it is very easy for us to drift away from what is right, and Satan is very subtle in encouraging us to do so. For example, for the sake of political unity, we are encouraged to think of every religion as leading to heaven and to rejoice regardless of whether it is a new church, a new mosque or a new shrine that has been set up in our village or town. We are expected to avoid preaching on the verse that "there is no other name given under heaven by which we must be saved" (Acts 4:12). In our secular lives, we are encouraged to believe that "the end justifies the means", and to argue that so long as I use part of my wealth in the work of the church, it does not matter how I got it, as long as I did not actually steal it. Such drifting away from biblical standards diminishes the difference that should exist between Christians and non-Christians. Unbelievers can then say that they see no point in being a Christian.

Paul tells Timothy that if he perseveres he will *save both yourself and your hearers*. What does Paul means by these words? Some commentators think that he is speaking about salvation in the sense of justification,[261] but Timothy and his congregation were already believers, so there would be no need for the future tense "will save". They are already saved.

Other commentators suggest that salvation here is being used as equivalent to our final glorification, the ultimate stage of our salvation.[262] On this interpretation, Paul is saying that our final salvation is tied to our continuing to live godly lives and hold to correct doctrine. But this interpretation does not really fit the context of this letter. Paul is not instructing Timothy about how to be justified or how to keep himself from being disqualified at the end. His main purpose in writing is to tell him how he should conduct his ministry as the leader of the church in Ephesus.

The best explanation seems to be that Paul is telling Timothy that he and his hearers will be saved, or kept safe from, the damaging influence of the false teachers.[263] These teachers not only taught false doctrine but also lived immoral lives. If Timothy takes care to live a godly life and to teach and preach pure doctrine, he will keep himself and those he teaches from being polluted by their influence.

Questions for Discussion

1. If you were to apply the challenge Paul lays before Timothy to yourself and rate your own life as objectively as possible, what would your score be?
2. Think about your pastor or some other Christian you work or live with, and rate his or her life in terms of these requirements. What is his or her score and why?
3. Which of the qualities required of Timothy are the most lacking in your corner of the church of Christ in Africa? What practical steps can you take to develop these qualities?

UNIT 13
1 TIMOTHY 5:1–2

PEOPLE MANAGEMENT

Most of those who are training to become pastors are between twenty-five and thirty years old. When they graduate, they assume responsibility for churches attended by five-year-olds and ninety-five-year-olds. They have to minister to Sunday school children, youth, couples, singles and the elderly. No matter who else assists them, everyone in the church looks to the pastor as the leader.

Timothy faced the same situation at Ephesus. So Paul gives him some guidelines to help him meet this challenge. Specifically, he gives him advice on how to relate to four groups, which in a sense represent every one in the church: older men, younger men, older women and younger women. Just as an elder must manage his own family well (3:4a), so Timothy must manage God's family well. His attitude to every member of a church should earn their respect and enhance his effectiveness.

Relating to Older Men

The older members of the church in Ephesus might be inclined to dismiss Timothy as being too young to tell them anything about life. Paul has instructed Timothy not to allow them to do this, but to live in a way that convinces them of his maturity (4:12). However, while in the process of convincing them, he is still to "command and teach" this group (4:11). How can he do this in a way that will not antagonize them?

In the society Timothy lived in, respect for elders was such a standard feature that it was believed that "abusive language towards an aged father invited divine punishment".[264] In extreme cases, it could even be a capital offence (Exod 21:15). The situation in Africa has been similar. Traditionally, a young person who had some concern about the behaviour of an older person would not approach them directly but would ask a relative or friend of the family who was of a similar age to the person to speak to them. Even today, a young person who directly rebukes an older person is generally considered to have very bad manners.

Paul shares the wisdom he has gained about how to nurture and encourage older people in the church. He advises Timothy that he should not *rebuke an older man harshly* (5:1). These words should not be read as implying that Timothy has been treating older people badly in the past. It is simply that "the problem of how to administer rebukes constructively is always a difficult one for those in authority, and never more so than when, as seems to have been the case with Timothy, there is a discrepancy of age".[265]

The man Paul is speaking of in 5:1 is not an elder or deacon but simply someone who is older than Timothy. Timothy must treat such men with gentleness and respect, not uttering harsh criticisms or speaking as if he were a teacher rebuking a disobedient pupil.[266] Instead of speaking as if he were superior to them, Timothy should *exhort* them, as if appealing to an equal.[267] Indeed, he must even speak as if he is subordinate to them, addressing each of them *as if he were your father*. This image reminds us that Paul thinks of the Christian community as a family, a household (see also 3:15).

African pastors need to balance the authority Scripture gives them to rebuke every believer with Paul's teaching to humbly and respectfully treat older men as fathers. This does not mean that sin is to be tolerated. But it is to be addressed wisely and with great humility. A young pastor who is well spoken of by the older members of the flock is guaranteed many years of effective ministry. One who alienates them by his arrogance will soon have no flock to lead.

Relating to Younger Men

Paul continues the family metaphor when speaking of how Timothy should relate to younger men. He is not to lord it over them or patronize them, but is to exhort them *as brothers* (5:1b).[268] They are his equals, not his subordinates. African traditional practice illustrates what this means. By virtue of being the firstborn, the oldest son (or now, in some cases, the oldest daughter) sometimes has the privilege of representing the parents. But this privilege does not entitle them to claim the right to inherit all their parents' land or other possessions. They are expected to share them equally with their brothers (and sometimes their sisters).

African pastors who take Paul's advice and treat the young men in their church as their brothers will create a bond of friendship that will give the men freedom to share openly about their lives and the problems they face.

Relating to Older Women

Timothy's relationship to the older women in his congregation is to be based on the same principle that governed his relationship to older men. He is to acknowledge the age difference between him and them and to treat them respectfully *as mothers* (5:2a).

In Timothy's day, an adult son who wanted to go against his mother's wishes had to do so very respectfully.[269] Similar respect was given to a mother in a traditional African homestead. Those who were openly rude to their mothers risked being beaten by their siblings. An old woman could rebuke a disrespectful younger person by saying, "I could have given birth to you".

However, it is also true that in traditional culture women had little say when it came to making decisions. So it can be easy for a young pastor to treat older women dismissively. But Paul insists that they must all be treated with the same respect that Timothy would show to his own mother, even when rebuking them and exhorting them to grow in the Lord.

Relating to Younger Women

Timothy's relationship with *younger women* should be characterized by *absolute purity* (5:2). The word Paul uses and the context make it clear that he is talking about sexual purity.[270] Timothy needs to watch his relationships with younger women, treating them *as sisters* to avoid being tempted into sexual sin, or even into the appearance of sexual sin.

Sexual relationships between brothers and sisters constitute incest, which is taboo in almost all societies, including those in Africa. Rather than seeking to have an incestuous relationship, a brother should constantly be encouraging his sister to behave morally and so be preparing her for marriage. Timothy is to have the same role in relation to the young women in his church. He should constantly be encouraging them to live pure and holy lives (2 Cor 11:2).

Paul may be making this point because this was "an area of special concern with some in the community".[271] It is also true that as a young man, Timothy would be particularly vulnerable to temptation and to accusations from his opponents. Many pastors have fallen into sexual sin through situations that began innocently. For example, a young woman may come to a pastor for counselling, benefit from his counsel, and return again and again. Along the way, the pastor may begin to forget that she is to be treated as a sister, and may say something inappropriate. If the woman also fails to show spiritual maturity, one thing leads to another. Soon they are in a sexual relationship that will destroy the young woman and the pastor and greatly injure the testimony of the church. If the pastor had followed Paul's instruction and regarded the woman as his sister, he would have maintained absolute purity by never speaking the first words that led to their sin.

These instructions mean that young pastors who are still unmarried must take care that their search for a spouse is done openly and honestly. Any courtship should take place in public places and in groups, as much as possible. Doing this will help them to maintain an effective ministry and avoid creating any suspicions in the minds of those they lead.

Questions for Discussion

1. This passage reminds us that we do not earn respect and become effective by holding positions of power but by the way in which we manage those we are placed over. To what degree do our political leaders bear this truth in mind? What about church leaders?
2. There have been many changes in the way younger people in Africa treat older people. In what ways are the changes good, and in what ways are they bad? How much should these social changes affect the way we apply this passage in pastoral ministry?

UNIT 14
1 TIMOTHY 5:3–16

RELATING TO PEOPLE IN NEED

Timothy not only has to deal with people of different ages, but also with people with different needs. His situation would be similar to that faced by a friend of mine in Machakos, Kenya, who was approached by a woman who used to go from house to house begging for money or food. James Mbuva was struggling financially himself at the time, but he gave her 20 Kenyan shillings from the little he had.

Later, he began to worry about what he had done. Was she really in need? Should he have given her money he could scarcely spare? He asked my advice. All I could say was, "Did the woman look as if she was really needy?" James replied that she did. "In that case," I said, "be glad that you have been able to help someone in need".

Paul may have been approached by Timothy with a request for advice about how he should handle the same type of situation, specifically as it related to widows. They were the neediest in Paul's day, as often in Africa today. They had almost no opportunities for employment and there were no social services to support them. When a man died without including his wife in his will, everything he owned was automatically given to his children. This practice left many widows in desperate situations if their children did not provide for them.[272]

Christ's evident compassion for widows (Luke 7:11–14; 18:1–8; 21:1–3) and the Christian community's care for each other (Acts 2:42–45) would have attracted many widows to the faith. As a result, it seems that the church in Ephesus had more requests for help than it could handle. Moreover, it seems that some who should not be receiving help were getting it, while others who desperately needed help were not. So

Paul sets out some guidelines that can be used to ensure that the limited resources available are used for those who need them most (5:16).

As we read Paul's instructions about the situation in Ephesus, we should also be thinking about how these principles can be applied in relation to the widows, orphans, refugees and street children of Africa.

Who Qualifies for Support?

Widows who are really in need are to be given *proper recognition* or "honour" (5:3).[273] Paul does not state what he means by "recognition" or "honour", but it is clear from verses like 5:4 that it would have included meeting their material needs. The names of these widows were to be entered in some sort of list of those entitled to support from the church (5:9).[274] Paul provides the following criteria for deciding whether someone's name should be on that list:

- *Demonstrated need:* Widows should normally be supported by their families so as not to burden the church. Only widows who have no *children or grandchildren* or any relatives who can support them need help from the church (5:4; 5:8; 5:16). They are *all alone,* and the only family they have is the family of God. A widow in this position knows she depends on God alone and *puts her hope*[275] in him as she *continues night and day to pray and to ask God for help* (5:5).

- *Age:* To qualify, the widow must be over the age of sixty (5:9). But why sixty? This cut off seems rather arbitrary. What about the fifty-nine-year-old widow who was in need? It is important to remember that the Ephesians, like many in Africa today, would generally not have known their exact age. Their society did not keep exact birth records. Thus the age of sixty was simply a round number that Paul probably settled on because in Jewish culture it was considered the start of old age.[276] Once a woman was sixty, there was no chance that she would remarry. Another reason for the age limit relates to the nature of the list that Paul refers to. Most likely, being *put on the list* involved formal registration[277] of these widows' commitment to the church, and of the church's commitment to support them for as long as they lived.[278] Paul did not want this list to become too long, for then the church might end up breaking its promise. So he restricted the list to widows over sixty. However, he is not saying that the church should not help younger widows in times of desperate need.

- *Record in marriage:* The church should support only a widow who has *been faithful to her husband* (5:9). Paul is emphasizing that the widows the church supports must have remained sexually and morally pure by being faithful during their marriages. (See also the discussion of the qualifications for elders in 3:2).
- *Reputation:* A widow who qualifies for help from the church should be *well known for her good deeds* (5:10). Paul give four examples of the types of deeds he has in mind:[279]
    - *a) Bringing up children:* Whether she raised her own children or orphaned children, her experience as a good mother is useful if she is asked to assist in caring for others (including children) in the church.
    - *b) Showing hospitality:* Hospitality was an important virtue at a time when people like Paul and his companions were travelling to spread the gospel. Many inns were little more than brothels and were not morally suitable for Christian travellers. A widow could serve the church by offering hospitality to these travellers. Hospitality is still an important ministry in Africa, especially where pastors or teachers travel great distances to visit a church.
    - *c) Washing the feet of the Lord's people:* Washing someone's feet was an act of kindness performed to welcome a traveller upon their arrival. Jesus' own example encouraged Christians to humbly serve one another in this way (John 13:4–17).
    - *d) Helping those in trouble*: Helping others involves more than meeting material needs. It includes showing kindness to those who are persecuted, oppressed, sidelined, or in any form of distress. In our context, these are often refugees and displaced peoples. We should offer them friendship as well as shelter and food.

Paul wraps up his list with a general reference to *all kinds of good deeds*. He has no intention of listing all the possible actions. What is important is that a widow has demonstrated her commitment to this kind of lifestyle and has earned a good reputation.

Who Doesn't Qualify for Support?

There are three categories of widows who do not qualify for support from the church:

Widows who can be supported by others

Paul is adamant that families and relatives have a responsibility to support any widows in their family. He feels so strongly about this point that he repeats it three times (5:4, 8, 16). In 5:4 he identifies the *children or grandchildren* as having a special responsibility, and then in 5:16 he broadens the scope beyond the immediate family, saying *if any woman who is a believer has widows in her care, she should continue to help them.* The general principle is that widows who have other sources of support outside the church should have their needs met there. In 5:4 he offers several reasons why this should be the case.

- Caring for parents is part of godliness. The Christian faith involves more than just believing certain things or having an abstract love for others. It requires us to act in ways that demonstrate practical love. Thus, children and grandchildren *should learn first of all to put their religion into practice by caring for their own family.*[280] This shows respect, which "is the first duty of children".[281]

- Children are not doing their parents a favour when they care for them – they are *repaying* a debt.[282] While children are growing up, they receive love, a home and security from their parents. Offering these to parents in return is a way of thanking them for the work they have done.

- Caring for one's parents *is pleasing to God*. In fact, God considered this principle so important that he enshrined it in the Ten Commandments, the fifth of which is "Honour your father and your mother" (Exod 20:12). For believers, the desire to please God should be the strongest motivation of all when it comes to supporting parents, stronger even than any social pressures to do so.

Believers who neglect their parents are not only disobeying God, they are not even living up to the standards of the society around them! They are behaving *worse than an unbeliever* (5:8a) and bringing shame on the church. After all, the ancient Greek philosopher Plato said that one's debt to one's parents is the first and greatest and oldest of debts, considering that all which a man has belongs to those who gave him birth and brought him up, and that he must do all that he can to minister to them; first, in his property; secondly, in his person; and thirdly, in his soul; paying the debts due to them for their care and travail which they bestowed upon him of old in the days of his infancy, and which he is now able to pay back to them, when they are old and in the extremity of their need.[283]

Those who fail to provide for poverty-stricken relatives have *denied the faith* (5:8b). They may not be guilty of apostasy and may not have verbally denied belief in Christ, but their actions imply a lack of real faith.[284] Ever since the earliest days of the church, one of its basic principles had been to care for the needy (Acts 6:1–6), and these people no longer uphold that principle.

The fact that some non-believers probably did not live up to the high standard that their society endorsed is no excuse for believers. Regardless of how others care for their parents, anyone who claims to be a Christian has accepted the Christian obligation to do so.[285] Failure to live up to one's obligations is culpable. As Ward puts it, "The man who switches off the light is worse than the man who has never known anything brighter than a candle."[286] The believer sins against light while the unbeliever has little light.

Ever since the earliest days of the church, one of its basic principles has been to care for the needy (Acts 6:1–6). Thus believers should not only care for their parents, but for any family member who is in need. That is why Paul mentions *relatives* in general in 5:8. In 5:16 he speaks of the responsibility of a believing woman to care not just for her widowed mother but for any *widows in her family.*

It is striking that in 5:16a, Paul clearly identifies the one who is doing the supporting as a *woman who is a believer.*[287] Is he implying that men need not support widows? No, for in 5:6 he speaks of a man providing for *his relatives.* Paul would also have been familiar with the ancient Jewish custom whereby a man took responsibility for a widow. The deceased husband's brother or a close relative would have been expected to marry her and bring her into his family (Deut 25:5). Some people groups in Africa have traditionally had a similar practice of widow inheritance.

However, this practice is only suited to polygamous societies, and by Paul's day it was recognized that God's plan for marriage is monogamy. Paul had underlined this point when he insisted that overseers and deacons must be the husband of one wife (3:2, 12). So it was necessary to find some other way to care for widows – just as the church needs to provide an alternative to widow inheritance in Africa.

What is said in the above paragraph does not, however, answer the question of why Paul says that it is the "woman" who is to care for widows (5:16).[288] Some commentators have suggested that Paul is talking about a young Christian widow who has the energy and time to support other widows. This position is attractive because it lets 5:16 continue the same subject of 5:11-15, that is, *younger widows*. However, it is unlikely that Paul would ask younger widows to give such support because these women would have their own needs. That is why he advises them *to marry, to have children and to manage their homes* (5:14).

Others argue that "woman" is being used here as a general term for female members of the church like Lydia (Acts 16:14-15) and Chloe (1 Cor 1:11). But this interpretation does not solve the problem of why Paul speaks specifically of women and not of men.

"Responsibility for the welfare of any widow would be taken by the housewife".[289] Kelly points out, "The reason why Paul does not impose the same obligation on a Christian man of similar position should be obvious. If such a man were unmarried or a widower, it would be most unsuitable for him to take over responsibility for a group of widows; whereas if he were married, the responsibility in all its practical aspects would naturally devolve upon his wife".[290]

Paul has already stressed the moral responsibility of believers to care for widowed relatives. Now he also gives a practical reason for it: to avoid the church being *burdened* (5:16). The church will then be able to use its resources to *help those widows who are really in need*. By supporting their own family members, these people are indirectly supporting other needy women.

Widows who live for pleasure

Paul described the godly widow who should be supported as one who "puts her hope in God" (5:5). In contrast to her, there is the widow who *lives for pleasure* (5:6). The Greek verb used here refers to self-indulgence in all areas, including sexual pleasure.[291] Some commentators interpret this verse as meaning that these women engaged in prostitution, but it is far more likely that these widows were simply, "totally self-centred, and given over to pursuit of selfish pleasure".[292] They are the same type of people described in James 5:5 as loving luxury for themselves and showing no concern for the needs of others. Instead of fixing her hope in God, the self-centred widow in 1 Timothy trusts in herself – and possibly in her own power to attract a husband. The tense of the verb indicates that this is her habitual way of life, not a one-time failing.[293]

Such a widow *is dead even while she lives* (5:6). She may be alive physically, but spiritually she is dead. She does not belong to the church, and thus is not eligible for its support. "She has cut herself off from the Christian community, either by deliberate choice or by neglect of its worship and fellowship, and has forfeited any claim to its care".[294]

Younger widows

Younger widows do not qualify to be placed on the list because *when their sensual desires overcome their dedication to Christ, they want to marry.* Thus, *they bring judgment on themselves, because they have broken their first pledge* (5:11–12).

What does this mean? Is Paul saying that it is wrong for a widow to remarry? Is the "pledge" he refers to the marriage pledge? Some argue that it is. They insist that no one should marry more than once. They would also insist that this is what Paul means when he says that an overseer, deacon or elder must be the "husband of but one wife" (3:2, 12; Titus 1:6 niv) and that a godly widow must be "faithful to her husband" (5:9, literally, "the wife of one man"). Those who interpret the words in this way say that these women are judged because they have abandoned this ideal. Most commentators disagree with this position. After all, only a few verses later Paul advises younger widows to remarry. He would not do this if a second marriage was a sin.

Another interpretation says that it is not wrong for a woman to want to remarry, but it is wrong for her to be so desperate for marriage that she will marry a non-Christian. This is based on the argument that the word translated "pledge" here literally means "faith".[295] "What seems envisioned in the present passage is remarriage that includes abandoning her faith in Christ; that is, her sensual desire is more important than her faith in Christ to the point that she would marry a non-believer in order to fulfil that desire."[296] However, this approach seems to inappropriately apply Paul's reference to following Satan in 5:15 to the natural tendency to remarry in 5:11–12.

The last, and most likely, interpretation understands the word "pledge" to be a reference to some type of contract. It is possible that every older widow whose name was added to the list of those being supported by the church had to promise to serve the church and remain unmarried for the rest of her life. Christ may have been thought of as her spiritual bridegroom.[297] Paul is warning Timothy that this pledge would most likely be too difficult for young widows to keep. It was not remarriage that was sinful, but the breaking of their promise. Those who had witnessed a young woman pledge herself to the church and Christ in this way would condemn her for unfaithfulness if she broke these promises. In these circumstances, remarriage would mean the young widow, and by extension the church, would not be living "above reproach".

Another reason why the church should not support younger widows is that it will leave them *idle*, with nothing to occupy their time.[298] Paul has already stressed that it is important that people keep busy (see 2:15). Without anything to do, the bored young widows will wander aimlessly from *house to house*, gossiping and meddling in other people's affairs (5:13).[299] Even if these visits are associated with their church duties, the young women may lack the wisdom to know what should or should not be asked or said. Some may become "inquisitive and meddlesome and express opinions which at the very least should have been left unsaid."[300] Some may even "make mischief, carrying from house to house private matters which have come to their knowledge in the course of their official visits."[301]

But if the young widows are not included in the church list, there is no organized provision for their material needs. This problem is made worse by the limited opportunities for professional work or trade at the time. So Paul thinks that getting married is the most sensible option: not only will their material needs be met, but "bearing children will satisfy the instinctive urges of their nature, and running a house will absorb their surplus energies".[302]

This is Paul's *counsel* (5:14). However, the nasb may be closer to the original with its translation, "I want". Paul used the same words in 2:8 when he gave instructions to the men and women in the church on worship and dress. He is giving his authoritative judgment as an apostle.[303]

But doesn't Paul's advice to "younger widows to marry" contradict his own words in 1 Corinthians 7:8–9, where he says the unmarried should stay unmarried? Not necessarily. Paul is responding to the reality of two different situations.

> Paul differentiates what is preferable and what is necessary in certain circumstances: to the Corinthian church Paul says that singleness is preferable, but if that is not possible then it is permissible to remarry; to the Ephesians he says that because of the problems caused by the Ephesian widows, it is best for them to remarry.[304]

Paul's main concern in both cases is that members of the church remain above reproach and give a good example to non-believers. If remaining single does not promote staying above reproach, it defeats its purpose.

We need to bear this point in mind when thinking about how best to serve young widows in Africa. What is the best way to meet their needs while maintaining the good name of Christ's church? In the modern world, it seems sensible to encourage widows and single women to seek training and use it to find honourable employment that adequately supports their family. The church can help them get the training they need and help them to find employment.

The word translated "to have children" (5:14) is the same word used for "childbearing" in 2:15. There, having children was presented as the alternative to disruptive teaching. Here, it is presented as an alternative to idleness, which leads to gossip, and becoming a busybody. Those who have children also have to "manage their homes". In Paul's day, this could involve managing a large household, with servants and extended family.[305] There is no conflict between this task and Paul's general teaching that the husband must manage the house (3:5, 12): "When wives rule their households they are not giving up their submissiveness but are acting as the female counterpart of their husband, the householder (Matt 24:43)."[306]

When young women dedicate themselves to constructive and godly tasks, the *enemy* will not have the *opportunity* to *slander* them or the church. This "enemy" may be Satan,[307] whom Paul mentions in the next verse (5:15; see also 3:6–7), or the church's human opponents.[308] Most commentators argue that Paul probably has both meanings in mind: the term "most likely refers to Satan, although of course the speaking evil of us is carried out through human instrumentality."[309]

Paul's instructions are necessary because some young widows have *already turned away to follow Satan* (5:15). We do not know exactly what these women had done. They may have drifted into immorality[310] or heresy,[311] or some other kind of sin.

The main reason for Paul's giving these instructions is set out in 5:7. Here the hcsb translation is closer to the original Greek. It reads, "Command this, so that they won't be blamed." "They" probably refers to the widows already enlisted in the church.[312] However, it could also refer to the relatives who are asked to carry out their responsibilities,[313] to both the widows and their relatives,[314] or even to the entire church. It is not important to specify who exactly is being referred to, because everyone in the church should help care for widows and build up the reputation of the church. Thus the tniv translates this verse as *so that no one may be open to blame.*

The emphasis on avoiding blame is a principle that Paul returns to repeatedly for all believers. He used the same expression when summarizing the qualifications for an overseer in 3:2. Believers are Christ's representatives on earth, and must not do anything that would bring any insult to their Lord's reputation.

Barrett provides an excellent summary of what Paul has been saying in 5:3–16:

> A society laying claim to philanthropic principles was under obligations to protect its weaker members, of whom none (in the ancient world) were more vulnerable than widows. If they could be otherwise cared for there was no need to burden the congregation, whose resources were doubtless small: if young enough, they should marry again, and thus come under the protection of a male head of a household; or their children or grandchildren might look after them. If these resorts

failed, if the woman was elderly and left alone in the world, the congregation might step in, but only if satisfied that the widow would bring no discredit upon it. The widow must have a good record; must be a true believer; must not be likely to use the opportunities afforded by her privileged position for idleness and gossip.[315]

Meeting Needs Today

Paul gave these instructions to Timothy because he wanted to be sure that those who were most needy were receiving help from their families or the church body. In his day, the most needy were the widows. In Africa today, the church still needs to serve widows, but it also has to consider how to care for orphans, prostitutes, street children and refugees. We should apply the same principles that Paul did, but adapt their practical application to our situation.

Paul's first principle was that believers have a responsibility to care for their own relatives. Pastors should thus encourage Christians to recover the traditional sense of community that bound families together. More than this, Christians should demonstrate the love of Christ that goes beyond the love that families would traditionally be expected to give. Church members should be strongly encouraged to assist any relatives who cannot support themselves. This support should not involve a widow being expected to become a second wife or to repay all that she is given.

Orphans should be adopted by their extended family in the church, if at all possible. This was in fact the traditional way of caring for orphans. But today the HIV/AIDS epidemic, wars and urbanization have produced such overwhelming numbers of orphans that it can be very difficult for extended families to adopt them all – and some have lost all contact with their extended families. In such situations, the church needs to get involved in helping. We should follow the example of the poor Kenyan grandmother, who on hearing that the orphan home lacked blankets gave them one of her own blanket, saying "I don't have any money to give, but I can imagine what it must be like to be lonely, helpless and cold". This grandmother is the type of older women whom Paul said that the church should be prepared to support.

Faced with overwhelming need, church members and leaders need to use wisdom and discernment in determining which relatives and children's homes they should support, and should give priority to those that are neediest. We must not be giving bursaries to children who could well be taken care of by their uncles and aunts. Nor should we tolerate the corruption that diverts funds intended for the destitute to benefit the children of well-off parents. If we permit that, we will indeed bring judgment on ourselves.

When the church calls on people to be responsible for their family members, it should also call on the government to do its part in caring for those it governs. Christians should get involved in helping to draft government policies and programmes that will help meet the needs of street children, widows, orphans, and refugees. Their needs include education and training that will enable them to find work. Then churches can become involved in helping to implement the programs. For example, rather than just condemning prostitutes and wanting the police to get them off the streets, respected women in the church could help single-mother clubs teach younger women skills they can employ to earn money in God-pleasing ways. In some cases, Christians will need to urge governments to act against corruption that keeps people trapped in poverty. They may also need to ask for legislation to change cultural practices so that women can inherit and own land, and keep their homes after the death of their husbands. These changes will enable them to support themselves and provide good homes for their children. They will no longer need to resort to prostitution to survive, and their children will be far less likely to end up as street children.

The church should also act itself and urge the government to act to meet the needs of the thousands of displaced people in Africa. Paul wanted young widows to have homes and families, because he knew the dangers of idleness. He would not have wanted to see so many men and women living in enforced idleness in refugee camps. We should set a high priority not only on feeding and clothing refugees but also on helping them to return to their homes. If they are to be able to do so, we will also have to act against those things that led to their being displaced in the first place. We as individuals and as churches will have to work to end wars and unnecessary tensions.

In sum, the principles underlying Paul's instructions for the care of widows are still highly relevant to the problems we face in helping the needy in Africa today.

Questions for Discussion

1. When it comes to the care of widows, the church in Africa has not always found adequate alternatives to widow inheritance. What practices do you propose as alternatives for the church to consider? What is your church doing to care for widows?
2. In what practical ways can the church be involved in making sure widows and orphans can support themselves when their husbands or parents die? Focus your discussions on how you can contribute to solutions that are already being implemented in your area.
3. Identify who else in your family or community might not be able to provide for themselves. What do they need? Do they have family that can help them or do they need help from the church? How can they be helped?

PRACTICAL CARE FOR WIDOWS

Mzee James and his wife Tabitha do not have great wealth, but they have a quiet and effective ministry to widows that all of us can emulate.

This couple keep a list of names of widows in their local church. Over the last five years, the list has increased by fifty per cent as many men have died of various causes, including AIDS. Each year, the couple review the list and arrange the names in order of greatest need. Then they do three things: 1) They pray for each woman on their list. 2) They speak brief words of encouragement to them whenever they see them, which is almost every Sunday. 3) They help financially according to their ability. In a given week, they may give Kshs. 200 to one widow and Kshs. 800 or more to another. At times, they are able to put something in an envelope for each of the widows on their list.

On special days like Christmas, James and Tabitha set aside something small to share with each of the widows, at times depriving themselves of a good meal. When they can, they provide short periods of work for the neediest widows. No widow who asks for help goes away empty-handed, even if all she receives is a small portion of what James and Tabitha were going to eat that day.

Though a few widows have assumed that the couple help people because they are wealthy, this is not the case. They are poor, but rich in the joy of helping others. In return for their generosity, the Lord has always provided their daily bread. He has been faithful in meeting their needs.

Mzee James is now 90 years old and his wife Tabitha is 80. In a few years they will pass on to share the glory of their Master whom they love and serve. However, they have left a lasting example that could minimize the suffering of many widows in Africa if other believers were to follow it.

The simple but effective principles that James and Tabitha leave behind include:

- If you are unable to help in any other way, pray for specific widows.
- Create a clear list of who you are helping, and review it occasionally.
- Help according to your ability, being honest before God that you have given all that you are able.
- Anticipate the Lord's provision for all of your needs.

UNIT 15
1 TIMOTHY 5:17–23

RELATING TO CHURCH ELDERS

Relations between pastors and elders can be difficult. I remember the situation of one African pastor who came to me for advice. He had taken responsibility for a church in an area where he was seen by many as a stranger. There he found that the church treasurer was in the habit of taking the offering to his home, where he would count it on his own. The pastor was unhappy about this practice as it could easily lead to dishonesty. But the elder concerned was very influential and could not easily be challenged. What could the pastor do?

I suggested that he should not rush to make accusations or attempt to remove the man from his position. He had no proof that the elder was stealing money. So instead of asking the elder to resign, he simply insisted that the money be counted at the church in the presence of a second elder, who would keep the records. The treasurer could continue to keep the money in his home because there were no banks nearby.

The treasurer was offended by the change in the counting procedure. He began to influence others against the pastor and to openly refer to him as "that stranger". So the pastor came back to me again. I again counselled patience, telling him to "preach the word honestly and give the matter time". He took my advice.

Some time later, church elections were held. The troublesome elder was not re-elected, and so could no longer be treasurer. The pastor's patience and gentleness avoided what could have become a drawn-out fight that could have damaged his ministry and harmed the church.

Timothy may have found himself in similar situations, and so Paul gives him advice on how to relate to the elders who serve with him.

Honour Elders

Paul starts by recognizing the truth that there are many elders whose dedication and integrity is beyond question. They *direct the affairs of the church well* (5:17a). They are worthy of respect because of their age and because of their position in the church. But a subset of this group are worthy of special honour. They are *those whose work is preaching and teaching* (5:17b).

It seems that there were different types of elders in the church. Some scholars argue that there were four categories of elders: a) the group of older men (mentioned in 5:1), who are simply older members of the church; b) the elders who are overseers, mentioned in 3:1 and in Titus 1:5; c) officials who rule well (5:17); and d) elders who are preachers and teachers (5:17).[316] The more common view is that Paul is only talking about two categories of elders: the men in the church who are older than Timothy (5:1), and all those who have some sort of position of responsibility in the church.[317] Their responsibilities often included preaching and teaching, but there were some whose skills were more in administration and caring for members. Barrett suggests that the duties of the latter group would probably have involved "general direction of the church's affairs, the administration of discipline, pastoral oversight, and presidency at meetings and services, including presumably the Eucharist, though this is not mentioned".[318] While all elders should be honoured, greater honour should go to those who have been chosen to lead, and in this group the one who does his job efficiently should also be honoured. But the elder who deserves the greatest honour is the one who preaches and teaches.

We sometimes get our priorities wrong. We tend to be excited about ministers who perform miracles or provide great entertainment. What we should be excited by is preachers and teachers who send us home rejoicing that we have learned more of the depths of the word of God. Nothing is more crucial for the growth of the church than the preaching and teaching ministry that helps believers grow to maturity in their faith and knowledge of God.

Those elders who performed their duties particularly well should be given special acknowledgement in the form of *double honour* (5:17a). The word translated "honour" here is closely related to the one translated as "recognition" in 5:3. There it was used in the context of material support for widows. The fact that Paul goes on to speak about working oxen and paid workers in 5:18 suggests that here, too, Paul is talking about material support. Elders who serve well should be paid for their services.

But what does the "double" mean when Paul speaks of "double honour"? It may mean that an elder who is performing his task should be paid twice as much as other elders,[319] or twice as much as the widow the church is supporting?[320] Or Paul may not be talking about doubling these elders' pay, but rather about their receiving both respect and a salary, whereas other officials receive only respect?[321]

In support of his argument that elders who serve well should receive some material benefit, Paul reminds Timothy that the Old Testament law prohibited anyone from using an ox to separate grain from chaff while muzzling it so that it could not eat any of the food it was producing (5:18a; see Deut 25:4). This prohibition was meant to keep the animal from being starved while it worked. Paul quoted the same verse to the Corinthians when explaining to them that people who work in the church must be allowed to earn a living by what they do (1 Cor 9:9b–11).[322]

This principle is underlined in the next statement, *workers deserve their wages* (5:18b). Here Paul is not quoting Scripture but is referring to a common saying at the time, which Jesus also quoted (Luke 10:7).[323] The point is that someone's reward should be in proportion to the work they have done. A pastor who scatters the sheep is not worthy of the name and should go home and do something else. A pastor who gathers the sheep together, however, needs to be paid an amount that will meet all his or her basic needs.

This principle is not always applied when it comes to pastors in Africa. A few receive good or adequate pay, but the majority are very poorly paid. They may receive even less than a casual labourer. This is partially due to a perception that pastors live "by faith" and should rely solely on God and be content with whatever they are given. Yet while it is true that God provides, the Bible makes it clear that the standard way in which God does this is through the people whom the pastor ministers to. They have a responsibility to support the pastor, and in so doing to contribute to building the kingdom of God. Congregations need to remember that pastors have to pay the same prices for sugar and bread as they do. They have to pay school fees for their children and buy clothing for their families just like everyone else. A pastor also deserves to have some good things and should not be expected to get by with the bare minimum.

This point was driven home to me when my wife and I returned to Africa after completing graduate studies. I was told that my salary would be Kshs. 1,500 (about $70.00 at that time in 1978) and my wife would earn Kshs. 1,000 ($50.00). We were expecting a baby and had many expenses related to settling down, so I asked if we could be given a higher salary. Our request was denied because any increase would make the gap between what we earned and the average pastor earned too large. Imagine what the pastors were living on! The irony of the situation is that the person who declined our request was a missionary who was requesting more than our salaries combined to support each of his children!

Be Wary of Accusations

The evil one likes to target pastors and elders. Thus it is not surprising that malicious accusations are often made against people who are in prominent positions in the church by those who want to discredit them. Such attacks may come from outsiders or from church members who resent being disciplined or rebuked by the elders.

Paul tells Timothy to use discernment in responding to such accusations. He does not deny that elders sometimes sin, and so he does not tell Timothy to refuse to listen to any accusation made against an elder. But he does tell him to insist that any accusation must be backed up by the evidence of *two or three witnesses* (5:19). This practice comes from the Jewish legal system (Deut 19:15), and is mentioned a number of times in the New Testament (Matt 18:16; John 8:17; 2 Cor 13:1). Timothy is to consider acting against an elder only when charges are adequately substantiated. Paul did not want elders to be "subject to charges on the basis of hearsay or possible personal antagonism by an individual".[324]

But what is to be done when the sin is such that there is only one witness? For example, I know of a case where a preacher raped a young girl. No one else witnessed the violation – indeed, it would not have happened had there been witnesses. Should the girl's tearful accusation be dismissed? Definitely not! We need to recognize that Paul was laying down a general principle rather than trying to deal with every possible case. A wicked elder should not be able to escape punishment by hiding behind Paul's instruction here.

In this kind of situation, the elder or pastor who hears the girl's story needs to investigate it carefully, exercising great discernment. The girl should be believed unless a thorough investigation reveals that she has some motive for trying to discredit the pastor, or that someone else has put her up to it, in the same way as Herodias used her daughter to get revenge on John the Baptist (Matt 14:3–12; Mark 6:17–29). If the girl is trustworthy and of good character and it seems likely that her accusation is true, then the pastor needs to be disciplined in accordance with church policies and in some cases the national law.

Rebuke Sin Publicly

If an accusation is found to be justified, Timothy needs to know how to deal with *those who are sinning*. The form of the verb indicates that he is referring to those who sin habitually as opposed to those who commit a sin on just one occasion.

Some commentators suggest that Paul is laying out a two-stage process when it comes to dealing with elders who sin. The first step would be to hear privately from two or three first-hand witnesses to the wrongdoing, and would probably involve a private confrontation with the elder. "If the accusation is valid and the sinning persists, then the elders should be confronted in public before the whole church."[325] This approach would mirror the process Jesus told his followers to adopt when a brother sins (Matt 18:15–17).

Persistent wrongdoing by elders must not be hushed up, but must be exposed by rebuking the offender *before everyone*, that is, in the presence of the entire congregation of believers. The reason for this public shame is *so that the others may take warning* (5:20). In this context "the others" are probably the other elders, who will be reminded that "they will be held accountable for their own actions by the church and God".[326] They will recognize that they must not exploit their positions but must live upright lives that will never expose them to public rebuke.³²⁷ The believers who witness this rebuke to an elder by a senior member of the church will also realize that the church is sincere and not hypocritical when it talks about the need to live a godly life.

The goal of the rebuke is thus not merely to humiliate and condemn someone. It is the application of "practical discipline in the interest of all".³²⁸ Although not mentioned, there must also be a hope that the sinner will repent. Jesus' words in Matthew 18:15–17 imply that this process of discipline does not only apply to the elders whom Paul is speaking about here, but also to all Christians who persist in a sinful way of life.

Those who wonder whether public rebuke is fair should keep in mind that we are talking about a persistent sinner, whose sin is likely public knowledge. By addressing it in public, the church is sending a clear message that it stands for purity, not wickedness, and that the most accountable persons are the leaders.

From time to time Africa has witnessed pastors or church leaders publicly violating the biblical principles of love, righteousness and justice. Whether done for personal or ethnic reasons, these violations call for public discipline. When the church fails to discipline those who sin in this manner, it fails to be the salt and light of the world (Matt 5:13–16).

Avoid Favouritism

It can be difficult to discipline others, particularly when those requiring discipline are one's friends or key leaders. Paul, therefore, thinks it is necessary to remind Timothy of the need for fairness by telling him *to keep these instructions without partiality and to do nothing out of favouritism* (5:21). The word translated as "without partiality" carries the idea of being prejudiced against someone and reaching a judgment before one has properly examined all the evidence.³²⁹ In Timothy's context, where he may be dealing with accusations against elders, Paul is reminding him that he must not dismiss complaints against an elder too easily or accept them too easily. He must not let his own feelings about certain elders lead him to treat some of them "as if they could do no wrong and others as if they could do no right".³³⁰

"Favouritism" is closely related to partiality, with the only difference being that the Greek word for favouritism refers to reaching an unfair decision even after the facts have been heard. It happens when someone hears all the evidence, but then chooses to overlook some of it or twist it in order to please the stronger party or protect the person one favours. Timothy is not to do this. He is to be scrupulously fair and must treat everyone the same.

As before, this principle applies not only to his dealings with the elders, which is the main topic here, but also to how he treats everyone in the church – including the widows and the young.

Paul underscores the importance of this instruction by introducing it as if he is making a formal statement in the presence of three witnesses: *I charge you in the sight of God and Christ Jesus and the elect angels* (5:21).[331] Paul is probably thinking of the same Jewish requirement that an oath be made before "two or three witnesses" (Deut 19:15). The reason for calling these witnesses is to remind himself, Timothy and others that the ultimate judge is God. When Timothy is carrying out his responsibilities to judge elders in need of discipline, he must remember that God will also judge him.

In this passage, the angels are described as "elect", which means "chosen". Paul may use this adjective to contrast them with fallen angels or to imply that God assigns certain tasks to certain angels. The involvement of angels in judgment is also mentioned in Matthew 25:31, Luke 9:26 and Revelation 14:10.[332]

Unfortunately, favouritism is very common in Africa. For example, one person may be assured that he will get the job, even before job interviews have been conducted. Often, the appointment is made purely because that person comes from the same tribe as the employer. This should not be the case, especially in the church. I have sometimes had to insist that church organizations should take particular care to ensure that their employees represent a range of people groups, even if this sometimes means rejecting a qualified candidate. A lack of diversity can all too easily be ascribed to favouritism.

Don't Rush Things

One way to avoid problems with elders is to be careful to appoint the right people. So Paul advises Timothy that he should *not be hasty in the laying on of hands* (5:22a). This action was part of the ordination rite that commissioned someone as an elder (4:14; see also 2 Tim 1:6).[333] People who show leadership ability should not be rushed into positions of leadership before they have had time to demonstrate their character and their commitment to the faith. The one appointing them needs to have taken the time to get to know them well and see evidence of their personal growth in the Lord.

One of the difficulties in applying this principle is that there are disagreements about exactly how long one should wait before appointing someone to an office. Some denominations will not ordain pastors until several years after they graduate from a pastoral training institution. Other denominations argue that when the church sends people for training, it is affirming that they are worthy to serve in the church and that their character has been observed while they were in training. Consequently these denominations ordain pastors as soon as they graduate. This approach has the benefit of avoiding creating a hierarchy of "pastors" and "reverends". It also places a responsibility on training institutions to see that everyone whom the Lord has called to ministry is given all the training they need to carry out all the duties of the ministry.

While I am not criticizing those denominations that delay ordination, I do object to the fact that in some cases ordination is too slow for reasons that have nothing to do with adherence to biblical standards. Candidates for ordination must generally have their names put forward by some individual or group of individuals. Sometimes, these groups can show favouritism and only nominate their friends and relatives. Such behaviour is sinful. The church should neither lay hands on people too fast nor too slowly.

Paul warns Timothy that if he appoints an unworthy elder who then falls into sin, Timothy would *share in the sins* (5:22b). Some commentators think that Paul is here warning Timothy against the temptation to join others in sinning.[334] But it is more likely that "Paul is concerned that by commissioning a sinner to leadership Timothy may to some degree be responsible for their ministry and the sins they may commit, possibly because Timothy may appear to condone their sin and because a failure to punish sin may encourage others to sin".[335]

Live a Life above Reproach

Keep yourself pure

The instruction to *keep yourself pure* (5:22c) may be a repetition of Paul's warning against participating in the sin of others. But these words could also be a summary of all that has been said so far. Timothy must be impartial and his life must be an example for others. Unless Timothy lives a holy life, he will have no power or authority to help others grow spiritually. As Paul's representative in Ephesus, he holds the highest office in the church. His own life must be above reproach if he is to be able to insist that elders must be above reproach.

Look after your health

In the midst of his instructions on how he should deal with and relate to church members, Paul also addresses one of Timothy's personal concerns – his physical health. He tells Timothy that he should *stop drinking only water, and use a little wine because of [his] stomach and [his] frequent illnesses* (5:23). It seems Timothy had abstained from all wine, probably in reaction to the tendency of some at Ephesus to get drunk (see comments on 1 Tim 3:3, 8). However water was often polluted at that time, and it is quite possible that Timothy's ailment arose from drinking the water.[336] Wine does have some healthful properties, if consumed in moderation. So Paul advises Timothy to take "a little" wine because it would help his body fight his illnesses. It is important for Timothy to take care of his health because he could only serve the church well if he was healthy and strong. In many cases "spiritual dullness and aridity come from the simple fact that the body is tired and neglected".[337]

We should apply the principle of good health in our lives too. Some of us may suffer poor health because of an imbalanced diet or lack of exercise. It is also possible that we are over-involved in good activities and service to the Lord, resulting in a lack of sleep and neglected relationships. We have a God-given duty to keep ourselves healthy in all areas so that we have many years to share Christ through the quality of our lives and our service to him.

Be careful with alcohol

This passage does not encourage drunkenness because the reason for the recommendation to drink wine is clearly stated. Drinking wine is not a sin. What the Bible condemns is drunkenness for it conflicts with self-control and control by the Holy Spirit (Prov 20:1; 23:29–35; 31:4–7; Eph 5:18). Yet because many find it difficult to exercise self-control with alcohol, it is better to abstain from drinking for pleasure. There is much wisdom in the saying: "those who say that they take a glass and no more, watch it; those who practice total abstinence, keep it".

People who are surrounded by a culture of drunkenness may also need to abstain completely in protest of the practice. Others may live among believers whose faith will suffer if they see a Christian drinking alcohol. These people should demonstrate maturity and abstain so that they do not "become a stumbling block to the weak" (1 Cor 8:9). Remember though, that while abstinence is the ideal in these cases, it ceases to be a virtue if it is done at the expense of good health. But care must be taken that the one prescribing alcohol as a remedy for some ailment is a medical doctor who upholds Christian values.

Questions for Discussion

1. Leaders are often criticized rather than honoured. How can you honour and encourage your pastors and elders?
2. Is your pastor paid well? If not, what are some practical ways of making sure that pastors receive more financial support?
3. Pastors and elders face many temptations. How have churches helped their leaders avoid them? What can your church do to make it less likely that they will be in situations where they will be tempted?
4. Have you ever done something hastily that you had to spend a lot of time and energy trying to undo? Share what you learned from this experience with your group.
5. What are some simple and appropriate ways of keeping ourselves physically healthy for the Lord's service?

A LEADER'S SOCIAL SKILLS

Pastor Samuel (not his actual name) has an impressive education, enough to make him a very effective pastor, but he has never been able to stay long in any local church. Everywhere he goes the congregation ends up asking for him to be placed elsewhere. Few churches give a specific reason for their request, but they all repeat the same general concern: "his character". None of the churches say that he struggles with anything like immorality or drunkenness. Their concern is simply the way he relates to other people.

Pastor Samuel never takes time to learn about the people and their way of doing things when he is appointed to a new church. When he joins a group, he takes over without any consideration of what they were doing or speaking about before he joined them. He does not address people appropriately – whether they are older or younger than him, he treats them all the same.

If things carry on like this, Pastor Samuel will soon end up without a job because no church will accept him. Several people have tried to talk to him about this issue. He always says he recognizes his mistakes, but when a similar situation arises, he shows the same poor judgment.

A man like this needs our prayers. At the same time, we should examine ourselves to see if we too sometimes lack wisdom in social interactions. We should learn the following lessons from his experience:

- Going to Bible college or graduate school is not the only type of preparation required for pastoral ministry.
- Churches may appreciate how much we know, but they also need to appreciate who we are.
- Appropriate behaviour in a pastor involves far more than just moral behaviour.
- All aspects of your character affect your ministry.

While simple rules of etiquette are not specifically mentioned in 1 Timothy 3, they play a key role in people's evaluation of a man or woman who claims to be called to serve the Lord. We should take pains to learn them.

UNIT 16
1 TIMOTHY 5:24–25

SIN AND GOOD DEEDS

One of the people who is most strongly condemned in the Bible is King Ahab, who is described as having "sold himself to do evil in the eyes of the Lord" (1 Kgs 21:25). He promoted the worship of Baal (1 Kgs 17–19) and his wife, Jezebel, had a man named Naboth killed because Ahab wanted his vineyard (1 Kgs 21:1–16). Ahab's actions led his people into sin. He so angered God that the Lord promised to bring disaster on him and his descendants (1 Kgs 21:21). Ahab was killed in battle and all his descendants were murdered by Jehu (2 Kings 9:7). Jehu was obeying God's command when he punished Ahab, and was rewarded with the promise that his descendants would "sit on the throne of Israel to the fourth generation" (2 Kgs 10:30).

But God also noted that Jehu had gone beyond the strict instructions he had been given. Besides killing Ahab's descendants, he also killed "all his chief men, his close friends and his priests, leaving him no survivor." He massacred at least forty-two other people as well (2 Kgs 10:10–14). God did not ignore this sin. The prophet Hosea declared that God would "punish the house of Jehu for the massacre at Jezreel" (Hos 1:4). Years later, King Zechariah, a descendant of Jehu, was assassinated in a conspiracy that fulfilled God's word that Jehu's descendants would not sit on the throne of Israel beyond the fourth generation (2 Kgs 15:12).

These stories remind us that our God is to be feared. He keeps his word when it comes to rewarding good and punishing evil. This is what

Paul has in mind as he concludes his message on relationships in the church.[338]

Obvious and Hidden Sin

Paul has already mentioned sin directly or indirectly several times in this letter.[339] He has spoken of sinful acts such as murder, adultery, the love of money, and being idle and a busybody (1:9–10; 3:2; 3:8; 5:13). He has said that some have already fallen into sin (5:15) and has encouraged Timothy to avoid sin and be an example to others (4:12).

Now, however, Paul makes a general statement about two categories of sinners: those whose sins *are obvious* and those whose sins *trail behind them*. The sins of the former group are clearly seen, the sins of the latter group are concealed.

Both categories of sinners face a similar fate: God's judgment. The only difference between them is how visible their sins are at a particular time. Some, whose sins are there for everyone to see, are clearly being led right into *the place of judgment* by those sins. Those whose sins are not yet out in the open are being pushed into the same judgment by their hidden sins. God knows every secret, and every sin will eventually be brought out in the open. We should thus not be upset when God takes his time in dealing with sinners.

Paul has been talking about the requirements for church leaders and the need to be careful when appointing them. He does not expect them to be sinless (after all, he admits that he himself is a sinner – 1:15). But his sin has been confessed and dealt with by Christ, who does not distinguish between public and private sins when it comes to the punishment due and the forgiveness offered.

Just as Christ is unbiased and impartial, treating all sinners the same, so Timothy must be careful to not show favouritism when appointing people as elders (5:21). He must not fall prey to the human tendency to judge obvious sins more heavily than hidden ones. So when considering whom to appoint as elders, he must not be prejudiced against someone who committed many public sins before he became a believer, provided those sins have been confessed and forgiven and the person is showing evidence of a changed life. At the same time, Timothy must not jump to the conclusion that just because he does not know of any sins someone has committed, that person is qualified to be an elder. They may have secret sins known only to God. This is one of the reasons why Timothy must not "be hasty in the laying on of hands" (5:22). He needs to rely on the Holy Spirit to lead him to the right people to appoint as leaders. A sinner whose sin is known and who has confessed it is in better standing with God than one who is still sinning in secret.

These words are also a warning to all believers. We should not be loudly denouncing those whose sin is known while showing favouritism to others who may be sinning in secret. Our task is to carry on doing good, not to judge others. We should also be moved to fear if we ourselves are committing secret sins that are known only to us and to God. We may enjoy the respect of other people, but we will not escape God's judgment.

Paul's words may have also served as a warning to the false teachers in Timothy's time and those who were following them. Their teachings encouraged people to sin, and they too would reap the consequences of sin.

Obvious and Hidden Good Deeds

Just as all sin will eventually be exposed, so will all good deeds. Paul emphatically states: *In the same way, good deeds are obvious, and even those that are not obvious cannot remain hidden forever* (5:25). Good deeds, like sin, may be obvious and easily seen by others. Or they may not be very visible, just like some sins that "trail behind", out of sight for the moment.

Some peoples' good deeds are visible to all. Sometimes this is because they parade their good deeds so that others will notice them. At other times, it is because their actions have major effects and attract public attention. For example, in 2008 some taxis in Kenya carried large photos of Kofi Annan with the label "Peace Maker" because he had helped to bring together the warring factions after the election. Nelson Mandela of South Africa and Wangari Maathai of Kenya were awarded the Nobel Peace Prize for their good work. On a more local level, a Mr. Edward Limo was awarded an honorary Bachelor of Theology degree because of his generous donations of land and property to different church bodies.

As we admire these individuals, we should ask ourselves, "What is our contribution to society and the church?"

Our good deeds may never receive such prominent recognition, but that does not mean that they are not valuable. God knows them all and he will honour each one. Some of this honour may be given on earth when others tell how they have been blessed by our kindness, or it may come in the future, when God exposes everything we have done.

In the context of this letter, Paul is again telling Timothy he must be impartial. Timothy must not reject some people as possible elders just because he does not know of any public good deeds they have performed. The good they have done may not be widely known. Rather, Timothy should be sensitive to what the Spirit of God puts on his heart and wait for God to reveal the person's qualities.

We, too, should remember that there is more to each person than we know. Many good deeds by people who have shaped the kingdom of God and his church are not publicly known. Only the Lord knows, and in due course, he will honour each one appropriately. So we should not show favouritism to some believers simply because of good deeds they are reported to have done. Ultimately, all believers are valuable because of what Christ has done for us. He has changed us from sinners into saints!

To sum up: While good deeds have an important place in the church, we should never despise some and honour others purely on the basis of their public reputation for generosity.

Questions for Discussion

1. This unit mentions some people who have made significant contributions to society or the church. Are there others whose names you could mention? What is it that stands out about them?
2. Are there some people you know in your church or community whose good deeds are not publicly recognized? Tell your group about what they do or have done and praise God for them.
3. In the context of your work, are good deeds done quietly or publicly? Is one approach better? If so, in what way?

4. Do you know of someone who was convicted by the Holy Spirit and publicly confessed a sinful habit that he or she had indulged in for many years without anyone knowing about it? How should the church handle a situation like this so that it ultimately has a positive effect on the church and on society?

UNIT 17
1 TIMOTHY 6:1–2a

MASTERS AND SLAVES

When I was a teenager, I loved the song:

> *Oh freedom! Oh freedom!*
> *Oh freedom over me*
> *And before I'll be a slave,*
> *I'll be buried in my grave*
> *And go home to my Lord and be free.*

At the same time, and without any sense of inconsistency, I also loved to sing:

> *All to Jesus I surrender;*
> *All to Him I freely give;*
> *I will ever love and trust Him,*
> *In His presence daily live.*
> *I surrender all,*
> *I surrender all,*
> *All to thee my blessed Saviour,*
> *I surrender all.*

The first song is a total refusal to allow anyone to enslave me or treat me like a slave. The second is a willing submission to slavery as I surrender everything to my Lord. It never occurred to me then that there was any contradiction between the two songs.

Even now, many years later, I sing them both without any sense of contradiction. When I sing the first, I am refusing to allow any human being to treat me as a slave; but when I sing the second song I am committing myself to live for and willingly serve my blessed Saviour – the same Saviour acknowledged as "my Lord" in the first hymn.

The New Testament never endorses slavery. There can be no doubt that the enslavement of one human being by another is wrong. But at the same time, the New Testament insists that there is nothing believers should not be willing to do if it will glorify their Saviour and Lord. This even includes serving another human being as a slave! Paul is endorsing this principle, but not slavery, in 6:1–2.

Paul's central question in every situation is "What type of behaviour will bring glory to our heavenly Master?" We should all be asking ourselves the same question, even if we work as employees, rather than slaves.

Slavery in the New Testament World

Some have accused Paul of condoning slavery because he does not condemn the practice or encourage slaves to revolt, but instead exhorts them to carry out their duties well. This approach is too simplistic because it does not view Paul's response in light of the social situation at the time. Slavery was a social reality in Paul's day. Many people, even many believers, were slaves. Some believers were slave-owners, and Paul addresses them too in his other letters (Eph 6:9; Col 4:1; Philemon).

Slavery in New Testament times was not necessarily related to the person's race or ethnic group. People became slaves after being captured in wars. Or poverty might force parents to sell a child or themselves into slavery. Some were born into slavery because their parents were slaves.[340]

The slave population of the Roman Empire is estimated to have reached 60 million during Paul's time, meaning that roughly twenty per cent of the population were slaves.[341] If Paul had advocated a slave revolt, he would have launched a civil war. The result would have been mass slaughter. Even if he had only advocated that slaves run away from their masters, he would have been responsible for countless deaths, for runaway slaves were often executed.

Moreover, not all slaves were unhappy with their situation. Some preferred the security they enjoyed as part of a household to the insecurity and poverty they would have faced if left to their own resources.

Paul and the other New Testament writers seem to have worked with the presupposition that human efforts would not change their society. They also had no way in which they could change the existing legislation. Any social change would have to be brought about by the Spirit of God at work in the society. What they did do was propagate the idea (radical at the time) that a slave owner and the slave had equal status before God (Gal 3:28). Thus the New Testament does not call for external change first, but rather for an internal change in relationships which will, over time, bring about external changes.

The Spirit has in fact been at work in our societies, and condemnation of slavery will no longer lead to a civil war. In fact, society now praises those who seek to end slavery. And many of us no longer live under dictators but in democracies, where we have a duty as citizens to speak out against evils in our society. So we do not have to assume that Paul's approach to social issues is the only one open to Christians.

The question also arises of whether there is still anything like slavery today. If a slave is defined as "a person over whose life, liberty and property someone has absolute control",[342] then we can certainly find slavery in Africa today. There are children who have been kidnapped or taken from their parents under false pretences and forced to work for very low wages. There are others who have been forced to become soldiers or prostitutes. And many orphans live in a state that is close to slavery. Their relatives take advantage of their helplessness and force them into domestic slavery. The orphans are expected to perform numerous household tasks before and after school whether they are tired or not (assuming that they are even allowed to attend school).

When we love God, we also love his people, both by virtue of creation and redemption. Speaking up for the helpless is an expression of that love. That is why social justice is as central to the gospel as the proclamation of God's love. Whenever people are deprived of their rights, we as believers are called upon to defend their rights.

Relating to Masters in General

Paul exhorts the Christian slaves in Ephesus to *consider their masters worthy of full respect* (6:1a). It is worth noting that this respect is not dependent on the master being a Christian. Slaves are to show equal respect to Christian and heathen masters.[343]

Paul explains why he wants them to act in this way. It is not because as slaves they are naturally inferior or because their masters deserve respect, but *so that God's name ... may not be slandered* (6:1b). Throughout this letter, Paul is very concerned about the way our behaviour affects Christianity's reputation (see, for example, 2:10; 3:7; 5:8, 14). He knows that if a Christian slave disrupts the social order and is disobedient or disrespectful, the gospel will get a bad reputation. This bad reputation will then extend to the God whom the believing slave worships. (God's "name" is not distinct from his being, but is equivalent to God himself).

As Christian employees, we can also expect people to judge our faith by our behaviour. Christians who are caught neglecting their duties bring disgrace to the kingdom of God. No Christian employee should ever be one of those who report to work on time, hang their jacket in the office so that it appears they are at work, and then slip out to conduct personal business. Rather, Christians should be among the most trustworthy of employees. Whatever job you have, you should "work at it with all your heart, as working for the Lord, not for human masters" (Col 3:23).

Paul is not only concerned about God's reputation but also about the reputation of *our teaching* (6:1b; literally, "the teaching"). There is no ambiguity about what Paul is speaking of here, it is the Christian gospel. However, translations like the tniv add the pronoun "our", and make it "our teaching", so the focus falls on those who are proclaiming the gospel. The kjv, by contrast, focuses on the ultimate source of this gospel, and thus translates these words as "his doctrine". This gospel, which originated with God and was proclaimed and defended by the apostles, was what Paul had passed on to Timothy, and what Timothy was to preach in Ephesus.

Relating to Christian Masters

Christian slaves might be tempted to think that a heathen master was of less value in the eyes of God, and so fail to show respect. But they might also make the opposite error and assume that because their master was their brother in Christ, they could treat him as an equal and need not show him any respect. Paul firmly says "no" to such an attitude. Their equality in Christ does not absolve them of their everyday responsibilities.

Instead of allowing disrespect and carelessness to creep into their relationship, the Christian slave is to work even harder for a master who is a *fellow believer* (6:2). The reason for this extra diligence is *because their masters are dear to them as fellow believers and are devoted to the welfare of their slaves* (6:2).[344] Besides this bond of love, there is also the probability that any service rendered to a Christian master is also indirectly service to God, for the master will use the proceeds to serve God. Thus while every master or employer is to be respected because God's reputation is at stake, Christian masters and employers are to be served even better because the Christian slave and his or her Christian master are in partnership in the service of God.

Unfortunately, too often this principle is not practised. Rather than appreciating Christian employers, some Christian workers seem to assume, "they are kind – I can slack off because they won't punish me for not doing my work." For example, when I held a Christmas party for employees, some of them did not bother to report to work the next day. When I increased their salaries, some of them headed out to spend the extra money on drink before reporting back to work. Food meant for emergency supplies was used before the workers used their own food.

We should never treat our employers this way. In circumstances where both employee and employer are believers, the Christian worker should seek to bless their brother or sister with honest hard work. Together they can serve the Lord.

Conclusion

There are more passages in the New Testament that teach us about the master–slave relationship. For a balanced view, all of them must be considered, including Ephesians 6:5–9, Colossians 3:22–4:1, Titus 2:9–10 and 1 Peter 2:18–25.

Timothy was ministering in Ephesus, and in his earlier letter to that church, Paul did include instructions to masters, and not just to slaves. We are not sure why he does not mention the masters in 1 Timothy, but it may be because the majority of the congregation were slaves or because there was a specific reason that the slaves needed to hear this message.

As a whole, these texts teach us that harmony and mutual respect become a reality when both master and slave behave as responsible Christians. Our position in society is less important than how we serve in that position. If you are an employee, give your best work to your employer. If you are an employer, treat those who work for you with the respect that you desire to be shown. Give your gardeners, maids, drivers or administrative workers the honour that a fellow human being, and in some cases a brother or sister in Christ, deserves. Every believer should work to please and honour God, who is glorified by their behaviour, and who will use it to transform society.

Questions for Discussion

1. Many of us are employers, employees, or both. In these positions, do we act in ways that bring honour to God's name? As an employee, do you work hard or do you secretly take long breaks and do personal tasks at work? Do you treat a Christian employer differently from a non-Christian one? Think of specific ways you can apply the principles set out in this passage.
2. What does it mean to "respect your employer" today? Is it disrespectful to be a member of a union or other legal institution that defends the rights of workers? Should Christians ever participate in a strike that is intended to paralyse the company they work for? Use Paul's instructions to help you answer these questions.

UNIT 18
1 TIMOTHY 6:2b–12

SOUND DOCTRINE AND GODLINESS

When I was twelve years old, I asked why the town where I was living was called Nunguni. I was told: "Long before you were born, a great tree was cut down here, and for some time afterwards there were many logs (*nungu* in Kikamba) lying around. That is why this town is called "the place of logs."

Many years later, when I took up a position at the Nairobi Evangelical Graduate School of Theology (NEGST), I asked someone why the place where NEGST was located was called Karen. I was told: "There was once a well-known farmer here called Karen, and the place was named after her."

When I went to Mumbuni in Machakos district, however, I did not need anyone to explain the origins of its name. The huge fig tree, or *mumbu*, that was planted there decades ago made it quite clear why it is called, "the place of the fig tree".

Many people can identify with my experiences with place names. Some names are so obscure that you have to ask someone who knows the history of the place to explain them. The remains of the tree that inspired the name Nunguni rotted away or were used for firewood. The Karen after whom the location of NEGST was named died long ago, and most of us have no idea what she looked like. But other names need no explanation. For over a hundred years the fig tree at Mumbuni has forced its strong roots into the soil and has withstood sun, wind, rain, and even abuse by children, all the time proclaiming: "I gave this place its name."

In the same way, there are people whose Christianity is so well hidden that an unbeliever meeting them for the first time might ask, "Why is that person said to be a Christian?" Then they may be told a long story about how an angel spoke to her, telling her to open their Bible and read John 3:16, and so on. There are others, however, with whom a newcomer spends an hour and then announces, "I know why she is called a Christian!" The difference between these people is the place they have given to sound doctrine and godliness in their lives. Those who are rooted in them stand tall like the fig tree of Mumbuni, proclaiming the message of our Lord and Saviour. But where sound doctrine and godliness are lacking, even the label "Christian" is misplaced. That is why Paul now takes the time to teach Timothy what he and all the believers at Ephesus must do and be if they are to be clearly identified as God's people.

Teach These Things

Paul introduces his instructions with the words *these are the things you are to teach and insist on* (6:2b). "These ... things", may either be the things he is about to say,[345] or the things he has just said (possibly the instructions for slaves,[346] or everything as far back as 5:3 where he began speaking about widows, or even all the way back to the instructions for worship in 2:1[347]). Paul has made similar statements a number of times in this letter (3:14; 4:6, 11, 15). These statements can be thought of as places to pause and pay attention to the teaching given so far, and prepare for the teaching still to come. In fact, if Timothy were to ask Paul, "What do you say I must teach and preach?", Paul's reply would definitely be, "Everything I have said so far, and also what I am about to say."

Definition of Sound Teaching

As pointed out in relation to 1:10, sound teaching is related to health, particularly spiritual health. Good spiritual health produces sound doctrine, and sound doctrine is the basis for good spiritual health.

Paul defines sound teaching as *the sound instruction of our Lord Jesus Christ* (6:3b). Academics argue about whether this means instruction "about" Christ or instruction "coming from" Christ, as the one who originally gave it.[348] Yet these two options overlap, for the content of the gospel is the person and work of Christ, who is also its ultimate source.

Paul speaks of sound instruction as being equivalent to *godly teaching*. The word translated "godly" is a comprehensive term that covers all dimensions of our relationships with God and with others that are pleasing to God (see discussion of 2:2). It involves both what we believe and what we do. Mounce refers to this word as describing "a life totally consecrated to God, with emphasis on how that consecration shows itself in the person's life".[349]

Character of False Teachers

Timothy is to teach sound doctrine, but there are others who do *not agree*[350] with sound words and godly teaching and instead teach *false doctrines* (6:3a; see also 1:3). In describing these people, Paul mentions two of their characteristics, two of their interests, and at least five vices that they generate. He focuses more on the character of the teachers than on the content of their teaching.

False teachers are generally *conceited* [351] (6:4). Such people have too high an opinion of themselves and have become "bloated with self-importance".[352] They are mainly interested in displaying their knowledge and being admired. Christ features only in the background of what they teach, or does not feature at all. It is easy for recent converts to fall into the trap of thinking like this, particularly if they are pushed into positions of leadership too soon (3:6). These people have no real grounds for their conceit, for despite their claims to know it all, they actually *understand nothing*.[353]

We have all met people like this. They hold beliefs that cannot possibly be correct, but are eager to get involved in arguments and insist on having the last word in any debate. It is a waste of time getting drawn into debate with them. They are so busy thinking about what they are going to say next that they do not listen to what you are actually saying. Christians should not be like that. We should listen carefully to what the other person is saying, and respond thoughtfully and lovingly. Assuring someone that you are listening shows them you care about them and goes a long way in drawing them to the Christian faith.

The false teachers Timothy has to deal with are not particularly interested in showing Christ's love, but have *an unhealthy interest in controversies*. They love to get involved in lengthy debates that go nowhere.[354] Their obsession with divisive questions does not advance God's work in any way (see 1:4).[355]

They also enjoy *quarrels about words*. These three English words translate one Greek word, which literally means "wordfights".[356] It could be that they fight about the meaning of words or that they use words as weapons in their fights.

With these attitudes and interests, the false teachers do not promote the growth of the fruit of the spirit (Gal 5:22–23). Instead, they encourage the destructive attitudes and behaviour listed in 6:4b–5: *envy* or jealousy; *strife*, that is, quarrels and arguments; *malicious talk*, that is, abusive language and slander; *evil suspicions* and mistrust of people because of slander spoken against them or because they have slandered others; and *constant friction* or irritation.[357]

Unfortunately, these vices are sometimes seen in church leaders in Africa. Competition between them produces envy and strife, which are spread by malicious talk. These sinful attitudes often cloud elections for church officers. Yet the church should be setting the example in love, unity, and truthful talk for the world to follow! All of us, leaders and people, need to examine our lives to make sure that we are showing a sincere love for God and each.

Paul expands on the last of these vices, saying that this friction occurs *between people of corrupt mind* (6:5).[358] Teachers of this kind are a continual source of irritation to each other as they fight about everything. Their minds are "corrupt" or "depraved" (nasb).[359] Paul is not saying that these people are as evil as they can possibly be. What he is saying is that it is not just their behaviour that is affected by evil, but also their reasoning power and their moral thinking. (This recognition that evil affects every part of us is traditionally called the doctrine of total depravity). When the mind is corrupted, "the eye of the soul is darkened and cannot catch the Divine light."[360]

The corruption in these teachers' minds has resulted in their being *robbed of the truth*.[361] The "truth" here stands for the Christian revelation, the gospel. Paul does not say who has robbed them of this truth because his focus is not on an external threat but on what these men have allowed to happen. They did not guard the truth by watching their lives and doctrine closely (4:16), and as a consequence they have lost it. As Ward says, "the truth has not been actually stolen from them; it has ebbed away. It begins to leave when a man neglects his own devotional life; he becomes a prey to false theories and pride, and in time welcomes them, especially if they are his own creation ('I do my own thinking')".[362]

The truth of the gospel is so simple that we are sometimes tempted to complicate it so that we can appear sophisticated. If we do this, we are in danger of losing the truth and replacing it with our own philosophy. We must guard against that temptation. After all, God chose the uncomplicated presentation of the truth so that all who hear it will be able to understand it.

As a result of losing their grip on the truth, these teachers have come to think that *godliness is a means to financial gain* (6:5b). Paul is not implying that ministers should never be paid for their ministry. He addressed that issue in 5:17. Here he is focusing on someone's motives. If their motive in their ministry is to get personal benefits, then their ministry is no longer Christian. They are not following in the footsteps of Christ, who did not come to get things for himself, but came to serve and to give his life as a ransom for many (Mark 10:45). A Christ-like attitude is shown by a young pastor who recently completed a master's degree at a good theological school in Africa. When he came to me for prayer, I was struck by his insistence that although he served in a poor area, "I will stick with them no matter how little they are able to pay me, for their souls are more important than a high salary". We should pray that this type of unselfish dedication to God will be multiplied in Africa. And we should also do our utmost to provide the financial and spiritual support that such servants of God need.

Contentment

Having said that it is a sign of a depraved mind to think that godliness is a means of gain, Paul hastens to correct any possible misunderstanding of his words. He is not saying that all Christians must be poor or that there is no gain in godliness. In fact, *godliness with contentment is great gain* (6:6). But this gain does not have to be defined in material terms.

Contentment was a favourite virtue of many Greek philosophers, who interpreted it as meaning self-sufficiency, "the ability to rely on one's own inner resources".[363] For Paul, contentment would not have meant self-sufficiency but Christ-sufficiency (see Phil 4:11–13). He is asserting that the greatest gain is not wealth but a secure happiness that nothing external can take away, a happiness that has a firm foundation in the person and work of Christ. It is a frame of mind which is "completely independent of all outward things, and which carried the secret of happiness within itself".[364]

The logic of contentment

People who are discontented are always looking for something to make them happy. They think that if they could just buy more clothes, or a car, or a house, they would be happy. But in the final analysis, will these truly make us happy? Can we even really say that they belong to us? It could be argued that the only things we really own are the things that are so much part of us that nothing can take them away from us. Put like that, it is clear that we really own nothing, for as Paul says, *we brought nothing into the world, and we can take nothing out of it* (6:7).[365] What we enjoy between "coming into" the world and "getting out" of it does not contribute to who we are. These are all secondary things, for we came complete and will also leave complete, but without any of them. Losing sight of "who we are" is what brings a lack of contentment. When "who we are" is discovered in our relationship with Christ, we recapture the joy that is ours, whether we have many or few possessions.

Possessions and contentment

As human beings we do need some material things in order to stay alive. Paul mentions our need for *food and clothing* (6:8). In defining these as the basics of life he is echoing Jesus' words about food ("what shall we eat?") and clothing ("what shall we wear?") (Matt 6:25–34; Luke 12:22–32). The word translated as "clothing" could also be translated as "shelter",[366] which makes its meaning broad enough to include a roof over our heads. But Paul is not talking about what we may or may not own. What he is doing is laying down a principle by which we can assess our satisfaction and our goals in life. Do we have the basics that are essential for survival? Everything else is an optional extra. He is reminding us that we should not focus on the accumulation of material possessions if we wish to live a contented life.

Dangers of a lack of contentment

If we are not content with what we have, we will *want to get rich* (6:9). The tense of the verb "want" in the Greek shows that this desire for riches is not a fleeting wish but a constant concern. Those who are discontented do not want money to meet a particular need at a particular time; they simply want money. As Ward puts it, these people "want to be rich and they are going to be rich, if by any means they can bring it about."[367]

Using "any means" is, of course, the problem, and it is the reason why such people *fall into temptation*. In itself, temptation is not a sin, but because of their discontent and desire to be rich, these people are particularly vulnerable to yielding to it. The exact form the temptation takes will, of course, differ from person to person.[368]

Those who succumb to the temptation inevitably find that they are led down a winding path into *a trap*. Paul does not say who has set the trap, but "the other two times *pagis*, 'snare', is used in these letters, the snare is identified as Satan's (1 Tim 3:7; 2 Tim 2:26), and Satan is pictured as being active in the Ephesian church (cf. 1 Tim 1:20)".[369]

The exact nature of the trap is not defined, but those caught in it become so enmeshed that escape becomes impossible. "Their moral sense becomes blurred."[370] This lack of clarity leads them to blunder into *many foolish and harmful desires*. Desires in themselves are not necessarily bad. Some may even be present in an innocent form before the temptation to become rich overwhelms the person and leads them into a trap. But as the person becomes more and more entangled, the desires intensify and become "foolish and harmful".[371] Theologically, they are foolish in that they are contrary to the mind of Christ who taught us to give rather than to accumulate. Practically, they are foolish in that they represent a pursuit of security on a route that leads to ruin and destruction. As Barclay puts it: "The desire for wealth is founded on an illusion. It is founded on the desire for security; but wealth cannot buy security. It cannot buy health, nor real love, and it cannot preserve from sorrow and from death."[372]

The end result of these harmful desires is not riches but a *plunge* into *ruin and destruction*. The word translated "plunge" is the same one used in Luke 5:7 to describe sinking boats. The foolish desires draw the people into deep waters, where they lose their footing and start to drown.[373]

It is sometimes suggested that the "ruin" represents material disasters whereas the "destruction" refers to spiritual ones.[374] But it seems more likely that Paul is simply using two synonyms because he wants "the repetition ... to drive the point home that the ultimate destiny of those who pursue riches is complete and total ruin".[375]

Let us look at a simple example of the process Paul is describing. A child who shows early signs of discontentment steals pencils from his classmates in school. When he leaves school and gets a job, he steals from his employer by taking goods or money from the till. When he is caught doing this, he is dismissed from his job, and resorts to robbery and carjacking. Eventually he is shot by the police. It is a tragic end to a life that could have been very different, if the person had not been eaten by discontent.

We should not only watch out for this sin in our own lives, but should nurture the virtue of contentment in our children. In doing this though, we must be careful not to group all desires together. As said before, desire in itself is neutral. The object a person desires makes the desire good or bad. A child who wants to become rich by creating a business or by becoming a professor after a lot of hard work should be encouraged. Their desire is to achieve something good, in the right way and hopefully for the right purpose. Usually evil desire does not regard the will of God and violates other people's rights.

It is not surprising that the desire to be rich produces these effects, *for the love of money is a root of all kinds of evil* (6:10). This seems to have been a common saying at the time.[376] It was a truth that Greeks and Jews, along with people everywhere, knew from experience. Thus we should not read these words as a full statement of Paul's theology about money, but should treat them as a proverb that he quotes to underscore what he has been saying in 6:9.

There are a number of misinterpretations of this proverb that we need to correct, some of which arise from the kjv translation, "the love of money is the root of all evil". First, it is not money itself which is the problem but the "love" of money. Once money, rather than God or others, becomes the object of one's love, getting rich becomes one's consuming desire.

Examples of this type of obsession with wealth are easy to find. Many African leaders have been included in lists of the richest people in the world, while those they ruled were among the poorest people in the world. But we should not just point fingers at the obvious targets. What about some of the people living in well-fenced rich neighbourhoods that back onto slums? It is not wrong to live in such a neighbourhood, but it is wrong if the reason you can afford a house there is because you have grown rich by exploiting the poor or underpaying your workers. Moreover, many people who are not yet rich are already obsessed with money. They spend all their time thinking of ways to get more money.

When those who are in love with money succeed in getting rich, their love of money makes it impossible for them to share it with others in need. This is not the way Christians should live. If God gives us wealth, we must use it to help people in need rather than accumulating large sums beyond what we require for our basic needs.

A second misinterpretation is that the love of money is the root of all evil. Paul says it is not the root but a root of evil. Evil can spring from many sources. Moreover, when Paul says "all evil", he does not mean that we have to try to relate each and every specific evil to the love of money. He is speaking of "all kinds of evil", that is, of many different categories of evil. Because of their love of money, people have "told lies, have defrauded, have exploited their fellows, have adopted violence as a policy, and have done everything from bullying to murder, with torture in between. They have betrayed their country, made money out of slums, and even married an innocent woman for the sake of her fortune."[377] The daily news confirms the truth of these words. We regularly hear of young people being sold drugs by unscrupulous vendors who do not care that the buyers may become addicts; of people being robbed and murdered by thieves; of corrupt civil servants taking bribes or stealing funds; and of policeman bribed to look the other way.

Some people, probably including some known to Timothy, have let their minds become so dominated by money that they *have wandered from the faith*.[378] The image here is of someone searching for something so eagerly that he does not take note of where he is going. When he stops and looks around, he finds that he is deep in the bush, far from the path he was following. The people Paul is speaking of have left something far more important than a path. They have left "the faith", that is, the Christian faith, not just as a set of doctrines to be believed but as something to be "known, obeyed, and practiced".[379] Where these people once trusted in Christ, they now put their trust in money.

But money is a treacherous thing in which to place one's trust. It promised them comfort and security, but it broke that promise and those who trusted it find that they have *pierced themselves with many griefs*.[380] This is not just something that will happen in the future, but is the present state of all who love money – including Paul and Timothy's opponents. We are not told what these griefs or pains are. They may be the inner torment of a guilty conscience, or some physical or material punishment sent by God to bring them to repentance. Probably, they involve a combination of these and all the sorrow and pain that sin brings.

Money is good and we are not wrong to want to earn enough of it to meet our needs. But money must never be sought at the expense of doing God's will. We are called to love God with all our hearts, minds and strength, and love others as we love ourselves (Luke 10:27). One way in which we show our love for God is by acquiring money in ways that are pleasing to him. Whether we find ourselves with more than enough money or just enough money for our basic needs, we should be content with what the Lord has given us.

Timothy's Role

Paul began this section by commending sound doctrine, warning against false doctrines, and pointing out how a love of argument and of material things can lead one astray from the Christian faith. Now he addresses Timothy directly. He begins with the word *but* to stress that he is contrasting a true man of God with a false teacher. He is not just talking about the difference between a man of God and someone who loves money (6:10), but is contrasting the characteristics of a godly teacher with the characteristics of a false teacher (6:3–10). Paul may even be thinking of everything that he has said about false teachers in this whole letter.

The title "man of God"[381] may be a technical or official designation for someone set aside to be God's agent. In this sense, it was used to refer to Moses (Deut 33:1; Josh 14:6), Samuel (1 Sam 9:6–8), Elijah (1 Kgs 17:18), Elisha (2 Kgs 4:7), and David (Neh 12:24).[382] By referring to Timothy in this way, Paul may be reminding him that God has set him apart for his mission at Ephesus. But "man of God" can also be used as a general term, focusing on the quality of someone's life (2 Tim 3:17).[383] Used in this way, it emphasizes that Timothy, like all believers, has been called to live a godly life. The latter meaning seems more likely because Paul goes on to give Timothy instructions about how to live, rather than a description of a particular mission he is to carry out. Timothy is being addressed as one man of God among many others.

Paul then gives four commands that anyone who wants to be "a man of God" should obey:

- *Flee these vices.* The first command is the only one that is expressed in negative terms (*flee*). All the others are positive actions. Timothy is to make a habit of fleeing from *all this*, that is, from the desire to get rich, the love of money, and all the vices that go along with them. But these are not the only things Timothy is to run away from. He must avoid all the vices mentioned in this letter, and any others that would interfere with his relationship with God and with those he is called to serve.

- *Pursue these virtues.* Paul lists six virtues that Timothy must work hard to cultivate. The instruction to "pursue" them makes it clear that these virtues must be actively sought.[384] Godliness does not just happen while we sit back and do nothing.

    1. *Righteousness* is a quality of life that is rooted in God's character as holy and is extended to others in the form of justice. Barclay writes, "It is the most comprehensive of the *virtues*; the righteous are those who do their duty to God and to their neighbours."[385] In the context of this letter, it means that Timothy must focus on serving God and others, and not on getting rich.

    2. *Godliness* is a virtue that has been mentioned a number of times in this letter (2:2; 3:16; 4:8; 6:5; 6:6). It refers to "a life fully consecrated to God".[386] A godly person is someone who lives with

an attitude of reverence, constantly "aware that all life is lived in the presence of God".[387]

3. *Faith* is personal trust in God, rather than trust in a body of doctrines about God, though the former is built on the latter. Faith is the attitude that makes one loyal to God, come what may.

4. *Love* is the type of love that is extended to others in spite of who they are or what they have done. Such love is rooted in God's love for us, which we have done nothing to deserve. It involves both feeling (caring about other people) and action (participating in their lives). Instead of using people for his own benefit, as his opponents were doing, Timothy is to focus on bringing benefits to others.

5. *Endurance* involves "standing one's ground".[388] Timothy needs perseverance as he endures physical ailments (5:23), opposition from opponents, and possibly even the indifference of others to his concerns. He should not let these things discourage and defeat him. Instead, he must use tools such as prayer, the example of Christ, and meditation on the Scriptures to strengthen his ability to endure.

6. *Gentleness* is not a sign of weakness, but of restrained strength.[389] As Barclay says, someone who is gentle "knows how to forgive and yet knows how to wage the battle of righteousness".[390] Gentle people are not arrogant, but treat people well. They are willing to correct others when necessary, but will do so very carefully and humbly. Timothy would need to exercise this virtue as he dealt with the false teachers and those who were being misled by them.

- *Fight the good fight.* Timothy is to *fight the good fight of the faith*. This is not a physical fight, but one in which faith is both the weapon and the realm where the struggle takes place.[391] Some take this instruction as a call to spiritual warfare, but the Greek verb does not necessarily refer to a battle. It could also be used to refer to something like a race, a boxing match or a wrestling contest in which the winner gets a prize.[392] What is important is that this fight involves an ongoing disciplined struggle.[393] Ward comments:

The whole figure implies not only effort but mastery. If we think of the foot race, Timothy must run to win: to reach the sinner before some further evil person could do further damage; to reach the suffering saint before some other person could suggest a complaint against God. If we think of boxing or wrestling, Timothy must outthink and outlive his opponents who advocated false theological and ethical doctrine; he must beat them in argument and in the quality of his own life. And if we think of some such event as throwing the discus, he must manifest the love of Christ which 'throws further' than the pretentious knowledge of the false teachers.[394]

In modern terms, Timothy must be like a soccer coach, training his team in Ephesus in the word of God so that they can score goals for God, while also training them to watch out for attacks from the opposing team, led by the evil one who wants to score goals by destroying the work already done in the lives of believers.

- *Take hold of the eternal life.* Timothy is to take a firm grip on eternal life.[395] This may be a one-time act of grasping salvation. But it seems more likely that Paul is using this expression to refer to all that has gone on in the past, is going on now, and will go on in the future, as a single whole. Timothy took *hold of the eternal life* in the past. He is to continue holding on to it now and in the days ahead. It is not something he can only do once he has won the fight, but is a central part of the fight in the present. This is because eternal life is a life of fellowship with God that begins when a person comes to faith in Christ and never ends. Enjoyment of this fellowship causes a person to hold onto it more tightly. It is held tightly, not because it can be lost but because loosening one's grip and sliding into sin decreases one's enjoyment of this fellowship. But holding firmly to the fellowship that is eternal life gives one a foretaste of the fullness of fellowship we shall enjoy in heaven, when we "shall see him [Christ] as he is" (1 John 3:2).

Timothy is said to have been *called* to this eternal life at some time in the past, *in the presence of many witnesses*. There can be no doubt that the one who did the calling was God, but what was the occasion? Some suggest that Timothy's calling happened at his ordination.[396] However, the focus here is on Timothy's salvation rather than his ministry. Paul speaks of Timothy having *made your good confession*. This suggests that Paul is thinking of Timothy's baptism.[397] That was the time when he made a public announcement that he had acknowledged ("confessed") that Jesus is Lord.

Questions for Discussion

1. What trends in Africa point to a departure from sound doctrine? What steps can we take to preserve sound doctrine for ourselves and those we serve?
2. How does contentment or the lack of it influence people's morality? In what specific ways have these attitudes influenced our politics, our economies, and our social and even religious contexts?
3. What practical things should the church do to encourage the rich to live with less and share what they have with the poor? How should we also be encouraging the poor to be content once their basic needs are met and to learn to share what they have with others?

UNIT 19
1 TIMOTHY 6:13–21

CONCLUDING CHARGE

It is not uncommon to present a summary of the most important concerns or instructions at the close of a meeting. Individuals often do the same as death approaches. This is what King David did some thousand years before Timothy received this charge from Paul. The elderly king summarized his charge to Solomon in three firm instructions: "be strong", "act like a man", and "observe what the Lord your God requires". He then gave a strong reason for obeying this charge: "so that you may prosper in all you do and wherever you go" (1 Kgs 2:2–3). Some five hundred years before David's charge to Solomon, the elderly Moses had charged Joshua, saying, "Be strong and courageous ... Do not be afraid; do not be discouraged" (Deut 31:7–8). Paul was now an old man, and could not be certain that he would have another opportunity to communicate with Timothy, and so he ends his letter with a charge that highlights the most important things that Timothy must do if he is to succeed in his assignment at Ephesus.

Witnesses to the Charge

Paul underscores the solemnity of the closing words in this letter not only by referring to them as a *charge*, an order that must be carried out to the letter (see 1:3) but also by calling on God and Jesus Christ as witnesses to what he is about to say (6:13). He used the same approach in 5:21, where he gave Timothy his charge "in the sight of God and Christ Jesus and the elect angels". Here in 6:13 Paul mentions only God and Christ Jesus, but he supplements his mention of them with a description that underscores their suitability as witnesses to the charge.

Paul describes God as the one *who gives life to everything* (6:13a). He uses the present tense, "gives", to convey that God gave life at creation and continues to give it as part of his work of providence. He is both our creator and preserver.[398] Yet although the focus here is on God's role as creator, there may also be an allusion to God's redemption of us and his gift of new life through his Son.[399] The implicit message to Timothy may be that God is the one who gives him the eternal life he is told to take hold of.

Christ Jesus is described as having *made the good confession* (6:13b).[400] The TNIV says that he did this *while testifying before Pontius Pilate*. Scholars often identify this confession as Christ's declaration that he was the king of the Jews (Matt 27:11; Mark 15:2; Luke 23:3; John 18:37). However, the words translated "before Pontius Pilate" can also be translated as "in the time of Pontius Pilate".[401] If this translation is correct, Jesus' "confession" was all that he said and did throughout his entire ministry.[402]

The Substance of the Charge

There are three elements to Paul's charge to Timothy: he is to *keep this command* (6:14), *command those who are rich* (6:17), and *guard what has been entrusted* to his care (6:20).

Keep this command

Timothy is told to *keep this command* (6:14), but it is not clear which command is being referred to here. There are five main possibilities:

- The things Timothy is commanded to do in 6:11–12.
- All that Paul has said in 1 Timothy.[403]
- Vows that Timothy made during his ordination (if we assume that the occasion mentioned in 6:12b was Timothy's ordination).[404]
- The law of Christ (the gospel) as a whole (if we assume that the occasion mentioned in 6:12b is Timothy's baptism).[405]
- Some specific baptismal charge.[406]

The possibilities fall into two basic categories: specific admonitions (for example, the specific commands in 6:11–12) and something more general (for example, the gospel as a whole). It seems most likely that this phrase encompasses everything Timothy has been entrusted with, including the content of 6:11–12.

Timothy is instructed to keep this command *without spot or blame*. But is it Timothy who is to be without spot or blame, or is it the command itself that is to be preserved free of any spot or blame?[407] This question is mainly of academic interest. In practical terms, the way to make sure that the commandment is kept pure is for Timothy to live a pure life in accordance with the commandment.

The commandment is to be kept *until the appearing of our Lord Jesus Christ*, an appearing that will happen *in his own time*, that is, at a time that suits God's timetable (see also 2:6). These words remind Timothy that he will have to face God's judgment on his character and ministry when Christ returns. Paul also reminds him of some of the qualities of the God whom he serves and before whom he will have to appear. God is *the blessed* (see also 1:11), *the only Ruler, the King of kings and Lord of lords*. We find similar descriptions of God in Deuteronomy 10:17 and Psalm 136:3 and the same words are applied to Christ in Revelation 17:14 and 19:16. God is also described as being the only one who *is immortal* (see also 1:17) and as living *in unapproachable light*. No one has ever seen him (see also Exod 33:17–23; John 1:18; 6:46). The awesome nature of the one he serves should lead Timothy to fall on his knees, asking God to enable him to carry out the charge well!

Paul's meditation on the nature and works of God leads him to burst out in worship himself, saying *to him be honour and might forever. Amen* (6:16; see also 1:17).

Instruct the rich

People can be proud of many things – their looks, academic achievements, long experience or the dramatic nature of their experiences. For the Ephesian Christians, the greatest temptation was to be proud of their wealth. This pride could cause them to ignore what Timothy is saying. So Paul makes special mention of it as he draws his letter to a close.

Timothy is to teach the rich to have the right attitude to material possessions. He must do this by telling them two things they are not to do. They must not be *arrogant* and consider themselves superior to the poor, and they must not put their trust in their wealth. Riches do not last forever and cannot offer security (6:17a).

Positively, the rich are to *put their hope in God, who richly provides us with everything for our enjoyment,* and to *do good, ... be rich in good deeds, and to be generous and willing to share* (6:17b–18).

We could summarize these instructions to the rich by saying that they are to take their hopes "off" riches and put them "on" God the Giver, which will result in their doing good deeds for others through their generosity and readiness to share.

Paul's words still apply today, for the rich still face the same temptation to rely on their wealth. Some wealthy members of our churches think that because they can make large contributions to fund-raising campaigns and building projects, they are superior to other believers and have a right to control matters in the church. Some others make the same mistake by thinking that a university education or a good job automatically gives them authority in the church – or even means that they do not need to attend church. But we are all on an equal footing before God. We need to remember that everything we have, whether it be wealth or education or a job, is a gift from God. We must never allow these things to become idols that prevent us from walking hand in hand with him. Instead, we must use the good gifts he has given us to serve our fellow-believers, other people, and the creation which he has entrusted to our care.

When the rich stop trusting in their wealth, the result will not only be that they perform good deeds in the present. There will also be future results. By giving away some of their earthly wealth, the rich are actually storing up *a treasure for themselves as a firm foundation for the coming age* (6:19). To give generously is not to lose wealth but to build wealth; establishing a firm basis on which to start life in heaven.[408] By doing this, they will *take hold of the life that is truly life*.[409] Paul is not saying that giving gifts is the way to earn salvation but rather that it is a way to enter into the full joy of salvation and fellowship with God. The eternal life that is "truly life" is something that "will be given hereafter in all its fullness, but it can be achieved even now, and is the only life which is worthy of the name".[410]

Guard what has been entrusted to you

The last command in the letter is directed to Timothy himself, as Paul says, *Timothy, guard what has been entrusted to your care* (6:20a). Previously, Paul addressed Timothy as a "man of God" (6:11) to remind him of who he was in relation to God. Now, Paul uses Timothy's own name to call his attention to the relationship Paul has with him.

Timothy has been entrusted with the sound doctrine Paul has taught him. In this verse, Paul does not focus on the passing on of the doctrine (as he does elsewhere in the letter), but on its protection. Timothy must guard it, just like banks guard the money that has been deposited in them. His vigilance will ensure that Paul's teaching is not distorted or diluted but is passed on to others in its wholeness.

To ensure that the doctrine is protected, Timothy must do two things: he must *turn away from godless chatter* and *the opposing ideas of what is falsely called knowledge* (6:20b).[411] These words remind us of Paul's earlier description of the false teaching Timothy has to deal with at Ephesus (1:6; 4:7). It is worldly and empty, and it adds nothing to true knowledge. It specializes in arguments and counter-arguments, but leads nowhere. In 6:4–5, Paul said that such arguments are the tools of all kinds of evils. They are part of Satan's scheme to try to distract God's people from promoting the kingdom of God.

Timothy is to avoid all such arguments and false teachings so that he does not risk following in the footsteps of some who have *departed from the faith* (6:21a). Here, "the faith" stands for sound doctrine as a body of beliefs. Timothy has been called to protect sound doctrine and he must give his full attention to that task.

Prayer

Paul concludes the letter with the prayer, *Grace be with you all* (6:21b). It is as if he is telling Timothy, "I know what a heavy task you have been assigned. You will need God's grace to keep going." It is the best prayer Paul could offer for Timothy as he served at Ephesus. But he is praying not only for grace for Timothy, but for all the believers in Ephesus, for in the Greek the "you" is plural.

Questions for Discussion

1. If you knew that you would be dying soon, what would be your last words to your children?
2. If you knew that you would be dying soon, what would be your last words to the members of your church?
3. What parts of sound doctrine are under the greatest attack today? How should we go about guarding what has been entrusted to our care?

2 TIMOTHY

INTRODUCTION TO 2 TIMOTHY

We all treasure the last message we receive from someone who is dying. That is what we have in 2 Timothy. It is not only Paul's last letter to Timothy but, as far as we know, the last letter he ever wrote.

Paul probably wrote this letter while he was a prisoner in Rome.[1] It was not the first time he had to write a letter in prison. But when he wrote to the Philippians and to Philemon, he was confident that he would soon be released to continue his ministry (Phil 1:25–26; Phlm 22). His confidence seems to have been justified.

Things are different now. He has been rearrested, and this time he knows that his ministry is at an end. What awaits him is execution (4:6–8). The writings of the early church suggest that he suffered this fate in ad 67 or 68 during the reign of the emperor Nero.

Paul does not fear death, and he knows that Timothy will faithfully continue his work. But Timothy is serving in a difficult place, and things will not get any easier. So Paul writes to encourage him and challenge him to persevere.

All of us have to come to terms with the need to pass our leadership responsibilities on to the next generation. Some people do this well, others do not. As we read these parting words from the great apostle, we need to pay particular attention to what we can learn from him.

UNIT 1
2 TIMOTHY 1:1–3

MAKING CONTACT

Paul is writing this letter to a man whom he regards as his spiritual son, and his opening words reflect the warm relationship between them.

Author

In 1 Timothy, Paul introduces himself as "an apostle … by the command of God" (1:1a). In 2 Timothy, however, he says that he is an apostle *by the will of God* (1:1a). This is the way Paul normally states what qualifies him to be an apostle (1 Cor 1:1; 2 Cor 1:1; Eph 1:1; Col 1:1). He did not choose to be an apostle and he was not appointed an apostle by someone else (Gal 1:1). It was God who appointed him to this position (see also 1 Tim 1:12–17).

Paul's words raise an important question for all of us who are in some kind of ministry: "Why am I doing this?" Is it because there was no other career open to me, or because my parents wanted me to work for the church, or just because I enjoy the work? Paul knew that God had given him a specific assignment. All those who are in Christian ministry should have a similar sense of calling.

The same principle applies to every believer. We all need to have the joy of knowing that we are doing a task God has given us – whether that be driving a taxi, running a business or raising a family.

Paul's first phrase tells us **how** he became an apostle, and the next phrase tells us **why** he became one: *for the promise of life in Christ Jesus* (1:1b – hcsb).[2] The words "of life" tell us the content of the promise.[3] In other words, what is promised is life. The words "in Christ Jesus" tell us the sphere in which the promised life is found.[4] Paul's well-defined mission is thus to proclaim the promise of life that is experienced by those who are in Christ. As Kelly puts it, "Paul's mission is to make known that this promise receives fulfilment through fellowship with Christ."[5] While we are not apostles, our mission is still the same as Paul's: we are to continue to bring others to know the life Christ offers those who place their faith in him.

Recipient

Paul addresses Timothy as *my dear son* (1:2). The same adjective translated "dear" or "beloved" (nkjv) or "dearly loved" (hcsb) was used to describe the relationship between Christian slaves and Christian masters (1 Tim 6:2). There, it denoted the spiritual bond between believers. Here, however, the word signals an even deeper bond, for Timothy is Paul's spiritual son.[6] "There are few bonds which are closer than the love between a spiritual father and his spiritual child."[7]

The same type of relationship often exists today between a believer and the person who led him or her to Christ. A similar special relationship can exist between us and those we have supported and rejoiced with when they were baptized or married. It is important that we maintain these relationships with our spiritual sons and daughters. We should not be too busy to follow up and find out how they are doing, for doing so will provide opportunities for further counselling and mentoring to help them grow in the faith.

Greetings

Paul greets Timothy using exactly the same words he used in 1 Timothy 1:1. He wishes him the same three blessings, *grace, mercy and peace,* and credits these blessings to *God the Father and Christ Jesus our Lord.* For a discussion of this greeting, see the commentary on 1 Timothy.

Paul's Attitude to Timothy

Older people sometimes complain about the attitudes of modern young people and their lack of respect for authority. But Paul does not complain about Timothy, or look down on him as an inferior. He longs to see him (1:4; 4:9) and shows real respect and appreciation for the younger man as he says *I thank God ... as night and day I constantly remember you in my prayers* (1:3). He is full of gratitude whenever he thinks of Timothy.[8] And he does this all the time, for that is what the phrase "night and day" implies. Paul is not saying that he was on his knees praying for Timothy all the time. Rather he is saying that his constant mood is one of prayer, and every time he thinks of Timothy, he gives thanks to God for him.

Paul's warm and positive attitude to Timothy is one that senior pastors should try to imitate in their relationships with those who serve with and under them. Rather than focusing on negative events and the occasions when they feel they were not treated with proper respect, senior pastors should occupy their minds with prayers of thanksgiving for the positive work God is doing in the lives of their assistants.

Paul's attitude to Timothy must have influenced Timothy's attitude to him. He must have responded with love, trust and a willingness to learn from the apostle.

Questions for Discussion

1. The relationships between senior pastors and their assistants are sometimes a source of conflict. Sometimes the problem stems from an assistant who wants to outshine the senior pastor. At other times the problem lies with the senior pastor who feels threatened when the assistant begins to receive more appreciation, and so does all he can to suppress the assistant. What principles can senior and assistant pastors draw from this passage that will help them build up rather than split the church?
2. Paul's relationship with Timothy provides a model for our relationship with our spiritual sons and daughters. What principles can you draw from this model? Are you regularly keeping meaningful contact with those who have looked up to you as their spiritual mentor? What else can you do to nurture these relationships?

3. Paul states that he is doing what he does because it is the Lord's will. How can we know whether the same is true of us? What kind of questions should we be asking ourselves to determine this? Should they be only spiritual questions about our "call" or should they concern whether we are obedient to the principle of total love for God and loving our neighbours as ourselves? Did we get our present jobs honestly, or did we pay bribes and have an innocent person fired to make room for us? Share your personal experiences and observations about how to determine that you are in the Lord's will.

RELATIONSHIPS BETWEEN PASTORS

Mzee Francis (not his actual name) was a second generation pastor who had served in one of his town's churches for over thirty years. Though he never went to high school, he was one of the best students when he trained for ministry at the diploma level. Over the years, he had gained a lot of ministerial experience, not only with his own church but also with other local churches. But at the same time, his congregation was changing as more and more people, including university students and lecturers, started attending the church. Some came primarily because of their loyalty to their denomination in which they had been raised before moving to the city.

The time came when even Francis could see that his sermons were not feeding many of the people in his congregation. His illustrations were all local, and did not appeal to them. His English was limited and his exposition of Scripture did not reflect depth of study. The situation was also causing concern to the denominational leadership. For a time, most of the preaching was done by invited guests, but this was clearly only a temporary solution.

At this time the Lord brought a young man whom we can call Luke (not his actual name) into the picture. Since the time Luke had begun training for ministry, he had identified pastoral work as his number one gift. He had kept this before him even as he went for further theological training overseas. When he returned to the country with his PhD in hand, Luke wanted to do pastoral work. The denomination asked him to be an assistant to Francis. Francis thought this was an excellent idea and Luke accepted the position without any reservations. It was a great opportunity to preach to influential citizens who attended the church and to many future leaders among the university students.

For several years, things went very well. Francis, as senior pastor, focused on the administration of the church and Luke focused on the preaching of the word. But when Francis preached (for he could not keep away from the pulpit completely) members would remark that they missed Luke's preaching. When members felt that Francis' administrative decisions were too narrow, they consulted Luke.

Eventually, Francis began to think of Luke as someone who was taking away all his glory. He no longer saw him as a gifted, educated man who had come to work alongside him, or as someone who might have some administrative ideas worth considering. Soon Francis' main focus shifted from his ministry to his personal glory. He kept reminding Luke that his position in the local church depended on Francis' approval. Francis became so hostile and Luke so discouraged that Luke left the church and decided to take his high education and pastoral gifts elsewhere.

In the Lord's grace, this local church is still alive and growing. But Francis and Luke are no longer in the picture.

What could have been done differently to prevent this local church from losing Luke's gifts? Some people think that Francis should have left when Luke came. However, the local church still needed Francis' wealth of experience. Others think that Francis and Luke should have been given firmer instructions to keep to their assigned tasks, Francis to administration and Luke to preaching. However, the same members who needed good preaching also needed the church to run well.

A third view (the one that Paul would agree with) was that Francis and Luke needed to be helped to see themselves as a team. Each had gifts and experiences that could bless the church. If they had cooperated rather than competed, all of their gifts could have been utilized and the church would have been greatly blessed.

Even little things matter when blending as a team. For example, when someone talked to Luke about an administrative issue, Luke should have responded immediately by saying, "Let's go and talk to Francis." When the two came to him, Francis should have thought through the matter with them right there as a team, rather than just issuing a ruling and refusing to allow any further discussion.

The church of Christ calls each of us, as a matter of primary importance, to bring our gifts together and as a team build the body of Christ (1 Cor 12:27–28). Our length of experience and level of training are tools for us to use together so that we succeed in our mission.

UNIT 2
2 TIMOTHY 1:3–7

WORDS OF ENCOURAGEMENT

Kenyatta Day is a Kenyan national holiday. It is celebrated on 20 October, the anniversary of the day in 1952 when Jomo Kenyatta and other political heroes were arrested and jailed for seeking independence for Kenya. Their love for Kenya helped them persevere in the struggle for more than ten years, until independence was finally won in 1963 and Jomo Kenyatta became Kenya's first president. During the 2004 celebrations, Kenyan President Mwai Kibaki reminded Kenyans of what these men had done and praised those who show the same qualities of self-sacrifice, unity, patriotism and hard work. He challenged all Kenyans to participate in building a Kenya that is a blessing to each citizen. He was using the natural and effective technique of encouraging people to learn from and be motivated by those who have gone before us.

Paul uses the same technique when writing to Timothy. He mentions how his own forefathers served God and reminds Timothy of the sincere faith of his mother and grandmother. He praises Timothy's own faith and challenges him to maintain and grow the God-given gift that Paul and others have recognized in him.

Models of Love and Service

Before discussing Timothy's relationship to God, Paul speaks of his own relationship to God. He has been called to be an apostle, but that is not a position of power but a position of ongoing service.[9] As he serves God, he is following in the footsteps of Christ, who did not come to be served but to serve (Mark 10:45). He is also following in the footsteps of his *ancestors* (1:3).

Paul's ancestors can be described as an "ethnic community of service".[10] They included men like Abraham, whose obedience to God led to the blessing of his descendants (Gen 12:3). There would have been many others like him in Paul's line, people who did not live to be served but made sacrifices so that others after them would be blessed. As believers, we too can claim to be part of a community of fellowship and service to God (1 John 1:3). The apostles Paul, Peter and John, and many other godly men and women are our forefathers.

Not only does Paul serve God, but he does so *with a clear conscience*.[11] As a prisoner whose guards may have been listening while he dictated this letter, he is eager to make this point. But the principle was also important to him, as is clear from his repeated emphasis on the importance of a clear conscience in 1 Timothy (1:5, 19; 3:9; 4:2) and in Titus 1:15. A clear conscience does not carry the scars caused by sin, which sear it so that it can no longer hear God's voice commending what is right, and exposing and condemning what is wrong. Someone whose conscience is clear is free from hypocrisy.

Paul freely admits that he longs to see Timothy. Timothy had wept when they parted, and the memory of those tears increases the intensity of Paul's desire to see him (1:4a).[12] We do not know where or when this sad parting took place. It may have been at Miletus (Acts 20:37)[13] or possibly just before Paul's present imprisonment (probably the same parting referred to in 1 Tim 1:3).[14] The latter seems to be the most likely as it would have been their most recent parting.[15]

Paul's words elsewhere in this letter show that he knows that this is his last imprisonment before he passes on to glory. An opportunity to see Timothy before then would fill him with joy (1:4b). Once again, we see the warmth in their relationship. In fact, this verse "may be regarded as a classic example of fellowship between ministers in general; and between the senior and the junior ... Here we have a 'flesh and blood' relationship."[16] The church needs to see more relationships like this, in which pastors and their team members model the unity and love found in Christ.

Timothy's Faith

The words *I am reminded* (1:5a)[17] suggest that something has recently happened or someone has said or done something that has brought Timothy vividly to Paul's mind. The particular aspect he has remembered is *your sincere faith*, or literally "the sincere faith in you". Timothy's faith is not something external that he puts on when it is convenient, as hypocrites do, but comes from his heart and radiates out of him. Paul and others can see that it is genuine and sincere (see also 1 Tim 1:5).

How will people remember us when something calls us to mind? I have been training students for thirty years now and have many memories of my students. They, no doubt, have memories of me. Are those memories positive or negative? All of us, whatever our situations, need to be aware that our actions are creating memories. How wonderful it would be if the first thought that leapt to someone's mind when they remembered us was our sincere faith.

In 1:3 Paul mentioned his own forefathers, who set a model for his service (1:3). Now he comes to Timothy's role models. He has learned what sincere faith means from his *grandmother Lois* and his *mother Eunice*.[18] This is the only text that mentions Timothy's grandmother and mother by name. These women may have come to faith during Paul's ministry in Lystra (Acts 14:6–7). All that we know about them is that his mother was Jewish and his father Greek (Acts 16:1).

As Christian parents, we should not minimize the influence we can have on the faith of our children. They watch how we do or do not live out our own faith. They will know if we live one life in public and another at home. Those who preach love on Sunday and show no love to their spouse, children and the needy; or who talk about humility but are arrogant to others; or who claim to know the truth but are dishonest in business – all are fuelling rebellion in their children. Sincerity and consistency, however, pull even a rebellious child towards the right path.

Those who doubt the impact their lives have on their children need to remember how effective traditional methods of education in Africa were. For example, I have a vivid memory of a medicine man who was called to my village to cleanse people from evil that had been spoken against them. Yes, I remember him dancing around without clothes, but what I remember most vividly was the young boy of my own age (about seven at the time) who followed him, carrying a bag containing all the man's equipment. He was the son of the medicine man. As he served his father, he was being trained to take over his responsibilities.

I have often seen parents use this same approach to teaching their children skills. Though our children now receive formal education in public schools, traditional forms of modelling are still very effective. They are particularly so within the home. The best thing we can model for our children is a faithful and sincere walk with Christ. Learning how to do this in all areas of life will prepare our children to be a positive influence for Christ in our society.

After remembering the models of faith that Timothy was blessed with, Paul continues *and, I am persuaded, now lives in you also* (1:5b).[19] The verb "am persuaded" is in the passive voice, which suggests that Paul was brought to his conviction that Timothy has the same faith by careful observation of Timothy's life. His words are a vote of confidence in Timothy.

When others observe our lives, can they draw the same conclusion about our faith as Paul could draw about Timothy's? Why is it that we are forced to wonder how some countries can be so corrupt when such a high proportion of the population claims to be Christian? We need to develop a craving for holiness that will lead us to act in a Christ-like way every day of the week. Only then will others be convinced that we are sincere in our faith.

A Challenge

Convinced of Timothy's faith, Paul challenges Timothy *to fan into flame the gift of God, which is in you* (1:6a). These words do not necessarily mean that Timothy has been careless about his assignment and has neglected his gift. This is unlikely given Paul's evaluation of Timothy's sincerity. More likely, Paul is writing as someone who knows that he himself will soon be dead and that tough times lie ahead. He wants Timothy to develop his spiritual gifts to the fullest possible extent because he will need all his spiritual energy and experience to minister to the church when he can no longer turn to his spiritual father for advice. Moreover, Paul knows that spiritual gifts that are not exercised do not reach their full potential. It is important that we use the gifts God has given us and that we encourage others to develop the gifts that God has given them.

Paul says that this gift is in Timothy *through the laying on of my hands* (1:6b). Some people raise questions about the details of this laying on of hands. They point out that 1 Timothy includes two references to such an event, one when prophecies were made about Timothy (1 Tim 1:18) and the other when "the body of elders laid their hands on you" (1 Tim 4:14). It is possible that these were actually one and the same event, and that Paul is simply giving more details in the second reference. But we cannot be dogmatic about this.

The next question they raise is why, if Paul is referring to the same event, he says that he was the one laying hands on Timothy, while in 1 Timothy 4:4 it was the elders who did this? Is this a contradiction? There are a couple of possible answers to this question. It may be that both Paul and the elders laid hands on Timothy as he embarked on his ministry in Ephesus. Alternatively, Paul may not be speaking of the same event but of something that happened many years earlier, when he alone did the laying of hands. The elders may have done this at a later stage in Timothy's career when he was set apart for ministry in Ephesus.[20]

On balance, it seems likely that all the references to the laying on of hands refer to the same event. In Timothy 4:14, Paul is speaking about Timothy's role in the church and chooses to focus on the elders' participation, whereas in 2 Timothy 1:6 he is speaking in the context of their own relationship, and so chooses to focus on his own participation in the ceremony. This laying on of hands was a testimony by Paul and other witnesses that Timothy had been given the privilege of being entrusted by God with a spiritual gift.

It is important to recognize that it was not the laying on of hands that gave Timothy his gift. It was a gift "of God", that is, it came from God.[21] What Paul and the elders did was recognize the gift and assign Timothy appropriate responsibilities in the church.

We still practise the laying on of hands today when, for example, bishops lay their hands on those being ordained for ministry. This does not make the one being ordained more acceptable before God; rather, it is a public statement by the bishop acknowledging that God has set the person apart for ministry. That is why bishops should not take this responsibility lightly. They must ensure that they are listening to God's voice, and not to social pressure, when they ordain someone.

Unfortunately, positions are still too often assigned on the basis of prestige or favouritism, without due consideration of the spiritual gifts required to fill the position. Thus we have people who do not have the gift of teaching appointed to teach in a Bible college simply because they have a master's degree. Someone with no gifts in administration may be appointed the principal of an institution simply because he or she has a PhD. Meanwhile, people who do have gifts of teaching or administration are assigned to positions that give them little scope to exercise these gifts. People's assignments need to be matched to their gifts if their service is to be satisfying and effective.

Meeting the Challenge

Paul issues his challenge to Timothy on the basis of the faith he has seen in him and the effects of God's work in his spirit. Some translations believe that the word *pneuma* in 1:7 refers to the Holy Spirit (tniv), while others take it as referring to the inner human spirit (nasb, niv). Regardless of which interpretation we accept, it is clear that the Holy Spirit energizes the human spirit.

With God's spirit at work in him, Timothy (and all other believers) need not be nervous or afraid, for *the Spirit God gave us does not make us timid* (1:7). Rather, it gives us *power, love and self-discipline*. Timothy will need power to carry out the tough task he has been given in Ephesus; he will need love to endure the inevitable opposition graciously; and he will need self-discipline or self-control to resist temptations to sin and to be able to live in a way that sets the best example to the church he pastors.[22]

Power to fight evil is very important in many African societies and there are many different ways to fight it. For example, the Kamba people in Kenya traditionally advise their children to quickly put a small stone in their mouth when they meet someone who might be a witch. They believe this will protect them from any evil the witch wishes against them. Education about hygiene and the Christian faith have made these practices decline. In their place, Christianity offers a "gospel of power". Paul is reminding Timothy that his power comes from God's Spirit, which is more powerful than anything, even death (Rom 8:11). Those who believe in Christ, have God's Spirit within them. They do not need to fear any man, woman, spirit or demon because they can rely on God's power within them to fight evil.

Pastors today can find encouragement in the fact that God still gives us the same gifts he gave to Paul and Timothy. There are many people in our congregations who enjoy church but do not love Christ. They want church to make them feel good about themselves. So they get angry and stir up trouble for the pastor if they are challenged about aspects of their life that are not in accordance with the way of Christ. In such situations, it is easy for a pastor to feel intimidated. We need to be reminded that "God did not give us a spirit of timidity" (niv). Pastors need power in order to continue ministering in the face of opposition like this. They need love to enable them to listen to those who challenge them and attack them, and to seek to gently win them over. Only self-control can keep them from engaging in a war of words that will destroy the church. Power, love and self-control are all elements of a holy character. A pastor or teacher who lacks this character will never have a fruitful ministry.

Questions for Discussion

1. Many people find it easier to demand service than to give it. In marriage relationships, for example, most problems are expressed using words such as "he does not" or "she does not", both of which focus on the service the speaker demands and is not getting. At times we extend this attitude to our relationship with God when we loudly complain of what he *has not* done but only mumble about what he *has* done. What principles can we draw from this passage that will cause us to join Paul and others as "a clan of servants"?

2. Have you ever had such a deep relationship with someone that the memory of them brings tears of joy to your eyes? How did such a relationship develop? How can such relationships be multiplied in places with frequent conflicts, such as the continent of Africa?

3. Paul and Timothy were both blessed with godly ancestors. What about you? Name some older Christians who have had an influence on your life. How did their influence change you?

4. The traditional relationship between parents and children has been eroded in modern Africa. Yet parents are still responsible for giving their children moral direction and life skills. Their children will be the leaders of tomorrow. What is your church doing to nurture relationships between parents and children and to prepare the young people in the congregation for their roles as adult church members? After listing what you are already doing, brainstorm other options that your church could consider. How can you get parents to interact more with their children?

5. Paul and the elders recognized the gift God had given Timothy. What gifts do you see in the Christian brothers and sisters who are with you now? What gifts do they see in you? How can you fan these gifts into flame? Is there any way in which others can help you to use your gifts?

6. As long as we are in this world, there will always be difficult situations. You may even be going through one now. How does the provision of the Spirit who gives us "power, love, and self-discipline" guard us from failing at such times?

CHILDREN AND FAITH

A common sight on Sunday mornings in sub-Saharan Africa is children walking home from Sunday school. There they are taught that Jesus loves them and sing songs such as "Jesus Loves Me" again and again. When an appeal is issued and they are asked to raise their hands if they love Jesus, many of them do so, often every week. To them it is natural to affirm their love for someone whenever they meet him.

These children who have declared their love for Jesus grow up and attend youth camps and rallies. There they are taught three truths: that every human is guilty of sin because Adam, the ancestor of all humankind, sinned; that Jesus died as our substitute on the cross, paying the penalty for our sins; and that if we believe these truths and turn to Jesus, we can be saved. They are urged to turn to him.

But what happens if one of these young people says, "I committed my life to him when I was a child"? He or she will be asked: "When you lifted your hand in Sunday school to say that you wanted to be a friend of Jesus, did you know the three truths you have just been taught? Of course, the child did not know them. So the young person is told, "Then you are not saved. You need to accept Jesus now." The young person agrees, prays the prayer of conversion, and the preacher adds his or her name to the list of those who came to faith during the youth camp or Christian rally.

This practice raises several important questions:

- *What does a child's love for Jesus amount to?* It amounts to being a friend of Jesus. It is Jesus who told adults (the disciples), "Let the little children come to me" (Luke 18:16a).
- *What does Jesus require from a child?* He requires simple faith that Jesus loves him or her and sincere love, not comprehension of a set of doctrinal statements.
- *How much knowledge is needed for a child to love Jesus in return?* Simply that Jesus loves him or her.
- *Where do the three important theological points listed in the second paragraph belong in the faith of a child?* They contribute to the young person's growing understanding of the degree of Jesus' love and why it is that we love him and believe in him. Understanding theology, which comes with mental development, does not mark the beginning of their

friendship with Jesus. It only widens their understanding of a friendship begun earlier in the child's life.

Paul builds on Timothy's childhood faith to strengthen him and encourage him to continue growing in it (2 Tim 3:14–15; see also 2 Tim 1:5). Why should we insist that young people today have to begin all over again?

We need to rethink what it means to be a friend of Jesus. A response to Jesus in love precedes knowledge of theological propositions. A child of a very tender age is able to comprehend that Jesus loves him or her, respond to Jesus' love by loving him also, and right there begin the journey of Christian faith. What follows over the years as the child matures into a young person and adult serves to build his or her understanding of the dimensions of this love.

UNIT 3
2 TIMOTHY 1:8–10

A CALL TO SUFFERING

Early in the twentieth century, a young boy was born in an area where the church was very poor. Christian service was equated with poverty. As the boy grew, he managed to obtain some education and became a successful businessman. He also became a believer. Over time, he became aware that most of the pastors and evangelists in his area were elderly, tired and struggling. They were not being joined by younger men because no-one wanted to waste his life doing something that would not bring material benefits.

There was general amazement when the young man announced that he was going to close his shop and work with the preachers. His relatives and friends asked, "How on earth can you close your promising business and join the people of the place of rust?" (the small church in the area was roofed with rusted iron sheets). But the young man would not be discouraged. He was convinced that God had called him to suffer so that others would hear the gospel.

The ageing pastors, the "Pauls" of that day, were greatly encouraged by his decision. They gave thanks for his coming to support their tired hands and continue their work. They assigned this modern-day Timothy the task of teaching in the school that was part of the local church. He proved a skilled teacher and a wise counsellor, whose pupils have gone on to serve Africa in significant ways. I am proud to have been one of them, a student of a man who was willing to sacrifice his reputation and his hope of prosperity for the cause of the gospel. His sacrifice changed people's lives, not only in his own village but also in the rest of Kenya, across Africa, and beyond.

Africa has had many other Pauls and Timothies. We, too, we are called to be models for those who come after us and to being willing to suffer for the work of Christ. How well are we doing? Keep this question in mind as you study Paul's teaching about suffering.

A Call for Courage

Paul has set the scene by praising Timothy's faith and reminding him of the gifts God has given him, which include power, love and self-discipline. Now, beginning with the word *so* or "therefore", he explains what Timothy is to do with his gifts. There are things he is not to do and things he must do.

Do not be ashamed

Timothy must *not be ashamed* (1:8a). Paul is not accusing Timothy of being ashamed already, but is simply stating that this temptation may come.[23] In Corinth, people who believed in the saving work of Christ on the cross were considered foolish (1 Cor 1:18–25). The situation would have been no different in Ephesus, and is no different today.

There are two things in particular of which Timothy is not to be ashamed. The first is *the testimony about our Lord*, or literally, "of our Lord". Paul's words could either refer to the testimony our Lord gave or to the testimony we give about our Lord by talking about him and living the way he wants us to live.[24] The second possibility is the better choice in this context. It is very easy to fall into the trap of being ashamed of testifying about our Lord: "If the preacher is sensitive to the atmosphere which surrounds an unbelieving congregation and dwells on it ... when he should have kept his eyes fixed on his master, then he will be sorely tempted to be ashamed of his own testifying to our Lord."[25]

These days, people seldom ask the person seated next to them in a bus, taxi, train or aeroplane about their status with Christ. (Except in the case of those who preach in buses that are waiting for passengers – and their motives may sometimes be suspect as they collect an offering before leaving the bus.) We fail to testify to our faith because we have accepted the lie that faith is a private subject that should not be discussed in public. Paul is encouraging Timothy (and us) to be bold and not afraid or embarrassed to talk about Christ.

The second thing Timothy must not be ashamed of is Paul himself, Christ's *prisoner*. It can be embarrassing to admit that we are close friends with someone who is in prison. So Paul reminds Timothy that he is not in prison because he is a criminal but because he proclaims the gospel. Rather than seeing the shame of imprisonment, Timothy must admire Paul's courage in proclaiming the saving death of Christ and his victory over death in the resurrection. Moreover, by describing himself as Christ's prisoner, Paul is making it clear that Christ is the one who has allowed him to be sent to prison: "The underlying thought is, not just that men have imprisoned him as a follower of Christ, but that Christ has made him his prisoner for purposes of his own."[26]

Paul is very aware that his life is under Christ's control. In an earlier letter, he said that Christ's love compels him to proclaim him (2 Cor 5:14). Paul has been so gripped by Christ and his love that he cannot refrain from doing and saying what Christ wants him to – which is the reason he is in jail.

How many of us today are this committed to Christ? There are some persecuted Christian brothers and sisters who do show this same level of commitment. But many of us must admit that we struggle with our commitment to Christ in our everyday circumstances, even where we face no threat of imprisonment when we proclaim him our Lord.

Timothy worships a Messiah who suffered a criminal's death on the cross and his mentor is in prison. He could easily feel ashamed to be associated with Christ and Paul. But the resurrection of Jesus and the conviction and courage of Paul should strengthen him to take his stand on the victory side.

Be willing to suffer

Having told Timothy what he must not do, Paul goes on to tell him what he should do. He uses the word *but* to emphasize the contrast with what he has just said. Instead of being ashamed of Paul, Timothy must join him *in suffering for the gospel* (1:8b),[27] that is, for the sake of the gospel.[28] If asked, many Christians today would say that they are not ashamed of the gospel, but are not fanatical about it. This answer suggests that they prefer to remain neutral observers of God's work and do not want to get involved in it themselves. But that is not good enough for Paul. Timothy must pluck up his courage and become an active participant in doing the work that will cause suffering. Later in this letter, Paul will specify what this call to join him will mean for Timothy's own ministry.

Timothy can take courage and comfort from the fact that he is not called to suffer helplessly but will face it *by the power of God,* that is, the power that comes from God (1:8c).[29] Paul has often spoken of this (1:7; Rom 1:16; 1 Cor 1:18, 24; 2:5; 2 Cor 6:7; 13:4). Armed with this power Timothy will be able to face any situation.

The tone of the writing leaves no doubt that Paul is experiencing this same power himself. He is in prison, but locks and chains do not limit what God can do. "The gospel was, and is, power – power to conquer self, power to master circumstances, power to go on living when life is unliveable, power to be a Christian when being a Christian looks impossible."[30]

Thank God that his power never changes or diminishes and is still available to us today. A Christian ministry run without it is simply another institution; with it, God's reign is present.

God's Call

The mention of God's power reminds Paul of what God has done: he has *saved us* and *called us* (1:9a). He treats these actions as a unit, for God's call includes all that God has done to redeem us.[31]

The idea that God calls us is very important to Paul and comes up in many of his letters (Rom 11:29; Gal 1:6). He always says that it is God the Father who issues the call (1 Cor 1:9). This is the case here also. The one who has done the calling is distinct from Jesus (see 1:10).

Paul begins by making two important points about God's call: It is a call to a holy life and it is not because of anything we have done, but is solely because of God's own purpose and grace.

A call to a holy life

If you look at different translations of 1:9, you will see that the nasb and nrsv speak of God having "called us with a holy calling", whereas the tniv says that we have been called *to a holy life*.[32] The exact translation makes very little difference to Paul's point, which is that "a holy God issues a holy call for believers to live a holy life."[33] A holy life is holy in all areas of life: "The man who has known the saving power of the gospel is a changed man, in his business, in his pleasure, in his home, in his character."[34]

Left to ourselves, we cannot possibly live a holy life, just as left to ourselves we would not choose to suffer for the gospel. But the God who has called us has the power to change sinners into saints and to enable us to obey his call. As Mounce puts it, "If God has been able to save Timothy, then he can empower Timothy as he lives out his calling in the midst of suffering."[35]

A call to the undeserving

We were not saved and called because we were living particularly virtuous lives or because we made a decision to follow God. No, we were not called *because of anything we have done*. Rather, we were saved because of God's *own purpose* (1:9b).[36] We were each saved for some particular purpose of God. His purpose exists apart from us, but because he is gracious he chooses to accomplish it through us.

God also calls us because of his *grace*. Here, "grace" means God's unmerited favour. We do not deserve God to do anything for us. As Barclay says, "It is not something we achieve, but something we accept … If we had to deserve the love of God, our situation would be helpless and hopeless".[37] Moreover, if our calling were dependent on our deserving it, we could never be sure of our salvation: "Our position would be at best precarious, and on a realistic estimate hopeless; but since it depends wholly on God, our confidence can be unshaken."[38] We should be grateful that God does not love the way we do. We tend to befriend only the people we find attractive, but God makes us his own and pays the price to make us attractive!

God's grace is not a new idea that has just occurred to God. It has been part of his purpose since *before the beginning of time* (1:9c). Elsewhere, Paul says God's grace was in place "before the creation of the world" (Eph 1:4). This grace was granted to us before time ever began because it is an essential element in God's plan to redeem the world. God had planned to use Christ as a mediator for us long before he lived on earth and died on the cross.[39] That is why Paul can say that God's grace was given to us long before we were born. Bernard puts it like this: "The grace of Christ, Incarnate, Crucified, Risen, is part of the eternal purpose of God for man, and since time does not limit the Deity, that which is unfalteringly purposed is described as actually given."[40]

The two passive verbs indicating that God's grace *was given* and *has ... been revealed* do not indicate who did the giving or the revealing, but there can be no doubt from the context that it was God.[41] And how did he do this? He did it *through the appearing of our Saviour, Christ Jesus* (1:10a). Here Paul is echoing what John says in the preface to his gospel when he describes the Word becoming flesh and living among us (John 1:14). Jesus was with God from the beginning, but his birth in Bethlehem brought eternity into history as he became one of us.[42] It was not merely an idea that God revealed to us, but a historical person who carried out God's plan of salvation.[43]

Our Saviour

Paul's words about God's grace naturally lead into a reflection on the one who has brought us that grace, our Saviour Jesus Christ. Before we get to that, it is interesting to note that in 1:9 Paul speaks of God the Father as the one who saved us, and in 1:10 he says that same thing about Jesus Christ, whom he describes as *our Saviour*.[44] It is thus not true to say that Jesus Christ is the one who intervenes to save us from an angry God, for both God and Jesus are our Saviours. The Father planned the way we would be saved, and the Son carried out that plan.

Paul has already mentioned Christ's place in the eternal plan of God when he spoke of his pre-existence and his gift of grace that was given "before the beginning of time" (1:9). Now he speaks of what Christ did when he became incarnate. He *destroyed death* and *brought life and immortality to light through the gospel* (1:10b). Paul stresses the two effects of Christ's death – on the one hand, it had the power to abolish death itself; on the other, it was able to bring eternal life.[45]

The destroyer of death

The Greek verb translated *destroyed* occurs twenty-five times in Paul's writings. It can mean "to abolish or wipe out"[46] (1 Cor 13:8, 10; 2 Cor 3:13; Gal 5:11) or "to nullify", "to make powerless" or "set aside" (Rom 3:3, 31; 4:14; 1 Cor 1:28; Gal 3:17; Eph 2:15). In the context of Paul's second letter to Timothy it means that death has been "put out of action".⁴⁷ If death were a car, we could say that its engine has been removed.

But what does Paul mean when he says death has been destroyed? People still die.

There are three possible interpretations of his words:

- Death's sting or pain is destroyed because there is life and immortality beyond the grave (1 Cor 15:54–56).⁴⁸
- Death is no longer a punishment for sin because God's gracious work through Jesus has dealt with our sins (Rom 5:12, 17).
- Death no longer means eternal separation from God or spiritual death, which affects all who have not found life in Christ.

It may not be necessary to decide between these three, for they overlap:

> As the penalty of sin [death] will not be experienced by the believer. . . . But he will still experience physical death. For him, however, as a believer the horrors have been removed ... The sting of death is sin (1 Cor 15:56) and sin has been dealt with by the Saviour. There remains for the believer no more than migration, and in this he is not unaccompanied. For he will be passing 'through Jesus' (cf. 1 Thess 4:14).⁴⁹

This conquest of death is why Jesus could say that Lazarus had "fallen asleep" (John 11:11). Paul also used the word "sleep" to describe a believer's death (1 Thess 4:15). This perspective gives believers extraordinary courage in the face of death. It explains Stephen's being able to pray for those who were stoning him until, as Luke puts it, "he fell asleep" (Acts 7:59–60). His killers thought that they had destroyed him, but he only slept the most refreshing sleep of his life, and would awake with a new and glorious body (Phil 3:21).

This truth offers great comfort in these days when we are tragically losing so many of those we love to violence or to diseases like HIV/AIDS. Those who die in the Lord have simply fallen asleep. And after falling asleep ourselves, we will continue to have fellowship with them in a more glorious state in a place where there will be "no more death or mourning or crying or pain" (Rev 21:4).

The bringer of life

The second aspect of Christ's work as Saviour is that *he has brought life and immortality to light*. This combination of "immortality" and "life" is equivalent to "immortal life" or, to use more biblical terminology, "eternal life", the life of the age to come. Paul says that this was brought to light *through the gospel*. Some commentators say that the gospel brings life and immortality to light by teaching us where to seek and find them.[50] Other say that they come to light because Christ's destruction of death and his proclamation of the fact allowed people to see that there is an alternative to the finality of death.[51] Death in itself is frightening, for it is a real separation from those we love and is something we have never experienced ourselves. But when we understand that it is temporary, like sleep, we are able to overcome our grief and fear. May the Lord increase the light of the gospel so that we can see death in this way!

Questions for Discussion

1. Think of someone you know who is very open about their Christian faith – perhaps he or she frequently mentions their faith in conversations, engages in church activities and possibly serves in full-time ministry. What is your reaction when you think of this person? What do your reactions tell you about how you regard Christian faith and service?

2. Many African societies had traditional ways of enhancing people's beauty. Some sharpened their teeth, others pierced their ears or scarred the body in different ways. These painful procedures were usually done without effective anaesthetics, but people endured the pain because they knew they would be more beautiful in the end. This is similar to how Paul's focus on teaching others about Christ enabled him to keep his mind off his physical suffering. How can you focus on the purpose God has called you to rather than on the challenges and discouragements you face along the way?

3. In many African nations we would expect the church to be on the front lines giving guidance about certain issues, but many times the church folds its hands until it is too late. Take, for example, the post-election violence in Kenya in December 2007 and January 2008.

Because the focus of the violence followed tribal lines, many believers and pastors shied away from calling murder by its name when it was their own people group who committed the atrocity. How does silence in times like these relate to being ashamed of Christ, our example of love and master of peace?

4. In this passage Jesus is described as the destroyer of death and bringer of life. How would focusing on these words help us to honestly say with the psalmist, "even though I walk through the darkest valley, I will fear no evil, for you are with me" (23:4)?

UNIT 4
2 TIMOTHY 1:11–18

THE EXAMPLE OF PAUL

In 2007, Nelson Mandela urged Robert Mugabe to step down as president of Zimbabwe. Mandela was one of the few who has the moral authority to do this, for he himself had willingly stepped down from being president of South Africa. He had not clung to power, and he urged Mugabe to do the same. Similarly when Paul calls Timothy to suffering, he is not asking him to do anything he has not done himself. He has ministered in situations like the one Timothy is facing in Ephesus, and he has endured the same things he is asking Timothy to endure. That is why he can offer himself as an example to the young man.

Paul's Model of Ministry

After telling Timothy what God has done, Paul comments on his own relationship to the good news of God's action: *of this gospel I was appointed a herald and an apostle and a teacher* (1:11; see also 1 Tim 2:7).[52]

- *Herald:* The herald's role was to publicly proclaim messages from the king, or to carry requests for a truce between warring parties, or to advertise goods that an auctioneer or merchant wanted to sell. By using this word to describe himself, Paul stresses the boldness and publicity with which an evangelist must proclaim the gospel. In many ways, the office of a herald is like that of a preacher. A preacher must proclaim the Lord's message to people, bring them the offer of peace with God, and invite them to accept the rich offer that God is making them.[53] It is interesting to note that both here and in 1 Timothy Paul mentions his responsibilities as a preacher first, before mentioning that he was appointed an apostle. He may be saying that his mission takes precedence over his authority. Christian leaders would do well to remember this when they are tempted to become so preoccupied with administrative work that they no longer take time to preach the word.

- *Apostle:* As an apostle, Paul is someone with a special commission. He has been sent on a mission.
- *Teacher:* As a teacher, Paul works as a pastor to train those who follow him to live according to the truth of the gospel.

Paul's Model of Suffering

Paul's work as a preacher, apostle and teacher had resulted in *suffering* (1:12). Paul may be speaking only of his current suffering in prison, or he may be speaking of the suffering that has become part of his life over his years of service as a herald, apostle and preacher.[54] The latter position seems more likely, given Paul's lifetime experience and his mention of Asia in 1:15. He has just been encouraging Timothy to join him in this life of suffering (1:8).

Paul has also been telling Timothy not to be ashamed, and now he shows Timothy that he practices what he preaches.[55] He could have good reason to be ashamed; he is in prison again and has been abandoned by many friends (1:15). In the eyes of the world, he is merely a travelling preacher and troublemaker.

We may all sometimes be tempted to feel ashamed. For example, a drunken young man in my area once shouted, "I am the most educated person in this village. I have a bachelor's degree in economics. My cousin has a master's degree, but it's only in theology." With his mind clouded by drink, he was expressing his real opinion of Christian ministry. African pastors are also sometimes embarrassed because they have little training for Christian service and because their salaries are so low that they are among the poorest in the community.

Similarly, ordinary believers in Christ are sometimes hesitant to acknowledge publicly that they are Christians. It is not that they fear persecution, as they attend church regularly. But they know that acknowledging their faith in other ways will lose them prestige. They are acting as if they are ashamed of the gospel.

Paul was not like that. He knew that others despised him and hated him, but it did not make him ashamed. The reason he could stand tall was that he knew God and trusted his power: *I know whom I have believed, and am convinced that he is able to guard what I have entrusted to him* (1:12).[56]

Paul does not say, "I do believe" but uses the perfect tense "I have believed". This tense shows that the act of believing was something that happened in the past and continues to have effects in the present.[57] At a particular point in his life, Paul entrusted himself, his life and ministry to God and entered into an experiential understanding of him. As Barclay puts it, "He knew God personally and intimately; he knew what he was like in love and in power; and to Paul it was inconceivable that he should fail him."[58]

Paul's experience of God as trustworthy in his own life and in Israel's history gives him confidence that God is still trustworthy. He has been convinced of this truth.[59] He knows that God has the ability to guard what has been entrusted to him.

In Paul's day, a person would entrust something they wanted to be kept safe to a friend or to an official in a temple (for temples also served as banks). That friend or official had a sacred duty to keep it safe so that it could be passed on to the depositor's children or whoever else was authorized to ask for it back. Paul is thinking in these terms here, and on the two other occasions when he uses the same image in his letters to Timothy (1 Tim 6:20; 2 Tim 1:14). In the other two references, he speaks of Timothy as the one chosen to be the guard and the thing to be guarded is the truth of the gospel. Here in 1:12, however, it is God who is the guard. But what is it that God is to guard? Is it something that Paul has entrusted to God, or is it something that Paul has been given by God?

If the deposit is from God to Paul, then what has been deposited is the truth of the gospel, just as it is in the other two occurrences. The strongest argument for this interpretation is that it means that Paul is always using the image the same way.[60] However, in this context it seems more likely that the deposit is from Paul to God. If so, Paul is thinking of his soul. He is in prison and facing death. It is encouraging for him to know that though the emperor can kill his body, his soul will remain safe. Paul may also be thinking of more than just himself. He may be entrusting to God all those who have been converted under his ministry. He is confident that God will care for them when he is no longer able to do so.[61]

We should not push this metaphor too far and interpret it as meaning that Paul was the owner of his own soul, or of anything else. Paul knew that everything he had, including his soul, came from God. When he uses this metaphor, he is focusing on the ability and faithfulness of the guardian, who will never lose anything that has been entrusted to his care (just as Jesus will never lose any of his sheep – John 10:29). Paul has the utmost confidence in the one to whom he has entrusted his entire life.

God will keep what Paul has entrusted to him *until that day*. The day in question is the day of judgment (see also 2 Thess 1:10).[62] Paul has no fear of God's final judgment because he knows that on that day he will receive the blessing God has promised to believers (Matt 25:34). Paul's peaceful assurance is like that of a child who knows that her father and mother have never punished a child unfairly. She feels no anxiety when her parents punish her siblings for some disobedience that she was not part of. She can continue to hold her father or mother's hand, secure in the knowledge that she is safe from their wrath. This is how we should face the future. We have nothing to fear on the day of judgment.

An Example of Suffering

Paul gives Timothy a specific illustration of his own suffering in ministry when he adds, *you know that everyone in the province of Asia has deserted me* (1:15).[63] Timothy knows about this because Ephesus was the capital of the Roman province of Asia. This province was not the same as the region we call Asia today. It covered the western part of Asia Minor and included Mysia, Lydia, Caria, large parts of Phrygia and the off-shore islands. It was bordered by Bithynia to the north, Galatia and Lycia to the east, and the Aegean Sea to the west.[64]

When Paul says that "everyone" has turned away from him, he is not meaning us to take this literally. After all, in the very next verse Paul states that the household of Onesiphorus has treated him well.

Paul is using the literary device of hyperbole to make the point that the people he would have expected to support him, people like Phygelus and Hermogenes, were embarrassed by him and abandoned him. They did not abandon their faith, but they did abandon their preacher.[65]

We know very little about Phygelus and Hermogenes because they are not mentioned anywhere else in the New Testament. They were probably either leaders of the group that rejected Paul or friends whom Paul expected to support him. It is possible that they were from Ephesus and were thus people whom Timothy would know.

We also know very little about Onesiphorus, except that he was definitely from Ephesus, for Paul asks Timothy to pass on greetings to his household (4:19). Paul's words about him also suggest why the others were not associating with Paul. They were avoiding him because he was a prisoner. Only Onesiphorus *was not ashamed of my chains* (1:16).

Paul may have been in chains because he had just been arrested.[66] After his release from his first Roman imprisonment (the one described in Acts 28), Paul may have resumed his missionary journeys and again visited Ephesus. While there, he was arrested, and Onesiphorus was one of the few who stood by him. This was a brave act for Paul was probably not arrested solely because he was preaching Christ, but also because his opponents accused him of threatening the peace. On a previous visit to Ephesus, his ministry had sparked a riot there (Acts 19:23–41).

Alternatively, Onesiphorus may have sought Paul out after he had been transferred to Rome as a prisoner. This would have involved far more than merely coming to visit him. It involved a lot of searching to find out where Paul was (1:17). Paul may have been in private accommodation, as he had been during his first imprisonment (Acts 28:16).[67] His position would then have been similar to a prisoner who is out on bail. More likely, he would have been in one of the overcrowded prisons where it would be "no easy task to find one obscure prisoner, among the large numbers in bonds in Rome for various offences".[68]

If Paul was a political prisoner, searching for him could have endangered Onesiphorus' own safety. No wonder Paul has such a warm attitude towards him and his household.[69]

Paul does not tell us exactly what Onesiphorus did for him, except that *he often refreshed me* (1:16). What does this mean? Did he encourage

Paul? Did he provide material support? The answer probably is that he did both: "by ministering as a Christian to his bodily needs Onesiphorus also refreshed and cheered Paul inwardly (compare Phlm 20)".[70] Material support would have been particularly necessary because, as in some African countries, it was expected that prisoners would be fed by their friends and relatives.[71] However, some scholars think that the support Onesiphorus gave was primarily the encouragement that his fellowship gave Paul.[72] It is also likely that he helped not only Paul but also the whole church in Ephesus, for a literal translation of 1:18b reads, *You know very well what service he rendered at Ephesus.*[73]

The three verbs "refreshed", "not ashamed", and "searched" are in the simple past tense, yet summarize actions done over an extended period of time.[74] When given the opportunity under any circumstances, this man supported Paul for as long as was needed, while others failed to do so.

Onesiphorus' visits to Paul in prison remind us of Jesus' words about visiting people in prison (Matt 25:31–46). This is an important aspect of ministry that we should not neglect. We can offer prisoners spiritual and emotional refreshment, and by showing them that people still care about them we can communicate the love of God to them.

Prayer for the Dead?

Onesiphorus' commendable service prompts Paul to say, *May the Lord show mercy to the household of Onesiphorus* (1:16) and to send greetings to the household (4:19).[75] The fact that he addresses the household rather than Onesiphorus himself suggests that Onesiphorus has died. So does the fact that 1:18 uses the past tense when speaking of his ministry at Ephesus, even though his household are still there (4:19).[76]

If this is true, then what are we to make of Paul's words, *May the Lord grant that he will find mercy from the Lord on that day* (1:18)? Was Paul praying for the dead man or only expressing a wish on his behalf? Scholars are generally agreed that praying for the dead was an acceptable practice among the Jews of the time[77] and that it was also common in the early Christian church.[78] But would Paul have done this? Some think that he did.[79] Others deny it and say that Paul's words do not constitute a prayer but are a wish, "a beautiful, loving sentiment, not an intercession."[80]

Does this mean that we should pray for the dead? This is a difficult question to answer. We must be careful not to answer it solely on the basis of this passage because it is not clear if Paul's words here were really a prayer. Moreover, even if they were, the prayer is "an exceedingly general one, amounting only to the commendation of the dead man to the divine mercy".[81] And as a believer Onesiphorus has already been promised mercy – not because he deserves it because of his good deeds, but because of God's grace (1:9).

When we read this passage, we should remember that "If we love a person with all our hearts, and if the remembrance of that person is never absent from our minds and memories, then, whatever the intellect of the theologian may say about it, the instinct of the heart is to remember such a loved one in prayer, whether he is in this or in any other world."[82]

It is interesting when we read this prayer (or wish) that it speaks of the Lord twice: "may **the Lord** grant that he will find mercy from **the Lord**". Paul may either be referring to God twice, or to Christ twice, or, as seems most likely, the first Lord may refer to Christ and the second to God.[83] The confusion may be deliberate, for it safeguards the truth that "the ground of God's mercy lies within God himself. Neither Onesiphorus nor Paul can evoke mercy of God. God grants mercy because he is merciful."[84]

Timothy's Ministry

Paul has called on Timothy to "join with me in suffering for the gospel" (1:8). Now he tells Timothy what this "joining" means in terms of Timothy's own ministry. He is to be faithful to what Paul has taught him (1:13) and he is to guard it so that it can be passed on intact to others. (1:14). If he does these things faithfully, he will inevitably also share in Paul's suffering for the gospel.

Remember what you were taught

Paul and Timothy have worked together for many years. The younger man has had many opportunities to listen to Paul teaching since they first met at Lystra (Acts 16:1). So now Paul reminds him, *What you heard from me, keep as the pattern of sound teaching* (1:13a). The verb "you heard" summarizes all that Timothy has learned from Paul while they have been together.[85] It would include the contents of Paul's letters to him and anything else he has heard Paul say about the gospel.

Given that Paul's next instruction is to guard what he has been given (1:14) and refers to Timothy's work in the church, it is possible that Paul is thinking of the way Timothy uses what he has heard in his own life when he tells Timothy not merely to remember this teaching but also to "keep" it. "Keep" is rather a weak translation of a word that means "hang on to it; don't let go" or "keep on holding on". The image it conjures up is of someone hanging onto a branch so as not to fall from a tree or a cliff, or clinging to a log to avoid slipping into the water and drowning.

The idea of danger is also present in Paul's description of his own teaching as "sound" or healthy. False teaching is poison to the soul, while sound teaching is a balanced diet with nutritional and medicinal qualities that nurture and cure parts of the soul that may be sick. It is our obligation as ministers of sound doctrine to point out what is nutritional and medicinal and warn against what is poisonous. We should not produce words that "distort the faith, lead astray morally, and even excite hatred".[86]

Paul tells Timothy to keep his teaching as a "pattern".[87] A pattern is something to be copied, when knitting, sewing or manufacturing something. It sets the standard for any reproductions of the original. In the same way, Timothy is to keep to Paul's teaching.[88] This does not mean that he has to stick to it rigidly and repeat it word for word. A dress pattern can be adjusted for size, and the dress can be made in different colours and from different fabrics, while still staying true to the original pattern. In the same way, Timothy has the freedom to decide how to convey what Paul has taught him: "The pattern leaves Timothy free to choose his own language, including that of illustration (word-pictures) in his preaching and teaching."[89]

Students need to remember this principle. A teacher's notes are not meant to be recited and reproduced. They are simply a foundation on which the student should build in order to become wise enough to share his own insights with others. The same principle applies to this commentary. No one should try and teach or preach its contents word for word. It is simply a base on which preachers and teachers can build as they apply what they learn to the situation in which they live and serve.

The fact that Paul's teaching to Timothy is not a "mathematical formula merely to be remembered, and used in calculations"[90] is emphasized by the instruction that he must keep the pattern *with faith and love in Christ Jesus* (1:13b).[91] Faith, meaning both his trust in God and his belief in God's word, will keep Timothy going even during periods of great suffering. It will keep him from questioning God's goodness. Love will guard him from reacting sinfully when things are difficult and will keep him from hating those who cause him suffering. He must not become like rowdy youths who beat up anyone they suspect of supporting a different political party. Instead he must defend the truth with a loving spirit.

Paul's message can be summarized like this: "Let what you have learned from me serve as your model for sound teaching, but let it do so as you yourself model faith (or faithfulness) and love."[92]

Timothy is to show these virtues "in Christ Jesus".[93] His relationship with Christ should teach him what it means to have faith and love and should strengthen him to act faithfully and lovingly.

Guard what you have been given

Paul tells Timothy to *guard the good deposit that was entrusted to you* (1:14a). As discussed above (see 1:12), faithfully keeping a deposit intact until it accomplished the purpose intended for it by the depositor was considered a sacred duty. The treasure with which Timothy has been entrusted is the truth of the gospel. Unlike the false teaching, it is unequivocally good.

Timothy is to guard this truth by doing everything necessary to keep it safe. This includes protecting it from the eroding and distorting effects of false teaching. This task would involve some suffering, for Timothy would probably be subject to verbal or even physical attacks when he refused to compromise on certain truths.

The task is too big for Timothy to tackle on his own. He needs *the help of the Holy Spirit who lives in us* (1:14b). With divine resources to back him up, victory is assured!

The "us" in 1 Timothy refers primarily to Paul and Timothy. But it also refers to all Christians, including you and me, for the Holy Spirit lives in us as well (Rom 8:9–11). He will strengthen us to serve Christ in faith and love and to pass the truth on to the next generation.

Questions for Discussion

1. Do you know of anyone or any group of people who are suffering for the gospel today? What is your role in relation to them? Are you acting like Phygelus and Hermogenes (1:13) or Onesiphorus (1:15)? How can you as an individual or with others encourage them emotionally? Can you also help them materially?

2. We sometimes carelessly tell someone who is suffering, "I understand what you are going through". But unless we have had a very similar experience, the words are meaningless. This is one reason we should view our bad experiences as equipping us to comfort and encourage someone else – just as Paul used his experience of suffering to encourage Timothy. Have you ever been through an experience that you would never wish on anyone, but something good came out of it? Share with each other, remembering that any experience in our walk of faith leaves us with a lesson to pass on to others.

3. We are called to guard the teaching that has been passed on to us. How do we do this? As part of your answer, think about the last sermon you listened to? What did it teach you? How are you applying it in your life?

UNIT 5
2 TIMOTHY 2:1–7

ENDURANCE IN SUFFERING

Genesis 29:15–30 tells the story of Jacob, his uncle Laban, and Laban's two daughters, Leah and Rachel. Jacob was staying with Laban, and he fell in love with Rachel. However, he was a refugee with no money, and he could not afford to pay lobola (the bride price). Instead, he agreed to work for Laban for seven years in order to earn her as his wife. So great was his love that the seven years passed quickly. But Laban tricked Jacob, and substituted his older daughter, Leah, for the young and beautiful Rachel. By the time Jacob discovered the deceit, it was too late. Deeply disappointed, he had to keep Leah as his wife. But his heart was still fixed on Rachel, and so he agreed to work for Laban for seven more years so he could marry her too. He was prepared to work for fourteen years and put up with a dishonest father-in-law if only he could have her as his wife.

Jacob is not the only man who has had to suffer in order to marry the woman he loves. They endure the suffering because they are focused on the one they love. In the same way, Timothy is to endure suffering because of his love for Christ and his gospel. This is what motivates Paul, who has called Timothy to join him in suffering and illustrated what suffering is like with examples from his own life. Now he tells Timothy how to endure this suffering.

The Power behind Endurance

Paul emphasizes the "you" when he addresses Timothy, *You, then, my son* (2:1b).[94] He may be intending to remind Timothy that he is not to be like Phygelus and Hermogenes (1:15) but is to follow the example of Paul and Onesiphorus. More likely, however, Paul is saying, "I have told you to join me in suffering for the gospel. Now, this is how you can endure the suffering."

The way to endure is to *be strong in the grace that is in Christ Jesus* (2:1b). Paul has regularly either implied or explicitly stated that Timothy must keep in mind that ministry is only successful by the power of the Holy Spirit working in someone who is in Christ (1:6–7, 9, 12–14). It is of his grace (*charis*) that God gives us his gift (*charisma*) to enable us to do his work. "Unaided, Timothy cannot fulfil his duties".[95] Paul knows this from his own experience (1 Tim 1:12; 2 Tim 4:17). This strengthening by the Spirit is to be Timothy's ongoing experience.[96]

The word translated "in the grace" in the tniv is probably better rendered "by the grace".[97] It is "by grace" that God acts to empower people.[98] Grace is what he uses to do this.[99] The place where this instrument is found is "in Christ Jesus": he is the one to whom we go to find grace for ourselves and from whom we draw grace to strengthen us.[100] Christ is like a bank from whose resources of grace we can make withdrawals time and time again – with no need or ability to ever make a deposit in the bank ourselves! It is as if a billionaire allowed us to use his credit card – and this billionaire will never lose his money in some stock market crash, or change his mind about helping us and take back his card. Christ is faithful and will not change. He is understanding and will not tire of our unending requests. His grace cannot be exhausted. It is always available, free of charge, and is able to deal with any circumstance. When we give up in times of hardship, it is because we have not drawn from the eternal bank of grace. No matter what comes our way, we can go through it with the grace we draw from our gentle, kind and understanding Lord. It alone is the source of success in Christian ministry.

The Fruit of Endurance

The fruit of Timothy's endurance will be that the gospel will spread as others take up the message that has come from Christ via Paul and Timothy. Using the strength he has received from Christ, Timothy is to entrust *the things you have heard me say in the presence of many witnesses* to reliable people (2:2a).

The "things" may be a particular set of beliefs that Paul presented in a specific setting while Timothy listened and others watched as witnesses.[101] The occasion might have been Timothy's conversion, baptism or ordination, with the last two being more likely.[102] However, Paul probably simply uses "things" to summarize all that he has taught Timothy over the years.[103]

Our interpretation of what the "things" are is affected by who we think the witnesses are. The nrsv translation, "through many witnesses"[104] implies that many witnesses have spoken to Timothy about what Paul has said. These witnesses could have included Barnabas, who was Paul's companion on his first missionary journey (Acts 13:2–4). Other witnesses might be Lois, Timothy's grandmother, and Eunice, Timothy's mother (1:5). But the Greek could also be translated literally as "with many witnesses". This is the translation the niv, nasb, nkjv and hcsb adopt with their version, "before many witnesses".[105] It implies that the witnesses were simply bystanders (not necessarily the same group every time) or elders who were present on various occasions when Paul was speaking.

Whether the "things" were a specific credal statement or simply a body of teaching, what is clear is that they were not something trivial. In fact, Paul considers them so valuable that he tells Timothy to *entrust* them to others, using a word very similar to the one he earlier used to describe a sacred trust (2 Tim 1:12; 1:14).[106] In Galatians 1:12, Paul says that he received his message from the Lord. Now he has entrusted it to Timothy, who is to entrust it to faithful believers, who will in turn entrust it to others like them (2:2b).

Paul is not setting up some kind of apostolic succession. Rather, he is recognizing that no one can monopolize the ministry of the gospel. For one thing, no one remains alive forever to carry on the ministry. There is thus a need for us to prepare others to take over our responsibilities.

We should have a sense of urgency about doing this, for we could be gone tomorrow!

Moreover, Timothy himself is due to leave Ephesus soon in order to join Paul (see 4:9, 12). The work should not come to a standstill while he is away. Neither Paul nor Timothy knows whether he will ever return to Ephesus.

Timothy must exercise discretion as he chooses whom he will pass the message on to. It is a treasure of great value, and so the responsibility of guarding it should only be given to *reliable people*.[107] Many translations read "reliable men" or "faithful men", but the tniv's use of "people" is correct because the Greek word *anthropos* is a generic term for all members of the human race. The main requirement is that these "teachers' hearts must be so stayed on Christ that no threat of danger will lure them from the path of loyalty and no seduction of false teaching cause them to stray from the straight path of the truth. They must be steadfast both in life and in thought."[108]

The gospel is a treasure, but unlike other treasures it should not be kept locked in a safe. It is the message of life and must be passed on for other peoples' spiritual enrichment. Thus Paul insists that those to whom Timothy passes it on must *also be qualified to teach others*. He mentions the same ability when discussing the appointment of overseers (1 Tim 3:2; and Titus 1:9).

Every institution of learning keeps records of those who have gone through it and loves to identify successful past students. Knowing that you have successfully prepared others to contribute to a good cause makes sacrifices and hardship bearable. For example, I sometimes teach an evening class in Nairobi, which means that I return home after dark. Nairobi is not a particularly safe city once the sun has gone down, and I do not like travelling its roads at night. What keeps me teaching the class is the response of the students, and the fruit I see in their lives. I rejoice when I see that the hardship I endure is producing others to serve the Kingdom of God. I am sure many of us could report similar experiences.

However, for such sacrifices to be worth making, the people being trained as teachers must be prepared to make similar sacrifices for others. As each of us cultivates this attitude of service, the church will multiply. When each person invests in another, the church will never be left without reliable leaders.

Models of Endurance

Paul tells Timothy to be ready to *join with me in suffering* (2:3a). In saying this, he is repeating the instruction he gave him in 1:8.[109] He wants Timothy to be on his team, suffering side by side with him in the cause of the gospel. He uses three illustrations to show what endurance involves: the life of a soldier (2:3–4), an athlete or sportsman (2:5) and a farmer (2:6).

The soldier

Timothy is to endure hardship *like a good soldier of Christ Jesus* (2:3b). Christ is Timothy's commanding officer,[110] but the relationship goes beyond this. Christ not only commands Paul, Timothy and by implication all believers; he is also the one who owns us all because he bought us with his own blood (1 Cor 6:20; 7:23; Eph 1:7; 1 Pet 1:18–19).[111] We are his soldiers because we belong to him.

But as we know all too well in Africa, not all soldiers are good soldiers. Being a good soldier involves far more than being able to shoot and hit a target. It also requires inner qualities like self-control and loyalty. A good soldier does not try to overthrow or betray his superior. However, there are many in this world who ignore that point and choose to model their behaviour on Judas Iscariot. Ambitious government ministers sometimes try to undermine a president; senior army officers may plan a coup. Within the church, pastors or priests may try to raise their own status by undermining the authority of a bishop. No matter how intelligent or skilled these people are, they do not qualify as "good soldiers" – particularly when the leader they oppose is upright and carrying out his duties well.

Paul knew soldiers well, for he had often been their prisoner (Acts 22:22-29; 23:17-33; 27:1; 28:16). So he expands on this image: *no one serving as a soldier gets involved in civilian affairs* (2:4a). In other words, someone who is a full-time member of the armed forces does not take on a full-time civilian job as well.[112] No soldier can try to juggle two jobs. You cannot run a shop and still be a soldier. If you try, you are unlikely to win any battles. In fact, Roman law explicitly stated: "We forbid men engaged on military service to engage in civilian occupations."[113]

The reason soldiers on active service do not even try to take on a second job is that *they want to please their commanding officer* (2:4b). This was their goal. In Paul's day, armies often centred on and were loyal to just one person. When a recruit joined the army, he had to swear an oath of loyalty to the emperor. The "commanding officer" was thus not just the officer who commanded the unit, but the king or emperor commanding the whole army.

Paul often applies military metaphors to Christian life (e.g., 2 Cor 10:3–5; Eph 6:10–17; Phlm 2), and that is what he is doing here. The soldier's commitment to full-time service and refusal of any civilian occupations parallels the way a Christian should be totally committed to Christ. We should not try to live with one foot in the kingdom of God and one foot in the world (see also Luke 9:62). Timothy's obedience to his commander, Christ Jesus, must be of the kind summarized in the army slogan, "obey first, complain later". The soldier has to trust the commander, knowing that the commander can see the whole field of action and that the orders to individual units are part of an overall strategy. In the same way, our first duty is to obey the voice of God and accept even that which we cannot understand. We have an advantage over ordinary soldiers when it comes to this, for our commanding officer is completely trustworthy. He will not abuse our loyalty to achieve selfish ends. Nor is he short-sighted in his planning or lacking information about his enemies. He will keep focused on the goal of fulfilling his mission of redemption. As we obey his commands, we will be moving towards victory.

Unfortunately, the church does not always obey its commander. When it fails to follow his strategy and instead lets society determine its agenda, it risks defeat. For example, our commander has told us to love one another (John 13:34–35; 15:12, 17), to be content with being last rather than fighting to be first (Matt 18:4; 20:25–28) and to remember that we are to be the light of the world (Matt 5:14). But we sometimes find fights and not love in our churches, the ambition to be served rather than to serve, and unethical behaviour borrowed from the world. No wonder we sometimes feel defeated!

It is important to address two misunderstandings of Paul's words here because some people have taken his metaphors too literally and without regard for the context. We need to be careful not to use models and images in ways that the biblical writers did not intend.

- **Paul is not commanding celibacy.** Some think that the instruction not to get involved in civilian affairs means that those engaged in full-time ministry should not marry and have children, but should live a celibate life. But the question Paul would ask is whether marriage will hinder or help our work towards Christ's ultimate victory. This question must be answered by each individual and couple. No one else can answer it for them. For some, marriage and children are better paths, for a good family can enhance ministry and not compete with it. Paul recognized this and was not opposed to marriage (1 Tim 3:2, 12; Titus 1:6). But he also recognized that celibacy can be valuable (1 Cor 7, especially 7:32–34). So he did not lay down rules, but instead gave people guidance to help them decide what they were called to do in their particular situation.

- **Paul is not condemning tent-making ministry.** Paul is not saying that someone engaged in full-time ministry should never have another job to provide additional income. For one thing, he sometimes did this himself, choosing to work as a tent-maker to enhance the effectiveness of his ministry (1 Cor 9:1–18). The question he would ask is, "Does your tent-making help or hinder you in achieving the purpose God has given you – the victories, prizes and harvests you are working towards?" While it is true that the Lord sometimes uses people's poverty to glorify his name, he more often uses circumstances in which we can meet the basic needs of our families. Victory may be better achieved if you do not have constant financial worries and if you have a well-fed and adequately dressed family in which the children can afford to attend school. If necessary, tent-making can become part and parcel of achieving your goal of pleasing your master. Forty hours spent working while worrying where food, clothing and school fees will come from may be far less productive than thirty or even twenty hours spent working with a settled mind. But ideally tent-making should only be considered when the church budget is unable to provide for your needs.

Having said this, we need to repeat a point mentioned earlier. Contentment is an essential element of godliness (1 Tim 6:6). If the motive for tent making is the love of money, the motive is sinful. Each person needs to carefully determine what their "basic needs" really are. For Paul and Timothy, it was simply food, clothing and shelter. For others, the basic needs may include school fees and some means of transportation. The issue is not what is on the list (for needs will change from year to year), nor how short or how long the list is. What is important is how that list ties into the goal of living in obedience to Christ, our commanding officer. Everything else must support that goal, and anything that interferes with it must be set aside, even if the thing we are putting aside is not wrong in itself. We must constantly examine our motives to see whether work we once undertook to meet our basic needs is being continued because of a love for money.

The athlete

Timothy is to endure hardship like an athlete. Timothy would have known what Paul meant by this image, for athletic ability was highly prized in ancient Greece. Ephesus, where Timothy ministered, had a vast athletic stadium where public competitions were held. He would have known that the great athletic competitions were not open to everyone, but only to those who met certain standards.[114] The ancient athletes had to swear an oath to the Greek god Zeus that they had followed the rules of preparation for ten months before participating in the games.[115] Paul may have been thinking of these rules for admission to the games when he said that only those who compete *according to the rules* were entitled to *receive the victor's crown* (2:5). Or he may have been thinking of the rules of particular sports.[116] There were such rules in his day, just as there are rules for sports like football or boxing today. We expect the referee to penalize and even disqualify players who break these rules. Similarly, Olympic gold medallists are sometimes stripped of their medals because they have broken the rules. They may have finished first in the race, but their victory counted for nothing because they had used performance-enhancing drugs or did not stay in their lane when running.

Most likely, Paul is thinking of both types of rules.[117] His point is simply that an athlete must endure the training and obey the rules in order to win the prize.[118] Endurance is a prerequisite for receiving "the victor's crown", that is, the wreath of laurel or olive leaves that was equivalent to today's trophy or medal.

Christian life and service also require us to persevere, enduring the training God puts us through to ensure that we are strong and fit for the particular "race" in which he enters us. As we run this race, we need to know and obey the rules God has laid down for it. One of these rules was mentioned in relation to the model of a solder above, where Paul reminded us that we need to live to please Christ. When we disobey God's rule that we must love, serve and be lights to the world, we are not being good soldiers or athletes and we will definitely not receive a "well done" from our divine referee.

Just as we are disappointed in a referee who does not know or uphold the FIFA rules in a football game, so we should be disappointed when a pastor ignores the rules that God has given. Just as a referee needs to ignore the boos from spectators when he makes an unpopular decision to apply a rule, so Christians need to ignore the boos from the society around us when we apply God's rules. We cannot ignore or change these rules. Instead, we must undertake careful and honest study of Scripture, have the courage and endurance to remind others of what it teaches, and live our lives prayerfully before Christ, the ultimate, all-righteous referee (1 John 1:9; 2:1).

The farmer

Paul's final illustration of what endurance means is a *hardworking farmer*. This type of farmer prepares the ground before the rains come, clears the weeds away, and carefully watches over the crop as it matures. By contrast, a lazy farmer leaves the ploughing to the last minute, and then does a poor job because the rains have started. He tosses the seed into the soil and leaves the crops to take care of themselves until it is time to harvest them. The weeds cripple the crops, which receive no fertilizer or protection from animals and insects, and the harvest is late and thin. Meanwhile the diligent farmer usually reaps a fine harvest and is *the first to receive a share of the crops* (2:6).

Those working in God's fields need to work hard. We have to plan what to plant and where and when to plant it. Once we have planted the seeds, we need to care for the growing crop. It is not enough just to proclaim the gospel as an evangelist; we must disciple those we have evangelized. We may need to study and undergo training for the ministry if the fields to which God has called us are to be well tended.

All of this calls for patience. A farmer who plants something that takes four months to mature should not complain that the crop is not yet ripe after two months. If he did, we would tell them to learn a bit more about farming! Christians also tend to become impatient and want to see the word of God that was planted in a person's life bear fruit the next day. Yet in most cases patience and endurance are needed while we give the Holy Spirit time to work.

The Overall Lesson

The illustration of the farmer clearly shows the rewards of hard work and endurance. So do the illustrations of the soldier and athlete. The soldier endures isolation from the affairs of everyday life, the athlete endures hours of intensive training, and the farmer endures backbreaking labour and patient waiting. All this suffering is for a purpose. They fix their eyes on what they hope to achieve: the soldier's eyes are fixed on victory in battle, the athlete's on the winner's crown, and the farmer's on the coming harvest. Their goals are worth achieving, but the path to them is characterized by hardship. But God never fails to recognize and reward the victor.

As Timothy takes the time to *reflect* on what Paul is telling him (2:7),[119] he will be challenged to go on and encouraged that his endurance and suffering are not in vain. That is why Paul can enthusiastically encourage him to "join with me in suffering for the gospel" (1:8). Many Christian workers regularly see at least part of their victory, prize or harvest as their hard work produces more disciples for the kingdom of God

Questions for Discussion

1. Paul uses the example of a farmer growing crops. Can you develop a similar example for pastoralists? What can we learn from the hardships they endure to protect their herds?
2. Paul's soldier, athlete and farmer would have been familiar figures to the people of Ephesus. Can you think of contemporary examples that might convey Paul's message to the people you work with?

3. Use a scale of 1 to 10 to rate the level of hardship which the people in your church are prepared to endure for the cause of Christ. (1 represents the lowest level and 10 the highest level.) If the score is on the low side, why is this? If it is on the high side, what effects do you see this endurance having in your community?

4. In what practical ways can we encourage each other to endure more for the sake of Christ?

5. What are the basic needs of someone living in Africa in the 21st century? Are your pastor's basic needs being met by the church? If not, how can the church provide for them?

UNIT 6
2 TIMOTHY 2:8–13

ENCOURAGEMENT IN SUFFERING

One reason we study history is because we can learn from it. If we pay attention, we can avoid the foolish decisions that some people have made and emulate the wise decisions of others. We can also be inspired by the example of those who have been willing to endure suffering for the sake of their convictions.

Peter Cameron Scott is one person who was inspired by the sacrifices of others, and in turn became a source of inspiration. When he first came to Africa as a missionary, he almost died of fever and had to return to Britain. There he visited the tomb of David Livingstone and read the inscription on his grave: "Other sheep I have who are not of this fold". These words and Livingstone's example inspired the discouraged young man to return to Africa a second time. He died in 1896 at the age of twenty-nine, less than two years after his return, but his sacrifice inspired others and planted the seeds for the Africa Inland Church.[120] Today, his name is honoured by two Kenyan theological institutions, Scott Theological College and Cameron Bible College (the latter at the location of his first mission station).

Stories like this should motivate us to follow Scott's example, and that of countless other believers in Bible times and since, who have freely forgiven those who hurt them, stood with courage against enemies of the Christian faith and willingly died for their Saviour. One such was Polycarp, the bishop of Smyrna (now Izmir in Turkey) who in ad 155 courageously faced death by fire rather than deny Jesus. Offered the opportunity to escape this fate, he replied, "For eighty-six years I have served him, and he has done me no evil. How could I curse my king who saved me?"[121] Paul would have agreed, for he tells Timothy that the main thing that motivates him and gives him the strength to endure is his memory of Jesus Christ and Christ's unchangeable promise.

Remember Jesus Christ

The greatest appeal Paul can make when he asks Timothy to join him in suffering is *Remember Jesus Christ* (2:8).[122] The verb "remember" is in the present tense, meaning "continually remember, keep in mind, be conscious of, keep before you". What he is to remember is not so much the work of Christ (what he accomplished for us), but rather who Jesus is. That may be why Paul changes the order from "Christ Jesus", which is used everywhere else in these letters, to "Jesus Christ".[123] It is the power of Christ's presence, and not just the memory of his work, that will inspire Timothy to exhibit the courage of a soldier, the perseverance of an athlete and the hard work of a good farmer.

Paul focuses on two aspects of Jesus Christ's life: his resurrection and his ancestry (see also Rom 1:3–40).

Raised from the dead

Here Paul does not focus on the power of God who raised Jesus but on the status of Jesus Christ as the one raised.[124] He reminds Timothy that Jesus is the living one, who is still living after passing through death, and so can continually be present with Timothy as he suffers for the sake of the gospel. Paul wants Timothy to say to himself, "Because Jesus lives after so much suffering and death, I am willing to embrace the same suffering, anticipating that I will also live with him in ultimate victory."

It is important to remind ourselves from time to time that the Jesus we serve is alive and has conquered death. This knowledge should give us courage as we face difficulties for his name's sake. Our suffering will also lead to glory! This combination of suffering and glory is incomprehensible to outsiders, but Christians know that if our lives are devoted to Christ, although we die in weakness, we will rise in glory.

Descended from David

Why did Paul choose to mention Christ's ancestry here? We do not know, but Fee suggests three main possibilities:[125]

- Paul is quoting some Christian creed without deleting parts that are irrelevant to his point here.[126] This seems unlikely because it is difficult to imagine Paul including something in his writing without concern for its relevance.
- Paul wants Timothy to focus on Jesus' humanity, and so he speaks of his human ancestry. Because Jesus was human, he walked the same path of suffering that Paul is asking Timothy to take.[127] Alternatively, Paul may be wanting to counter the gnostic teaching that Jesus was a spiritual being who was not fully human.[128] But if Paul had wanted to focus on the incarnation, the description of Jesus as "descended from David" would probably have preceded the words "raised from the dead".
- Paul wants Timothy to focus on the fulfilment of God's promise. Hultgren, who also believes these words were part of a creed, says, "The promise of God has been fulfilled in Jesus Christ, son of David, who has been raised to sit at God's right hand as his Messiah (cf. Matt. 22:41–45; Acts 2:22–36; Hebrews 1:3–5)."[129]

The third possibility seems the most likely. Paul is saying that the living Jesus, who was raised from the dead, is the Messiah. He fulfils the prophecies that the Messiah would come from the lineage of David (see, for example, 2 Sam 7:12–16). As the Messiah, Jesus is the Lord's Anointed and nothing can thwart the Lord's plans and purposes for him.

Remembering God's faithfulness to his promise in the Old Testament encourages Timothy, and us, to believe that he will also be faithful to carry out his plans through us. We are now in a special relationship with God (John 1:12). We can thus face suffering with the assurance that God's good purposes in our lives will come to pass, no matter what path we have to tread first.

Paul follows his triumphant assertion of who Jesus is with the simple statement, *This is my gospel* (2:8b). This is what Paul teaches. Others, particularly Timothy's opponents in Ephesus, may teach a different gospel. But Paul's gospel is about a risen Lord and God's anointed.

This gospel of power, a gospel with God's signature of approval, is the same gospel we preach today. It is a privilege to be part of God's team proclaiming such a powerful message. Those who dilute it by denying the deity of Christ or making him merely one of many ways to God must be corrected and even rebuked. The truth of the gospel must be guarded.

Remember Paul's Example

Because of his proclamation of the gospel, Paul himself is following Christ's example and can say, *I am suffering* (2:9a).[130] He may be thinking of all the suffering he has endured during his years of ministry or only of his present suffering.[131] Probably, he is thinking of both, although in what follows he talks about his present sufferings.

Enduring chains

As he writes, Paul is *chained as a criminal* (2:9a). He is not a thief, murderer or traitor – not at all! But the Roman authorities are treating him as if he is.

We do not know much about Paul's second Roman imprisonment. It was probably around the time when the Emperor Nero blamed Christians for the fire that raged through Rome for six days and seven nights in July ad 64. There were suspicions that Nero himself was responsible for the fire, but Christians were made the scapegoats. This set in motion the first great persecution of Christians, and many were arrested and killed. If Paul was one of those arrested, he would have been sentenced to death as a criminal. But Paul is not worried about how others see him. He knows that he is in prison because of his association with Christ and his followers. For the sake of the gospel, he is happy to endure even "the worst indignities to which he, a Roman citizen and an innocent man, was subjected." [132]

What about us? We sometimes hear about believers who have been victimized. For example, some lose their jobs or are beaten for refusing to join in a scheme to steal from their employer or from public funds. Would we be willing to be like them and like Paul and take a stand for the truth? Or does even the mildest attack cause us to slink away in defeat?

Those who are prepared to face persecution for the gospel are blessed (1 Pet 4:14). It may be difficult for us to comprehend this blessing from our limited perspective, but we can count on it, for God, who cannot lie, has promised it. The blessing may not be in material goods but may be inner peace, good relationships and miraculous provision for our needs.

Celebrating the gospel

Paul contrasts his own chains with the freedom the word of God enjoys, for it *is not chained* (2:9b). Here *God's word* is equivalent to the gospel. God is its source[133] and Paul is only its trustee (1:14; 2:2) and proclaimer (1:11). So although he may be jailed, the word of God is still enjoying its freedom.[134] It is still being preached by others (just as it was when Paul wrote Philippians 1:12–14 during his first Roman imprisonment), and it continues to minister to Paul even while he is in prison, giving him the courage he needs.

Paul may also be speaking in more general terms, and making the point that no one can "arrest" God's word or stop if from accomplishing what God wants it to (Isa 55:11).[135] History shows that anyone who attempts to stop God's word acts foolishly – the mere attempt shows that they have not learned from history! The gospel has weathered many storms, but it continues to live on. Even today, in most African countries, the Bible is still treated as a special book. And that it is, for it is God speaking. When the Creator speaks, what creature can change what he has said?

Suffering for the elect

Paul's *therefore* in 2:10 refers back to all he has been saying about Jesus Christ and the gospel in 2:8–9. Because of the wonder of who Christ is and the power of his word, Paul is prepared to *endure everything*. The "everything" embraces his present suffering in prison, his past suffering and the suffering that lies ahead.[136]

Paul will endure whatever comes if it promotes salvation of *the elect*. The word "elect" in this context means "chosen by God" (just as in the Old Testament the Israelites were God's chosen people and, in a modern context, elected politicians are those chosen by the people). But who exactly are the chosen ones for whom Paul is willing to suffer? There are at least three possibilities:

- Those whom God has chosen but who have not yet been saved.[137]
- Those who already been saved by the time Paul writes this letter.[138]
- Both of the above groups, or in other words, those who have already been saved and those who have yet to be saved.[139]

The last option seems the most likely, for Paul probably did not think of the elect in categories.[140] The only difference he would have recognized was that those who had already come to salvation needed to be nurtured, while those who had not yet come to Christ needed to be reached. His endurance would be an example to his fellow believers and was necessary for outreach to those who had not yet come to salvation.

Salvation is found *in Christ Jesus*[141] and is *with eternal glory*.[142] The journey of salvation began with God's election of believers in eternity (Rom 8:29–30), continues in history as individuals believe and are saved (John 3:16), and will be completed in the future when Christ returns, at which time we will enjoy our salvation in its full glory (1 John 3:2). The future completion does not mean that we are not already saved now, but it explains the contrast between the suffering we are called to endure in the present and the glory that awaits us.

When we suffer, it is easy to focus on ourselves and what we are going through. Here Paul helps us look beyond ourselves and see how others will be blessed through our perseverance. If we follow Paul, we will be prepared to sacrifice our comforts so that others will be blessed. We will be prepared to endure suffering to the point of death, knowing that our testimony will encourage those who hear or read about us.

The Unchangeable Promise

Paul follows his call to suffering with a reminder of God's promise to those who endure. He introduces the reminder with the words, *Here is a trustworthy saying* (2:11a).[143] This is the last of the five "trustworthy sayings" in the Pastoral Epistles.[144]

In some translations, what follows is introduced by the word "for", which is omitted in the tniv. It is omitted because it was probably the first word in the verse of a hymn that Paul is quoting. While it made sense in its original context, it does not fit in here.[145]

The clue that 2:11b–13 is a quotation from one of the earliest Christian hymns is its structure.[146] It consists of four matching lines, each starting with the word "if". Paul probably added the words "for he cannot disown himself" at the end of line four. In fact, he may even have written the entire hymn himself. He was certainly capable of writing it, given the beauty of such passages as 1 Corinthians 13 and Romans 8:28–39.[147]

If this is a Christian hymn, when would the early Christians have sung it?[148] There are two competing views. The first is that it was composed to be sung at baptisms and thus focuses on conversion and life after conversion. The second is that it was sung to encourage those facing martyrdom and thus focuses on enduring suffering and persecution.[149]

Both of these two interpretations would fit the context of 2 Timothy. "All we can be sure of is that Paul's motive in quoting it was to press home the connexion between the Christian's fellowship with Christ in suffering and glory."[150] While we may never be certain of the original context of the hymn, we can still understand the point Paul is making when he quotes it.

The hymn presents two ways of living the Christian life, the right way and the wrong way, and spells out the consequences of each choice.

The right way

The hymn begins, *If we died with him* (2:11b). The verb is in the past tense, so this death has already happened, and is not in the future.[151] To understand how this is possible, we need to remember that Paul has been talking about suffering and sacrificing ourselves for others, or in other words, about dying to sin and self-centredness (Rom 6:1–11). This is the same death that Paul talked about when he said, "We were therefore buried with him through baptism into death in order that, just as Christ was raised from the dead through the glory of the Father, we too may live a new life" (Rom 6:4). He repeats this point in Romans 6:8: "Now if we died with Christ, we believe that we will also live with him" – words which almost exactly parallel 2 Timothy 2:11b.

The result of dying with Christ is that we enter into a mystical union in which our lives are "hidden with Christ in God" (Col 3:3). When this hymn was sung at baptisms, the death to self had just happened, and the new believers would *live with him* as their daily lives become more Christ-like. On the other hand, when those singing this hymn were facing martyrdom, the future tense of *we will live* would focus their attention on the resurrected life that lay ahead.

In the context of 2 Timothy, where Paul is facing execution, it is likely that in the first line he is referring to the beginning of our life as believers, and in the second he is pointing Timothy to the promise that there is life beyond death for those who suffer for Christ.

The next line of the hymn promises that *if we endure, we will also reign with him* (12a, b). Here the verb "endure" is in the present tense. Those who have died to their previous lives need to keep on living the new life with Christ. If they do, they will "reign with him" (see also Rev 20:6). The Scriptures do not give us many details about what this reign will involve. All we know is that it includes reigning over death since believers will be raised to be like Christ and so will never die (1 John 3:2), and that we will be with Christ, the ruler, forever.

There is an interesting progression in these opening lines of the hymn. They start with our conversion (when we die), go on to our life with Christ in which we endure suffering, and end with our future life, the life of the resurrection, in which we will also reign with him.[152] The hymn encapsulates the tension we live in as believers, the tension between the "already" – what God has already done – and the "not yet" – the full coming of his kingdom in the future.

The wrong way

The mood of the hymn now changes from triumphant celebration to serious warning: *If we disown him* (2:12c). What does this mean? Is Paul saying that he, or Timothy, or some other believers may actually disown Christ?

Some commentators argue that this is the case because some Christians may deny Christ in the future.[153] Others insist that Paul is merely mentioning this as a highly unlikely scenario.[154] But the problem with dismissing this possibility is the way this line parallels the other two lines in the hymn. The "if" clause in the first line referred to something that has definitely happened (we died with Christ). The "if" clause in the second line refers to something that is happening (we are enduring suffering). So it seems likely that the "if" clause here is referring to something that will happen. It could actually be translated, "If we disown (or "deny", nasb) him, and we will".[155] But this translation is very disturbing! So we need to look at the passage even more closely.

The first thing we notice when we turn back to it is that lines two and three contradict each other. We cannot both "endure" and "disown him". We can do one of these, but not both. This is particularly clear when we realize that the verb indicates that the action is a habit, not merely a temporary denial like that of Peter (Matt 26:69–74).[156] Paul is speaking of full-blown apostasy, involving a continual moving away from Christianity into an open expression of denial.

The impossibility of combining enduring and denying suggests that Paul is speaking about two different groups of people. The one group are enduring Christians who have a genuine faith. The other consists of people who associate with Christians or are nominally Christian, but who are not committed to Christ and will not be prepared to suffer for him. The church contains both groups, as Christ predicted when he told the parable about the good seed and the weeds growing together (Matt 13:24–29; 36–43). Knowing this, Paul can predict that some within the Christian movement will fall away, not because they have lost their salvation but because they had none to begin with. They were only polite associates of Christianity. Only God, who knows the heart, is able to separate these people from the genuine believers. The rest of us can only assume that where there is wheat, there will be weeds.

But, some people will ask, why does Paul use "we" when he says, "If *we* disown him'? Doesn't that mean that he is thinking that all of us, including himself and Timothy, can fall away? No. The "we" here is what is called a speaker's or editorial "we". It means "some of us".[157]

Paul uses the future tense when he says that Christ *will disown us* (2:12d) to communicate that those who disown Christ can still change their status and join the group of those who will endure. But if they do not, the inevitable consequence is that they will be disowned,[158] because they never belonged to him.

These words are a warning to people like Hymenaeus and Philetus (see 2:17) who are members of the church but are beginning to adopt a philosophy that leads them to deny the reality of the resurrection. Their thinking is going in a dangerous direction. If they do not turn around, they will eventually end up disowning Christ, and being disowned by him. This is what Christ himself stated in Matthew 10:33: "Whoever publicly disowns me, I will disown him before my Father in heaven." Hultgren puts it well, "Jesus Christ cannot vouch in eternity for a man who has refused to have anything to do with him in time."[159]

In every church there are people who neither publicly confess Jesus as their Saviour nor deny him. Such people must ultimately decide to embrace the Christian faith more intimately by accepting Jesus as Saviour or to stop their journey completely and declare that they have never been followers of Jesus. Because such people do not have the Holy Spirit in them to encourage them, they tend to deny Christ when a situation calls for Christians to suffer for their faith.

The final line in the hymn is *If we are faithless, he remains faithful* (2:13a). The present tense verb indicates that this is a settled attitude towards God, and the conditional clause speaks of something which is certain.[160] Many people are unfaithful to God and show no loyalty to him, but their faithlessness does not change God's character in dealing with humankind in general.

While this line of the hymn speaks specifically of unbelievers, it also offers comfort to believers. We may sometimes fail during times of trial and temptation, but our failure does not change Jesus' faithfulness.

Paul's readers may agree that Jesus is unchangeably faithful – but they may still ask, "Faithful to what?" So Paul add the words, *he cannot disown himself*. Jesus is always faithful to who he himself is. He is God, and God does not change. But which particular aspect of God's character is Paul focusing on here? If he is focusing on God's holiness, he may be making the point that God will respond to unfaithfulness with the punishment it deserves. However, it seems more likely that Paul wants us to focus on God's love.[161] In his love, God bears with our faithlessness and waits for us to see the foolishness of following the wrong way and make a complete turn to "die with Christ" and "endure" suffering for the cause of the gospel. This focus on love balances the focus on justice in line three ("if you disown me, I disown you"). It is not meant to make Timothy and other readers careless about being faithful. Rather, it is meant to encourage them if they fail. God's acceptance of them is not based on their being perfect but flows from his grace and faithfulness.

Remember!

Many of us put things we would like to be reminded of on a wall. We may hang up pictures of friends and family, a calendar with a verse from Scripture, or a handwritten page with some words we found particularly moving. In a sense, Paul is telling Timothy to place three things on the wall so that they are always before him: the risen Christ, a committed Paul, and the unchangeable promise of God.

We could summarize Paul's message to Timothy like this: "When you feel that your suffering for the gospel is more than you can bear, remember our Lord Jesus Christ in whose life both suffering and glory went hand in hand. Remember me, your mentor, who does not mind being treated like a criminal if my only crime is my determination to preach the word. And remember that God is faithful even if you sometimes fail. Your goal should be to endure for the sake of Christ, our faithful Lord who has promised that we will reign with him."

Paul's message is also for us today. We serve the same unchanging Jesus, we can look to Paul and others as our models, and God's promise still stands. Rather than looking for a weapon when enemies attack, we should arm ourselves with these memories. Then we will be ready when suffering arrives.

Questions for Discussion

1. What pressures are Christians experiencing today from society in general, groups representing special interests or nominal Christians?
2. What should the church be doing to make sure its members do not give in to these pressures?
3. Identify some people who are models of suffering for Christ in your region or nation. What makes these people stand out as models?
4. Have you ever faced a situation in which you were called to make a decision that could have resulted in suffering? How did you deal with it and what factors made you respond the way you did?

UNIT 7
2 TIMOTHY 2:14–16, 22

MINISTRY TO OTHERS AND OUR PERSONAL LIVES

On 10 October 2004, a group of about ten human rights lobbyists defaced a national monument in Central Park in Nairobi. The monument commemorated former president Daniel Arap Moi (president from 1978 to 2002), whom they accused of failing to safeguard human rights. On the same day, a bishop addressed thousands of Christians in Nyayo Stadium and described Moi as a peacemaker and a God-fearing man. The human rights lobbyists focused on the failures of the former president and held him responsible for the actions of those under his authority; the bishop focused on the fact that Moi peacefully handed over power to his successor, President Mwai Kibaki. Two truths, two foci, and two totally opposing judgments.

Moi is not the only person to be subject to public scrutiny. All of us are constantly being evaluated either positively or negatively by a variety of people. Paul reminds Timothy of this, but stresses that he is being evaluated by an even higher judge, one who never misses something he should know nor overlooks anything. Timothy, and we who serve God today, should constantly be aware of God's scrutiny.

Ministry to Others

The human rights activists held Moi accountable for what was done by his subordinates and for the instructions he gave to the members of his government. As a leader, Timothy too is responsible for the behaviour of those who follow him. Thus he is to keep reminding them of what they need to know and warning them about how they should be living.

Keep reminding them

Timothy is to *keep reminding God's people of these things* (2:14a). He is to do so regularly.[162]

Because the original Greek does not include the words "God's people", there has been some debate about who exactly is to be reminded. Is it the whole congregation or is it only the "reliable people" referred to in 2 Timothy 2:2?[163] The former is more likely, because the reference to the reliable people is a full twelve verses before this. It also seems that Paul divides Timothy's listeners into two categories: those to be reminded and those to be warned. Those to be reminded are then all those under Timothy's spiritual care who do not need to be warned.

A second question concerns what exactly they are to be reminded of. Paul uses only the vague words, "these things". The "things" may be the faithful saying found in 2:11–13; the faithful saying and whatever teaching is alluded to in 2 Timothy 2:2; all that Paul has said so far in the letter; or all that Paul has said so far, in and beyond this letter.[164] The last option makes good sense. Paul would consider everything he has said to Timothy to be relevant and important for the Ephesians to know.

Young pastors sometimes forget that their congregations already know much of what is being preached. Many of the believers in Ephesus would have learned the essentials of the Christian faith from Paul himself, for he had served there for about three years (Acts 19:8, 10; 20:31). They would be like some of the older believers in our churches today who have heard sermons on almost every possible topic or theme. They do not come to church to hear something new but to hear the same old story told in a fresh and relevant way. The preachers' task is to remind them, to bring back to their memories the truths they have heard over and over again, and to challenge them to act on them in the present. The truths remain the same, but they need to be applied in each new day and circumstance.

Warn them

The word translated "warn" is used in two other places in Paul's letters to Timothy, and in both places it is translated as "charge" (1 Tim 5:21;

2 Tim 4:1). There Paul gave Timothy a charge; now Timothy is to charge others.[165]

Timothy is to utter this warning or charge *before God* (2:14b). He is to speak "in [God's] presence and with his authority".[166] He will then have no need to be discouraged if those he solemnly charges do not obey, for he will have faithfully discharged his duty and it is not him they disobey but God.

Like Timothy, our duty is to simply do our best. Critics will always be looking for points of failure. For example, they may seize on the fact that a pastor's children are sometimes disobedient. Some will quote Proverbs 22:6 to suggest that the pastor is a failure. But the most fundamental question that needs to be asked is whether the pastor did his or her best. If the answer is yes, there are no grounds for feeling guilty.

The substance of the warning is that people should not be *quarrelling about words*. In other words, they are not to get involved in disputes where their sole aim is to win the argument and gain a personal reputation as a great debater.[167] Paul is not saying that we should never engage others in debate or write a letter to the newspaper. What is important is our motive. We must not get into debate to promote our own glory but only to uphold the glory of God and defend the truth of the gospel.

Paul gives two reasons for issuing this warning: such quarrelling *is of no value, and only ruins those who listen*".[168] It is useless because it does nothing to promote the kingdom of God (see also 1 Tim 1:4). "What Paul is underlining here is the danger of getting involved in that kind of theological discussion which is in the end purely verbal, having nothing to do with the realities of the Christian religion."[169] Quarrelling is not only useless, it is also destructive. It breaks down what has already been accomplished in people's lives. It is "unlikely to achieve anything beyond overthrow of the faith of those who listen".[170]

When we study God's word and read commentaries like this one, we need to watch how much of our time is spent on secondary things. For example, we should not spend so much time arguing about whether 1 and 2 Timothy were written by Paul that we never get round to studying what is taught in these letters. Details of authorship and the place of writing are relevant matters, but they should never be allowed to overshadow the content. The former are not sources of spiritual nourishment, but the latter has a life-changing message that we need to proclaim.

Personal Qualities

The line between personal life and ministry may at times be blurred. So Paul reminds Timothy that he is not to be so involved in ministry that he forgets the needs of his own soul. He should not spend so much time examining the lives of others that he allows his own to rot spiritually. This point is driven home by the placement of "yourself" as the second word in the Greek sentence translated, *Do your best to present yourself to God as one approved* (2:15a).[171]

Timothy is to do his best not in one particular area but in everything he does.[172] All his actions should be designed to elicit God's approval, not merely the approval of other people. He is a *worker* employed by God and should be doing his utmost to satisfy his employer. If he does this, he will have nothing to be ashamed of.

Having sketched this general idea, Paul goes on to give Timothy specific instructions about how to achieve this goal. He tells Timothy what he should and should not do, and spells out the characteristics of a God-approved worker. In all these instructions, both the positive and the negative, he is helping the young man to understand the practical working out of holiness in the pastorate.[173]

What to do

There are two things that Timothy must do if he is to please God: he must correctly handle the word of truth (2:15) and pursue righteousness, faith, love and peace (2:22–23).

Correctly handle the word of truth

The word translated *correctly handles* (2:15b) is a combination of two Greek words. One of them means "straight" or "make level" (as in Hebrews 12:13) and the other means "to cut".[174] The literal meaning is therefore "to cut straight". Applied to a worker, it would describe the way a farmhand ploughs a straight furrow so that the seeds are planted in a straight line, the way a carpenter cuts a piece of wood so that it fits exactly where it belongs, the way a tailor cuts cloth to fit the customer perfectly, or the way a road builder lays out a straight road to avoid unnecessary distance for the traveller.

Timothy is to be like these workers and is to follow a straight path as he communicates the word of truth. He is not to be turned aside by arguments about words or useless talk, but must stay on the correct path of service. His one desire should be to help people to live well by accurately interpreting and applying God's word. He must use sound principles when interpreting Scripture and must not twist the Scriptures to make them say what he wants.[175]

The expression "the word of truth" stands for the gospel. This is clear from the use of the same expression in Ephesians 1:13 and Colossian 1:5. The "of truth" may describe the nature of the gospel, communicating that it means what it says. It could also be an equivalent to "namely", in which case the expression means "the word which is itself truth". However, the best choice in this context may be to see "of truth" as describing the content of the word.[176] Truth is found (contained) in the words Timothy is to expound, as opposed to the words which others are disputing about.

The content of our words is very important, especially when preaching. A fifteen-minute sermon containing words of truth can more effectively build lives than a forty-five minute sermon containing one humorous story after another. Preachers are not meant solely to entertain, and while there is nothing wrong with telling a humorous story to illustrate an eternal truth, a story for the sake of entertaining does not qualify as a "word of truth".

Today, the "word of truth" is often interpreted as referring to the Bible, rather than just the gospel. Paul's words still apply: we need to handle God's word correctly. We should not veer to either of two possible extremes. On the one hand, there are the people who argue that the only teacher they need is the Holy Spirit. They quote passages like John 16:13 and downplay the role of Bible training. And there are others who approach the Bible as if it is nothing more than a work of literature. They analyze it as if they can understand all the depths of its teaching by using their minds. Both groups fail to recognize that the Bible is a book given under the guidance of the Holy Spirit to real people living in a particular time and place. Correct study of the word of truth calls for the application of our minds as well as humble dependence on the Holy Spirit. Failure to study the Bible diligently results in superficial teaching or preaching, and neglecting the role of the Holy Spirit results in dead speech. It is the living Spirit of God who helps all those who listen to apply the word to their life situations.

Pursue righteousness, faith, love and peace

The second thing that Timothy has to do in order to maintain God's approval as a good worker is to pursue "righteousness, faith, love, and peace" (2:22b).[177] When we come to the list of what Timothy is not to do, we will see that this instruction contrasts with the instruction to "flee evil desires" (2:22a).[178]

The imperative "pursue" is in present tense, indicating that Timothy is to make a habit of doing this, just as he must make a habit of fleeing from evil. We can get some idea of the intensity that this word implies if we think of how people used to set about a hunt. They would prepare by wearing clothes that would not hinder them from running fast. They would arm themselves with bow and arrows and take along a dog in case the quarry went into thick bush and needed to be chased out. The hunters might spread out so as to block possible escape routes. The desired animal would be carefully tracked and once it had been spotted, it would be pursued until it was captured. The hunt was a serious matter, but the reward of a feast of meat made the effort worthwhile. Paul would tell us to pursue virtues with the same degree of determination, for at the end of the day, we will receive the "well done" that we are waiting for from our beloved Lord.

Timothy is told to pursue these virtues *along with those who call on the Lord out of a pure heart* (2:22b). There is some disagreement about whether this phrase should be linked with all four virtues, or only with the last one, peace.[179] Those who limit it to applying only to peace argue that the first three virtues (righteousness, faith and love) are to be exercised in relation to God, while peace is related to the fellowship between people that will flow from the first three. Thus Timothy should pursue righteousness, faith and love in his relationship with God and cultivate a peaceful atmosphere as he relates to other people.

However, it seems unlikely that any of the four virtues needs to be limited to either the vertical or horizontal relationship for they are all tied together. Timothy is to pursue righteousness, faith, love and peace as he relates to others, but without losing sight of the fact that he can only exercise them from a pure heart if they are based on his relationship with God. Righteousness focuses on giving what is due to both God and people; faith focuses on the loyalty and reliability that come from trusting God; love never seeks anything but the highest good for others; peace focuses on the right relationships experienced when in loving fellowship with God and with others.[180]

"Those who call on the Lord" is another way of saying "Christians". The addition of the phrase "out of a pure heart" indicates that Timothy is to work with those who are truly Christians, and not merely associates or hypocrites. He is to work "with them", a translation that encourages unity, or "along with them", a translation that suggests mutual encouragement and interdependence.[181] While both ideas are essential, Paul seems to focus more on how Timothy should relate to God and to other people than on what people will contribute to Timothy's development, and so the first option is preferred.

What not to do

There are two things that Timothy is *not* to do if he to please God. He must avoid godless chatter (2:16) and flee the evil desires of youth (2:22).

Avoid godless chatter

"Godless chatter" is talk that has no value in promoting the kingdom of heaven, but instead promotes worldliness (see also 1 Tim 6:20). There are two reasons why Timothy should make a habit of avoiding such godless talk.[182] The first is that as a general principle *those who indulge in it will become more and more ungodly* (2:16).[183] This statement needs to be interpreted within the total context at Ephesus. Paul's letters to Timothy have been full of references to "meaningless talk" (1 Tim 1:6), "godless myths" (1 Tim 4:7), "controversies and quarrels about words that result in envy, strife, malicious talk, evil suspicions and constant friction" (1 Tim 6:4–5), and "godless chatter and the opposing ideas of what is falsely called knowledge, which some have professed and in so doing have departed from the faith" (1 Tim 6:20–21). Clearly, there were major problems involving those promoting an opposing gospel.

The false gospel they were spreading did not seek to honour God but instead promoted ungodliness among those who believed it.

Christians cannot shun all debates, because at times they need to defend the gospel. But they must use wisdom when choosing what arguments to get involved in. There is no point in getting involved in fruitless discussions that produce only envy and strife.[184] Barclay offers a useful rule of thumb: "If at the end of our talk, we are closer to one another and to God, then all is well; but if we have put up barriers between one another and have left God more distant, then all is not well."[185]

For example, I sometimes wonder whether it is worth getting involved in arguments with those who suggest that our Bible translations are inaccurate when it comes to homosexuality. Too often, such arguments are simply defences of entrenched positions, with no real concern to discern the truth of the matter. The time spent in such debates might be better spent in prayer that the Lord will touch some who practise homosexuality and lead them to repentance so that they walk with the Lord in the sexual area.

Having said that, it is important to note that there is some ambiguity about the subject of the verb translated "become more and more". The tniv takes the subject to be the false teachers, who become increasingly corrupt. However, it is also possible that it is chatter that becomes worse and worse. Thus the nasb translation of this verse is "avoid worldly and empty chatter, for it will lead to further ungodliness" (see also the nrsv). This ambiguity is not necessarily a bad thing, for it "draws attention to the inevitable progress in ungodliness of both teaching and teachers."[186] The two go hand in hand. However, the mention of two of the false teachers by name in 2:17 suggests that Paul is focusing primarily on the teachers. Their teaching leads them further and further away from God. Timothy is not to allow himself to be drawn into their debates.

The second reason why Timothy needs to avoid worldly and empty chatter is that it *will spread like gangrene* (2:17a).[187] The word translated "gangrene" was used to refer to "a sore which eats into the flesh."[188] Today, we might use the image of cancer rather than gangrene. Just as cancer spreads and destroys the body, so false teaching will eat into the spiritual flesh of the church. The danger is not limited to those who currently embrace the teaching, for it has an "insidious tendency to spread and infect other people, just as gangrene spreads and eats up the neighbouring tissue."[189] Or we could use the image of HIV/AIDS. The human immunodeficiency virus works invisibly within the body at first. It hides while it slowly destroys the infected person's immune system. Then suddenly it appears as full-blown AIDS and destroys the person.

Paul speaks of the false teaching devouring the church, for the word translated "will spread" could be literally translated "will have pasture".[190] Where there is pasture, there is food and a flock of errors will multiply. If Timothy gets involved in long discussions about the teaching, he will be helping it to spread. By refusing to discuss it, he will be cutting off its food supply.

Of course, this is not the only instruction Paul gives to Timothy concerning how he is to relate to the false teachers. Here Paul tells Timothy to avoid them, but earlier he had told him to rebuke them. We need to read each instruction in the context of the whole of both letters.

We can draw on the principles set out in this passage when deciding how to deal with false teaching today. First, we must exercise discernment in deciding whether we should get involved in the argument. If we do get involved, we may find that some of those taking part refuse to listen to the truth of the gospel, and so need to be rebuked. At times, we may even need to excommunicate such people. If they are allowed to remain in the congregation, they will eat into the fellowship of God's people like cancer or HIV/AIDS – planting hatred and not love, self-importance and not sacrificial service, lies and not the truth.

Flee the evil desires of youth

Another habit that Timothy is to cultivate is fleeing *the evil desires of youth* (2:22).[191] Paul is calling on Timothy to show maturity, for he cannot afford to act like a youngster[192] given his responsibilities at Ephesus. When we read this, we need to remember that Timothy was probably already in his thirties (see commentary on 1 Tim 4:11). The mere fact that somebody is older in years does not mean that he will not be tempted to make the same mistakes as the young.

Paul does not specify exactly what youthful desires he has in mind. Given the kjv translation of the word as "lusts", we may leap to the conclusion that he means illicit sexual desires, but although those are included, the word has a far broader meaning.[193] Like the English word "desire" the Greek word Paul uses can refer to things that are both positive and negative. Its basic idea is "a strong yearning", and it is in this sense that Paul uses it when he speaks of how much he, Silas and Timothy long to see the Thessalonians (1 Thess 2:17). When writing to Timothy, Paul restricts its meaning to "evil desires", that is, the strong emotions that can cause young people to sin. These emotions include the following:

- *Impatience.* The young are often in a hurry to get things done. They want to fix everything that is wrong in the church or society in one day and are impatient with those who do not share their vision for, say, a new church building.[194] They have not learned the truth of the Kiswahili proverb, *haraka, haraka, haina baraka* (hurry, hurry, has no blessing). Too much hurry can destroy rather than build up. True leaders take the total context into account when setting the pace. If they are too far ahead of those they lead, they will become martyrs. While they must have dreams and a coherent vision, they must also take time to bring their congregation to accept these.

- *Arrogance.* The young can be intolerant and arrogant in expressing their opinions.[195] Many have not yet learned to listen to others and understand their points of view. Despite their lack of experience, they are sure they are right. They are the type of people described in the Kamba proverb, *mwiilungi nde iluu* (someone who does not allow others to examine him believes he has no faults). This arrogance can manifest itself in their understanding of the gospel and in relation to the policies of the local church or denomination.

- *Argumentativeness.* Some young people love to argue. They do not necessarily listen to the responses to their arguments, but simply keep on talking because they need to have the last word. Such people have not learned that actions are more effective than words. Nor do they recognize that everyone has some degree of knowledge, whether gained through formal education or experience. You may have an advanced degree in some specialized field, but someone else may know far more than you do about some aspect of life. Young people need to learn that if they listen to those who know more than they do in some areas, the others will be more prepared to listen to them when they speak about their area of expertise. All experienced teachers know that they can still learn a lot from their students.

- *Love of novelty.* It is easy for young people to dismiss something simply because it is old and to desire something simply because it is new. This attitude feeds into their tendency to undervalue the wealth of experience found in older people. For example, a young person may return from a ministry seminar with a brand new way of doing things and want to sweep away some traditions that have held churches together for years. Or they may challenge conventions about what type of clothes Christians wear, the type of music they listen to, the songs they sing, and the way they dance. It is easy to dismiss these conventions as old-fashioned, but it is worth thinking about the function they served. They helped to keep the church we inherited pure. We need to think about the implications of our choices for the kind of church others will inherit from us. Will our new ideas glorify God in our times?

Sadly, there are many stories in Africa about young people who have been instrumental in tearing churches apart following their "discovery" that salvation must be followed by speaking in tongues. Some students have even accused godly parents of not being Christians simply because they did not speak in tongues. Maturity says, "This is an idea that may be right, but let me investigate it carefully. Once I am convinced that it is right, I will try to introduce it into the church gradually, in an atmosphere of peace."

Advising someone to be patient is not the same as advising them to compromise the truths of the gospel – far from it. Paul has earlier called on Timothy to uphold the truth of the gospel, but the point at issue here is how he goes about doing this. He must show maturity and wisdom even as he refutes false doctrine. Ward reminds us that we should not overreact at the first sign of any heresy for "heresy is at times 10 percent theological error and 90 percent stubborn self-will. Intolerance of the person may merely confirm him in his stubbornness."[196]

We are not told whether Timothy actually suffered from any of these 'evil desires' or whether Paul is simply advising Timothy to continue on his present course, which involves fleeing from them.[197] Or Paul may simply be giving good advice based on his experience of life in general, which would suggest that these were temptations that might arise for a young man like Timothy.[198] This last option seems the most likely given the young man we have got to know through Paul's letters. He is someone who will overcome, but who still needs encouragement due to his age and the challenging nature of his ministry.[199]

Questions for Discussion

1. Have you ever observed an incident involving something that Paul might refer to as one of 'the evil desires of youth'? What happened, and how did it affect those involved? If the one at fault was a leader, how was his or her ministry or institution affected?
2. How should we respond to those we disagree with? What dangers do we need to avoid?
3. Have you ever been evaluated by a group? If so, how did you respond to the group's appreciation of you or your service to them? How did you take the group's points of criticism?

UNIT 8
2 TIMOTHY 2:17–21

HONOUR OR DISHONOUR?

In some schools in Africa, the best three students in each class are recognized at the end of each term. This recognition is done at an assembly with all parents present, and those honoured are very excited. But they also know that the work has just started – others will be working hard to compete for recognition the following term. At times, the excitement of working hard for this public approval is interesting to watch, especially in the lower classes where the young pupils have not learned to conceal how they feel.

All of us want to be noticed – but sometimes we are noticed for the wrong reasons. This is the case for the two men whom Paul refers to in this chapter. While thinking about Jesus Christ and Paul would inspire Timothy (2:8-10), the memory of these two men serves only as a warning about what to avoid.

Who Not to Imitate

The two people who are not to be role models for Timothy are *Hymenaeus and Philetus* (2:17a). Hymenaeus was mentioned in 1 Timothy 1:19–20 in association with someone called Alexander. There Paul called him a blasphemer and said that he had been delivered to Satan. In 2 Timothy, Hymenaeus is associated with Philetus, a man who is not mentioned anywhere else in the New Testament.

These two men were carriers of the deadly disease that Paul referred to as "gangrene". Changing the metaphor, Paul says that they have *departed from the truth* (2:18a).[200] The word translated "departed from" communicates the idea of "missing the mark" (see also 1 Timothy 1:6; 6:21).²⁰¹ The mark they missed is "the truth", that is, the apostolic gospel. Instead of maintaining it, they have wandered away from it.

At this point Paul gives us the clearest statement so far about the exact nature of the false teaching at Ephesus. Hymenaeus and Philetus were claiming *that the resurrection has already taken place* (2:18b). What does this claim mean, and why would they make it?

It seems likely that they were arguing that resurrection is only a spiritual and not a physical reality, and that spiritual resurrection takes place during this life. They may have been making this claim because they had misinterpreted Paul's teaching that baptism is a symbolic representation of the death and resurrection of believers (Rom 6:4; Col 2:12). They may have mistaken the symbol for the reality.²⁰²

Some think that the false teachers were linked to some organized set of beliefs such as Gnosticism, which despised the body and the material world.²⁰³ However, it seems unlikely that there was a full-blown gnostic system at the time Paul was writing. That would come later. The most that can be said is that the seeds of Gnosticism may have been present. A misunderstanding of Paul is sufficient to explain their claims.

It is possible that what was most offensive about these false teachers was not their wrong doctrine but their unwillingness to listen to Timothy's correction on the issue. (Admittedly, this needs to be weighed against the strong language Paul uses when speaking about them.)

The false teachers may also have been influenced by the beliefs of the Jewish Sadducees, who denied any possibility of resurrection. Or they may have been influenced by Greek, and especially Stoic, thinking. The Greeks believed that the human soul was an immortal spark that was reabsorbed into God at death, but they did believe in anything as physical as the resurrection of the body.²⁰⁴

Unfortunately, the effect of the false teaching was to *destroy the faith of some*. The present tense communicates a sense of this happening again and again as the false teachers make their position known.²⁰⁵ The word translated "destroy" could be better translated as "upset" (nasb, nrsv) or "overturn" (hcsb). Those affected may not actually have left the faith, but they have begun to doubt the Christian teaching about bodily resurrection, which is one of the most basic Christian beliefs (1 Cor 15:16–17). To deny bodily resurrection is not only wrong but also leads to other errors. Those who believe this may argue that Christians have already been made divine (possibly at baptism) and do not need the things of the material world. This asceticism easily slides into the idea that one can save oneself by self-denial. Alternatively, they may turn to libertinism, assuming that it no longer matters how they live because there is no future hope for which to keep themselves pure. Thus the false teaching created a climate in which there was a tendency towards wrong theological beliefs and carelessness in the way people conducted themselves.

There are certain issues on which Christians can agree to disagree, but there are others that are central to the Christian faith, and thus are not negotiable. One of these is the truth that Christ physically rose from the dead and that those who believe in him will also rise from the dead. This resurrection will be followed by judgment of the believers' lives. Denying this doctrine has a profound effect on our moral lives because it means that we are not going to be held accountable for how we have lived. Similarly, to deny that Jesus is God is also to deny that he can save us, and thus demolishes any possibility of salvation for anyone.

Paul instructed Timothy to keep away from those promoting false teaching, and we should do the same. We must be careful not to be drawn into doing anything that will help false teaching to spread and wreak havoc in the lives of believers.

What to Trust

The teaching of Hymenaeus and Philetus has destroyed the faith of some believers. But Paul's firm *Nevertheless* contrasts this unstable faith with the unshakeable foundation that God himself has laid (2:19a).[206] This foundation *stands firm* – its status is solid.[207]

But what is this foundation? Several possible answers have been suggested:[208]

- *The church at Ephesus.* Although some have had their faith upset, the main body in Ephesus, the unshakeable core of genuine Christians, will remain steadfast.[209]
- *The church universal.* Instead of focusing specifically on the Ephesian church, some think that Paul is thinking of the whole church of

which the Ephesian church is only a small part.²¹⁰ Paul may have been thinking of Jesus' words in Matthew 16:18: "I will build my church, and the gates of death will not overcome it." Even if everyone in Ephesus starts to follow the false teachings of Hymenaeus and Philetus, God's universal church will not be shaken. Some who support this view also point out that in 1 Corinthians 3:11 Christ is said to be the foundation of the whole church, and in Ephesians 2:20 the foundation is said to be the apostles and prophets. These verses are not contradictory but complementary. The teaching of the prophets and apostles centres on the person and work of Christ.

- *The Christian faith, that is, the truth of the gospel.* The gospel is an objective fact that remains true regardless of what anyone teaches or believes. No matter how often Hymenaeus, Philetus and others at Ephesus deny the future resurrection of believers, it will still take place.

These views about what constitutes the foundation are not mutually exclusive. The faithful believers at Ephesus are members of the universal church, and the universal church is rooted in the truth of the gospel. However, it seems that the focus of this verse is on the steadfastness of the church universal, including the faithful ones at Ephesus.

It is unlikely that the Scriptures are the foundation that Paul is talking of, for he speaks of foundation as being *sealed with this inscription,* and then proceeds to quote Scripture. The image that Paul is using here is of someone engraving something "on the foundation of a building in order to indicate ownership and sometimes the function of the building" (see also 2 Cor 1:22; Eph 1:13),²¹¹ It is the ancient equivalent of a company mounting its logo on its corporate headquarters to indicate that it owns the building.

The inscription on the foundation of the church takes the form of two statements: "The Lord knows those who are his" and "Everyone who confesses the name of the Lord must turn away from wickedness" (2:19).

The Lord knows those who are his

The statement *the Lord knows those who are his* comes from Numbers 16:5.²¹² The context was the rebellion of Korah, Dathan, Abiram, On and 250 other leaders against Moses and Aaron. In the Septuagint (the Greek translation of the Old Testament that the Ephesians would have known) Moses' response to the rebels is, "God has visited and known those that are his".[213] Applying this to Timothy's situation, Paul is saying that God knows who the true believers are. He not only knows their identity but also "knows them in the intimacy of fellowship."[214] The faithful are both secure in God's hands and in their relationship with him as a friend.

These words are both an encouragement to Timothy and a warning and challenge to the false teachers. God has created everyone, but when it comes to redemption, some people are the Lord's and others are not. Timothy is the Lord's, and he should continue with confidence on the right course he is already taking. But those who have embraced the false teachings need to take notice that being in error is a sign that they do not belong to God.

Turn away from wickedness

The second statement is that *everyone who confesses the name of the Lord must turn away from wickedness*. Mounce describes this as "one of the most strongly worded demands in Scripture that obedience to the ethical demands of the gospel is mandatory, not optional".[215]

The words are not a quotation from any one Old Testament passage but draw on Leviticus 24:16, Numbers 16:26, Joshua 23:7 and Isaiah 26:13, 52:11. "Confessing the name of the Lord" is equivalent to claiming that one is a believer. And those who are believers have no choice but to take a route that keeps them away from wickedness. In Ephesus, this means that they need to keep away from the teaching of people like Hymenaeus and Philetus, whose wickedness is probably not only false teaching about the resurrection but also immoral practices that arise because of this denial.

The command to turn away from sin also provides a way to identify true believers. But Barclay's words are worth noting:

> The church consists of those who have departed from unrighteousness. That is not to say that it consists of perfect people. If that were so, there would be no church. It has been said that the great interest of God is not so much in where

a man has reached, as in the direction in which he is facing. And the church consists of those whose faces are turned to righteousness. They may often fail and the goal may sometimes seem distressingly far away, but their faces are ever set in the right direction.[216]

God is the one who examines hearts and motives. He knows the damage Timothy's opponents have caused, and he knows the hearts of Timothy and others who are faithful. Instead of being discouraged, Timothy is to take comfort in God's knowledge and stay faithfully on course. God is in charge. He can be trusted upon to "discriminate between his loyal and disloyal servants."[217]

These are very comforting words when so much seems to be going wrong in the church. We have lowered our standards to avoid offending those with particular interests. Even the most corrupt are not rebuked because we fear losing the money they contribute. There are many other examples of error we could mention. But despite these discouraging circumstances, we can find assurance in the knowledge of the Lord, who sees and knows those who belong to him. Many may pretend to love God, but he examines each life and determines whether we pass or fail his test.

God's Grading System

Paul has just discussed the fact that some people's faith has been overturned but that God's foundation is unshakeable. However, some people may be asking why things have gone wrong in Ephesus. How do the events there relate to God's perfect knowledge of those who belong to him?

Anticipating their questions, Paul uses "a simple illustration to account for the presence of false teachers in the church."[218] He points out that *in a large house there are articles not only of gold and silver, but also of wood and clay; some are for noble purposes and some for disposal of refuse*. The nasb translation is closer to the original Greek when it says that some of the vessels are for honour and some for dishonour.[219] These are the two contrasting grades that God as the examiner can assign. Some will receive honour and others dishonour.

The honoured category contains the vessels made of "gold and silver", and presumably includes Timothy and others who are faithful to the apostolic teaching. The dishonoured vessels are made of "wood and clay". This category probably includes Hymenaeus, Philetus and those who are unfaithful to the apostolic teaching.

But, someone will argue, a house needs both articles of gold and silver and articles made from wood and clay. This is true. But what is important here is that some articles are of greater value and usefulness to the owner than others (see also Rom 9:21).

The logical conclusion then is that Hymenaeus, Philetus and those like them are of some use to God. If so, what type of use? Ward suggests that "even those with heretical views can be used by God to throw into high relief the true believers whose views are sound (compare 1 Cor 11:19)."[220] However, this does not seem to be the point that Paul is trying to make here.

It seems that Paul wants to show that there are different categories of people within the church. Some are people of solid faith ("gold and silver") while the faith of others is shaky ("wood and clay"). If Hymenaeus and Philetus are actually unbelievers (as opposed to merely erring believers) they do not belong anywhere in the house.

The principle laid out above can be extended to imply that there may well be unbelievers in the church. This second level of interpretation is in alignment with Jesus' parables about the weeds growing among the wheat (Matt 13:24–30, 36–43) and the net containing edible and inedible fish (Matt 13:47–50). With this interpretation, Hymenaeus and Philetus may clearly be unbelievers.

The illustration thus makes two distinct points. The first is that Christians are at different levels of faith and that this corresponds with how God uses them – a thought comparable to Romans 9:21. Secondly, the church body has weeds growing among the wheat. Timothy and the faithful belong in the category of honour and are wheat. On the other hand, Hymenaeus and Philetus belong in the category of dishonour (a miserable fate). They are weeds.[221]

On the Honour Roll

In 2:21, Paul specifies what constitutes a good mark from the divine examiner: *Those who cleanse themselves from the latter will be instruments for noble purposes, made holy, useful to the Master and prepared to do any good work*. The path that results in honour is the path of cleansing oneself. However, the opening clause is actually an 'if' clause in the Greek, indicating that each individual has to choose to follow this path.[222]

What are believers to cleanse themselves from? The "from the latter" in the tniv suggests that it is from the ignoble purposes mentioned in the previous sentence. But Paul simply says "from these" (nkjv), leaving the content undefined. Within the context, it is safe to see "these" as the false teachings.[223] Paul was addressing the current situation in Ephesus and inviting all who heard his letter to respond by cleansing themselves from the false teachings.[224]

Those who do will be "made holy" (or "sanctified", nasb) and "prepared" by God.[225] By purifying themselves they invite God to set them apart (sanctify them) for his use. He will give them all they need to do the task that he, "the Master", assigns. The term *despotes*, translated Master, is the one from which we get the English word "despot". However, our Master is no cruel despot but is the one who owns and controls all lives and the plan of redemption. It is an honour to be useful to him.

The quality needed to receive a passing grade from God is honour – not honour in the sense that one receives privileges, but that one is entrusted with more service.[226] Honour is achieved by combining human responsibility (cleansing oneself) with divine activity (sanctification and preparedness).

Many grading systems use four passing levels: A, B, C and D. The effort students put into a course determines the grade they receive. But human examiners can make mistakes or be influenced by other factors that cause them to give grades that are better or worse than a student deserves. But when God is the examiner, there is no possibility of error. He is all-knowing and righteous. The challenge falls on us to work hard to receive "higher grades" from God when he examines how we live our lives in relation to him and our fellow human beings.

Questions for Discussion

1. Can you identify some groups in our day who you believe are teaching error, rather than truth? What is the effect of their error?
2. The introduction to this unit spoke about students receiving public recognition for their achievements. What will it be like when God gives a public praise in the great assembly in heaven? What will it feel like?
3. How much should we strive for God's praise? How should we go about earning it?

UNIT 9
2 TIMOTHY 2:23–26

THE MARKS OF A GOOD LEADER

On 18 March 2009 the National Council of Churches of Kenya issued a statement that said, "the impression and expression of most Kenyans is that they have a moribund president and an ineffective prime minister".[227] The president was considered moribund because he kept quiet and did not address the nation even during times of crisis. The prime minister was viewed as ineffective because "he complains about those he supervises instead of streamlining them". Regardless of whether all Kenyans agree with this evaluation, it communicates that leaders are always under the scrutiny of those being led. Good qualities earn them commendation while negative characteristics expose them to criticism. Some of these qualities are found in leaders' personal lives while others relate to how they carry out their duties.

Because our personal and professional lives overlap, it can be difficult to separate the qualities that should characterize someone's personal life from those that should characterize their work life. Nevertheless, it can be useful to focus on the qualities that are specifically required of a minister, and that is what Paul does here.

Not Quarrelsome

Paul tells Timothy, *Don't have anything to do with foolish and stupid arguments* (2:23).[228] He repeats this point again and again in these letters in order to stress the uselessness of "arguments" or "speculations" (nasb) about controversial questions that make no positive contribution to the cause of the kingdom of God (see 1 Tim 1:4, 7; 4:7; 6:4, 20; 2 Tim 2:23; Titus 3:9). Here, he describes the arguments as "foolish" and "stupid" ("ignorant", nasb). They are stupid in that they lead nowhere, and ignorant because those arguing are uninformed. Someone who is "ignorant" is someone who has not learned how to think[229] – and this is true of the false teachers.

Paul's reason for this instruction is that foolish arguments *produce quarrels* (2:23). Such arguments are not driven by a search for truth. All that happens is that each participant constantly reasserts his or her point without listening to anything that the other party has to say. When such debates break out in the church, they destroy fellowship and any expressions of genuine Christian unity. The result is that "uninformed men rejoice in a verbal victory and angels weep at the damage done to the witness of the church."[230]

Few of us know how to respond to the hurt feelings generated by such quarrels. It is certainly wise to refuse to get involved in them. The word translated "don't have anything to do with" is used elsewhere in these letters when people are to be avoided (Titus 3:10), or when the church is to have no official association with some people (1 Tim 5:11). When the word is used with reference to false teaching, as here and in 1 Timothy 4:7, it means avoiding doing anything that will promote such teaching.

This attitude to arguments reflects the requirement that *the Lord's servant must not be quarrelsome* (2:24a). Literally, this could be translated "a slave of the Lord ought not to fight". A slave or servant of the Lord not only serves the Lord but also belongs to him.[231] As such, he must be under the Lord's full control and, therefore, must be like the Lord himself.

But, some may argue, here Timothy is told not to fight, whereas in 1 Timothy 6:12 he was told to "fight the good fight" and in 2:3 he was told to be "a good soldier of Christ Jesus". How can he be a good soldier and not fight? The answer is that Timothy is to fight evil, not people. His enemies (and those of every Christian) are "spiritual powers of evil and not his brothers in the family of Christ."[232]

Because the particular fight that Paul has been talking about in this chapter involves words and arguments, the tniv's translation as "quarrelsome" is in order. Leaders who get involved in quarrels that do not promote the kingdom of God have lost their sensitivity to the will of the master who owns them.

Kind to Everyone

Paul's instruction that the Lord's servant should be *kind to everyone* (2:24b) is a positive statement compared to the negative instruction above. That is why he introduces it with *But*. The "everyone" includes not only Timothy's supporters at Ephesus, but also those who oppose him. The Lord's servant is to be like his master in showing love even to his enemies (Matt 5:43–48).

This attitude contrasts with the belief that the harsher the words, the more effective they are. Harshness drives people away, while kindness draws those who have wandered away back towards the right course. And this must be Timothy's aim, for what is important is not his opponents' attitude to him as a person but their attitude to what he stands for, namely, the truth of the gospel.

When a Christian leader has to rebuke someone, this must be done "with the gentleness which never seeks to hurt."[233] It takes a lot of skill to do this. One must choose words that are effective but also permeated with Christ-like love if the person is not to feel rejected and unloved.

This same principle applies to all who have to correct others, whether it is parents raising children or pastors caring for believers.

Able to Teach

This ability *to teach* (2:24c) was also mentioned as one of the requirements for elders (1 Tim 3:2). Teaching ability is not just a skill that can be learned, it is also a matter of character. Good teachers should be like magnets, drawing people towards the gospel they preach. They cannot do this if people are put off by their characters.

No matter how well trained teachers are, if they cannot make disciples they are not actually teaching but merely talking. The same is true of a pastor whose message is rejected by those who hear him because of the pastor's character. Christian ministry is not only an activity but also, and primarily, an example of Christ-like living.

Not Resentful

Only those who are consciously striving to be like Christ can succeed in "bearing evil without resentment",[234] or as the nasb puts it, being *patient when wronged* (2:24). Our natural tendency is to get upset and respond harshly when we are wronged, but Timothy is to be forbearing even in such circumstances.

Barclay puts it well when he says that any Christian leader worthy to be called a slave of Christ, "must be able to accept insult and injury, slights and humiliations, as Jesus accepted them".[235] Ward makes a similar point: "Even when the teacher makes a kindly approach, he may meet with no response and no answering warmth. On the contrary his hearers may be surly, rude and critical. When this happens he has to be forbearing. This means that he puts up with the wrongs done to him and the pain occasioned and does so without resentment".[236]

This is another test that leaves many of us wanting. We are called to self-sacrifice for the sake of effectiveness in ministry. The principle is the same as the one Jesus laid down for his followers when he said, "If anyone slaps you on the right cheek, turn to them the other cheek also" (Matt 5:39). This may seem like stupidity, but its goal is to win the souls of men and women to Christ rather than responding to them on the same level as they are responding to us.

Gently Instructing Opponents

Paul describes those who oppose him[237] as being held captive by the devil to do his will (2:26). However, captives can be freed and there is hope for them, but that hope is directly tied to how Timothy carries out his ministry. Many who are in error, theologically or morally, are blinded by Satan. They need someone who can lovingly open their eyes, enabling them to see their error and walk rightly before God.

Timothy's gentle correction of the false teaching will begin a chain of events that will lead to his opponent's escape from the snare of the devil. It is worth looking at each of the links in the chain separately.

The starting point

The false teachers' status is that they have been trapped by the devil *who has taken them captive to do his will* (2:26).[238] The words stress that they are prisoners who are being kept alive by their captor for reasons of his own.[239] While their state is a fulfilment of what is predicted in 1 Timothy 4:1, they are responsible for their actions and must be helped to change their ways.

The tniv unequivocally suggests that the devil is one who has captured them and whom they now serve. However, the original is a little more ambiguous. There is no doubt that the devil set the trap, but who is the one holding them captive whom they now serve?[240] Is it the devil (2:26b) or the Lord's servant (2:24a) or God (2:25b)? Any of these possibilities could be true. Satan does hold some people as captives. Christian workers can hold those who believe captive to the word of God.[241] God may hold believers captive to his will until they choose to do it, as happened to Jonah in the Old Testament. However, in this context, the most natural interpretation of the phrase is that the devil is doing the holding. There is a sense in which this condition overlaps with demon-possession, although usually demon-possession is far broader in its effects and includes a state of mental imbalance. What we have here are people whose minds are working well, but who continually make ungodly choices. Satan has full control over their wills.

Gentle correction

Timothy's duty is to make sure that the false teachers are *gently instructed* or corrected (2:25a). The Greek word translated "gently" has a slightly richer meaning than the word translated as "kind" earlier in this passage (2:24).[242] It combines gentleness with humility or meekness.[243] It communicates the idea of "restrained strength", as found in the "strong arms of the father, which do not crush the little child".[244] The same word is used to describe one of the fruits of the Spirit in Galatians 5:23. It is the attitude of Christ, who was himself gentle (Matt 11:29).

The verb translated "instructed" can mean either "to instruct or educate" (tniv, hcsb) or "to discipline, chastise or correct" (nasb, nrsv, nkjv). While both notions can fit this context, it seems that here Paul is focusing on the constructive re-education of those who are misguided.[245] When discipline is required, Timothy must do it with gentleness; "his hand like the hand of a surgeon, unerring to find the diseased spot, yet never for a moment causing unnecessary pain."

God's act

Timothy may doubt his ability to change his opponents' views or may be tempted "to batter them, into submission to the truth."[246] So Paul gently reminds him ultimately it is God who changes people's hearts. Timothy's task is simply to speak lovingly *in the hope that God will grant them repentance* (2:25b). God is sovereign and controls the outcome. There is no guarantee that God will grant repentance.[247] What Paul is saying is that "God will grant repentance totally dependant upon his will, which neither you nor I can predict, though we wish he would grant it to everyone to whom we minister."

The word translated "repentance" is used of changing one's mind. In this case, it involves someone changing their mind about what is true or false. Timothy's opponents were currently committed to false teaching, but his prayer must be that they will change their minds about it, and come to *a knowledge of the truth*".[248] The words "of the truth" focus on and specify the content of knowledge – truth.[249] In these letters, "truth" is a synonym for the apostolic gospel.

The false teachers claimed to have knowledge (1 Tim 6:20), but they did not have knowledge of truth; what they had was knowledge of errors. (The possibility of different kinds of knowledge may explain why the tniv has the indefinite article "a" before the word "knowledge".)

Barrett suggests that the constant references to knowledge in these letters (1 Tim 2:4; 2 Tim 3:7; Titus 1:1) have "an anti-Gnostic ring". Paul is making the point that "There are men who profess to have knowledge (gnosis) of the truth; it is to be hoped that they repent and so gain real knowledge (epi-gnosis)."[250] In summary, we have a statement that labels everything contrary to the apostolic teaching as "not true knowledge". In the time of Timothy, the knowledge may have been a philosophical system (though not full-blown Gnosticism). Today the philosophical system may be different, but the principle remains the same. Those who want true knowledge should turn to the apostolic teachings recorded in the Scriptures. The teachings of the apostles and prophets contain the foundational truths on which we must build (Eph 2:20). Anything that is contrary to them is not true.

While the word "truth" may be used here primarily to describe the content of the message, this truth goes beyond the mind and touches the heart. It moves "beyond theoretical knowledge to fullness of knowledge gained by experience (cf. 1 Tim 2:4)".[251] In the same way, repentance involves more than just a change of mind; there must also be a change of attitude and behaviour (see Acts 20:21; 26:20; Heb 6:1). Doctrine and practice go hand in hand. The question is whether this point is fully recognized in the curricula in our theological institutions. Are they designed to address both the students' knowledge and their characters?

The end point

When Timothy has done his work well and in the right spirit, and God is pleased to grant repentance, the former opponents of the gospel gain a new status. They begin to enjoy knowledge of the truth as they *come to their senses and escape from the trap of the devil* (2:26).[252]

Paul's reference to being in a trap makes us think of animals in a zoo or birds in a cage. The animal can pace to and fro, and the bird can fly from one end of its cage to the other. But whichever way they turn, they encounter bars. There is no way out. We could call animals in such situations slaves of human beings. Timothy's opponents are in the same position, except that they have been trapped by the devil. No matter which way they turn, they cannot escape his trap that he has laid "for the feet of the unwary",[253] hoping to catch the spiritually careless.

The verb translated "will come to their senses" literally means "to sober up" or come to one's senses after drinking. It implies that the people who are trapped are drunk. This image suggests that "the perception of the teachers has been dulled and confused – they cannot sort out the evidence properly. Their conscience has become insensitive – they do not realize what they are doing. Their wills have no power – they did not and do not resist the allurements of falsity."[254]

When Timothy's ministry is coupled with God's granting of repentance, his opponents gain clear minds and can at last escape from their captivity. They will no longer be enslaved to the devil.

When Paul spoke of the devil's trap (or snare) in 1 Timothy 3:7, he saw it as something the devil would use to bring the church and its message into disrepute. Here, the devil seems to be using the trap to stop us from enjoying the Lord's spiritual blessings (although Paul does not say so in so many words). He traps us into accepting wrong thinking about God's good plan for our lives, and so manages to keep us spiritual dwarfs. (For example, he encouraged the teachings of Hymenaeus and Philetus that the resurrection had already happened.)

A change of mind about wrong beliefs accompanied by a change of attitude towards what is right brings freedom from the devil's trap. Our freedom provides an opportunity for us to enjoy God's spiritual blessings in all their fullness. This was what Paul wanted for all believers, even those who opposed Timothy in Ephesus. Timothy's gentle re-education was crucial to achieving it.

In saying that God gives the gift of repentance, Paul is not denying that we have the ability to choose good or evil. We could theoretically use that ability to get us out of the trap. But there is a point where the will is so weakened by the tricks of the devil that it will not choose what is right without God's miraculous intervention. The devil loves it when we are so securely trapped.

Each of us may be lured into a different trap. Some of us are trapped by theological doubts about fundamental matters of the gospel, such as whether Jesus Christ is the only way to God and whether there is a life after death. Others of us may be trapped by moral lapses, such as sexual immorality, bribery and alcoholism. Living as Satan's slaves year after year, just like the animals in the zoo, is not the best kind of life. May God give us the power and courage to step out of the cage and proceed on our journey to see Jesus as he is (1 John 3:2).

The message of the gospel is God's key to people's release. Those of us entrusted by God to minister his word must take this responsibility very seriously. Our faithfulness or lack of it determines the freedom or slavery of many.

Questions for Discussion

1. What traps could the devil be laying for you? What can you do to avoid them?
2. How do we accept that God is at work in our lives to change us without abdicating our responsibility to make the change happen?
3. How do we combine kindness and the need to rebuke? Are they mutually exclusive? If not, how do we balance them?

UNIT 10
2 TIMOTHY 3:1–5a

CHARACTERISTICS OF THE LAST DAYS

Murder, rape, armed robberies, family feuds! Every day the African media report terrible incidents. You probably know of some that have happened near you. I scanned a local newspaper for a month and found reports of the murder of a 13-year-old girl, the rape of two sisters during a robbery, a pastor assaulting another man, the murder of night watchmen, a toddler raped by his stepfather, a son assaulting his father, and so on.

You will often hear an older African man or woman say, "Things were never like this in the past!" If one walked at night, one used to fear only wild animals. These days, one has to fear people who will rob and kill at the slightest provocation. Helpless victims of accidents can now expect that they will also be victims of thieves. The rich no longer help the poor, but seek only to line their own pockets. We read daily of civil wars, border fights, tribal clashes, *coups d'état*, and the like. How should we be living in such times? How should a pastor be ministering in such times?

These are the questions Paul sets out to answer in this chapter of his letter to Timothy. But first he sketches what things will be like in the days ahead.

The Challenge Ahead

Paul has told Timothy what is expected of him as a workman approved by God. But Timothy must not think he is going to have an easy time carrying out these instructions. Paul tells him of the challenges he will face, underlining the importance of what he has to say by introducing it with the solemn phrase *But mark this* (3:1a). The Greek verb translated as "mark" could also be translated as "know" (see hcsb), and also contains an aspect of "understanding" or "realizing" (see nrsv and nasb). Because it is in the present tense, we know that Timothy needs to continually keep everything Paul is about to tell him in mind.

These challenges relate to what Timothy can expect to happen and how men and women will behave during the last days.

Characteristics of the Last Days

Both Jews and Christians divide history into the present age and the age to come. *The last days* (3:1b) are the final days of the present age. Jews believe this age will end with the Day of the Lord, when the Messiah will come. Christians believe that the Messiah has already come and that the present age will end when Jesus Christ comes for a second time to usher in his kingdom. Thus when Paul and the other New Testament writers speak of "the last days" (or "later times" or "the last times" (Acts 2:17; 1 Tim 4:1; Jas 5:3; 2 Pet 3:3; Jude 18), they are speaking about the period preceding the second coming of Christ. The last days began with Jesus' ascension and the coming of the Holy Spirit (Acts 2), and they continue until Jesus comes again. They are the last days because there is no other major event in God's plan of redemption between the two comings.

These days will include *terrible times* (3:1b).[255] The word translated as "terrible" is used to describe something that is both violent and dangerous. (For example, it is used to describe the violent demon-possessed men of Gadara – Matt 8:28.) These terrible happenings do not just lie in the future. Paul's words to Timothy in the rest of this letter show that the situation is already violent and dangerous.

In Ephesus, Timothy can expect violent opposition to the very existence of the Christian church and all it stands for. Some of the attacks may be physical, but others will be spiritual as people are swept away by false teachings and wicked behaviour.

Of course, it is not the "days" themselves that are dangerous, but the behaviour of the people living in those days. So Paul gives Timothy some idea of what to expect of men and women.

Characteristics of People in the Last Days

The people who make the last days violent and dangerous have some unpleasant characteristics. Paul lists eighteen vices that characterize the times (3:2–5). These vices can be grouped into four overlapping categories: a love of the wrong things, mistreatment of others, ungodly attitudes and uncontrolled behaviour. One final characteristic describes people who appear to be godly, but are not so in reality. It is worth noting these vices because when we are surrounded by such people, we may come to accept their values. None of them should be present in the lives of believers.

Loving the wrong things

Jesus stated that the first commandment was that we should love God, and the second was that we should love other people (Matt 22:37–39). But in the last days, people will love the wrong things.[256] Love for God will be replaced by a love of self, money and pleasure, and by a hatred for the good. All the other vices that Paul lists here stem from this failure to love the Lord. It affects both our relationship with God and our relationships with others.

Loving themselves

When people do not love God, they become *lovers of themselves* (3:2a). The result is that "divine and human relationships are destroyed, and obedience to God and charity to other people both become impossible."[257] These people put themselves on the throne of their lives and thus deny the very essence of Christianity, which is dying to oneself. They decide that they will make their own rules, and become so "intent on their own interests that they are often reluctant to listen to the minister."[258] Such people would make life very difficult for Timothy.

Lovers of self are still common today. We see this attitude in the lazy clerks who refuse to perform simple tasks, like finding a file, regardless of how much trouble and distress it causes the person needing access to the file. Poor and elderly pensioners may have travel long distances to a government office ten times before they are helped – unless they offer a bribe. Those who should be serving them put their own comfort and concerns ahead of those of everyone else.

Loving money

Like the clerks mentioned above, many people redirect the love that should be given to God and his people towards money. Paul warned Timothy about this in 1 Timothy 6:9–10 saying, "the love of money is a root of all kinds of evil". Those who are *lovers of money* (3:2b) assume that money can do anything and become proud in their attitude to God and other people. They think that their wealth brings them security and see no need for salvation or for growing in the knowledge of God.

The Ephesians were vulnerable to this temptation because Ephesus was a great trading centre. But the problem is no less acute in Africa. We see the same love of money when business owners in Ethiopia and Kenya hoard food so that prices will rise, or redirect food to more profitable markets, regardless of the hardship this causes ordinary people.

This is not to say that Christians cannot be involved in trade and cannot make money. But it does mean that we need to have a healthy attitude towards money. We should not try to become rich in ways that are displeasing to God. To give two other examples, we should not keep the extra money if someone overpays us or engage in dishonest business practices. If our hard work does result in us becoming rich, we need to remember that all that we have comes from God, and that we must still serve him.

Loving pleasure more than God

When it comes down to it, many *are lovers of pleasure rather than lovers of God* (3:4d). In other words, they prefer pleasure to God. Here Paul may be using the figure of speech called meiosis or understatement. If so, what he means is that "they always please themselves and do not love God at all".[259]

It is not that pleasure in itself is wrong. We can find pleasure in many areas of life, including our work and social relationships. But when we have to make a decision, the deciding factor should not be what we will enjoy most (even if it is wrong) but what will bring honour to God.

Hating the good

God is the ultimate good, and he has told us what goodness is in his commands and through our human consciences. Every part of the way of life he wants us to follow is good. But some people are *not lovers of the good* (3:3e), and instead hate everything about a godly way of life. They prefer evil, and revel in its false joys. Such people enjoy deceiving and abusing others and terrorizing society. Their eyes are completely blinded by Satan.

Mistreating others

Human relationships are damaged when love for God is replaced with a love of self, money or pleasure. Those who no longer love God become abusive, disobedient, slanderous and treacherous towards others.

Abusing others

The word translated *abusive* (3:2d) can also be translated as "blasphemers", as in the kjv. However, here Paul is speaking mainly of human relationships, not about blasphemy against God. He is referring to self-loving and arrogant people who speak evil of others and cause them harm (see 1 Tim 1:13). Their words destroy relationships and pose a threat to Christian unity and to the church.

The abuse referred to here is more than just words spoken in haste and immediately regretted: "The insult which comes from anger is bad but it is forgivable, for it is launched in the heat of the moment, but the cold insult which comes from arrogant pride is an ugly and an unforgivable thing."[260]

Christians are called to speak words of blessing. Yet, as James says, the tongue is very difficult to control (Jas 3:1–12). We need to be careful to think before we speak so that our words contribute to the kingdom of God and bless those who hear them.

Disobeying parents[261]

Kelly, who defines the "abusive" behaviour above as "unnatural conduct in relation to other people", describes being *disobedient to parents* (3:2e) as "unnatural conduct in relation to one's own family".[262] Duty to one's parents was very important in the ancient world and is still highly valued in many parts of Africa today (although this value is fading in some areas). Many cultures believe that disobedience automatically brings a curse on the disobedient child. Paul, too, considers it a sin when "youth loses all respect for age and fails to recognize the unpayable debt and the basic duty it owes to those who gave it life."[263] Christians who disobey their parents harm the reputation of the Christian faith, which teaches obedience to parents (Eph 6:1).

However, Christians also need to remember that obedience does not necessarily involve agreeing with everything our parents say or do. Obedience is a matter of our attitude to them. It requires us to recognize their role in our lives and show them the honour and respect they are due.

Many parents today complain that their children do not listen to them. While it is true that such disobedience is to be expected in the last days, this is no excuse for giving up the attempt to communicate with them. We need to work to find ways to communicate with our children. When children feel that they are respected and loved, they will be more open to hearing the advice of their parents. They will not feel that obedience entails losing their sense of their own identity.

Slandering others

The word translated as *slanderous* in 3:3c is *diaboloi*. It is closely related to the word translated as "devil" (for example, in 1 Tim 3:6). The devil is the one who slanders or accuses us before God, but the person Paul is talking about here is someone who slanders or accuses other people (see also 1 Tim 3:11). Slander is rooted in malice and its motive is the destruction of another person. It represents the complete opposite of Jesus' command to love one another (John 13:34) and is one of the cruellest sins. If a person's property is destroyed, it can be replaced. However, if someone's good name is taken away, "irreparable damage has been done."[264] The damage is irreparable because while "it is one thing to start an evil and untrue report on its malicious way; it is entirely another thing to stop it."[265]

It is characteristic of these last days that men and women are happy to destroy people with slander. We see this being done in the context of politics, business and the church, and even within broken families.

Betraying others

Those who are *treacherous* (3:4a) are more than just unfaithful friends. They are people who have an unforgiving spirit and seek revenge for some perceived offence, humiliation or defeat. They want to pay the person back by harming them. The same Greek word can also be translated "traitor" or "betrayer".[266] It is used to describe Judas in Luke 6:16 and the Jews in Acts 7:52.

Ungodly attitudes

People who have no love for God and who treat others badly also have bad attitudes.

Boastful and Proud

The attitudes of being *boastful* and *proud* (3:2c) are closely related, but they are not identical. Both characterize someone who is arrogant and Paul uses them both to describe the people God has given over to a depraved mind (Rom 1:30).

The difference between them is in how they manifest themselves. Those who are boastful reveal their inner pride in their "words, gestures, and outward behaviour".[267] They make no attempt to hide it. Pride, on the other hand, is hidden in the heart, in the form of an inner arrogance.

Both boastfulness and pride spring from self-centredness and show themselves in relationships. However, it is possible for someone to keep their pride a secret. "The arrogant person might even seem to be humble; but deep down there is contempt for everyone else."[268] But God knows everything hidden in our hearts, and he judges both the boastful and the proud.

Ungrateful

It is probably no accident that in Paul's list the vice of being *ungrateful* (3:2f) immediately follows disobedience to parents. After all, one of the worst forms of ingratitude "is that which repudiates the claim of parents to respect and obedience."[269] Shakespeare was well aware of this when he had King Lear lament, "How sharper than a serpent's tooth it is to have a thankless child!" People who are ungrateful are self-centred and think that they are only getting what they deserve. They refuse to acknowledge that we all owe what we have attained to God and to others, and that we should acknowledge this debt by expressing our gratitude for what we have been given.

In Africa, where there is no form of social welfare, many parents invest much of their money in educating a son or daughter. Rather than saving their money in a bank, they pay high school fees to ensure that their child can have a bright future. For such a child to turn his back on his aged parents and refuse to support them is a sign of rank ingratitude. But we sometimes forget that the same principle applies when it comes to acknowledging our heavenly Father, who has given us the ability to achieve whatever wealth, education and status we now enjoy.

Unholy

The word translated *unholy* (3:2g) denotes an attitude that dismisses spiritual matters as unimportant (see also 1 Tim 1:9). People who have this attitude casually disobey God's written laws and also violate the unwritten laws regarding the decencies of life that are written on the human conscience. They care about nothing besides themselves and their desires. Barclay puts it like this: "People who are ruled by their passions will gratify them in the most shameless ways. Those who have exhausted the normal pleasures of life and are still unsatisfied will seek their thrills in any new pleasures which are on offer."[270]

In Paul and Timothy's context, the unwritten laws would have included the requirement to bury the dead and the prohibition against marrying a sister or mother. In Africa today we can add "respect for the dead" to the list of unwritten laws. This law is violated when people rush to the scene of an accident not to rescue anyone but to steal from the badly injured or dead. Such a violation of human decency is totally at odds with African traditional practice and the Scriptures.

Without love

Someone who is *without love* (3:3a; see also Rom 1:31) is lacking natural affection. They do not know the love which is rooted in the family bonds linking a child to its parent or the parent to their child.[271] Nor do they have any concern for others in their community. We could even substitute the word "inhuman" for "without love". When people's closest social ties mean nothing to them, times are indeed terrible. Yet such lives will proliferate in the last days.

Unforgiving

People who are *unforgiving* (3:3b) may be so bitter that they are unwilling to come to terms with someone with whom they have quarrelled. The Greek word also allows for the possibility that they are dishonourable people who break agreements they have made, but the idea of a lack of forgiveness seems more prominent.[272] They demonstrate "a certain harshness of mind which separates people from their neighbours in unrelenting bitterness."[273] They are unwilling or unable to be "reconciled to a fellow human being."[274]

It is almost impossible for any of us to please everyone all the time. The same act that pleases one person offends another. Because of this, forgiveness is an essential element in human relations. An unforgiving attitude strikes at the root of fellowship because people are on edge or stay aloof when a person who cannot forgive is around. Harmony does not last long with an unforgiving person in the group.

Conceited

Some people in the last days are *conceited* (3:4c; see also 1 Tim 3:6; 6:4).[275] In other words, they are "inflated with a sense of their self-importance"[276] This vice is often accompanied by "hasty and headstrong action".[277] Conceited people tend not to listen to advice or to apologize when they hurt others. They consider themselves to be "Mr. or Mrs. Right" and assume that all others are in the wrong.

Uncontrolled behaviour

As people move further away from God and separate themselves from good, they begin to engage in increasingly destructive behaviours. Such behaviours will become more and more prominent in the last days.

Without self-control

People who are *without self-control* (3:3d) have no ability to reign in their tempers and no limits to their passions.[278] They strike out at anyone who disagrees with them or annoys them in any way. They respond to any desire that their sinful nature arouses. Their behaviour gradually destroys their relationships, and eventually their own bodies as they sink further and further into evil.

These people are not deliberately rebellious.[279] In fact, they would like to do what is right, but they cannot resist temptation.[280] They are weak and easily led, and lack spiritual and moral backbone. Instead of controlling their desires, they are enslaved by them.

Brutal

The Greek word for *brutal* (3:3e) can also mean "untamed".[281] It refers to the brutality of animals, for example, when a lion tears a gazelle to pieces. It communicates "a savagery which has neither sensitivity nor sympathy".[282] People of the last days are characterized by tearing each other to pieces.

We see plenty of evidence of brutality in our day. What else can explain the behaviour of those who set fire to buildings in which innocent women and children have taken shelter? Or who steal goods and then wantonly kill those whom they have robbed? Or massacre people from certain groups? The brutality of such heinous crimes exceeds that of any wild animal, which has no conscience.

Rash

The word *rash* (3:4b) means "reckless" and "thoughtless".[283] Those who are rash are so mastered by passions and impulses that they are "totally unable to think sensibly".[284] They will stop at nothing to gain their ends,[285] and throw "caution to the winds, no matter what disaster or punishment such an attitude may bring upon fellow citizens".[286] We see an example of this type of behaviour in Acts 19:28–36, where the city clerk at Ephesus warns a furious mob that they should "not do anything rash" that would get them into trouble.

The word "reckless" is often used today to describe dangerous driving that risks the lives of pedestrians and other motorists. Reckless speech can also do great harm. We should always stop and think before plunging into action.

Empty religiosity

Paul's final statement is that people in the last days are guilty of *having a form of godliness but denying its power* (3:5a). This can be treated as a concluding remark or final vice. It is considered a separate vice in this commentary, making Paul's list a total of nineteen vices.

Religion has two components: its outward form and its internal power. The outward form can be hypocritically assumed and can persist without the power, or remain after the power is lost.[287] All that is left is an outward shell. This is the state of the people Paul is writing about here. They parade their "Christianity", preaching and teaching what they conceive to be true faith. However, their way of life demonstrates that they know nothing about the regenerative, transforming power of Christianity that is rooted in Christ and follows the apostolic teaching.[288] If there was power in their teaching, the vices would not be part of their lives. Genuine faith produces godliness, and godliness confirms the existence of genuine faith.

In Romans 1:16, Paul referred to the gospel as the "power of God for the salvation of everyone who believes". This salvation includes both justification and sanctification, for the gospel both brings us to Christ and nurture us in Christ. To deny the power of the gospel is equivalent to claiming to be one's own "saviour", which is impossible in the kingdom of God.

We may ask ourselves why the church in our age lacks the degree of godliness we would expect. Why do we find hatred, fighting, immorality, injustice and other ungodly characteristics in the church? The answer lies right here. Without the power that comes from personal knowledge of Christ, people cannot live lives worthy of those who are disciples of Christ.

As ministers of the gospel we should not value quantity more than quality. Thousands of people may attend our church, but if they lack power, their witness is totally ineffective.

Even during these last days, our duty is to lead people into a relationship with Christ. That is the only way to access this power.

Questions for Discussion

1. Believers in Africa hear many sermons against corruption, yet there does not seem to be any noticeable reduction in the level of corruption. What practical ways can we adopt to help us "walk our talk" and achieve a fair and just society?

2. When church leaders criticise the government, their words are often met with a charged response from a government official, making it clear that the official does not consider the church leader a spiritual shepherd. Whether directed towards people in government or personal friends, how can we offer criticism so that the person receiving it is blessed by it rather than humiliated?

3. Have you ever watched an innocent person suffer because others are slandering him or her? What effect did the slander have on the person? What motivated the slanderers to speak this way? If this happens where you work or even where you worship, what can you do to make things right?

UNIT 11
2 TIMOTHY 3:5b–9

PEOPLE TO AVOID

Every now and again we hear about someone being approached in the street and invited to participate in a time of prayer for multiplication of what is in their wallet or purse. Not surprisingly, all the stories end with the one being prayed for losing everything that was in the wallet. Those offering to pray for wealth were thieves.

Then there are stories like the pastor and his wife in Kenya who claimed to have the power to pray for miracle babies for infertile couples. But suspicions were aroused when the miracle babies were born just three months after the prayer! The couple tried to explain this by saying that "God had agreed to set aside the usual nine months between conception and birth".

People like this have a form of godliness but deny its power. Our God can do miracles, but he does not do them on demand to make money for individuals. Nor does he interrupt the natural order that he has established just because we are so full of ourselves that we think we can command him to act. The God of the Bible is the Creator and Preserver of all. He is not to be ordered but obeyed and served. He is the Master and not a slave to our wills.

Even in Paul's day, there were people who misrepresented God. Paul describes some of their techniques to Timothy, and warns him to avoid any contact with them. It is striking that the people he focuses on are not outwardly the most depraved of the sinners he spoke of in the previous section. Rather, they are false teachers, who mislead others under a cloak of religion. If Timothy were to associate with them, he would be seen as agreeing with them and supporting them in what they do.

Stay Away from Evil People

Immediately after mentioning the people who have "a form of godliness but [are] denying its power" (3:5a), Paul issues a strong warning in the present tense, *have nothing to do with such people*. The present imperative makes it clear that this is a warning that Timothy should always obey.[289]

The verb translated "have nothing to do with" or "avoid" (nasb) is a very strong one. It implies that Timothy is to shy away from them with horror.[290] But this response arouses some questions. Surely we are supposed to reach out to people with the love of God and rescue them from their evil ways? How can we do this if we have no contact with them?

The question is a difficult one. How do we find a healthy balance between avoiding and mingling with such people? The answer lies in remembering certain principles that can help us in such situations.

- **Remember your role:** Paul is speaking to Timothy in his role as a church leader.[291] If Timothy is seen to be associating with people who mislead and exploit others, the reputation of the entire church will be affected. This could have a very negative effect on the church's ministry.

- **Follow Jesus' example:** Jesus Christ is the supreme example for us to follow. He did not stay away from sinners, yet he never sinned (Matt 11:19; 1 Pet 2:22–23). His separation was not one of quarantine but "a separation of spirit, a freedom from contagion or infection".[292] Our basic call is not so much to stay away from sinners as not to be like them. Christ sternly rebuked the religious leaders of his day who did not serve others but instead pursued selfish personal ambition. But he was also prepared to talk to leaders who were prepared to listen. He spent a long time with Nicodemus, a Pharisee, talking about what it means to be born again (John 3). In doing this, he was demonstrating what it means to see all relationships from within the context of agape love. It involves loving people (including our enemies – Matt 5:44) because of their intrinsic value as beings made in the image of God. We carrying on loving them whether they come to faith or deny the gospel, but we do this without compromising the truth of the gospel. On this basis, a believer can befriend the worst of characters so long as the goal is to win them by showing them the love of Christ.

- **Use your time wisely:** While Jesus associated with sinners, he did not spend a lot of time with those who would refuse to listen to him. That is why he was not interested in speaking to someone like King Herod (Luke 23:7–9) or having an extended conversation with the rich ruler (Luke 18:18–22), but he gave all the time needed to attend to the needs of people like Bartimaeus (Mark 10:46–52) and Zacchaeus (Luke 19:1–10). He was committed to reaching sinners for salvation, not to getting into arguments with people determined to persist in their sin. Pastors in particular "should avoid certain people when it is clear that they are set in their obstinacy. … This is not because hope has been abandoned but because of the practical necessity of avoiding further controversies and even 'fights' and the positive need to deal with those who are receptive to teaching and pastoral care."[293] A few minutes spent talking with a receptive person may achieve more than a full day spent arguing with a person who is not interested in what you have to say. It may be better to spend time praying for such a person than seeking to engage him or her in endless debates.

- **Show humility:** When it becomes necessary to avoid having anything to do with someone, this should never be done with a "holier than thou" attitude. Rather, it should be done in a spirit of humble commitment to the Lord and a resolve to be obedient to him. We must seek the Lord's guidance, and act with a humble spirit, remembering that we ourselves owe everything to God's grace.

Five Reasons to Stay Away from Them

Paul gives Timothy five reasons why he should avoid certain people.

Their methods

Timothy should have nothing to do with these people because *they are the kind who worm their way into homes and gain control over gullible women* (3:6a).[294] The words "worm their way" and "gain control over" (or "enter into" and "captivate", nasb) describe both what these men do and the type of people they are.²⁹⁵ While we do not have to assume that every one of the false teachers engaged in this type of behaviour,²⁹⁶ the group as a whole was prepared to accommodate it.

Paul may have had particular homes in mind.²⁹⁷ He may have been thinking of some families that Timothy would know, or of homes belonging to a certain class of people. The rich and influential, for example, are often the targets of unscrupulous manipulators who want to make money out of them.²⁹⁸

The false teachers gained "control" by persuading the women to follow them as their disciples. Given Paul's insistence that false teaching involves both wrong beliefs and wrong conduct (1 Tim 4:1, 2; 2 Tim 3:8–9; Titus 1:10; 3:9), it is probably safe to say that the teachers controlled these women by the mental, emotional and moral guidance they gave. They may even have taken advantage of these women sexually. We see this kind of behaviour in our times when counsellors take advantage of counselees due to their vulnerability. Such counsellors are not shepherds but thieves (John 10:10), and their sin deserves the strongest condemnation.

The women these men prey on are referred to by a diminutive that could literally be translated as "little women".²⁹⁹ Paul is not talking about their physical size but about their lack of spiritual and intellectual maturity. The tniv captures the mood of what Paul is saying with its translation, "gullible women". Such women are easily deceived.

We should not misread Paul here. He is not saying that all women are gullible. We know that he had great respect for some women who worked alongside him, like Priscilla and Junia (Rom 16:3, 7; 2 Tim 4:19). But because women in general tend to be more intuitive and welcoming than men, women are particularly "susceptible to proselytism, bad as well as good".³⁰⁰ They are more prepared to come to faith than men, which is one reason why there are more women than men in our churches. However, this characteristic can be abused, and that is what the false teachers in Ephesus are doing. They find their best harvest among the women.

The spiritual weakness of these women shows up in several aspects of their characters:

- ***They are loaded down with sins*** (3:6b). Just as some Africans carry heavy loads on their backs or shoulders when cheap transport is scarce, so these women carry a heavy load of sin, which is weighing them down.[301] Satan has piled the sins there, and he is now using them to keep the women under his control. He is using this load to make them vulnerable to false teaching. The false teachers have identified this point of vulnerability and are using it to enter and dominate their lives. This is a standard technique that false teachers still use today as they search for someone's weak spot. The women themselves may still be living sinful lives and looking for some way to relieve their consciences.[302] Alternatively, they may be burdened by the memory of past sins and will not accept that God has justified and forgiven them (as he did Paul – 1 Tim 1:12–15). So they continue to obsess about these sins. They have not listened to Paul and Timothy's teaching about justification or believed God's promise to forgive sin, something that Jesus promised when he said, "Come to me, all you who are weary and burdened, and I will give you rest" (Matt 11:28). John was referring to the same truth when he said that "if we confess our sins, he is faithful and just and will forgive us our sins and purify us from all unrighteousness" (1 John 1:9).

- ***They are swayed by all kinds of evil desires*** (3:6b). In the Greek, the word translated "desires" is neutral and does not necessarily refer to evil desires. However, the context makes it clear that here Paul is referring to evil desires. The "desires" may include sexual sins, but are probably broader than that.[303] It is probably best to view them as "lusts of all kinds of the flesh, including not only the desires of the flesh, but the wandering and undisciplined movement of the spirit".[304] They include anything that Satan can encourage us to prefer to doing the will of God. It seems that these women followed their impulses whenever temptations came their way.[305]

- ***They are always learning but never able to acknowledge the truth*** (3:7). The women who entertained the false teachers were gullible but not necessarily unintelligent. Their problem was that they had allowed themselves to become fascinated by speculation and theory for its own sake, and were not searching for real answers to real problems. To put this another way, they had developed "overmuch curiosity as to the solution of unpractical problems of speculative theology."[306] The result was that they had become the intellectual prey of the false teachers. Either because they had never been exposed to correct teaching or because "prolonged exposure to the heresy had dulled their senses",[307] they were no longer able to "come to the knowledge of the truth" (nasb),[308] that is, to knowledge of the gospel.[309] Their mentors were opposed to the truth (3:8), and so there was no way the women could learn the truth from them.

Paul's words must not be read as implying either that all women are like this group of women in Ephesus or that we should not be using our minds and seeking to learn more about our faith. What his words do mean is that we should not automatically go chasing after every new theological fashion. When we read, we must read critically, using our minds to evaluate what an author is saying in light of sound doctrine, and accepting only what is compatible with this. We should not simply believe everything that we see in print. We should also be careful that we do not give immature Christians books that will lead them astray. While some of them may need to know about controversies, they are best introduced to the arguments by reading books that interact with them critically.

Their predecessors

The situation Timothy is facing is nothing new. Paul reminds him that the great Jewish leader Moses had faced similar opposition. Jewish tradition identified the magicians who opposed Moses before Pharaoh (Exod 7:11, 22; 8:7, 18–19) as two brothers named *Jannes and Jambres* (3:8).[310] These names are not mentioned in the Old Testament, and Paul is not claiming that they were their real names. He is simply using names that his readers would have recognized in order to make his main point, which is that just as the magicians *opposed Moses, so also these men oppose the truth* (3:8a).[311] Moses, God's servant and messenger, faced opposition, and so will Timothy.[312] He should not be surprised by it. False teachers always oppose the truth.[313]

Given the lessons of history, we should not be surprised that we, too, encounter opposition and false teaching. Many of the positions put forward today are simply updated versions of ancient heresies. For example, those who deny Christ's deity, like Jehovah's Witnesses, are simply following in the footsteps of a man named Arius (died ad 336) who asserted that Jesus was created by God. All such false teaching is encouraged by Satan, whose goal is always to loosen our grasp of the truth by presenting us with alternatives that he claims are better suited to the spirit of the times.

Their characters

Timothy should avoid any dealings with such men because they have *depraved minds* (3:8b).[314] Paul does not tell us who or what has made them depraved, but it is safe to assume that it is either Satan or the heresies the men teach (1 Tim 4:1; 2 Tim 2:26).[315] The idea is that their minds have been corrupted so that they reject anything to do with godliness. Because the mind controls decisions, a depraved mind affects their "moral and intellectual capacity."[316] Evil has infected their thinking and blunted their sensitivity to spiritual things.

To follow a leader whose mind has been corrupted against godliness is to be walking a path that will eventually lead over a cliff. It is thus extremely important that we spend time with a believer who is being led astray in order to make them aware of the danger they are in. We should not calmly stand by while believers come under the sway of groups who deny essential doctrines like the deity of Christ.

Their status

We would never expect to learn maths from a teacher who had not passed courses in mathematics. The same is true when it comes to spiritual things. These teachers have failed the test, and *as far as the faith is concerned*, these people *are rejected* (3:8c). The Greek word used implies more than that they have just been examined and found wanting by other people. It also implies that they have been rejected by God.[317] They have been disqualified, and are no longer participating in the race of faith (1 Cor 9:27). Paul's reference to "the faith" here means the apostolic faith, the body of sound doctrine that he has repeatedly stressed in these letters to Timothy.

Before we decide to follow people or believe what they are teaching, we must ask, "Are these people qualified to teach according to God's standards?" If they do not pass the Lord's test for godliness and sound doctrine, we are wise to drop out of their class and avoid their teaching. This may even involve leaving a church that is promoting ungodliness.

Their end

Paul's final word about these ungodly men is *they will not get very far because ... their folly will be clear to everyone* (3:9). The men may be successful at the moment, but in the end they are doomed.[318] In fact, the main area in which the false teachers are making progress is in ungodliness (2:16). They are going "from bad to worse" (3:13).

In focusing on their ultimate failure, Paul again reminds Timothy of Jannes and Jambres, whom he refers to as *those men*. The two magicians had succeeded in replicating some of Moses' early miracles or plagues (Exod 7:11, 22; 8:7) but they could not sustain their success and failed to replicate all of them (Exod 8:18–19; 9:11). The same thing will happen to the false teachers.

This principle applies to anything false. It may "flourish for a time, but when it is exposed to the light of truth, it is bound to shrivel and die."[319] Just as light chases away darkness, so truth will expose what is hollow and foolish.

The key point is not so much that something that is false will be ineffective as it is that the truth of God's word will ultimately always win. It is very comforting to remember this when we confront false teaching in our day. Any success it has is temporary because the victory ultimately belongs to God and the truth of his word.

Our duty is to remain on the right course and defend what we know to be true from attack. However, we must not become so preoccupied with debates that we fail to proclaim the truth. Satan's schemes can be very crafty. At times he will keep us occupied with something good (such as confronting false teachers), so that we are kept from doing what is best (expounding God's word). We should always be alert to such distractions.

Questions for Discussion

1. Sometimes sin creeps up on us and before we know it we find ourselves engaged in something wrong. For example, a casual meeting with someone may be followed by having tea or coffee together, and later by a suggestive phone conversation between you. If you have ever been in a situation where you gradually slid into sin, without being aware of it at first, share your story with the others in your group (if you are comfortable doing so). How could you have acted differently? What is the best way to deal with similar situations?

2. Have you ever watched someone or something trying to run while carrying a heavy load? What happened? Satan weighs us down with our sins to trap us. How can we obey the injunction in Hebrews 12:1 and off-load the sins that hinder us from running the Christian race effectively?

3. Do you know people who repeatedly move from one church to another? What reasons do they have for moving? Is it because the church is not presenting the gospel truthfully or are they searching for a more exciting church?

4. Paul describes the kind of people we should stay away from. Later he presents himself as a model for Timothy to follow (3:10, 14). What examples are before us today that we should avoid?

UNIT 12
2 TIMOTHY 3:10–17

WORDS OF WISDOM

On 17 March 2000, a fire in a church at Kanungu in Uganda took the lives of five hundred members of a secretive religious cult. But this fire was no accident. It had been deliberately started by the leaders of the group. As horrified Ugandans investigated what had happened, they discovered mass graves at other sites owned by the group. At least 1000 people had been murdered – but not before they had been commanded to sell all their goods and give the proceeds to the leaders! These leaders had betrayed their followers. And they had done this by "deception, false prophecies and lies through selective readings of the Bible". They "exploited the general view among Ugandans that religious people are always innocent, humble, harmless and peace-loving which helped them plan and carry out mischief and crimes without being detected at all."[320] These people were exactly like the false teachers Paul has described, people who claim to be Christian leaders but actually abuse their position and lead their followers astray. All such people will eventually end up being publicly exposed as frauds.

On a less dramatic scale, other Christian leaders have preached against certain sins, and then been shown to be guilty of those same sins themselves.

But Timothy need not worry that the leader he is following is a fraud or a hypocrite. He has been taught by someone who is not afraid to expose his own life and teaching to scrutiny. And his mentor is someone who has seen how God has preserved him through many challenges. He can confidently tell Timothy to persevere despite persecution and despite the apparent success of false teachers. More than that: he can point him to the true source of authority and wisdom.

Paul's Example

Paul reminds Timothy of what the younger man has seen in him, saying *You, however, know all about ...* (3:10, 11). But this translation is an interpretation, rather than a strictly accurate translation.[321] The nasb is much closer to the original Greek when it says, "Now you followed ...". This following may refer to the many years for which Timothy was Paul's close associate or to what Timothy is doing at present.[322]

The word translated "followed" can refer to following someone physically, following someone mentally (by attending to their instructions), or following someone spiritually (living the kind of life they exemplify).[323] All these meanings apply to Timothy's relationship with Paul, although the last two are the most important in this context. Paul is telling Timothy: "My life is an open book before you – you know the details. You have learned well all along. Now carry on living up to what you know."

Paul's words are a challenge to all of us. How many of us can really open up our lives to our disciples? If we did, they might be shocked by what we revealed! May the Lord help us to be in private what we are in public.

The nine aspects of Paul's life that Timothy has followed can be subdivided into three categories: Paul's duties, Paul's character, and Paul's experiences. This list contrasts with the list of vices listed in 3:2–5. Paul is using his own life to illustrate the difference between ungodliness and godliness. Believers should avoid the one while pursuing the other. As they do so, they will be cultivating the fruit of the Holy Spirit (Gal 5:22–23) and living a life controlled not by false teachers but by the Spirit.

Paul's Duties

Teaching was a duty for Paul because he knew that he had a responsibility to guard the truth and pass it on faithfully to others.[324] His teaching was sound (or healthy) and promoted life (1 Tim 1:10). Timothy himself had grown spiritually through it, and he now has a responsibility to preach it and teach it to others (2:2).

This second letter to Timothy is the last of the thirteen letters by Paul that form part of the New Testament. Timothy must have been familiar with the contents of several of these letters, including the one Paul had earlier written to him (1 Timothy). So he was not uninformed about what Paul taught. We are even more fortunate than Timothy, because we not only have access to all of Paul's letters but also to all twenty-seven books of the New Testament, in addition to the Old Testament. Together the sixty-six books of the Bible form the basis for our teaching.

Paul's Character

Six of the nine items in Paul's list relate to his character, reflecting Paul's belief that a godly life is very important for the promotion of the Christian faith.

- *Way of life.* Paul's "way of life" is the way he conducts himself, his habits in general, which Timothy has imitated. Timothy knows the purity, the simplicity and the determination that have characterized Paul's life. He should continue to imitate them.

- *Purpose.* In the New Testament the word translated "purpose" is often used to refer to God's purpose of salvation (e.g., 2 Tim 1:9). Here, however, it is used in relation to Paul's driving force, the motive underlying all he does. Paul's motive was not financial – he did not prize money more than lost souls. Nor was it to promote himself – he only defended himself when it was necessary to do so in order to defend the truth. Nor was it to find security – he did not stop proclaiming the good news of the kingdom even when his life was in danger. Timothy would have no doubt that Paul lived for the gospel.

- *Faith.* In this context, "faith" focuses on Paul's personal response to God's promises, but does not exclude what he believed about God. It was because he believed God had certain characteristics that he could put his faith in him. Because he believed Jesus was the only Saviour, that was what he preached to everyone, whether Jews or Gentiles. Timothy knew that Paul had put his faith in God and his promises, which never fail.

- *Patience.* Patience has been defined as, "the ability not to lose patience when people are foolish, not to grow irritable when they seem unteachable. It is the ability to accept the folly, the perversity, the blindness and the ingratitude of others and still to remain gracious, and still to labour on."[325] Timothy has had many opportunities to observe Paul's patience. He has been present as Paul has dealt with false teachers and with all kinds of responses from those he is teaching or to whom he is preaching, as well as with many troubles and afflictions.

- *Love.* Personal sacrifice for the sake of others is the focus of *agape* love, the kind of love Paul exemplified. God is the ultimate example of this love, and also its source. He places love in our lives so that we can love him and others. In our human relationships, which Paul is focusing on here, love bears with everything people do, refuses to be angry or bitter and never seeks anything but the good of others. Timothy would have known that Paul could only show this kind of love because of his relationship with God. Paul was loving in response to God's love.

- *Endurance.* It is no surprise that when Paul speaks of love he follows this by speaking of endurance. This same linkage occurs every time Paul mentions endurance in the letters to Timothy and Titus 2:2 (1 Tim 6:11; 2 Tim 3:10; Titus 2:2). These two virtues go together. "Endurance" is not just putting up with something, "not a passive sitting down and bearing things but a triumphant facing of them so that even out of evil there can come good. It describes not the spirit which accepts life but the spirit which takes control of it."[326] This attitude is only possible if we have a genuine love for God and others. Without it, difficult situations can drive us away from God, lead us to isolate ourselves from others and settle into bitterness towards them. Obviously, there is also a close link between endurance and the patience that Paul mentions in this list. But whereas patience is an attitude towards people, endurance and perseverance are attitudes towards our circumstances.

Paul's Experience

The experiences that Paul focuses on are all related to *persecutions* and *sufferings* (3:11a). Paul mentions three specific incidents, not because they were the first or the most severe he ever experienced, but because they were the ones that would have had the most indelible effect on Timothy's mind. Paul was thrown out of *Antioch* of Pisidia (Acts 13:50) and moved on to *Iconium*. But there too trouble broke out and he was forced to flee (Acts 14:1–6). He fled to *Lystra*, Timothy's home town (Acts 16:2). There Paul was stoned and left for dead (Acts 14:19). Although Timothy may not have seen all these events himself, they would certainly have been talked about while he was growing up. It was probably while Paul was in Lystra that Timothy's mother and grandmother, and possibly Timothy himself, were converted. The family would have had no illusions about the life that lay ahead when Timothy took Paul as his mentor.

Paul says that all these persecutions *happened to me*, and later in the same verse says that he *endured* them. He faced them squarely, secure in his faith that God was in control. [327]

Paul ends his account of his experience of persecution and suffering with the words, *Yet the Lord rescued me from all of them* (3:11b).[328] He was not "rescued" in the sense that he escaped the suffering, but in the sense that he did not die. He knows that the day of his death is in the Lord's hands. Many times we give up too soon. When we feel like giving up we should remember how the Lord rescued Paul. This thought should help us endure a little longer.

Expect Persecution

Paul does not take his safety for granted, but he knows that God has been with him whenever he was in danger. He can thus confidently tell Timothy to expect that God will watch over him too. We can have the same confidence as we serve God in our day. But we can also be confident that we, too, will have to face suffering. Paul assures Timothy that *everyone who wants to live a godly life in Christ Jesus will be persecuted* (3:12). That "everyone" includes more than just Paul and Timothy. It applies to all believers who are serious about their faith and continually want "to live a godly life" (see also 1 Tim 2:2).[329] The "in Christ Jesus" indicates that the godliness in question is not just devotion to any religion but specifically to Christ. The godly lives of committed believers stand in contrast to the ungodly lives Paul described in 3:1–9.

The certainty of persecution is a constant theme in Paul's teaching (Acts 14:22; 1 Thess 3:4). But it is not only Paul who predicts that we "will be persecuted".[330] Christ made the same prediction (Matt 5:10–11; 10:22–23). As long as our chief enemy (Satan) and his forces are on the loose, Christians can expect opposition.

While the godly are suffering, *evildoers and impostors will go from bad to worse* (3:13). The word translated as "while" in the tniv would be better translated as "but" (as is done in the nasb, nrsv and nkjv). The "but" emphasizes the contrast between the experiences of the godly and that of evildoers. The godly will struggle, but the evildoers will have a smooth ride as they slide deeper and deeper into ungodliness and move further and further away from God. They will develop "new heresies, new methods of fostering unbelief, new tools and outlets for old sins, new hypocrisies, and wider propaganda".[331] The more sophisticated a person who is not in Christ becomes, the more creative is his or her ungodliness. We have witnessed this in our own times. To give only one example, as people have learned to use computers, they have not only found them very useful tools for doing many good things, but have also been able to use them for all sorts of evil purposes.

The evildoers are described as *deceiving and being deceived*.[332] They have believed a lie (probably instigated by Satan, the original deceiver) and in turn go on to deceive those around them. They are caught up in a system in which everything conspires to draw people away from godliness.

Timothy's Responsibility

Timothy is surrounded by ungodliness and can anticipate persecution. But he must not despair. So Paul addresses him forcefully, *But as for you*, with an emphasis on the "you".[333] The word "but" underlines the contrast there must be between Timothy and the evildoers.

Timothy must make it his habit to *continue* in what he has *learned* (3:14).[334] He has learned these things over the years he has been associated with Paul, and the learning has had an effect – he is now an informed believer.[335] He has been entrusted with the truths of the Christian faith (1 Tim 6:20; 2 Tim 1:12, 14) which he is to treasure and pass on to others.

Not only is Timothy informed, he has also *become convinced of* the truth of what he believes.[336] As Mounce puts it, "Both objective learning and experiential validation are necessary parts of Timothy's growth as a believer.[337] This is an important point. Too many of us simply pass on truths we were taught by someone else. We have not put in the time and trouble to investigate them and become convinced of their truth at a personal level. If we do not do this, we are actually like the atheist who used to attend church with his Christian wife. When the congregation recited the Nicene creed, he would join in. But rather than saying "I believe" he would say, "They believe". We may laugh at this story – but our laughter should be somewhat uncomfortable. Are we doing the same thing, without being truthful enough to admit it? The church desperately needs authentic teachers who preach from personal conviction.

Paul has good grounds for anticipating that Timothy will do as instructed: the source of Timothy's knowledge and his upbringing, which has grounded him in the Scriptures.

- Timothy's faith is strong because he knows that those *from whom [he] learned it* (3:14b) were trustworthy.[338] This group would have included his mother Eunice, his grandmother Lois (2 Tim 1:5) and his mentor, Paul, as well as others.[339] Timothy should be very reluctant to disappoint any of those who have taught him. If we are to be strong to continue in what we have learned, we need to choose our mentors very carefully. We must be certain that they are accurately passing on the true message of the gospel before we entrust our souls and spiritual development into their hands. For example, if someone opens a new church in our town, we need to take time to assess the pastor's ministry before enthusiastically becoming his or her disciple. Only if they are faithful in proclaiming the Christ of the Scriptures should we be prepared to follow them.

- Timothy's faith is also strong because he has *known the Holy Scriptures* since early childhood (4:15a).[340] As a Jewish boy, he would have been learning about the Old Testament ever since he was five or six years old.[341] He may even have known some of the gospels, if they were already circulating in an oral form when he was a young man.[342] His knowledge of God's word is thus deeply rooted. Children in our day begin to learn about Jesus as early as the age of two, when they start singing short choruses in Sunday school that teach them about Jesus at a level they can understand. However, we often fail to help these children comprehend the work of Christ personally when they reach an age where they can understand more. We need to create a time and place within church structures to instruct children in these truths, as personally as possible, so that they can choose a relationship with Christ.

Timothy's Roots in Scripture

Paul's reminder to Timothy of his deep roots in the Scriptures prompts him to expand on why such knowledge is so valuable and how the Scriptures should be used in ministry.

The purpose of Scripture

The Scriptures are important for Timothy because they *are able to make you wise for salvation* (3:15b). The present tense of the words "are able" focuses on the abiding power of the Scriptures to convey wisdom in Timothy's day and in ours.[343] The wisdom that they convey relates not to wealth or human relationships but to receiving salvation.[344] They do not contain "simply facts or even sacred history, but a revelation of God's saving purpose".[345] They bring people to salvation by leading them on the path of wisdom. This wisdom contrasts with the folly of the false teachers (3:9).

The path to salvation is *through faith in Christ Jesus*. He is the object of our faith. Paul has essentially described the process of salvation: gaining knowledge of the Scriptures, becoming wise, exercising faith and attaining salvation. Using the metaphor of a journey, we could say that Scripture is the guide we are expected to follow, wisdom is the path we walk on, faith is the key we use to open the door or gate, and salvation is the destination we are walking towards.

It is wonderful that God does not leave any ambiguity about the way of salvation. He makes it very clear that it comes only through his son Jesus Christ. Any other teaching is a counterfeit, a mirage that cannot quench the thirst of those seeking salvation. Christians should lift up Jesus as the Saviour of the world and should do so with deep conviction and determination, no matter the circumstances. Every person, whether rich or poor, great or small, educated or uneducated, needs to be offered real salvation.

This need and the knowledge that salvation comes only through Christ underlies Paul's second reason for Timothy continuing in what he has learned. Like Timothy, we carry a treasure in the gospel and we must continue to preach it until everyone around us knows this truth. At times we are tempted to limit our reach to the groups that are easy to share with and neglect those that are more difficult. Yet we should be reaching out not only to the unsaved in general but also to those who are hard to witness to.

The authority of Scripture

Timothy has been reminded of the purpose of Scripture and of how long he has known the Scriptures, but now Paul goes on to remind him of why the Scriptures are so authoritative and why Timothy can cite them when he faces challenges. The reason is that *all Scripture is God-breathed* (3:16).

The word translated "Scripture" can mean writing in general, but Paul is using it to refer to the Old Testament, just as he did in Romans 4:3, 1 Corinthians 15:3–4 and Galatians 2:8, 12. However, it also includes any parts of the New Testament that would have been recognized as authoritative when this letter was written (around ad 67).

There has been a lot of debate about exactly how this phrase should be translated.[346] The neb translation, for example, reads "Every inspired scripture", changing the "all" to "every", which shifts the focus from Scripture considered as a whole to individual passages of Scripture. It also takes the word translated "inspired" or "God-breathed" as an adjective describing these passages, rather than as a statement about the source of all Scripture. This translation is possible, but it has the problem that it can be read as suggesting that only some Scriptures qualify as inspired, while others are of human origin.

The strongest argument against this reading is that Paul nowhere spends any time telling Timothy how to distinguish the specific Scriptures inspired by God from those that are not inspired by him. It is clear that he does not make this distinction. Thus the majority of scholars prefer the translation given in the tniv, although there is still some debate about whether the first word should be translated "all" or "every". While this decision is important for an accurate translation, it makes little practical difference to the meaning of the text. If every individual passage of Scripture is inspired, the end result is that all Scripture is inspired.

But what does the word "inspired" mean? It translates a Greek word that literally means "God breathed".[347] We should not interpret this as meaning that God takes something that already exists and breaths on it to make it come alive (as happened to Adam at creation – Gen 2:7) or to confer authority on it (as Jesus did when he breathed on the disciples and said "receive the Holy Spirit"– John 20:22). Rather, Paul is dealing with where Scripture comes from. It came from God just as breath comes out of a person.

The fact that God breathed Scripture does not mean that he took over the human authors so completely that they were merely dictating words they heard from God. Rather, it means that God worked with the individual authors' minds in such a way that he was the ultimate source of their message (see also 2 Pet 1:21). What they wrote carried his authority. That is why Timothy can use Scripture as his authority in his ministry.

Four uses of Scripture

Having reminded Timothy of the source of the authority of Scripture, Paul tells him another quality of Scripture: it is *useful*. Some commentators believe that this quality is Paul's main focus here. They argue that Timothy did not need to be told about the inspiration of Scripture because he already believed it was inspired. Instead, he needed to be reminded that he would be wise to use Scripture in his ministry.[348]

How is Scripture profitable for Timothy's ministry? Paul lists four ways it can be used: *for teaching, rebuking, correcting and training in righteousness* (3:16b).

- *Teaching.* One of Timothy's primary responsibilities is to teach. In Scripture, he will find what he needs to do this because it is: a) the "sourcebook of doctrine both religious and ethical"; b) the "record of the power of God in the lives of men" and c) the "stimulus to deeper discipleship".[349] Scripture must be the textbook from which he teaches.

- *Rebuking.* Scripture exposes false teachings and the errors of those who hold them. As a pastor, Timothy must mercilessly tear to pieces "all theories, all theologies, and all ethics" that contradict sound doctrine.[350] This does not mean that he must go on a witch-hunt looking for false teaching, nor does it mean that he must savagely attack the person holding the error. This function is closely linked to the use of Scripture to correct others.

- *Correcting.* While rebuking false teaching or doctrine, Timothy must gently correct those who hold it. He must be merciless to the heresy but kind to its proponents. His goal is to save the person, and Scripture is profitable for "convincing people of the error of their ways and for pointing them on the right path".[351]

- *Training in righteousness.* Those who are trained are unlikely to go astray and therefore will not need to be rebuked or corrected. Timothy must use Scripture to teach Christian beliefs and guidelines for conduct so that believers can live constructive Christian lives that are pleasing to God.[352] Teaching and training overlap. The difference is that teaching addresses mental knowledge, whereas training focuses on the practical result of learning sound doctrine – a changed life.

God gave us his word so that we can be taught his will and know it. When we go wrong, his word can correct us, and if we persist in doing wrong, it can be used to rebuke us. The goal of all Scripture is to see us grow in righteousness. But it can only accomplish its goal if it is used faithfully and fully. It is not good enough to simply teach and train if we never rebuke or correct. We have to do those as well, regardless of whether what we say offends a wealthy member of the church.

The purpose and result of Scripture

The result or purpose of all this teaching, rebuking, correcting and training in righteousness is that all God's people are *thoroughly equipped for every good work* (3:17).[353] A literal translation of the Greek states that it is the "man of God" who is equipped. This title was used to refer to Timothy in 1 Timothy 6:11. Here, however, it refers both to Timothy and to anyone who has accepted training in righteousness. The tniv translation *all God's people* is thus perfectly acceptable.

Those who have listened and responded to the Scriptures are "thoroughly equipped" – they have everything necessary to do "good work".[354] This is not to say they are all equally expert in carrying out every single task. That would be impossible, for nobody has access to all the spiritual gifts. Here, the phrase "every good work" is equivalent to "any good work"[355] and covers all the possible tasks that God might entrust someone with. Each individual will be equipped for the task God entrusts to him or her.

Timothy's responsibility is to root people in sound doctrine and his resource for doing this is the authoritative Scriptures. Our goal is still to maintain the purity of Christ's bride, his church, until he comes again. Like Timothy, we need to derive our authority from the Scriptures and use them to equip others for promoting righteousness. Questions or objections do not limit Scriptures God-given authority. We must take God at his word and use Scripture with confidence.

Questions for Discussion

1. Is there someone in your life whom you view as a good model to follow? What is it about them that leads you to think of them in these terms?

2. How would you evaluate the use of Scripture in the congregation to which you belong? Is it used only for exhortation or also for correction and rebuke? Share specific examples of the result of using Scriptures in any of the four ways discussed in this unit, without mentioning names of those involved.

3. What contemporary experiences count as persecution of Christians? Do Christians respond to the situations with endurance or do they compromise? How can we support each other so that we endure persecution?

UNIT 13
2 TIMOTHY 4:1–2, 5

PAUL'S FINAL CHARGE TO TIMOTHY

In African traditional practice, old people who sensed that they would soon die would send for all their children. Then in the presence of the whole family they would give their last words of general advice, as well as specific instructions for each son or daughter. On such occasions, everyone present wonders what the old person is going to say to them. Some will rejoice as their parent gives them praise and blessing. Others will be filled with remorse and regret because they have not done well in the eyes of their father or mother. Only the most insensitive do not attach deep significance to these words. This sense of significance is even greater because of the traditional belief that "the heavens" will bring the parent's curses, blessings or prophecies to pass.

Timothy would have valued Paul's final words as much as we value the final words of our own parents.[356] We, too, can benefit from listening to these words, for they contain important instructions about our own calling. Paul charges Timothy to continue to work as faithfully as he himself had done.

Divine Witnesses

For a charge to have legal status, it had to be issued in the presence of two or three witnesses. So Paul invokes the two greatest witnesses he knows to observe the charge he is issuing to Timothy: *In the presence of God and of Christ Jesus ... I give you this charge* (4:1a; see also 1 Tim 5:21; 2 Tim 2:14). Given these witnesses, Timothy has no choice but to take the matter very seriously.

As a further reminder of why Timothy must take this charge very seriously, Paul points out that Jesus is the one *who will judge the living and the dead*. No one will escape his judgment when he comes for the second time. Paul does not go into details about this judgment here, but from other passages we know that it will involve rewarding believers for their work for the kingdom (1 Cor 3:12–15) and declaring that unbelievers will not experience heaven but the lake of fire (Rev 21:8).

The immediate goal of Paul's statement is not to terrify Timothy with the prospect of judgment but to encourage him. No matter what others may say about his ministry, his ultimate judge will be Christ. Having this perspective helps us to avoid being touchy when someone criticizes us, or being self-important and focused on our personal rights and prestige, or being self-centred, demanding thanks and praise for everything we do.[357]

Paul's words are also a warning to Timothy's opponents, who may well be listening as this letter is read aloud to the congregation. The ultimate judge will scrutinize every move they make to hinder his ministry.

The words translated "will judge" should literally be rendered "about to judge".[358] Paul lived with the expectation that Christ's second coming could take place any time. We should do the same. No other divine act of redemption is expected before Christ's second coming. Now is the time for us to receive God's free offer of salvation and be ready for Christ's glorious return.

Paul and Timothy certainly understood the significance of being in the presence of God and Jesus Christ. But we seem to forget it. We sometimes treat them with less respect than we show to prominent members of society. For example, I was once asked to meet the president of Kenya briefly after I had preached in a church where he was present. As I walked towards the house, my escort kept whispering, "*Tafadhari harakisha!*" ("Please move faster!"). I thought I was walking fast enough, and I doubt that the president would have complained about my pace. But to the guard, the president was so important and his time so precious that I ought to move at a pace just short of a run.

The experience left me wondering why we as believers sometimes approach God so casually. Is it because we have not experienced God in the powerful way Isaiah did (Isa 6:1–5)? Or is it because he is so much a father to us that we take him for granted? When we come into the presence of the Lord, we must always keep his nature and our relationship with him in proper perspective. He is our creator, provider, and protector. He is Yahweh (the faithful covenant God) and also Elohim (the majestic one). He will be our judge. Surely he is due the greatest honour, reverence and respect!

The Basis for the Charge

The basis for Paul's charge is Christ's *appearing and his kingdom* (4:1b).[359] It is because Christ Jesus will return that Timothy's assignment at Ephesus is important. As a Christian minister, he is to continue the work of establishing the kingdom of God, with Christ at its centre.

The Greek word translated "appearing" (*epiphaneia*) was used to refer to the visit of the emperor to any province or town. Great preparations would be made for such an important visit. In the same way, God made great preparations for Christ's first appearing (2 Tim 1:10) and now Timothy and other believers are to prepare for his second coming (1 Tim 6:14; 2 Tim 4:1, 8; Titus 2:13). We should look forward to it with anticipation. At that time Christ will acknowledge his own and reward the faithfulness with which they have served him.

Christ's reign is the focus of the kingdom of God. While his realm will only be established following his second coming, his reign has already begun, for he is already seated in glory (1 Tim 3:16) and is at work changing people's hearts. At his second appearing, however, he will come as king and no one will be able to question his righteous judgment. As one who anticipates that Christ will appear again, and believes in Christ's kingdom and its consummation at his appearing, Timothy is to adhere to the charge Paul gives him.

African hospitality requires thorough preparation when a visitor is expected. The living room and bathroom are put in order, the compound is cleaned, meals are modified to ensure that the guest will enjoy them, and other adjustments are made in everyday living. If we see any dirt on our shirts while we wait for the guest, we hurriedly change what we are wearing. If there is discord between the parents or fighting among the children, we do not let our guests witness the chaos. We decide that we will settle our differences later and focus on making the best impression on our guest. I could list many other examples showing how preparation for a guest affects every aspect of our lives.

We do all this for each other as human beings. How much more should we do to prepare for Christ's coming! He is our Lord and Saviour and we should be determined that when he comes he will find us at our best for him. There should be no sin spots or discord in our lives when he arrives.

While our motive for preparing for Christ's arrival is that we love him, the Scriptures warn that we also need to prepare for him because he will pass judgment. Those who live as if they are their own creators, rejecting God and his way of salvation, will face God's wrath. Those who wait for him as their beloved Saviour will enjoy his eternal fellowship.

The Content of the Charge

Paul's charge to Timothy includes nine instructions for Timothy to follow. Five of them are found in 4:2 and are important for promoting Timothy's ministry. The remaining four are in 4:5 and focus on Timothy's personal growth.

Instructions for ministry

Preach the word

The verb translated *preach* also means "to proclaim", like a herald proclaims good news.[360] Paul considers himself a herald (1 Tim 2:7; 2 Tim 1:11). In this context, the good news is the gospel concerning Christ's work of salvation and his coming. This instruction "sums up what the Apostle believes to be Timothy's urgent practical duty in the present critical situation."[361] Preaching the word is Timothy's "one comprehensive duty" that "is to fill his whole horizon and absorb his whole intellect. It is to be the dominant purpose of all his days."[362]

A messenger has not completed the job until the message is delivered to the person it is meant for. As long as there are believers to encourage in their Christian walk and unbelievers to be told about the way of salvation and the coming judgment, the ministry of preaching is still needed.

Each of us has a part to play in our time that no one else can do for us. Paul's message to Timothy is also a message to each of us – "Preach the word". May the Lord help us to obey.

Be prepared in season and out of season

Being prepared "in season" and "out of season" means being prepared "whether the moment seems opportune or not".[363] Barrett translates the phrase as "on all occasions, convenient or inconvenient."[364] Timothy should not miss a single moment or opportunity for carrying out the work of the ministry. He should perform his task in any situation and speak the word whether people are disposed to hear it or not.[365]

Paul is not telling Timothy to be discourteous when he says that he must speak at inconvenient times. We should be careful about choosing the right time to speak, "for there should be courtesy in evangelism as in every other human contact."[366] However, we should not use the excuse that the time is inconvenient for us or our listeners when our motive is that we are too shy to speak about Christ.

Given the importance of hearing God's news of redemption, there is no wrong place or time to share it. Yet when the one we are sharing it with requests us to speak at another time or place, we should be courteous and adjust accordingly. The gospel is good news, but not news to be forced down anyone's throat. The Lord wants people to understand what is being offered to them and to choose it of their own free will. Our duty is to make sure they understand this.

Correct, rebuke and encourage

Correct ("reprove", nasb) and *rebuke* are similar responsibilities, but are not the same (see commentary on 2 Tim 3:16). Correction is for people who have to be informed that they are sinning, whereas rebuking is for people who do not listen when they are corrected. Titus is also to *encourage* ("exhort", nasb) everyone.[367]

These three verbs can be seen as summarizing the way a preacher appeals to his hearers. Correction appeals to reason and reasoned arguments to refute error; rebuking triggers the conscience by bringing a message of judgment; and encouraging seeks to touch the will by urging people to repent and persevere.[368]

The three verbs may also suggest a logical order for dealing with people who have erred. Our ministry starts by focusing on everybody as we encourage and exhort everyone to persevere in the faith and to repent if they have sinned. This encouragement may be enough to persuade many to remain faithful. However, there are some who will not do so, and it may become necessary to correct or reprove them. When this fails, the only remaining option is to rebuke them. Yet even rebuking must be done with the intention of winning the sinner. "No rebuke should ever be such that it drives another person to despair and takes away all heart and hope. People should not only be rebuked; they should also be encouraged."[369]

Paul's next words tell us how these things must be done: *with great patience and careful instruction* (4:2b). It is possible that these qualities are particularly associated with the word "encourage", but they are also needed when reproving and rebuking.[370]

The word translated "patience" describes "the spirit which never becomes irritated, never despairs and never regards anyone as beyond salvation."[371] Timothy is to remain optimistic that people's lives will change, since no one is beyond the changing power of Christ. He is to be patient and to give wise counsel on how to do well in the Christian life. "Always persevering" and "always enabling" are to be his mottos in ministry.

Admittedly, there are people in our churches or institutions who make great demands on our patience! Our duty is not to give up on such people but to offer patient instruction until they make the necessary changes in their lives. This, of course, does not mean we must instruct them endlessly. Rather, our instruction must go hand in hand with the discernment that enables us to know whether we are making progress or wasting our time. It is better to spend time with an unbeliever who is willing to be instructed than with a churchgoer who is determined never to change.

Instructions for personal growth

Keep your head in all situations

This instruction to *keep your head in all situations* (4:5a) could also be translated "Be sober in all things" (nasb). The Greek word used has the idea of keeping calm and sane.³⁷² One who is sober does not panic, does not go to extremes, does not make wild decisions and does not take offence or act in anger.³⁷³ Timothy is to be such a person in all areas of life, and especially in his ministry. Any minister who is this clear-minded will be effective. It is a quality of life and type of response to people and circumstances that blesses others and does not offend them.

Endure hardship

Paul never promises that Christians will not have to *endure hardship* (4:5b). In fact, he promises the opposite. Hardships are sure to come, especially when working as a minister of the gospel. However, the goal of ministry outweighs any amount of hardship, and so he exhorts Timothy to suffer evil without giving up.

Every believer should expect to experience some hardship for the sake of Christ. Christians in the business world will receive opposition when they put service to others before profit. Christian teachers will endure hostility from other teachers when they ask whether it is right to strike just before important examinations. Christian police officers will be harassed when they refuse to participate in a bribery scheme that their boss is involved in. In every walk of life or profession, the Christian will stand out as odd. But we are called to endure this hardship for the sake of the kingdom of God.

Do the work of an evangelist

The work of an evangelist (*euangelistes*) is to make the gospel (*euangelion*) known. Timothy's work is to preach the gospel (*euangelizesthai*). Paul viewed this as the main purpose for his own ministry (1 Cor 1:17). In two places in the New Testament (Acts 21:8; Eph 4:11), the specific office of being an evangelist is mentioned, but that does not seem to be what Paul is talking about here. He is simply telling Timothy what kind of work he is to do: he is to teach and expound the gospel.³⁷⁴

Evangelists are preoccupied with telling the good news that there is a Saviour for the world who is willing to save all who believe. They carry out their ministry in hope that those who hear the news will accept it. Evangelism is the first step. Once a person comes to faith, shepherding (pastoring) begins.

While every believer has a duty to evangelize, this duty is particularly incumbent on people like Timothy, who have not only believed but have also acquired skills to present the good news effectively. Timothy has learned these skills by watching how Paul went about evangelism.

Discharge all the duties of your ministry

The last charge Paul gives to Timothy can be translated literally as "fulfil your ministry" (nasb)[375] or "your service" (as in 1 Tim 1:12). Paul knows he is about to die. It is as if he is telling Timothy, "I have done my work; now you make sure that you complete yours." The verb he uses carries the idea of "do it; do not neglect it".

Our call to ministry has multiple dimensions. It involves maintaining a healthy relationship to God, our Master. It also involves sacrificial service to the church as we work to establish fellow believers in the faith. Finally, it involves the attempt to make positive contributions to humanity in general, which is yet to be reached with the gospel. In Barclay's words, "Christians should have only one ambition – to be of use to the church of which they are a part and the society in which they live."[376]

Christians' involvement with society in general should, of course, always go hand in hand with a healthy relationship with God. Their involvement should draw society towards God and not pull Christians towards the world. This means, for example, that Christians should get involved in politics – but must be guided by Christian values as they do so. Politics need not be a dirty game; it can be a God-given ministry. Africa needs people with excellent political skills who exemplify the virtues of righteousness, truth and justice to help us manage our differences.

Questions for Discussion

1. What is the significance to you of knowing that one day Jesus will judge whether or not we should be rewarded? How should this affect the way you serve him now?
2. How do you rate your ability to make good judgments as to when to exhort, correct or rebuke? There are some parents, for example, who always rebuke their children and never encourage them. What

principles can we draw from this passage to help us be better parents, lead more effectively, and build souls rather than destroy them?

3. Undeserved criticism and misrepresentation are always difficult to deal with. For example, at one time, I had to instruct the accounts department of an institution to borrow designated funds to pay staff salaries. Someone who had other differences with me was very bitter about this and called me a "thief". My immediate response was to order him out of my office. Have you ever had such an experience? Did you handle it better than I did? What principle is laid down in this passage that will help us achieve greater victory in such situations?

4. Have you ever tried to talk to someone about salvation and had the person carry on doing something trivial and non-urgent in order to avoid listening to you? What did you do – leave the person alone or insist that they listen to you? If you insisted, what was the end result? Is there a similarity between this situation and one where a child refuses to take prescribed medicine? Is there a guiding principle we can apply to help us evangelize without being a nuisance?

UNIT 14
2 TIMOTHY 4:3–4, 6–8

PROBLEMS AND REWARDS

On 9 October 2004 Professor Wangari Maathai of Kenya was awarded the 2004 Nobel Peace Prize "for her contribution to sustainable development, democracy and peace".[377] The award brought not only fame but also a cheque for more than a million dollars. She was the first African woman to receive this prize, and only the sixth African to win a Nobel prize since they were first awarded in 1901. She joined the company of Albert Lutuli (1960), Desmond Tutu (1984), Frederik Willem de Klerk (1993), Nelson Mandela (1993) and Kofi Annan (2001).

Wangari rejoiced that the world had noticed her work as founder and leader of the Green Belt Movement, which had sought "to empower women, better the environment and fight corruption in Africa for almost 30 years".[378] Her struggle to plant trees and oppose deforestation had at last been honoured. As she put it, it was "too good to be true!"

Over the years, Wangari kept determinedly to her course, despite much opposition. She stood firm against those who do not care for the environment and would not care if more forests were destroyed. She continues to stand tall, telling others: "There is value in saving the environment – plant two trees for every one you cut." Her actions have matched her words and have brought her global recognition.

Paul is like Wangari in that he, too, has determinedly carried out the task to which he was called, despite great opposition. Now, as the end of his life approaches, he anticipates the reward that he will receive from the Lord. But this award is not like a Nobel Prize, restricted to only a few. Christ's reward is available to Timothy, to you and to me at the end of our faithful service to him.

The Urgency of the Charge

Timothy has been assigned a great responsibility, and he must carry it out urgently. The days ahead are going to be very challenging, and so he must preach and teach now, while people are ready to listen. He must be the one to do this because Paul's voice will be silenced.

The days ahead

Paul's words, *For the time will come*, imply that the things he is predicting will certainly happen.[379] The first signs of this attitude are already evident, but things will only intensify as the end approaches. *People*, including the Ephesians among whom Timothy works, will display three closely related characteristics that will make his ministry difficult.

- **Their nature.** These people will not be prepared to listen to *sound doctrine* (4:3a), that is, to the true gospel that Paul and Timothy (and Titus) preach (1 Tim 1:10; 6:3; 2 Tim 1:13; Titus 1:9, 13; 2:1).

- **Their desire.** Rather than listening to sound teaching, these people have *itching ears* or, as another translation puts it, they want "to have the ears tickled" (4:3b).[380] They are not interested in finding or obeying the truth but rather have that type of "curiosity that looks for interesting and spicy bits of information".[381] They have heard what Paul and Timothy have to say, are bored with it and want something new. They are only too happy to listen to the false teachers because their message is "sensational or novel".[382]

- **Their actions.** Given their taste for novelty, these people *will turn their ears away from the truth, and will turn aside to myths* (4:4).[383] Their lack of interest in the truth leads them to turn away from sound doctrine (see 1 Tim 2:4; 3:15; 2 Tim 2:18; 3:7–8; Titus 1:1). They replace it with "myths" (4:4; see 1 Tim 1:4; 4:7). Rather than pursuing what God desires, they follow their own appetites and curiosities. There are always teachers willing to cater to such desires, and so these people *gather around them a great number of teachers* (4:3c).[384] The number of false teachers will continue to accumulate because the people will not find ultimate satisfaction in such teaching. Only God's message of salvation through Jesus Christ, our mediator can truly meet their spiritual needs (1 Tim 2:5).

Since Timothy is obedient to God, he cannot vary the truth of the gospel to suit people's tastes. He will have an uphill task when it comes to reaching them. One of the most difficult things to do is to share a message with people who have decided not to listen to it. The task is only endurable because the message is so valuable that not proclaiming it endangers the lives of those who reject it. So Timothy should ignore people's rejecting attitude and keep on announcing the good news.

Rejection of the truth will increase, rather than decrease, as we approach the final "later days". Therefore, while there is still some evidence of a positive response to the gospel, we should not waste time but should eagerly share the truth.

Paul's future

After talking about Timothy's role, Paul uses an emphatic "I" (parallel to the emphatic "you" in 4:5) as he turns to talking about his own situation. His message could be summarized as "You, Timothy, are staying on, but I am dying". He uses a present tense, *I am already being poured out* (4:6a), for even although his blood has not yet been spilt, he is so certain that this is coming that he can speak of it as already happening.[385]

Paul uses a vivid metaphor to describe his situation, saying that he is *like a drink offering*. In Africa, some cultures offer libations to the ancestors, and similar offerings were common in many cultures. But what Paul is probably thinking about here is the Jewish custom of pouring out a drink offering as part of some temple sacrifices (Exod 29:40; Num 28:7).[386]

Changing the metaphor, Paul says that *the time has come for my departure* (4:6b), meaning that he will be leaving this life. The Greek word translated "departure" was used in a number of contexts. It would be used to describe unyoking an animal from the shafts of a cart or plough after it had finished its work, unchaining a prisoner, pulling up the stakes of a tent as one prepares to move on to another place, and loosening the mooring ropes of a ship as it sets sail. All of these meanings could have been in Paul's mind. He is looking forward to a rest after his hard work for the kingdom. He is eager to be released from the Roman prison into the liberty of the courts of heaven. As a frequent traveller along the roads of Asia Minor and Europe, he would have known all about taking down tents and preparing to move on. Many of his missionary journeys had also involved travel by sea, and he must often have stood on deck as sailors cast off the mooring ropes and his ship began to glide into deep water, heading for the next port. Now at last he is on the final leg of his last and greatest journey into the presence of God.[387]

Paul's perspective on death is a source of great peace as death approaches, and even when it comes very near. Our times are in God's hands, and when death comes we pass from time into eternity. If we could comprehend this truth, we would accept any believer's death with gratitude to God for the life they lived and the home prepared for them in heaven.

Paul is convinced that his time "has come". He even speaks as though he is already leaving.[388] His future will be spent with the Lord, and no longer with Timothy. Therefore, Timothy is to take up his responsibilities with all urgency and seriousness.

This is what Christian ministry is all about. We will all follow Paul into death. The crucial question is whether we have prepared anyone to pick up the task and carry on from where we stop. No matter how effective we are in ministry, we should not let our success give us the illusion that we will always be here. A good leader prepares a successor to lead even better. This applies whether our task is teaching, preaching or any other activity. If we die without leaving someone to take over from us, we were not good leaders.

Paul's Example

Looking back over his long life, Paul can say, *I have fought the good fight, I have finished the race, I have kept the faith* (4:7). He has faithfully completed his assigned mission.[389] However, the English translation is not quite accurate, because it emphasizes the "I" in each of these expressions by putting it first. But in the original Greek, "Fight", "race", and "faith" are placed first. Paul is not showing off about what he has done. Rather, he is stressing the tasks that contribute to promoting the truth of the gospel, and encouraging Timothy by telling him that he successfully completed them all.

Paul is not speaking of just any fight, race or faith. He speaks specifically of **the** fight, **the** race, **the** faith. These are unique struggles because their focus is the gospel.

- The "good fight" does not describe the way Paul fought, but the kind of fight he has been involved in. It is inherently a good fight, a battle in a cause worth dying for. As in 1 Timothy 6:12, this image does not necessarily refer to a war. Paul may have been thinking of a wrestling match, for wrestling was a popular sport in Greece.[390] Nor is Paul claiming that he is "the greatest". He is speaking like a player after an intense soccer game, who will say, "That was a good game". He is satisfied with what he has been called to do and with how he has done it. He is now prepared to have Timothy continue the fight (see 1 Tim 6:12).

- "The race" in which Paul is involved is not a sprint in which one person is the winner. Rather, it is a relay race that will involve many runners before it is won. So when Paul says "I have finished the race", he is not saying that he has won the race. Rather, he has completed his part of the race and is now handing the baton to Timothy to continue. "For Paul the race is now over, not just his life, but his ministry. But what he has finished is the course, the race laid out by his divine master, not the full distance."[391] Timothy is to be a single-minded athlete with staying-power who takes the baton and completes the next leg of the race, regardless of persecution.[392] Following the principle of 2 Timothy 2:2, Timothy will pass the baton to someone else, and so it will be handed on from one Christian to the next until Christ returns.

- Paul has "kept the faith", but what faith is this? Is it objective faith in the form of a creed, belief or doctrine, or is it subjective faith, that is, Paul's personal response to God?[393] This argument may be somewhat artificial, for doctrine and beliefs should generate a personal response of faith that is as deep as the person's commitment to the beliefs. This is the normal pattern. However, sometimes rebellion in people's hearts keeps them from responding in faith. As for Paul, he did not waver from the objective truth of the gospel once it was entrusted to him, and he remained steady in his personal commitment to his master "through thick and thin, in freedom and in imprisonment, in all his perils by land and sea, and now in the very face of death."[394]

It is a great honour for anyone to be able to make the three claims that Paul does here. They are the mark of a life lived for the purposes God intended. We all know people who could make the same claims; the important question is, can we?

Paul's Reward

Having finished his fight and his race, Paul now looks forward to the reward: a victor's crown. He describes this crown as *the crown of righteousness* (4:8a). But what does this mean? Is the crown actually the gift of righteousness that God bestows on believers? Or is it something distinct, some other reward that is given to those who are righteous?[395]

Those who think that the crown is something distinct from righteousness argue that Paul is continuing to use athletic imagery. In Greece, a victorious athlete was crowned with a laurel wreath. The wreath and the honour accompanying his victory were two separate things. In the same way, the crown and the righteousness to which Paul looks forward are two different things. The crown he hopes to receive will be imperishable (unlike the fading laurel wreath – 1 Cor 9:25). Kelly suggests that "the crown of righteousness" is actually eternal life.[396]

The problem with this position is that it could mean that believers will end up wearing many crowns, for the New Testament also speaks of a crown of rejoicing (1 Thess 2:19 – nkjv), a crown of life (Jas 1:12; Rev 2:10 – nkjv) and a crown of glory (1 Pet 5:4). In light of these passages, it seems more likely that Paul is saying that righteousness will be one of the qualities of glorified believers. They will be made perfectly righteous, joyful and glorious, and will never die.

There is no need to get involved in arguments about the exact nature of the crown (or crowns) that await us. What is important, and what we can be certain of is that believers can enjoy a righteousness they have never experienced before, a glory that can never be attained in this world, and life in all its fullness. It is certainly worth enduring hardship for the sake of attaining this award!

The one who will award this crown is *the Lord, the righteous Judge* (4:8b). As a righteous Judge, the Lord makes no mistakes about what is true or valuable. He knows all things and he is righteous in everything he does. Paul will soon be facing a Roman judge who will condemn him to death as a criminal. But as a man "whose life is dedicated to Christ [Paul] is indifferent to the verdict of men. He cares not if they condemn him so long as he hears his master's 'Well done'."[397] The righteous judge knows the truth of the matter, and he is the only one whose verdict matters in the long run.

While it is important that we are aware of how other people evaluate us and can learn from their opinions, there is also a time when it is appropriate to turn a deaf ear to what they say. Words that are spoken to discourage rather than encourage us should enter one ear and leave immediately through the other. The same applies to criticisms intended to destroy our work for malicious reasons rather than to build it up from a pure heart. Meditating on or being preoccupied with maliciously spoken words creates discouragement, hatred and defeat, trapping us in the devil's snares. We should always remember that Christ is the ultimate judge, who congratulates us or rebukes us when it is right and for our good.

Paul expects to be awarded *on that day*, meaning the day of judgment (see 2 Tim 1:12, 18; 4:1). Others may fear that day, but for him and other believers it will be a day of rejoicing as they hear the judge say, "Well done!"

Paul is confident that he will not be alone when he receives his crown. The same crown will be awarded *to all who have longed for his appearing* (4:8c). This "appearing" is Christ's return, when he comes for a second time as judge (see 1 Tim 6:14; 2 Tim 4:1; Titus 2:13). True believers long for this day when they will see their Lord, and when he will overthrow evil and reward his faithful followers. This longing is "a steadily burning flame which has continued from its original outburst up to the present moment".[398] Certainly Paul has longed for it as he has lived and preached the gospel. He has been waiting for his Master to come and examine his work. Thus Paul writes with a sense of fulfilment that he has done his best and in anticipation of the joy he will experience when his master returns.

The type of longing Paul speaks of here is best seen in children eagerly anticipating a coming event. It may be months before it will happen, but they keep talking about it with their friends. They repeatedly ask their parents how many days they still have to wait. They are excited about it! Believers should have a similar excitement about the prospect of seeing Jesus face to face, and should be longing for it to happen soon. We should share the prayer of John as he meditated on Christ's return while writing the book of Revelation: "Amen. Come, Lord Jesus" (Rev 22:20b).

Timothy can find encouragement in Paul's words because he can look forward to meeting the Lord in this way. In fact, Paul's joy is available to everyone who fights the same fight, finishes the race and keeps the faith.

Questions for Discussion

1. What experiences have you had with God in the past that may serve as a basis for confidence as you face the future?
2. Teenagers often prefer listening to their peers to listening to their parents. It is thus very important that we teach our children good values while they are still prepared to listen. What is your church doing to teach children values and to help parents teach them? What could your church do better? What role do you see for yourself in helping with this?
3. Death is the enemy we all fear. What principles can we draw from this passage that may help minimize our fear even when death is knocking at the door?
4. One day our energy will be gone. What kind of fight will you look back on – will you have fought people or fought the darkness brought by sin? Will you be able to say that you have lived the Christian faith (run the Christian race) in a manner that glorified God? What can we learn from Paul to help us take pride in our achievements for Christ when our time on earth is drawing to an end?

UNIT 15
2 TIMOTHY 4:9-22

CONCLUDING MATTERS

I recently watched two African women parting ways. Initially, one woman said goodbye to her visitor at the door of the house. Then she escorted her visitor to the gate. At the gate, the two talked for another five minutes before shaking hands to say goodbye again. But the conversation wasn't over yet! After another two-minute exchange, the women shook hands for the third time and the visitor finally left. What exactly was happening here? Were the two women gossiping? Probably not. This type of lengthy parting is quite normal for good friends in Africa.

Paul is a like a good African when it comes to saying goodbye. We keep thinking that he has finished and said his goodbyes to Timothy, and then he brings up another important point.

Paul's Final Instructions

In his final instructions to Timothy Paul expresses some real human needs. One of them is the need for Timothy's company as the end approaches. Men could learn from the fact that Paul sees no need to conceal the fact that he has emotions. Too often we believe that "real men never cry" and that they swallow their tears if they do. But we are not supposed to be superhuman and to suppress or hide all our emotions. There is a time to weep. All that is needed is to determine when is the appropriate time. A pastor does not want to be labelled a cry-baby, yet he should remember that Jesus wept and was respected for doing so (John 11:35-36). It is not beneath our dignity to show emotion when it is called for.

Come soon

Paul does not yet know the date of his trial or execution. However he suspects it will be soon, and so he urges Timothy not to delay in coming to visit him in prison: *Do your best to come to me quickly* (4:9).

The journey to Rome was a long one. It would involve Timothy travelling north to Troas, where he would pick up some of Paul's belongings that had been left there (4:13). From Troas he would probably take a ship to Philippi, and then follow the great Roman road known as the Egnatian Way across the north of the Balkan Peninsula to Dyrrachium, where the road ended on the shores of the Adriatic Sea. He would then sail across the Adriatic and land at Brindisi in the south of Italy. From there, he would follow another great Roman road, the Appian Way, for some three hundred miles (500 km) before reaching Rome. This journey would have taken at least two months to complete. Assuming that Paul's letter to Timothy had to reach him via the same route, it would be three or four months from the time Paul wrote it before Timothy could possibly arrive in Rome. Thus Paul's encouragement to Timothy to arrive *before winter* (4:21) suggests that the letter was probably written in late spring or early summer.[399] Such a date would leave Timothy just enough time to get to Rome before winter storms ended all travel by sea and made travel by land very difficult.[400]

Bring support

From the book of Acts we know that at different times Paul travelled with Barnabas, Silas, Luke, Mark, Timothy and others. It seems that he did not like to travel alone; nor was it safe to do so. Now, however, he is almost alone in Rome. His companion *Crescens has gone to Galatia* (in modern Turkey) and his other companion *Titus* has gone *to Dalmatia* (in modern Croatia). They may have gone for personal reasons or because Paul sent them to look after churches in those regions. He does not accuse them of neglecting him. However, he does express his disappointment in someone called *Demas*, who has left him *because he loved this world* (4:10). It appears that Demas was not prepared to endure the kind of suffering that association with Christ and Paul would bring.

The only person who is still with him is *Luke* (4:11) – the author of the Gospel of Luke and the book of Acts. He accompanied Paul for parts of his missionary journeys (as we can tell from his use of "we" in Acts 20:6; 21:15; 28:16) and was with him during his first Roman imprisonment (Col 4:14; Phlm 24). Luke's use of medical terms in his writings tells us that he was a physician. This may explain why he was travelling with Paul when he did. It may be that Paul needed medical care at the time.

The mention of *Tychicus* being sent *to Ephesus* (4:12) sheds light on the decision Paul was mulling over when he wrote to Titus. In Titus 3:12 he says he was not certain whether he would send Artemas or Tychicus to Crete to relieve Titus. Since he is sending Tychicus to Ephesus, he most likely sent Artemas to Crete.

The chronology appears to work like this. By the time Paul wrote 2 Timothy, Artemas had relieved Titus of his duties at Crete, and Titus had carried out Paul's instruction to meet him at Nicopolis (Titus 3:12). That city would have been an ideal springboard for Titus to move on to further work in Dalmatia (4:10). Meanwhile, Tychicus will probably carry this letter to Timothy and take over from him so that Timothy can set out to join Paul in Rome.[401]

While looking forward to fellowship with Timothy, Paul would like to have another companion as well, and so Timothy is requested to *get Mark and bring him with you* (4:11). Presumably he was expected to meet Mark somewhere on his way to Rome.[402] The reason Paul wants Mark in Rome is *because he is helpful to me in my ministry*. He does not specify exactly how Mark is helpful, but it could be that he would help Luke in providing for Paul's personal needs in prison. He may also have spoken Latin well, for his name is Roman, not Jewish. Fluency in Latin would have been useful in Rome, the centre of the Latin language.

This reference to Mark is an excellent example of how people can change. Ten years earlier, Paul had objected to taking Mark with them on his second missionary journey (Acts 15:36–39). Mark had been a quitter, and Paul thought he would hamper the mission. But now Mark has matured, and Paul is more than willing to recognize that change. The person he once rejected is now a valued co-worker (see also Col 4:10; Phlm 24).[403]

We are badly mistaken when we evaluate people based on outdated information. While their history cannot be erased, people change and we need to acknowledge their change.

Bring my clothes and my books

Paul's request for Timothy to *bring the cloak that I left with Carpus at Troas, and my scrolls, especially the parchments* (4:13) is one of the most personal notes in all his letters.[404]

We do not know why these personal belongings had been left in Troas. Possibly that was where Paul was arrested, in which case he may not have had time to gather his belongings from the place where he was staying at the time. With winter approaching, he needs his cloak to keep him warm. The type of cloak he refers to was very similar to the poncho worn in South America. It was made of heavy material with a hole in the middle, and often included a hood. It provided shelter from cold and rain by covering the wearer "like a little tent, reaching right down to the ground".[405]

The scrolls Paul requested could have been made of papyrus or parchment. Parchment was the higher quality material because it was reusable and more durable.

Scholars have speculated about the possible content of these scrolls. They may have been copies of the books of the Old Testament[406] or collections of Old Testament proof-texts (that is, Old Testament passages that Paul recognized as relating to the truths he was teaching).[407] Or they may have been blank scrolls on which he could write. Still another possibility is that they were personal documents to which Paul had a sentimental attachment, or even legal documents that Paul needed for his trial, such as a certificate proving his Roman citizenship.

Watch out for Alexander

Paul concludes these specific requests with a specific warning against someone Timothy probably knew called *Alexander the metalworker* (4:14). Alexander was a common name, but it seems likely that this man is the same Alexander referred to in 1 Timothy 1:20. If this is true, it is possible that after Paul excommunicated him, Alexander became determined to get even. He may have set out to cause trouble for Paul. If so, he was obviously successful, for Paul says that he *did me a great deal of harm*. It is possible that he was even behind Paul's arrest. The verb translated as "did" was often used in a legal context when someone was an informer, "informing against" someone else.[408] Or he may have harmed Paul when he was in Rome by testifying against him in court. Or he may have done something else, unrelated to Paul's present condition.

Besides the personal harm Alexander caused Paul, he also *strongly opposed our message* (4:15). He may have frustrated Paul's work on one occasion or numerous times.[409] Paul speaks of "**our** message" to make it clear that Alexander is also likely to oppose Timothy or anyone else who preaches the same message as Paul. For this reason, Timothy must continually *be on ... guard against him*.[410]

It is worth noting that Timothy is not told to do anything about this man except beware of him. The warning is prompted by Paul's concern for Timothy's safety; it is not a disguised call for revenge.[411] Paul is content to leave Alexander's fate in the hands of God, the righteous judge. He knows that *the Lord will repay him* (4:14).[412] This repayment may come in this life or on the day of judgment.

We would do well to imitate Paul's example and leave those who harm us to God's judgment. They may prosper in the present because God sends his rain on everyone, whether they love him or oppose him (Matt 5:45). But in the long run, their work will not prosper (Ps 1:4–5). It is not that we pretend that nothing has happened, but rather that we leave our case with the court of heaven. Paul knew that taking Alexander to court would distract him from his work of glorifying God.

Believers are not doing wrong if they seek justice in human courts – that is what the courts are there for. The Lord has established them to exercise justice on his behalf. But we need to think carefully about whether going to court will glorify God and open the eyes of those who have harmed us, or whether it will only deepen their spiritual blindness. For example, some people rush to court whenever the neighbour's cattle stray into their field, or the neighbourhood children break a branch off their tree, or someone makes a noise that disturb their sleep. Believers who act like this are seen as court lovers not Christ followers. We should be prepared to forgive accidental offences.

What about deliberate offences? Here, too, we have the option of going to a human court or leaving the matter to the courts of heaven. For example, if someone injures (or even amputates) your left hand, you may choose to take them to court or you may decide to leave them to God, and ask the Lord to strengthen your right hand to function as if you had two hands. Neither decision is wrong in itself. In every situation, we should base our actions on what will bring more glory to God.

The Lord's Faithfulness

Paul now gives Timothy a brief account of his experience in the Roman legal system. He presents what has happened in terms of his relationship with people (4:16) and with God (4:17). What he has to say could be summarized as "human absence, divine presence".[413]

Human absence

The particular aspect of his experience that Paul speaks of is his *first defence* (4:16a). In the past, some commentators argued that this "first defence" was Paul's first Roman imprisonment (Acts 28).[414] Today, however, most scholars believe that the word translated "first defence" is a technical term for a particular step in a Roman court case. The "defence" involved the defendant appearing before a magistrate to reply to the accusations against him. This was when the precise charge against the prisoner would be formulated.[415] The goal was to gather basic information, and to decide whether to proceed with a full trial.

If the preliminary examination revealed that more information was needed, the second stage of the procedure would begin.[416] Further investigation would be ordered. This investigation could drag on for as long as was necessary in order to establish the facts of the case. During Paul's first Roman imprisonment, this took about two years (see Acts 24:1, 23, 27; compare with Acts 28:18, 30).

From the record in Acts and the words here, we can assume that after his first arrest in Jerusalem, Paul experienced imprisonment, a preliminary examination and further investigation, after which he was released. He then undertook further ministry (during which he wrote 1 Timothy and Titus), before being arrested again (possibly in Troas – see above) and imprisoned for a second time. He has now had the preliminary examination (4:16) and the further investigations have begun. While these are going on, Paul writes this second letter to Timothy. Because of the way things went during the preliminary examination, Paul senses that this imprisonment will result in his conviction and execution. But the further investigation is still underway, and given how long this took during his first Roman imprisonment, there may be time for Timothy to reach him before his final trial and death.

During Roman legal proceedings the prisoner could be represented or given advice by someone called a *patronus* or advocate.[417] But Paul clearly had no such help, for he says, *no one came to my support*. He had neither a lawyer, nor any friends willing to testify on his behalf. Instead, *everyone deserted me* (4:16).[418]

Although Luke was with Paul (4:11), he was probably not eligible to offer the type of legal support Paul needed. Nor was Tychicus, assuming he was still in Rome during these proceedings (4:12). But those who could have helped Paul distanced themselves from him. Associating with Paul as an official witness or advocate in his defence was dangerous, and they shied away from such exposure. They all reacted in the same way as Demas had, and probably for the same reason (4:10). No wonder Paul felt abandoned.

Divine presence

Though deserted by others, Paul was not alone. His *but* at the start of 4:17 stresses that the human desertion served to highlight the divine assistance he received, which gave him support, strength and protection (4:17).

Support

Paul did not receive any human support at his trial, but he reports that *the Lord stood at my side* (4:17a). The verb used here means to come to someone's aid or help them, but it can also have the technical meaning of "to bring before (a judge)".[419] Paul is saying that the Lord became his "legal adviser". This is what Christ promised in Matthew 10:19–20: "But when they arrest you, do not worry about what to say or how to say it. At that time you will be given what to say, for it will not be you speaking, but the Spirit of your Father speaking through you" (see also Mark 13:11.) The "Lord" is Jesus Christ, who is himself the ultimate judge (4:1, 8). What better legal advisor could there be?

Strength

When Paul says the Lord *gave me strength* (4:17b), he means more than just physical or intellectual strength. He also received the emotional strength that gave him courage and boldness to meet the situation.[420] He had known this strength in the past (Acts 9:22) and often spoke of it in his letters (Rom 4:20; Eph 6:10; Phil 4:13; 1 Tim 1:12; 2 Tim 2:1).

Paul's experience is not unique. Others who have stayed close to the Lord have also received this strength in difficult situations. Where others would have given up, these people have persevered. Their secret is the inner enabling of God.

The Lord strengthened Paul *so that ... the message might be fully proclaimed* (4:17c). The "message" here is the "apostolic preaching of the gospel".[421] Paul used the legal hearing as an opportunity to proclaim the message of salvation! And not only did he proclaim the gospel, he did it with a sense of exultation. He saw what was happening as the climax of his ministry, the fulfilment of prophecies that he had received (Acts 9:15; 23:11; 27:24).[422] He puts the words *through me* at the very start of the sentence to emphasize his excitement. God had given him the privilege of proclaiming the gospel so that *all the Gentiles might hear it.*

"All the Gentiles" is hyperbole, for clearly Paul did not preach to every single non-Jew living in the world at that time. But he was preaching in the most multicultural and powerful city of the Gentile world, and those hearing him would have represented many different countries. News of his message would spread as people talked about what they had heard.[423] Paul counted it a great privilege to have had this opportunity. He must have felt wonderful that despite being forsaken by men, God had strengthened him and used him. What a glorious climax to his life's work!

Protection

The Lord protected Paul and *delivered [him] from the lion's mouth* (4:17d). Who or what was this "lion"? Various suggestions have been made. It could have been Satan, who is described elsewhere in the New Testament as being "like a roaring lion looking for someone to devour" (1 Pet 5:8). Paul was delivered from him by being given the strength not to yield to weakness or betray his faith during the trial. Or it might have been the emperor Nero, if he was the judge at Paul's trial, or the whole Roman Empire as a system working against Paul. It could even be a literal lion, for some Christians were indeed sentenced to be torn apart by wild animals. But it appears more likely that Paul is not thinking of any particular lion. He is simply using a common expression to describe deliverance from great danger (see, for example, Pss 7:2; 22:21; 35:17).[424]

The preliminary investigation could easily have led to Paul being pronounced guilty and executed immediately, but he was delivered because the judge or judges who examined him did not come to a conclusive decision. This temporary reprieve gave him an opportunity to write this letter, and possibly even to see Timothy again. It was an act of God.[425]

We can all probably remember experiences that cause us to say, "If it was not for God, I would not be here." I have had several such experiences. There was the very dark night when my father and I made several attempts to cross a swollen river, and later discovered that we had been dangerously close to a deep hole where the water would have swept us away. Now, when my father and I discuss the greatness of the Lord, we often remind each other, "Remember the River Kaiti!" We should never take our safety for granted or say we were "lucky". The truth is that God is watching over us.

Such experiences should not merely be historical incidents recorded in our memories or our diaries. Like Paul, we should use God's wonderful work in our lives as a source of courage to help us face similar or even more complex situations in the future. We should also share our stories with others as an encouragement to them. We should tell the stories to our children, to our friends, and to those we mentor.

Confidence in the Lord

Paul was delivered from immediate death, but he is still in jail and facing the likelihood of execution. But he does not despair. Instead, he has confidence in the Lord. He trusts in the Lord's deliverance, takes hope in the promise of God's heavenly kingdom, and praises him. 4:18.

The Lord's deliverance

Paul has been facing many difficulties: Alexander the metalworker had harmed him, (4:14–15), many friends have abandoned him (4:16), and he has been in imminent danger of death (4:17). Each situation taught

Paul more about what it means to depend upon the Lord. He can now confidently look to the future and say, *The Lord will rescue me from every evil attack* (4:18a). He recognizes that the Lord is above each and every evil deed. He has delivered Paul in the past, and he will continue to do so.

What Paul has in mind here goes beyond physical deliverance. He senses that this imprisonment will end in death (4:6). In human terms, he seems "to be the victim of circumstances and a criminal condemned at the bar of Roman justice; but Paul saw beyond time and knew that his eternal safety was assured".[426]

Some commentators think that Paul is expressing confidence that the inner or outer temptations he encounters, which might undermine his faith or courage, will not derail his faith.[427] This conclusion seems unnecessary. Paul is simply stating that his adversaries may destroy his body but cannot touch his soul (see also Matt 10:28).

Like him, we should remember that "it is always better to be in danger for a moment and safe for eternity, than to be safe for a moment and jeopardize eternity"[428] or lose our Master's "well-done" on our arrival there.

The heavenly kingdom

God's kingdom is a present reality for believers in the sense that God reigns over them. But entrance into this realm is also a hope that "Christians look forward to at the consummation of the age"[429] (1 Cor 6:10; 15:50; Gal 5:21; Eph 5:5; 1 Thess 2:12; 2 Thess 1:5). Paul is confident that the Lord *will bring me safely to his heavenly kingdom* (4:18b).

Paul may be deliberately mentioning the heavenly kingdom to contrast it with the earthly kingdom that will soon condemn him to death. The Roman empire will execute him, but the Lord will lead him safely into his heavenly kingdom. He will lose nothing when death comes. Instead, he will gain the enjoyment of God's eternal kingdom by leaving the temporary kingdom that holds him captive.

Expression of praise

With his eyes fixed on his eternal destiny that no person, not even the emperor, can prevent him attaining, Paul praises the Lord saying, *To him be the glory forever and ever. Amen* (4:18c).

Most doxologies are addressed to God the Father (see, for example, Gal 1:5; Phil 4:20; 1 Tim 1:17) but for Paul, what is due to the Father is also due to the Son. So the "him" here is probably the Lord Jesus Christ (4:1, 8, 14). But far more important than whether the doxology addresses the Father or the Son is the question of when we should ascribe glory, praise and honour to him. For Paul, personal reflection on God or the Lord Jesus Christ always leads to him bursting out in praise. The Lord who has delivered him before and will deliver him again is worthy of all glory and praise.

As we walk with the Lord, we too should sometimes burst out in spontaneous praise to God. All that he has done, is doing and will do is so wonderful that it should move us to worship. For example, recently four of us were in a car when an out-of-control car suddenly hurtled towards us. The two women behind me gasped, "Oh God!" We just managed to avoid an accident, and when it was clear that the Lord had spared us from death, the two women simultaneously said, "Thank you, Jesus" and "God loves us!" This type of spontaneous prayer and praise should characterize our lives. Our help comes from the Lord. He is the one who grants us protection.

Parting Words

Paul closes his letter with personal greetings to his acquaintances in Ephesus (4:19). Paul had first met *Aquila* and his wife *Priscilla* in Corinth shortly after their arrival there from Rome. They had then joined him in his journey from Corinth to Ephesus, where they had become leaders in the church (Acts 18). They had briefly returned to Rome at one stage (16:3), but are now back in Ephesus.[430] *Onesiphorus* himself had probably died (see commentary on 2 Tim 1:16–18), and that is why Paul's greeting is directed to his *household*, rather than to the man himself.

The mention of these shared friends reminds Paul of two others whom Timothy might like information about, as when he last saw them they had been travelling with Paul. So Paul reports that *Erastus stayed in Corinth* and that he *left Trophimus sick in Miletus* (4:20). We cannot know exactly why they stayed behind, but it is easy to construct a plausible scenario that looks something like this.[431] Paul was arrested at Troas. In the chaos accompanying his arrest, his cloak and books were left behind there. Trophimus and Erastus accompanied Paul up the coast to Miletus, but there Trophimus fell ill and had to be left behind. Erastus went further with Paul, but was then instructed to go to Corinth and remain there. Alternatively, if Paul travelled to Rome by ship, his ship might have put in at Corinth, and Erastus could have been left there to care for the Corinthian church.

If this scenario is correct, Trophimus would probably be recovering by the time Paul wrote this letter (assuming that he had not contracted a chronic illness or died). Paul's goal in mentioning him does not seem to be to request prayer for him but to let Timothy know why Luke is the only one of his trusted fellow workers with him in Rome (4:11).

However, although none of Paul's close associates is with him, he is not totally friendless. He sends greetings from *Eubulus ... Pudens, Linus, Claudia and all the brothers and sisters* (4:21b). We know nothing about these three men and one woman, all of whom, except Eubulus, have Latin names. Presumably they were not important enough to have been called to give testimony at Paul's first defence, or else they had not yet been converted at that time. The ancient church fathers Irenaeus and Eusebius do mention a Linus who is said to have been the bishop of Rome and a successor of Peter.[432] But we do not know whether he was the same man.

Finally, Paul prays for Timothy: *The Lord be with your spirit*. He then blesses all those others who will read this letter, saying: *Grace be with you all* (4:22).[433] These people may have been Timothy's associates in Ephesus, such as Priscilla, Aquila and the household of Onesiphorus,[434] or the entire Ephesian Christian community.[435]

Paul expects to see Timothy before long. But in the meantime, and as always, his prayer is that Timothy will feel the Lord's presence in his life and ministry, and that the Lord's grace will be with him and will freely supply everything he needs.

Paul's prayer is for Timothy's "spirit", but this is only a figure of speech referring to his whole being. Yet at the same time, Paul knows that Timothy needs a lot of spiritual encouragement. And so, with this prayer of encouragement, Paul concludes his second letter to his dear son in the faith and friend in the ministry. What a wonderful spiritual father he has been to Timothy!

Questions for Discussion

1. Some people experience dramatic demonstrations of God's protection, while others are protected in less visible and more subtle ways. What circumstances in your life make you say, like Paul, "the Lord protected me" as you went through them? Share your experience and thank God for his goodness in each one.

2. At times we can better understand why God allowed our lives to unfold the way they have when we look back on them. What bearing does God's previous work in your life have on your present and possibly your future? Is there evidence that you have learned from your past? Have you learned that because God took care of you before, he will also take care of you today and tomorrow? How do you evaluate yourself? Share with others and ask the Lord for continued spiritual growth in each of those in your group.

TITUS

INTRODUCTION TO TITUS

It is usually easier to continue something one has started than to take over work that someone else began. If we want to finish their work successfully, we need a clear understanding of what they had in mind. It will help to have detailed instructions on how to proceed. In modern terms, the predecessor needs to provide clear, detailed handover notes to his or her successor.

Titus finds himself in this type of situation in Crete. Paul had started a work there, but now Titus has been left to deal with "what was left unfinished" (1:5a). In this letter, Paul provides him with the instructions he needs to carry on and finish the task.

Studying this book makes it clear that Paul's concern is not only that Titus organize the church in Crete well. He also wants Titus to establish believers who will not easily be swayed by false teaching and who will live up to the expectations that God has for people who call themselves Christians.

We need to keep this ministerial lesson in mind as we go through Titus. Organization has its place in building up the kingdom of God, but virtues that conform to the nature of God take higher priority. A congregation with a well-written constitution and by-laws is not the end. The organization must result in holy lives in a congregation that everyone feels comfortable belonging to because Christ's love is felt there.

UNIT 1
TITUS 1:1–4

ESTABLISHING CONTACT

A weary father enters the gate of his home, tired after labouring all day. Glancing around, he sees that the cows have not been fed nor the yard swept. Sighing, he walks into the house, stepping over the dusty shoes left lying at the door. Animated voices fill his ears and children burst into the room. They run to greet him. Resisting the temptation to scold them for what they have not done, he smiles and greets them warmly. There will be plenty of time later to tell them to do their chores. But he only has one opportunity to greet them.

This father understands that what matters most to a child is whether the father's face shines when he comes home. Children are very sensitive to a parent's moods. When their father or mother comes home from work, class or a journey and immediately launches into complaints about everything that is wrong, the entire day is clouded. But when the greeting signals a joyful reunion, children live in a climate of security and know that they are loved. True, the issues that need attention have to be dealt with, but not in a way that makes them more important than loving relationships. This applies not only when it comes to parents and children, but also to husbands and wives.

Paul's greeting to Titus has the warmth of a father greeting a child he loves. The strength of this relationship will make Titus eager to hear what Paul has to say. We should remember this principle when it comes to our own relationships, whether at home, at work or in a church. The way we greet others will create an impression that can have positive or negative effects on everything else in our relationship.

The Author

This letter was probably written on a scroll of papyrus or parchment, not on individual sheets of paper. Rather than forcing a reader to unwind the entire scroll before finding out who wrote the letter, the Greeks and Romans sensibly put the author's name right at the start. This is what Paul does here as he introduces himself to Timothy.

Identification of the author

In 1 and 2 Timothy Paul began by describing himself as an "apostle of Christ Jesus", but here he introduces himself to Titus as a *servant*, using a word that could equally well be translated "slave" (1:1). He does not often refer to himself in this way in the opening words of a letter. He only does so in his letters to the Romans, Philippians and Titus – all letters to places where there does not seem to be any serious questioning of his authority. It thus seems that Titus' situation in Crete was not as difficult as Timothy's in Ephesus. (Paul does not hesitate to describe himself as a servant at other points in his letters – see Galatians 1:10 and 2 Timothy 2:24).

The title "servant/slave of God" combines humility and honour. It shows humility because slaves had no freedom or rights. They were the property of the one who bought them. Paul thus views himself as God's property. But the title could also be one of honour, for Paul shares it with people like Abraham (Ps 105:42), Moses (Num 12:7), Joshua (Josh 24:29), David (Ps 89:3), Daniel (Dan 6:20) and the prophets in general (Jer 7:25; Ezek 38:17; Amos 3:7; Zech 1:6). All of these great men were in a special relationship to God and it was a great honour to be counted one of them by sharing the same title.[1] While Paul was probably thinking primarily of himself as God's slave, the other connotations of the title should not be ignored.

What is unusual in Titus is that Paul speaks of himself as *a servant of God*. He may have chosen to use "God" here simply because in the very next phrase he describes himself as an apostle of Jesus Christ. But in all his other letters, he describes himself as a servant of Christ.[2] His willingness to use either "of God" or "of Christ" reflects his belief that anything which belongs to the Father belongs equally to the Son (see commentary on 2 Tim 4:18).

The other title he uses, *an apostle of Jesus Christ*, is discussed in the commentary on 1 Timothy 1:1.

The titles Paul chooses to use make an important point about how he sees his relationship to others, including those he is writing to. We should be like him in seeing ourselves as God's servants, reporting directly to him. We can speak with God's authority when carrying out the ministry he has assigned us, but to avoid becoming proud of our successes or arrogant in exercising this authority, we need to remember that we are only servants in God's vineyard.

It must offend God when people who claim to have performed miracles parade them as if they were their own doing. I do not question that God is able to do miracles, but I am cautious about some of those who claim to have performed them. Many men and women are willing to do anything to get religious fame. Assuming the miracles are genuine, God is the one who should be honoured. He should be the focus, not the person he used as his instrument. Whatever work God gives us to do, whether it is preaching, teaching, healing or any other acts of service, we must remember to communicate the fact that we are only servants.

Purpose of the author

Paul continues his introduction by spelling out the particular tasks he has been assigned, the things God wants to use him *for*.[3] These responsibilities give him the right to speak authoritatively to Titus and to the church.

For the faith of the church

The first thing God wants to use Paul for is *to further the faith of God's elect* (1:1b). These words mean either that Paul is to bring God's chosen to saving faith or that he is to strengthen the faith of believers. The first task is evangelistic, the second is pastoral. It is not necessary to choose between these two options, for Paul did both.[4] He probably defined the "elect" both in terms of the status believers had before they came to faith in Christ and the status they gain when they come to faith and enter into a new relationship with God (Rom 8:29–30, 33; Col 3:12).[5]

We are called to the same task that Paul was in that we are to bring people to faith in Christ and then help them to grow in their faith. "Hit and run" evangelism is of little value because Satan is very quick to show new believers reasons why coming to faith in Christ was a mistake. Unless these people are followed up and nurtured in their faith, they will stagnate and never grow to maturity.

For the knowledge of the truth

The second thing God wants to use Paul for is to further believers' *knowledge of the truth* (1:1c). Whereas his first task was to bring them to a subjective commitment to the faith, his second is to inform them about the objective facts of their faith,[6] for although faith begins with a simple response of the heart, it must also involve the mind.

The "knowledge" believers need is not limited to intellectual understanding. It encompasses the full understanding that results from experiencing God and his word. It produces more knowledge of God's word, a closer walk with God, and evident spiritual maturity. Such knowledge enables those who have it to distinguish truth from error when it comes to what to believe and how to behave.[7]

Finding the right balance between subjective faith and objective knowledge seems to be a problem for the church in Africa. Many who sincerely invited Jesus into their hearts in Sunday school have not been given the teaching they needed to become grounded in their faith, and so their adult lives show no evidence that they ever came to know Christ as Saviour. On the other hand, some who faithfully attended Sunday school or catechism classes acquired only a head knowledge of doctrine, without their hearts being touched. Our hearts and heads must meet if our faith is to make a difference in how we live from Monday to Saturday.

One way church leaders can help this happen is by arranging for smaller classes. In a class with more than fifty children, a child can learn to answer questions correctly and qualify for baptism. But we can only know whether that child has come to faith in Christ if we know him or her as an individual. In small classes, teachers have the opportunity to talk to children about their personal faith. Teaching such a class is thus one of the most important ministries in the church. Unfortunately, it is also one of the most neglected because it is treated as a place to teach rote answers to set questions. This perception must be corrected if African Christians are to become deeply rooted in their faith.

There is an intimate relationship between knowledge of truth and *godliness*, or between "right belief and right conduct".[8] They are twins. One does not gain knowledge and then set about becoming godly (although this is what the tniv translation could be read as implying). Rather, the two go hand in hand, so that a better translation of the phrase would read, "the knowledge of the truth which is according to godliness" (nasb).[9] This point is illustrated by the heretical teachers who claim to teach truth, but whose lack of godliness reveals that their "truth" is false (Titus 1:16). To deny this intimate connection between truth and right conduct is to deny one of the basic tenets of Christianity. That is why godliness is one of the key themes in Paul's letters to Timothy and Titus. It can be said that "the goal of Paul's apostleship is the personal response of faith, a faith based on an accurate knowledge of the truth of the gospel, and a faith that naturally and necessarily shows itself in godly behaviour."[10]

The fact that truth and godliness are twins should prompt deep reflection in the African church. A high percentage of Africans claim to be Christians, yet there is no equivalent level of godliness in African countries. How is it that people with Christian names like Peter, Paul and Mary are so often guilty of corruption, theft and immorality? We need to ground our people not only in Christian beliefs but also in how their beliefs should integrate with and transform their lives.

For the hope of eternal life

Translations like the niv, which speaks of "a faith and knowledge resting on the hope of eternal life", imply that possession of eternal life is the goal of the faith and knowledge Paul has been speaking of. But Paul' statement that he carries out his ministry *in the hope of eternal life* (1:2a) can also be read as Paul's third purpose for his ministry.[11] His goal is to promote the hope of eternal life *as well as* faith and knowledge of truth, not as a consequence of them. The reason this distinction is important is that eternal life is not something given to us at the end of our lives, but is something we receive at the very beginning of our journey of faith in Christ Jesus. We already have eternal life, although we will only experience its fullness in the future (see also 1 Tim 1:16). Moreover, in the New Testament "hope" does not refer to wondering whether something will or will not happen. Rather, it is a confident assurance based on God's promises.

The hope Paul is speaking of here is the assurance of eternal life,[12] *which God, who does not lie, promised* (1:2b). In describing God in these terms, Paul is quoting the Old Testament: "God is not a human, that he should lie, not a human being, that he should change his mind. Does he speak and then not act? Does he promise and not fulfil?" (Num 23:19). He is stressing that his ministry has deep roots and a solid foundation. Because God is trustworthy, so are his promises. The Christian hope of eternal life is secure.

This is one of the major differences between Christianity and all other religions. Christianity offers what *God* has *promised*. Other religions only suggest ways to find what people are looking for. Take African traditional religions as an example. Their sacrifices are offered in the hope that God will accept them and respond to the worshipper's needs. But Christianity offers certainty, for it is built on the known will of God.

But as we read Paul's words, questions arise in our minds. When did God make this promise? Who did he make it to? Two possible answers have been suggested, based on different translations of Paul's words at the end of 1:2. If they are translated as "long ages ago" (as in the nasb), then Paul is referring to the Old Testament era.[13] In that case, the promise was probably given to the prophets, although not necessarily on one specific occasion. The verb "promised" can be taken as summarizing everything that God revealed about his plans for humanity over time.[14]

Alternatively, the words can be translated as *before the beginning of time* (as in the tniv, nrsv, hcsb and nkjv). In this case, the promise was made before the world was created and it was made to the pre-existent Christ, who received it as our representative, acting on our behalf.[15] This interpretation, which seems preferable, is based on the use of the same phrase in 2 Timothy 1:9.

God's promise was made in eternity, but it was revealed in history *at his appointed season* (1:3). The same Greek words are also translated "at the proper time" in 1 Timothy 2:6 and "in his own time" in 6:14, each translation reflecting the context in which the words are used. Here the context is the same as Galatians 4:4, and the focus falls on the manifestation of the hope of eternal life within history when Christ became incarnate. So, the "appointed time" in Titus 1:3 was the time chosen by God as the right time for his son to appear in the world.

Why did Jesus appear when he did? The answer provides further confirmation that God is ultimately in charge of history. When Alexander the Great (356–323 bc) popularized the Greek language and united many small kingdoms, God was in charge. He was ensuring that communication across cultures would be easy, for the Greek language would be widely understood. When the Romans took over from the Greeks and exercised their skills in road construction and good governance, God was in charge. He was ensuring that missionaries like Paul could use the extensive network of Roman roads to travel easily across the vast Roman Empire without any need for visas. They could travel in relative safety because the *pax Romana* (the Roman peace) inhibited major wars.

The time when Christ came was also a time when older faiths had failed to answer people's basic questions. The philosophical answers being offered to replace them were often too complicated for ordinary people to understand. Thus people's hearts were "open to receive the message of salvation which the Christian missionaries brought".[16]

God was in charge, and he is still in charge. We live in a time of worldwide economic and environmental problems, a time when terrorism makes us look at others with suspicion and when the balance of power in the world is shifting. In these uncertain times, one thing is certain: God is in charge. He controls the big things and the small things, the affairs of the world and the affairs of our lives. So we have no need to worry – we can face the future with confidence (Matt 6:25–34).

The Method of the Author

The next phrase in 1:3 is difficult to understand in the original Greek, as is apparent from the variety of translations: *which God has brought to light through the preaching entrusted to me* (tniv); "he brought his word to light through the preaching entrusted to me" (niv); "manifested, even His word, in the proclamation with which I was entrusted" (nasb). Literally, it would be translated "manifested his word in the proclamation". The problem arises because the grammar of the sentence is not clear, and so it is difficult to tell whether the thing that is brought to light is the "hope of eternal life" or the "word".[17] Both positions are possible. However, I would suggest that hope of eternal life is what was manifested at the proper time;[18] the method of the manifestation is the word of God;[19] and the sphere of the manifestation is proclamation (nasb, hcsb, nrsv) or preaching (niv, nkjv).

But what is meant by "the word" here? On this point at least, almost all commentators agree. The "word" is not to be interpreted as referring to Jesus (as in John 1:1), for in these letters "the word of God" always means the gospel (see 1 Tim 4:5; 2 Tim 2:9; Titus 2:5).[20] Paul is speaking about the *message* about Jesus and not about the *person* of Jesus.[21] This is the message that he has been preaching.[22]

Paul's preaching ministry was *entrusted to [him] by the command of God our Saviour* (1:3b). Other passages make the same point. Paul did not choose to become a preacher; he was assigned this responsibility (Gal 2:7; 1 Tim 1:11; 2 Tim 1:11). The phrase translated "by the command of God" could equally well be translated "by order of God". Paul is not complaining or showing resentment about this task. On the contrary, he loves proclaiming the gospel and considers it a privilege to do so. The reason he mentions the command is to stress that his mission is backed by the highest possible authority (see commentary on 1 Tim 1:1).[23]

God continues to choose people for the crucial ministry of proclaiming the word today. He is the one who makes the choice, and he expects that those he selects will willingly obey him. In saying this, I am not saying that he ignores those who are not entrusted with this ministry. God assigns all believers tasks to do. He calls each of us to serve humanity in some way. Some are called to study the law and ensure that justice is done, others to care for and educate children, others to provide affordable medical services to their communities, and so on. But there are people whom God calls to serve him specifically by proclaiming the word. Like Paul, this group have been entrusted with the message of the gospel.

When we proclaim the gospel, we tend to think of Christ as our Saviour. But it is striking that here Paul once again speaks of God as our Saviour. As discussed at length in the commentary on 1 Timothy 2:3, both are involved in our salvation.

The Recipient

Paul is writing to Titus. We can piece together a rough portrait of this man from the comments made about him in Paul's other letters. He was a Greek who was not a Jewish proselyte before he became a Christian, for he was not circumcised (Gal 2:3). He may possibly have been related to Luke, if Luke is the brother referred to in 2 Corinthians 8:18 and 12:18, and if "brother" there is not simply a reference to a fellow-believer. It is impossible to be dogmatic on this point.

Titus' uncircumcised state was an important issue when he was part of the team that accompanied Paul to Jerusalem for the debate on the requirements for Gentile converts (Gal 2:1).

It seems that he was also a competent administrator, for Paul chose him to organize a collection for the poor in Jerusalem (2 Cor 8:6, 10). He was someone who could handle difficult situations, for Paul sent him to Corinth to deliver one of the most severe letters he ever wrote (2 Cor 8:16). Now he is handling a difficult situation in Crete (Titus 1:5). The description of Titus as a "man who could bring order where there was chaos and peace where there was strife"[24] may not be far-fetched.

In the recent past, Africa has badly needed men and women like Titus to be God's instruments of healing and reconciliation. Africa still needs them in its villages, churches, national politics and international relationships. We are grateful whenever we see God using people to reconcile neighbours fighting over a piece of land or to bring opposing parties in a local church into a good working relationship. We have also witnessed God using people who give their time and money to reconcile warring nations and groups within nations. At whatever level we are engaged in a ministry of reconciliation, God sees it and rewards us because he loves peace among his people.

We need to pray for more people like Titus who are brave enough to take up the task of reconciliation and who have the credibility to be accepted by the warring parties.

Paul addresses Titus as *my true son in our common faith* (1:4). This is the same way he addressed Timothy (1 Tim 1:2). It indicates their very close spiritual relationship in matters concerning the gospel. While it may mean that Titus was converted through the direct ministry of Paul, it could simply be saying that Titus has been faithful in carrying out Paul's instructions.[25]

The prepositional phrase "in our common faith" (literally, "in a common faith") functions the same way "in the faith" does in 1 Timothy 1:2. It tells us the context of the spiritual bond between Paul and Titus. When Paul describes their faith as "common", he may mean that they share a common set of beliefs (as in Jude 3)[26], or that they both received salvation in the same way, despite Paul being Jewish and Titus being Greek.[27] "Common" could also communicate their equality in the faith; they are brothers, partners and fellow workers.[28]

None of these views excludes the other. However, given that Paul has just called Titus his son, it is unlikely that he is thinking of him here as a "brother, partner and fellow worker" (although he was all these). Moreover, the father-son relationship implies that Paul has nurtured Titus' spiritual development, and makes it more likely that the focus falls on their shared response of faith rather than on their credal beliefs.

The principle underlying Paul's words here is important when it comes to the relationship between missionaries and local believers, or between mother and daughter churches. Too often, this relationship is framed in terms of "we need to help them because they are poor and don't have the money and education we have". But important as it is to help the poor, the driving force should not be our one-sided desire to help but our common faith in Jesus Christ. This should drive us to work together. Regardless of whether missionaries come from the West or from other regions of Africa, they should relate to local believers as fellow Christians and all should serve as partners working together to achieve a common purpose.

Greeting

Paul greets Titus with, *Grace and peace from God the Father and Christ Jesus our Saviour* (1:4b). This is very similar to the greeting he used when writing to Timothy, but it does not include "mercy" as a third blessing, and it addresses Jesus as "our Saviour" rather than "our Lord". The variations may not be deliberate, given that both Saviour and Lord are appropriate titles for Jesus. However, Timothy certainly needed the

Lord's abundant mercy while he worked in Ephesus, a seemingly more difficult field than Crete, where Titus is.[29]

Paul freely uses the title "Saviour" for both God and Jesus in this letter to Titus (1:3, 1:4; 2:13; 3:4). Both are involved in our salvation, for it originated in God the Father and was implemented by God the Son. Paul's prayer for Titus is that he will be blessed with grace and peace from the highest sources – the givers of salvation.

Again, Paul models the attitude church elders and younger members should have towards each other. In many African churches, there is tension between the older and younger generations. The younger members sometimes flaunt their education before the less educated older members, who react by desperately protecting their status and power. This competitive spirit brings no blessing to the church of Christ. What is called for is humility, in which each prays for God's blessings on others, whether they are of equal, greater or lesser status. We should never fight to protect or raise our personal status and success in the church. Instead, we should rejoice at every success that anyone achieves, for we are one team in Christ, working towards the same purposes.

Questions for Discussion

1. In these few verses of introduction, Paul lays great stress on the fact that knowledge of God must result in living like him. We have seen that there is great discrepancy in Africa between the claim to be a Christian and living like one. How can we address this problem as we handle the word of God?

2. Paul was not afraid to say good things about Titus. What statements, phrases, or even words would have made Titus' face glow as he read the introduction to this epistle? Why is it important that Paul wrote them? How can we follow Paul's manner of building rapport with the people we relate to?

UNIT 2
TITUS 1:5–9

ESTABLISHING THE CHURCH AT CRETE

There is a traditional saying, "The blind do not lead the blind across a river". If two blind people try to ford a river without help, both are likely to drown. Neither can see where the water is shallow or anticipate deeper channels where the river bends. Their lack of vision prevents them from identifying safe crossing points.

The young church on the island of Crete is a bit like a blind man walking, and it may be heading for trouble. Titus's task is to make sure that it is led by people whose eyes can see the direction it needs to go in.

Taking Time to Finish the Work

The large island of Crete is only mentioned twice in the New Testament. In Acts 27:7–21 there is an account of how the ship that was taking Paul to Rome sailed along the coast of Crete and hoped to winter in a harbour there. In Acts 2:11 we are told that Cretans were present in Jerusalem on the day of Pentecost and heard the disciples "declaring the wonders of God" in their own language. Some of those who were in Jerusalem on that day may have gone home and founded the church in Crete. Or it may have been founded by Paul in the course of a missionary journey that is not recorded in Acts. Certainly, Paul must have been there at some stage, because he speaks of having "left" Titus there.

However the church began, Paul tells Titus, *The reason I left you in Crete was that you might put in order what was left unfinished* (1:5a).

Some translations correctly translate the opening words as "for this reason" (nasb, nkjv).[30] The "for" links what follows to Paul's earlier description of Titus as his "true son in our common faith" (1:4). This link is important. It was because Titus was spiritually ready that Paul could assign him this task in Crete.

As we think about how to turn Africa around, we need to ask ourselves whether our pastors are spiritually ready to lead congregations. They may have completed theological studies, but do they also have spiritual maturity? We cannot expect a body of believers to be at a higher spiritual level than the person who leads them. Nor can we expect loving relationships between church members when there is unhealthy competition or bad relationships among pastors. These evils often come to the fore during church elections. Sadly, some will resort to malicious talk and even bribery in order to gain an office. Paul would regard such people as totally unqualified to lead.

Titus' task is to put things in order, which means to correct things or set things right.[31] The verb used could refer either to reforming something that was being done badly or to completing something that has not been finished. Paul's reference to the things "left unfinished" suggests that the latter is the primary meaning here. It seems that "while Christianity has caught on in a number of districts, the church in Crete is evidently in a pretty disorganized state".[32] Titus has the task of continuing and completing the work of establishing the church there. His responsibilities include appointing elders and teaching the basics of godly living.[33]

It is important to note that Paul was not the sort of church planter who only wanted to found a church. He was committed to establishing churches that would last. Today, too, those who feel called to be missionaries and church planters must not be motivated solely by the desire to win praise as people who can start churches. They must be committed to ensuring the well-being of a continuing church and must be willing to stay with the people they reach for Christ until the church is firmly established. If something like poor health or other circumstances makes this impossible, they or those who sent them must make a determined effort to ensure that there is someone to replace them, just as Titus replaced Paul.

Appointing Elders

There is some debate about whether appointing elders is part of "what was left unfinished" or whether it is an additional task. The tniv implies the latter by using "and" when it says: *and appoint elders in every town* (1:5b; also nasb, nkjv). It could be argued that a better translation would be "that you might straighten what was left unfinished, *especially* that you may appoint elders"[34] (neb). The appointment of elders is such an important part of the general task that it needs to be highlighted.[35]

Why is this part of the task so important? The answer is that elders have a vital role to play. They lead a church in the direction it should go in. But merely having elders is not as important as having the right kind of elders. A church is better off without *any* elders than with poor elders who lead it in the wrong direction. So Paul did not rush to appoint elders before he left Crete. Titus will take the time needed to identify qualified people to serve as elders rather than appointing unqualified elders who will make serious mistakes that later have to be rectified. He has been clearly instructed to do this, for when Paul says *I directed you* (1:5b) the "I" is emphatic and the "directed" has the force of an authoritative command.[36] In a sense, Paul is telling him, "This is what I told you to do, and I expect that you have been acting accordingly."

Paul expects Titus to have the time needed to carry out this task before meeting him in Nicopolis (3:12), and so presumably some progress has already been made. This implies that Titus is already familiar with the requirements for elders. But Paul is repeating these instructions because the issue is so important that he does not want any mistakes made. Moreover, Paul knows that Titus will share his letter with others. So he makes it clear that Titus has his authority and support as he exercises control over spiritual matters and appoints elders "in every town" on the large island, not just in the town where he is well-known to the church.

In instructing Titus to appoint elders, Paul is not making a theological statement governing all situations. It was simply the case that the church in Crete was young, and the best approach there was to appoint the elders. In some churches today elders are still appointed, while in others they are elected by the members. The method does not matter; what is important is that those who lead the church have the right qualities to be leaders.

General qualifications of elders

The general requirements for elders mentioned here are very similar to those listed for elders and deacons in 1 Timothy 3:1–12, so it is worth reading the commentary on that chapter in conjunction with these comments on Titus.

Paul summarizes the qualifications of an elder with the word *blameless*, which he repeats for emphasis (1:6, 1:7). In 1 Timothy he used the same word to describe deacons (3:10), and a synonym to specify the same requirement for elders (3:2). An elder must be someone whose behaviour will not bring the church into disrepute.

It is not only the elders' reputation as individuals that is important, but also their reputation as spouses and parents. Thus Paul specifies that an elder must be *faithful to his wife* (1:6). This requirement parallels the requirement for elders in 1 Timothy 3:2, for deacons in 1 Timothy 3:12, and for enrolled widows in 1 Timothy 5:9. It is discussed at length in the commentary on those passages.

Paul is also concerned that the elder's relationship with his own children should help, not hinder, the cause of the gospel. In 1 Timothy 3:4, he phrased this requirement in terms of the children's general behaviour, saying they should be obedient and respectful (see also 1 Tim 3:12). However, here he focuses on the children's relationships with Christ and specifies that an elder should be *a man whose children believe* (1:6). The word translated "believe" could also be translated as "are faithful" or "loyal".[37] So Paul might be saying that an elder's children must be "faithful to God, faithful to the family, faithful to a child's responsibility, faithful to the church".[38] But here the word probably means more than merely "loyal": Paul is stating that the elder's children need to be believers too.[39] If they are in a relationship with Christ, their behaviour will not bring shame on the church.

It cannot be denied that ministry is hampered when the leader's own child does not believe the word of God that is being taught. As Ward points out, "Children who are not believers are a living, permanent contradiction of an elder's message and may – but not always and not necessarily – point to his own failure. In any case they 'cramp his style'. Every time he offered a rebuke or made an appeal he would be open to the charge, 'what about your own children?'"[40]

The responsibility here is not laid on the children so much as on the parents. Have they brought their children to salvation? Or have they been too busy and too wrapped up in their own affairs to pay attention to their families? Barclay reminds us, "It is no virtue to be so engaged in public work that the result is neglect of those at home. All the church service in the world will not make amends for neglect of a church official's family".[41]

Paul expands on what he has been saying by adding that the children of an elder should not be *open to the charge of being wild and disobedient* (1:6). The word translated "charge" is used in 1 Tim 5:19 in the context of a formal accusation against an elder. Paul is talking about more than just private gossip and the spreading of rumours. He is saying that some people may try to parade any bad behaviour by the elders' children in public in order to discredit the elder and the gospel. The elder's children must not leave him vulnerable to such attacks.

One of the accusations levelled at the children might be that they are "wild". The Greek word conveys the ideas of debauchery, dissipation and riotous living – the kind of lifestyle adopted by the prodigal son (Luke 15:13). Someone who is wild is "wasteful extravagant and incapable of saving and spends everything on personal pleasure. Such a person loses it all and in the end suffers personal ruin."[42] Their lifestyle is uncontrolled and often involves drugs and alcohol.[43] They delight in immorality, abusive language and the like.

The charge of being "wild" can have serious effects. In Africa, where people live in communities in which people know each other, it is not uncommon to hear people say they will not believe in Christ because of the bad behaviour of the church leaders' children.

The accusation that they are "disobedient" could also be translated as "undisciplined", or "rebellious".[44] Having disobedient children may indicate an elder is unable to exhort or encourage people to do what is right. This failure to lead in a smaller area of influence like the family disqualifies someone from being entrusted with wider responsibility in the church (and should also disqualify people for public offices).[45] The results of our parenting reflect how well we balance love and justice: a critical ability for church leadership.

Where an elder's family is behaving badly, an elder may need to voluntarily resign from his or her position for the sake of the kingdom of God. However, church administrators should remember that there is always an element of personal choice when it comes to behaviour.[46] An elder's child may have been brought up in a godly way in a godly home, but can still refuse to surrender to Christ. If this is clearly the case, the pastor should not be victimized for the child's behaviour.

Due to the profound effect that home life has on ministry, we should constantly reflect on issues relating to families in leadership seminars and in formal courses at theological institutions. We cannot afford to concentrate on academic and spiritual matters and ignore the practical problems involved in raising a family well.

Church leaders should also remember that the state of their families is the first (though unspoken) point in every sermon they preach. Being an example of a healthy family opens the doors and invites listeners to accept the rest of the sermon. We should thus strive to be good husbands, wives and parents. Our listeners will know whether we have done our best and will generally accept that we cannot be held responsible for the behaviour of every member of the family.

Specific qualifications

Many of the specific qualifications for elders in Titus are the same as those listed for overseers and deacons in 1 Timothy 3 and thus this section contains numerous cross-references to that chapter.

Undesirable qualities

Three of the five undesirable characteristics mentioned in Titus 1:7 are also mentioned in 1 Timothy: *not given to drunkenness, not violent, not pursuing dishonest gain* (see commentary on 1 Tim 3:3, 8). But Paul adds two additional characteristics to be avoided:

- *Overbearing* (or "self-willed", nasb) people are obstinate and arrogant. They assert their rights and insist that their opinions and interests outweigh those of others.[47] Such people cannot serve Christ for they want others to serve them. But Christ calls us to serve others and not insist on getting our own way. Sadly, missionaries are often found to be overbearing. Whether they are reaching out to people of a different race or people group or to people from their own region, some missionaries treat those being reached as though they need only to receive and have nothing to offer. When relationships begin this way, the people rebel at the first opportunity. Lasting ministry starts with clear understanding and genuine practice of the principle of equality in Christ.

- *Quick-tempered* people are also not qualified to serve as elders. Their lack of patience clouds their judgment. This applies whether their anger is of the type that flares quickly and subsides just as fast or is the type that smoulders and "is continually fed to keep it alive".[48] Not only does persistent anger make people spiritually sick, it also harms relationships because it makes those who have to live around them withdraw. Thus consistent evidence of either of these types of anger disqualifies a person from being an elder.

Desirable qualities

Two of the seven desirable qualities in an elder mentioned in Titus 1:8–9a mirror those discussed in Timothy: elders should be *hospitable* and *self-controlled*. Two other qualities are contrasted with their opposites: elders must *love what is good* and be *holy* (unlike the false teachers who are "unholy" and "not lovers of the good" – 2 Tim 3:3–3). In addition, elders should be able to be characterized as follows:

- *Upright* people treat everybody with respect. They weigh situations carefully without prejudging issues. Their decisions are not influenced by someone's social status or their personal relationship with them. People who are upright do not nurse grudges or cling to misconceptions. They think through issues on the basis of the merits of the case.
- *Disciplined* people are able to refrain from doing anything unlawful and use moderation when doing things that are lawful. This quality is mentioned among the fruit of the Spirit (Gal 5:22–23) and is closely related to self-discipline (2 Tim 1:7) and self-control (1 Tim 3:2).
- *Holding firmly to the trustworthy message as it has been taught* is more a theological qualification than a moral one. Elders must be people who can stand firm and guard the truth entrusted to their care (see commentary on 1 Tim 6:20). This requirement is similar to the one that elders must be "able to teach" (1 Tim 3:2), but goes further than this. Not only must an elder know what truths to teach, he must

also be "heart and soul devoted to, and by implication convinced of, the truth of the apostolic message".⁴⁹

Commitment to the trustworthy message is necessary so that elders *may encourage others by sound doctrine and refute those who oppose it* (1:9b). If God's truth is deeply rooted in an elder's heart, "if he clings to it, meditates on it and dwells in it; then he will have spiritual vitality and liveliness whereby he may be able to deal with the opponents. With growing sensitiveness he will observe not only the points of doctrine where the antagonist is wrong but also the motives which lie behind his contradiction."⁵⁰

"Encouraging" and "refuting" are the same tasks given to Timothy in 2 Timothy 4:2. The first involves exhorting people to get on the right course. Elders can only do this if they themselves know what constitutes "sound doctrine". When used in a technical sense, as it is here, "sound" means "theologically healthy". The Greek word "suggests not only freedom from error, but also teaching which is able to impart healthiness, that is, salvation."⁵¹ The concept of "soundness" comes up repeatedly in this letter to Titus (1:9, 13; 2:1, 8; see also the commentary on 1 Tim 1:10).

Those who oppose sound doctrine (like the people mentioned in 3:10) need to be refuted. This means that the elders should expose their errors in a way that convicts them that they are in the wrong.

The goal of both the encouragement and the refutation is not to discourage believers but to build them up and give them hope.⁵² Our goal must always be to bring people to maturity (Eph 4:11–13). Sometimes people wander off into error because their faith is immature. We should be helping them to get back on their feet, not removing their names from the list of church members. They are like patients who need help from a trusted doctor, not directions to the morgue!

Discerning the true state of someone who is in error requires a heart filled with God's love, especially when dealing with difficult people. Sadly, there may be some who stubbornly refuse to listen when corrected and who have to be left to go their own way. Dealing with these people is the topic of the next unit.

Questions for Discussion

1. Are our church leaders blindly leading the blind, or do they see beyond the great challenges we face in Africa and seek to direct the church onto the right course? What characterizes a blind leader in our day? Provide examples to show why you think someone is a blind or visionary leader.
2. Identify situations where you have seen a need for the qualities Paul lists for elders. How did the elders handle them?
3. Which qualities do you need to work on if you wish to become a leader, whether of a Sunday school class, a youth group, a small group or a church? How will you set about cultivating these qualities?

UNIT 3
TITUS 1:10–16

UPROOTING ERROR

African farmers have to contend with many different kinds of weeds. Some are easy to uproot because their roots grow just below the surface. Others cannot be pulled up by hand but are easily uprooted with one strike of the hoe. But some weeds, especially certain grasses, send their roots a great distance under the soil. The farmer must carefully trace their path to the point where they started in order to uproot the whole plant. What the weeds have in common is that they must all be pulled up by the roots or they will grow again. The difference between them is how troublesome it is to uproot them.

The same is true in ministry. Error, like weed, must be dealt with or it will eventually weaken or kill the church's testimony for Christ. Some error is easier to deal with than others, but an error is an error, just as a weed is a weed. It must be uprooted.

Silence Those in Error

Paul has just instructed Titus to appoint blameless elders who "can encourage others by sound doctrine and refute those who oppose it" (1:9). Why are these people needed? It is because they are the ones who can ensure that those who are in error are *silenced* (1:11a). They will be able to do this because they are people of impeccable character. Anyone who is inclined to find fault with God's people will be silenced by being left with nothing to say and nothing to gossip about! Those who are disposed to argue with them will be silenced by their sure grasp of doctrine and their ability to discern what is important and what is not.

The opposition Titus will face will often come from within the church. This much is clear from Paul's use of the word *rebellious* (1:10a), for one has to be part of something to be able to rebel against it.[53] The same word is translated as "disobedient" when speaking about elders' children (1:6). These people are rebelling against the gospel, and by extension against the lordship of Christ and the leadership of Paul.[54]

While these people are unwilling to listen to Titus, they have a lot to say themselves! They are *full of meaningless talk* (1:10b). What they have to say has no substance or significance. They are just talking for the sake of talking (see also 1 Tim 1:6). They love to use their verbal skills to impress others, but their words are worthless because they make no contribution to helping those listening to them become more Christ-like. Unfortunately, we sometimes see such talk in our churches. Some people offer long prayers or testimonies, or preach long sermons, but their aim is only to impress the congregation with their oratory, not to build them up in their love for God and others.[55]

Paul feels free to say that such people are full of *deception* because they fail to adhere to the truth of the gospel. What they have to say is not only not sound doctrine, it is also not true. Titus is to silence all such people, *especially those of the circumcision group* (1:10c). Some commentators suggest that the word translated as "especially" should be translated as "namely", implying that only the Jews were causing these problems.[56] While we cannot be dogmatic on this point, most translations prefer the word "especially". It is likely that both Jews and Gentiles were part of the group that was making ministry difficult for Titus, but that the Jewish component was more prominent.[57] But regardless of who exactly is causing the trouble, Paul's main concern is that these people are undermining the message of the gospel.

Paul refers to these people as "the circumcision group". This label does not seem to be referring to their theological position but to their ethnicity. They were probably not urging others to be circumcised, but were simply ethnic Jews, who were circumcised whereas Greeks were not.[58]

Rebuke Them Sharply

Paul's next instruction to Titus is *rebuke them sharply* (1:13b). But who does the "them" refer to? The closest noun is "Cretans". Does this mean that Titus is to rebuke all the people of Crete? That seems unlikely, for he is to preach to them and seek to reach them with the good news. Does Paul mean all the Cretan Christians? Should he be rebuking them to make sure that the heresy being spread by the false teachers does not infect the whole church?[59] Again, this seems unlikely, for the elders are also called to "encourage others by sound doctrine" (1:9). Most likely, Paul wants Titus to rebuke those residents of Crete who claim to be believers but are actually opponents of the gospel (1:9b).[60]

But what about that reference to Cretans? Paul's own description of the false teachers in 1:10-11 is harsh, but the words he quotes are brutal: *one of Crete's own prophets has said it: "Cretans are always liars, evil brutes, lazy gluttons."* In case Titus doubts these words, Paul adds, *He has surely told the truth* (1:12–13).

Paul does not name the "prophet", but the church father called Clement of Alexandria identified him as the poet called Epimenides of Knossos who was reputedly one of the seven wisest men of Greece.[61] Epimenides lived in Knossos, a town on the island of Crete, in about 600 bc.[62] He was famous as a religious teacher and wonder worker with unusual powers of foretelling the future.[63]

Some other church fathers identified the poet as Callimachus of Cyrene, who lived approximately 305–240 bc.[64] However, it seems likely that Callimachus was merely quoting an earlier poem by Epimenides.

The line quoted comes from a hymn to Zeus, the greatest of the Greek gods. The poet was outraged at the presence of a monument in Crete called The Tomb of Zeus. So he wrote this:

> Cretans are chronic liars;
> for they build a tomb, O King;
> and called it thine; but you die not;
> your life is everlasting.[65]

The poet's point was that Zeus, the greatest of the Greek gods could not die. By naming their monument a burial site for Zeus, the Cretans were guilty of the greatest lie ever told![66]

The Cretans still had a bad reputation at the time Paul was writing. They were referred to as part of the *tria kappa kakista*, "the three bad K's", which were *Krete*, *Kappadokia* and *Kilikia* (today spelled as Cretans, Cappadocians and Cilicians). The Greeks coined words and passed down proverbs that equated Cretans with liars.

We, too, make generalizations about different people groups. But we should not use Paul as an example to justify stereotyping. In fact, Paul acknowledges that there are exceptions to these gross generalizations when he says that a Cretan poet is speaking the truth when he says that Cretans are liars. The poet is a Cretan, but not a liar!

Similarly, we should not assume that every long-distance truck driver is immoral. Many of them do have concubines in every town where they spend the night. But not every truck driver is like this. Some are believers. Nor should we stereotype the members of different people groups in Africa. While generalizations may have some basis in fact, they do not apply to every member of a particular group. For example, in the West it has become common to refer to certain emails that promise riches but do not deliver them as Nigerian e-mails. Those who use this term do not mean that every Nigerian who sends an e-mail is a scammer. In the same way, Paul is not making a blanket statement about all Cretans. He is speaking about the people he referred to as deceivers in 1:10 and is saying that the prophet's words are an accurate description of them.

Paul refers to Epimenides as a prophet because that is how the Cretans thought of him. He is not a prophet like Isaiah, Jeremiah, Ezekiel and the other prophets in the Bible who accurately conveyed God's word. He is more like Caiaphas, who spoke the truth despite himself (John 11:49–51).[67]

Paul's awareness of their "meaningless talk and deception" (1:10) justifies his quotation of the statement about Cretans being liars. He may include the rest of the line about their being "evil brutes" and "lazy gluttons" simply because this was part of the original saying. Yet when we look at the rest of his description of how these opponents behave, it seems that Paul might well have considered them "evil brutes". They do not tend and spare the flock, but mercilessly tear it to pieces for their personal gain (1:11b). They are "lazy gluttons" because they prefer not to work and instead prey on foolish people who give them financial support.[68] This is the opposite of what Paul and Peter say is the work of a church leader (Acts 20:28; 1 Pet 5:2–3) and is a fulfilment in Crete of what Paul predicts will happen in the church at Ephesus (Acts 20:29).

Titus' consistent approach to these people must be to "rebuke them sharply".[69] Paul does not mean that he must only address them in short, sharp sentences. What he means is that Titus must be like a surgeon, cutting into flesh to expose and remove a tumour. "Sound doctrine" is healthy doctrine, which nourishes Christ-like character. The unhealthy doctrine of the false teachers is causing poor spiritual health in those who listen to them. So Titus must perform spiritual surgery. He must not be content merely to rub in ointment, which does nothing more than alleviate the symptoms of the disease without addressing the cause. Instead, he must insist that his opponents completely abandon their teaching.[70] Error cannot be left to die out on its own. It must be uprooted or it will destroy the congregation as cancer does the body (2 Tim 2:17).

However, we must keep in mind that the purpose of surgery is to save and heal the patient. We must take great care that in cutting out the tumour we do not maim healthy parts of the body. And we must do our utmost to avoid causing any unnecessary pain and suffering.

Paul followed this principle in his exercise of discipline in Corinth (1 Cor 5:5). When the one in error responds to rebuke by repenting, there is a patient healed. When those rebuked refuse to listen, we have to accept that we have done what we could. They may die in their sickness, but that will not be because we failed to try to bring healing with the word of life.

The Urgency

Paul gives a number of reasons why it is important that Titus stop the work of the false teachers.

The damage being done

The false teachers *are disrupting whole households* (1:11a). The verb used here is closely related to the one used when Jesus overturned the money changers' tables (John 2:15).[71] This gives a clear indication of the degree of disruption involved. Hence in some translations the verb is translated as "ruining". It may be that the faith of every member of these families is shaken by the false teaching, or it may be that the false teaching causes conflict because some members of the family have converted to the heresy while others continue to hold firmly to sound doctrine.[72] Alternatively, given that Paul refers to the church as "God's household" (1 Tim 3:14), it may be that the false teachers are disrupting entire congregations in some of the towns in Crete.[73] All of these possibilities could be true. False teaching starts with one person speaking to someone else, who then shares it with others. Before long, many people are wondering if what they are hearing is true. Families start to argue about it, and soon whole congregations are split as some side with those presenting the new teaching while others adhere to the truth of the gospel.

Their methods and motives

The false teachers are ruining these households *by teaching* (1:11b). The verb translated "by teaching" can also be rendered "because they teach".[74] Both elements are important. The teachers cause disruption by what they do and because of what they do. It is therefore urgent that they be silenced.

What they are teaching is *things they ought not to teach*. What they should be teaching is sound doctrine. But they are not – not because they do not know better, but because their type of teaching will bring them material benefits. They are like the teachers mentioned in 1 Timothy 6:5–10 who also wanted to enjoy *dishonest gain*. No wonder Paul insists that elders must not be guilty of this (Titus 1:7). These teachers are "religious mercenaries, who are trying to win converts all for the shameful purpose of making money."[75]

If you want to get rich quickly in Africa, founding a church is supposedly high on the list of ways to do so! From my observations, this is not far from the truth. Many pastors are motivated more by the offerings people bring than by concern for people's souls. They paint their greed in the colours of Scripture. For example, some teach that the principle of first fruits (which they interpret as the "law" of "first fruits") means that people must give the church their first month's earnings when they start a new job. Such pastors energetically resist any attempts to correct this misinterpretation of the principle because they benefit from it. They see themselves as the owners of the church, which they think of as a business. May the Lord help us place souls before money and seek to be true to the meaning and intention of Scripture!

Their actions

The false teachers Titus is dealing with in Crete resemble those Timothy had trouble with in Ephesus. These people *claim to know God, but by their actions they deny him* (1:16; see also 2 Tim 3:5).

The false teachers' claim to know God may be a simple claim that they have a relationship with God. If they are the Jews whom Paul specifically mentions in 1:10, they may be claiming that they have a special knowledge of God that is not available to Gentiles.[76] Or the teachers may be claiming to have a special secret knowledge of God that is only open to a few initiates. This type of philosophy would eventually develop into full-blown Gnosticism.[77] The Cretan heresy may actually be a blend of early Gnosticism and some Jewish teachings.

Although the false teachers claim to know God, their actions do not bear this out. In fact, their actions are equivalent to either denying their claim to know God or denying that they know him. The latter is the position taken in the tniv and many other translations, and it is attractive because God is at the centre of sound doctrine, and so denying sound doctrine amounts to denying him. But in fact the word "him" is not part of the original Greek text. Translators add it because they are influenced by the words in 2 Timothy 2:12b. Paul does not tell us who or what is being denied. It seems more likely that what the teachers are denying is their own claim.[78] Their actions do not support their claim to know God.

This type of situation is not uncommon in churches in Africa. It has been said that many Christians have one leg in the church and the other in African traditional beliefs. The sick are taken to church for prayer on Sunday and to the witchdoctor on Monday – a reflection of believing in the power of prayer while at the same time doubting it. There must be consistency. Jesus wants us to be wholly his. Every Christian in Africa should be a Christian every day of the week and in all circumstances, in good or poor health, when wealthy or poor, when the rains come and when they do not.

Their characters

The false teachers' actions are merely a reflection of their characters, which Paul describes in 1:16:

- *Detestable* people are in a very bad state. The noun form of this adjective is often translated as "abomination" (for example, in Luke 16:15, nrsv, nkjv). Paul would have been well aware of how this word was used in the Old Testament to describe things that roused God's "anger, hatred, opposition and destruction"[79] or caused him to feel "horror and disgust".[80] For example, Proverbs 6:16–19 lists seven things that are detestable to the Lord: "haughty eyes, a lying tongue, hands that shed innocent blood, a heart that devises wicked schemes, feet that are quick to rush into evil, a false witness who pours out lies and a person who stirs up dissension in the community." Deuteronomy 17:1 says that offering animals with defects to the Lord is also detestable. Paul is saying that God finds the behaviour of the false teachers revolting. If they do not repent, they will face his judgment.

- *Disobedient* people are similar to detestable people in that what they do arouses God's disgust. Saul, for example, was rejected by the Lord as leader of Israel due to his disobedience (1 Sam 13:13–14). The false teachers are committed to disobeying God by refusing to accept the gospel proclaimed by Paul, Titus and anyone else who holds to sound doctrine.

- *Unfit for doing anything good* signals that by being disobedient and detestable, the false teachers have disqualified themselves from serving God. They can no longer carry out the good work that is an essential part of the gospel. People who are always trying to enrich themselves and promote alternatives to God's way are of no use to God or anyone else.[81]

The description of the false teachers is not a declaration that God has totally rejected them. Rather, it is a description that is meant to get their attention. Think of how you would react if someone came to you and warned you that your boss spits when your name is mentioned! You would be deeply upset. You would try to find out what you had done to make him so angry and disgusted with you. If you do not seek to put things right, you will soon be out of a job. It would be even worse if the person who did this was your father!

Paul is not using strong language just because he is angry with the false teachers. He is like the friend referred to above, warning them of the danger they are in and the urgency of setting things right. They had better start worrying, because the one who gives them life is very displeased with them! He knows what they are up to, and he is only withholding his judgment to give them time to repent. This is the message that Timothy must urgently convey.

It is one thing to use harsh words to hurt someone's feelings or spoil their reputation. It is another thing to tell them exactly what they are like (no matter how ugly the picture) because we want them to come to repentance. The former is motivated by hatred; the latter by love.

Unfortunately, we often hear people in Africa using strong words without any sign of love; the goal is simply to destroy the one criticized. But our goal must always be to bless the other person even when we are severely rebuking what he or she has done. We demonstrate our love by taking the time to verify the facts before we speak. Love should drive us to be absolutely certain that the rebuke is merited before it is offered. And when we speak, we should not condemn the other person while presenting ourselves as paragons of virtue, for that shows pride, not love.

Of course, it can be difficult for others to discern our motivation. God is the only one who can truly judge our hearts. But we can demonstrate the purity of our motives by praying for blessings on the one we have had to speak out against – provided our prayer is sincere and not merely a hypocritical veneer intended to make us look good to others.

The Goal

Any delay in dealing with false teachers gives them more time to deceive people. They can do so because they appear to be on the right course, but they are not. However, our goal must not just be speed in dealing with them, it must also be to bring them to a position where *they will be sound in the faith* (1:13b).

As noted earlier, the word translated as "sound" is a medical term that means "healthy" (see 1:9). The "faith" here refers to the body of beliefs that Christians hold. Paul's point is that people need to accept the interpretation of the gospel of salvation presented by the Lord Jesus Christ and his apostles (1 Cor 3:11; Eph 2:20). This was the gospel that Paul preached and Titus is passing on.

Paul explains the purpose of the rebuke by describing what the false teachers will *not* do once they have been healed and made whole. Firstly, they *will pay no attention to Jewish myths* (1:14a). These myths may include the many legends that had grown up about the Old Testament patriarchs (see commentary on 1 Tim 1:4).[82] The mention of Jewish myths is a further indication that the primary source of the problems in Crete was Judaism and not the Greek myths and philosophies circulating at the time.

Secondly, once rebuked the people will no longer listen to *merely human commands* (1:14b). These commands come from the same source as other rules Paul described as "based on merely human commands and teachings" (Col 2:22).[83] God's commands, when understood and accepted in the right spirit, are a delight to obey. Jesus could say that "my yoke is easy and my burden is light" (Matt 11:30). But human commands are burdensome and sap our joy. They are also dangerous because they tend to replace God's law and so endanger the soul (Mark 7:8–9). God's law has its rightful place (Rom 13:8–9; Gal 5:14) and there it enhances rather than hinders the gospel. But when people twist God's law to suit themselves, they move away from God. In the context of Titus, God's commandments are equivalent to the sound doctrine preached by Paul and Titus.

The human commands may have insisted on asceticism (if so, they were like false teaching being promoted in Ephesus – 1 Tim 4:3). Believers were being encouraged to reject the good things that God gives by people who themselves *reject the truth*. The verb translated as "reject" means "separating from". It is used to describe people turning away from Paul (2 Tim 1:15) or from the truth (2 Tim 4:4). These teachers are separating themselves and those who follow them from sound doctrine.

Paul then explains the principle that should guide us when others pressurize us to do specific things or to give up some everyday things. They may claim that these things are sinful and that by giving them up we will attain a higher level of spirituality. But Paul insists that *to the pure, all things are pure, but to those who are corrupted and do not believe, nothing is pure. In fact, both their minds and consciences are corrupted* (1:15).

Here Paul is speaking of ritual or ceremonial purity. His point is that to people who are morally pure, everything is ritually pure (compare 1 Tim 4:4). On the other hand, to those who are morally corrupt and rebellious, nothing is ritually pure. Their own corruption infects everything they see or do.

This point is one that is made repeatedly in the New Testament. Jesus stressed that defilement comes from our sinful hearts, not from our bodies or from what we touch (Matt 15:11; Mark 7:15). In Acts, Peter was sent a vision to teach him how this principle applies to relationships with Gentiles so that he was ready to preach to Cornelius and his household (Acts 10:10–16, 28). Paul refers to the same principle in Romans 14:14, 20 when discussing the larger principle of taking care of people whose faith is weak. Here in Titus, he is using the principle to make the point that human commands about what to eat or not eat, what to touch or not touch, and what to do or not do are unnecessary. Nothing will change the pure status of a person who is pure at heart. At the same time, nothing outside a person defiled at heart will make them less defiled. In fact, defiled people defile the good things God created.

Barclay comments that the corrupted person's "mind soils every thought that enters into it; the imagination turns every picture which it forms into a source of lust ... Every motive is misinterpreted. Every statement is given a double meaning." This happens because the person's mind and conscience are defiled:

> We come to decisions and form conclusions by using two faculties. We use intellect to think things out; we use conscience to listen to the voice of God. But if the intellect is warped in such a way that it sees the unclean everywhere and in all things, anywhere, and if the conscience is darkened and numbed by continual consent to what is evil, it becomes impossible to take any good decision at all.[84]

Take this situation as an example. At a party, the hosts serve a fruit drink to which alcohol has been added. The guests only discover this later in the evening. One of the guests is a pastor who has taken a strong position against drinking alcohol. Does he consider himself defiled because he drank alcohol even though it was against his principles? No. Alcohol itself is not wrong, and he had not deliberately acted against his conscience. But if a known alcoholic was also a guest, he might take great delight in pointing out that "the pastor drank alcohol!" He lays totally unwarranted blame on the pastor.

Another example would be that of two young Christians of the opposite sex who go to a private place to pray. When their hearts are pure, there is nothing wrong with them doing this. But when those whose minds are not pure hear about this, they assume that immoral behaviour was involved. With their corrupt minds, they cannot believe in innocence and purity.

The corrupted "do not believe".[85] They have chosen not to trust that God's provision in the gospel is enough for their relationship with him. They have not accepted the message of Paul and Titus that salvation is through Christ's perfect obedience on their behalf. Therefore they replace God's good law with human commandments that undermine the work of Christ. By doing this, they promote unbelief.

The principle that all things are pure to the believers who are pure in heart is sometimes misunderstood or abused. Some people think that it means believers can do anything they like, including what is sinful. But a pure person will not want to be associated with sin, but will be concerned for purity in thought, word and deed. Nor can good and evil be bundled together and labelled as "pure". Paul's principle needs to be interpreted in its context, which concerns the multiplication of human rules and regulations.

Questions for Discussion

1. It seems that the believers at Crete were being swayed by the philosophies of their day. As African believers, we are also influenced by African traditional beliefs. How do we relate these beliefs to the gospel? Which traditional aspects of African culture are found in the gospel and should be kept, and which are not found in the gospel and must be done away with?

2. Is everyone who holds a different view from ours wrong? What fundamental issues must not be compromised, and what issues can we disagree on without being divided as members of the same church?
3. There was an inconsistency between what the false teachers said and what they did. Do Christians have a similar problem? Identify some common areas of failures of consistency. What is the remedy?
4. When governments or powerful people are threatened in their leadership, they often try to silence critics by summoning them to official meetings in an attempt to intimidate them or try to discredit them by exposing some scandal in their past or in their family. Sometimes they hire thugs to beat them up or have them thrown into jail on trumped-up charges. They may even execute them, as happened to Ken Sara-wiwa in Nigeria when he exposed the corruption and exploitation in the oil industry there. It also happened in Uganda, where Archbishop Janani Luwum was murdered by Idi Amin and other Christian leaders like Festo Kivengere were forced to flee into exile. Similar things have happened to opposition supporters in places as far apart as Zimbabwe and Kenya. In what ways is the ministry of silencing those who oppose the truth of the gospel different from what these powerful people of the world do? When thinking about this, focus on the nature and purpose of the rebuke.

UNIT 4
TITUS 2:1–6, 9–10

DOCTRINE AND LIFE

Many farmers in Africa eat the crops they harvest. When the rains fail, they go hungry because they do not have enough money to buy the food they would typically grow. Higher food prices during times of drought only make the situation more difficult. But when the rains fall and the harvest is plentiful, farmers remember the season for a long time.

Many Kenyan farmers remember the season they call Elunino, referring to the El Niño weather pattern of 1997–1998. Farmers tell stories about harvesting ten bags instead of five, or forty bags instead of twenty – double their normal harvest! But their stories do not end there. While they rejoiced, other Africans planned to exploit them.

At harvest time, a new grain preservative appeared in the market. Many farmers bought it, thinking they would save money on this new product that was cheaper than the preservative they normally bought. They applied it to their bountiful harvests as they stored them. But the preservative was a fake and did not deter weevils. At this point in their stories, many farmers shed tears, remembering how weevils destroyed their harvest, leaving them with nothing.

The farmers' stories remind me of the situation Paul describes when he writes to Titus in his letter. The farmers are like believers who want to enjoy what the Lord has provided. The deceptive merchants are like the false teachers who prepared, packaged and sold the ineffective product. The fake preservative is like the false teaching, and the older, effective preservative is like sound doctrine. Satan and his agents are like the weevils (though we know Satan was responsible for much more than just the final destruction of the harvests, because he was the one behind the entire scheme).

Many people, including those Titus ministers to, will accept a cheap gospel so that they do not have to "pay" very much. A cheap gospel does not call for self-denial and total surrender to God's word. But this is the only way a believer can keep what is good and prevent it from being destroyed! If the gospel that people accept is not genuine, it will only provide a reason to weep.

The Importance of Sound Doctrine

Paul does not shy away from belabouring the point that believers must know sound doctrine. In the first chapter of Titus, he alludes to this in 1:9, 11, 13 and 16. He describes the false teachers as deceitful and corrupt, and then he turns to Titus with an emphatic *But as for you* (2:1a nasb). The words emphasize that there must be a marked difference between Titus and his opponents.[86]

In contrast to the habits of the false teachers, Titus must make a habit of *teaching what is appropriate to sound doctrine* (2:1).[87] Sound doctrine encompasses the beliefs and practices, or in other words the ways of thinking and living, that bring spiritual health rather than sickness (1 Tim 1:10; Titus 1:9, 13).

It is striking that Paul does not follow this instruction with statements about Christian theology but instead starts to talk about details of Christian living. Sound doctrine obviously involves more than just knowing the catechism. It also means living a life that reflects what we believe. It is only by maintaining this link between theology and life that the church will remain the church.

Paul's instructions make it clear that every member of the church is called to live in a way that "is appropriate to sound doctrine". The same principles apply to all, but the application differs depending on each person's position in society. So Paul addresses the specific requirements for men and women of different ages and different social status in the society of his day.

In his other letters, Paul used similar categories when talking about relationships within a family (Eph 5:22–6:9; Col 3:18–4:11) and so does Peter (1 Pet 2:18–3:9). But in his letter to Titus Paul is less concerned about families and more concerned about how believers' conduct affects the reputation of the church. Unbelievers should not be given any reason to criticize the church, and nothing believers do must repel unbelievers. They must be living examples of the difference that sound doctrine makes.

Older Men

On Crete, just as in many African societies today, older men were the leaders in society and in the family. In fact, in Africa village elders sometimes constitute the first level of government. But age is not the sole criterion for being considered an elder. Even more important than age is having an exemplary character. The four qualities Paul lists for older men in 2:2 would still qualify them as leaders in communities today.

- *Temperate*. Being temperate means having a clear mind. This quality is also discussed in the context of elders and deaconesses (1 Tim 3:2, 11). To restrict it to meaning that someone's mind is not clouded by wine is to make a mistake. People's minds can be clouded by many things, including their expectations, social status and past relationships. All these things can influence our judgment, often without our being aware of it. As much as it lies within their power, older men should seek to clear their minds of any negative influences that hinder them from making decision that are acceptable to God. Decisions made by those whose minds are clouded are unlikely to promote what is best for the community or for the church, and may even prove damaging. This danger is particularly acute given that in the first century, just as in many rural areas of Africa today, elders' decisions were binding.

- *Worthy of respect*. Church leaders like Titus (2:7), deacons (1 Tim 3:8) and deaconesses (1 Tim 3:11) must be people others can look up to, not look down on. If they are respected, people will be more prepared to listen to what they have to say. So if we want people to hear the message of the gospel from us, we must remove anything in our lives that the devil could use to undermine respect for us. No one listens to a liar who lectures on the importance of being truthful;

someone who is filled with hatred cannot effectively teach about love; a proud person cannot preach about humility. None of these people would be listened to with any respect. Similarly, there is no place for church leaders, preachers or teachers who are not worthy of respect. If they are not respected, their ministry will be completely ineffective.

- *Self-controlled.* People who are self-controlled have mastered not only their sensual desires but also their emotions. They may become angry, but they can still control their tongue and their behaviour. This quality is also important in church elders (1 Tim 3:2; see also Titus 1:8; 2:5). Leaders should not be quick to say something or to act on their first emotional responses to a situation. If they do, they will end up saying things that they may regret later, and their impulsive behaviour may hurt others rather than help them. Good leaders take time to think through a situation. For a relatively simple issue, they may not need to reflect for more than a few minutes, but when it comes to more complex issues they may want to take time to consult others and to spending a night bringing this matter before the Lord to seek his wisdom.

- *Sound in faith, in love and in endurance.* Faith and love were qualities discussed in the commentary on 1 Timothy 4:12, and faith, love and endurance were discussed in relation to 2 Timothy 3:10. It is because we have faith in God and his way of redemption that we become his children (John 3:16) and surrender our daily affairs to him. It is because we love God and his people that we remain in fellowship with them (1 John 1:3). And it is because we endure that we will reign with Christ (2 Tim 2:12). We all need faith, love and endurance if we are to enjoy God's blessings now and for eternity. Because these qualities are better caught than taught, it is important that people not only receive teaching about them but also see them being practised by elders and church leaders. In fact, these qualities should be demonstrated by all leaders, whether in churches, schools, business or government. All leaders should remember that their behaviour shapes the behaviour of those who follow them. Africa would be a better place if African leaders set a better example.

Older Women

Whereas Paul's guidelines for older men relate only to their character, his instructions regarding older women relate to their character and ministry.

Their character

Like the older men, older women should also be of exemplary character. Paul mentions three specific characteristics in 2:3a:

- *Reverent in the way they live.* The word translated "the way they live" can be used in a narrow sense to talk about the way women dress (1 Tim 2:9). Here, however, Paul is referring to all aspects of a Christian woman's bearing and appearance, in public and in private. She must be someone who lives in the awareness that she is always in the presence of God and must bring honour to him in what she does, what she says and what she wears. In bringing honour to God, she will also bring honour to her family. Her husband will take great joy in being married to a woman of good character, and her children will be proud to hear their mother spoken well of in the community. This virtue is the female equivalent of the call for older men to be worthy of respect. How this virtue will be expressed in practical terms will differ from community to community and even from one generation to the other. The way a Christian woman lives reverently in most African rural areas may differ from the way a woman does so in Nairobi, Kampala or Accra. And this may differ from how Christian women live reverently in New York. But the principle is the same: live reverently as one who has the holy ministry of glorifying God.

- *Not slanderers.* The evils of gossip and malicious talk were discussed in relation to deaconesses in 1 Timothy 3:11. Slanderers are people who broadcast bad news as soon as they receive it, without verifying it or caring about the people involved. Their motive is to improve their own reputation by running down the reputations of others. It is not safe to be friends with anyone like this. The only people who can enjoy their company are fellow-slanderers! They do great harm to the reputation of the church. Even some of us who would deny that we are slanderers are quick to pass on gossip about others while being easily offended when a person says something about us that they have not verified is true. Such behaviour is contrary to the principle Jesus taught us, namely, "love your neighbour as yourself" (Matt 19:19; Matt 22:39; Mark 12:31; Luke 10:27), and "do to others what you would have them do to you" (Matt 7:12).

- *Not heavy drinkers.* Those who are "addicted to much wine" lack self-control (the virtue required of older men – 2:2). They do not decide how much they are going to drink – the wine makes the decision for them. The older women who are to train the younger women need to have clear minds if they are to exercise good judgment and teach the right things. In his first-century context, Paul does not call for total abstinence from wine, but he does stress that addiction to wine is unacceptable in elders and deacons (1 Tim 3:3, 8; 5:23), At most, Christians should be moderate drinkers, but it is far better to abstain completely.

Their ministry

Paul specifies two tasks for older women, both of which involve ministering to younger women. The aim of their ministry is to forestall behaviour that will cause anyone to *malign the word of God* (2:5b). The importance of protecting God's honour is a constant theme in Paul's letters to Timothy and Titus (see comments on 1 Tim 6:1 and Titus 2:9–10).

Teach younger women

Paul's instruction that older women should *teach what is good* (2:3b) should be noted by those who deny women any ministry of teaching and preaching. However, public ministry is not the main focus here, because what Paul is talking about is teaching through private conversations and personal example. He wants these women to instruct younger people through their words and deeds. Women can exercise this influence without even saying a word through "the testimony of a godly life".[88]

This fact places a tremendous responsibility on older women (and in fact, on all believers). No matter what our age or social status, there is always someone younger than us whom we are influencing. Younger people learn by watching those older than them. And they often imitate what they learn. It can be said that each generation defines the character traits of the next.

It was once common for Africans to make sure that the older members of the community passed their wisdom, skills and good behaviour on to the younger ones. Some groups still do this formally. Boys are taught important lessons about life when they are initiated into manhood, and girls may have to go through similar rituals before being considered eligible for marriage. The church has often rejected these traditional initiation rituals because they include some non-Christian elements. However, the church needs to provide alternative means of passing on the important traditional values that do align with Christian values. This can be done by encouraging the efforts of groups like Boys' and Girls' Brigade and Scripture Union, which work to teach boys and girls what it means to live for Christ as youngsters and as adults. The activities we offer our youth should be geared to helping them grow to maturity in Christ and encouraging them to love their neighbours – who are not just the members of their own community but every member of the human race. Churches that have strong youth ministries are to be commended and those who do not should be encouraged to begin one. The ministry of the youth pastor is at least as important as that of the senior pastor.

Train younger women

The second task Paul assigns to older women is to *urge the younger women* (2:4). The verb translated "urge" in the tniv has a number of different meanings. Thus the kjv translates it as "teach", the nkjv as "admonish", the nasb as "encourage", and the niv as "train". It originally meant to make someone discreet or prudent, or to bring them to their senses, but it later came to mean "training".[89] Paul is not saying that the younger women were doing something wrong. Rather, his point is that by observing the older women's good behaviour, the younger women will take them as role models. If they are already doing the things they see the old women do, they will be encouraged; if they are not, they may change their behaviour.

This kind of mentoring relationship between older and younger women is very important these days as women move into new roles. They need guidance not only on how to live as Christian wives, but also on how to live as Christian university students, businesswomen, teachers, doctors, lawyers and so on. Many of the parents of young Christian women have not known these roles, or have lived in rural settings very different from the urban communities where their children now live. So it is vitally important that churches find ways of filling this vacuum. Opportunities need to be created for women with good reputations to advise younger ones.

Younger Women

In the ancient world, husbands and children were regarded as "the glory of young womanhood"[90] and there were very few opportunities for women outside the home. Thus Paul assumes that all the young women in Crete will be married, and the specific virtues he wants them to learn are all related to their roles as wives and mothers (2:4–5). Although women now have wider opportunities, the virtues he mentions are still very important, for the state of the families that make up the church is a direct reflection of the success of the church.

- *Love their husbands and children.* The older women are to teach the younger married women that the first object of their love should be their husband, followed by their children.[91] In saying this, Paul is probably not focusing on the order of relationships but on the point that when a father and mother love each other and both transfer that love to their children, they create a happy home. So even though Paul is here speaking of wives, his point applies equally to husbands. We may think it strange that women need to be taught how to love their own children. Learning how to love their husbands is more understandable! But "love does not always flow out of a person, even a wife and mother, as from a mountain spring. Love in the family requires thoughtfulness, and the mother has to work at it."[92] As young women work at loving their husbands and children, they need living models. What they do not need is interfering busybodies. Fortunately, the Christian qualities that Paul has already listed for older women should prevent them from falling into this trap. They are called to be humble advisers on married life.

- *Self-controlled.* Young women are not alone in needing to show self-control – the same requirement was laid down for older and younger men and church leaders (1 Tim 3:2; Titus 1:8; 2:5). However, young women may have to exercise self-control in different areas than men.

For example, young mothers will probably find that children try their patience, so that they have to exercise great restraint in order to avoid punishing a child in anger. Or a young woman may watch another family become wealthier while hers continues to struggle. Her resentment of the difference can result in bitterness towards her husband. For this woman, self-control involves controlling her anger and her desire for possessions in order to build her home and strengthen her marriage.

- *Pure*. These women must also be *pure*. The concept of "purity" is general enough to cover all areas of life, and not just sexual matters. This is clear when we note that chastity seems to have been uppermost in Paul's mind when he instructed Timothy to be pure in his relationships with younger women (1 Tim 5:2), but also instructed Timothy to maintain purity when appointing elders (1 Tim 5:22), where no sexual component was present. In practical terms, purity is seen in a young woman who treats her stepchild exactly the same as her own child. It is also seen in a woman who does not attempt to prevent a neighbour's child from doing better in school than her own child. Purity springs from a righteous character and becomes evident in all areas of a woman's life.

- *Busy at home*. Paul is not saying that younger women should never leave the house. But what he is concerned about is that some of them may spend too much time flitting around from house to house, being idle busybodies whose main enjoyment is spreading gossip. He wants them to throw their energy into the life of their home. While Paul's instruction must be viewed within the culture of his day, when the stay-at-home wife was the norm, it remains true that "there is no greater task, responsibility and privilege in this world than to make a home".[93] In every generation, many people owe their success to the mother who nurtured them or the wife who supported them. When applying the principle of being "busy at home" in Africa today, we could say that it means that spouses and parents must not make plans or accept jobs that will undermine their ability to care for each other and for their families.

- *Kind*. Some commentators link the word translated as "kind" with the phrase "being busy at home", and come up with the translation, "fulfill their house duties well".⁹⁴ But there is little justification for this translation. Kindness is itself a virtue. It denotes goodness in general. Within the family setting, kindness covers all the woman does to express her love for her husband and children. But it goes beyond being a kind and benevolent wife and mother. She should also be a good neighbour, not someone who is constantly quarrelling with her neighbours. A kind woman is highly esteemed in African communities. Her husband is proud of her and when she is in need everyone rallies around her. In traditional Africa, kind behaviour was often associated with the group or "clan" a woman came from, so that it would not be unusual to say "the women of that clan are kind". The same should be said of every African Christian woman – but the clan she belongs to is the clan of Christ, and it is his clan whose honour she upholds.

- *Subject to their husbands.* It was easy for the new believers in Crete to confuse the freedom the gospel gives with freedom from social norms. "Under the influence of Christian ideas of liberty, women were claiming emancipation, in a manner that often clashed with ancient notions of fitness and decorum."⁹⁵ This would bring the church into disrepute and create a misunderstanding of the message of the gospel. So Paul tells believing wives to submit to their husbands (see also Eph 5:22; Col 3:18).⁹⁶ When a wife became a believer, she should not become wilful or domineering. Instead, she should be an even better wife than she had been before. This applies regardless of whether the woman's husband is Christian or non-Christian.

In this letter, Paul refers only to the wife's responsibility to maintain a harmonious marriage and does not deal with the husband's corresponding duty to love his wife (Eph 5:25; Col 3:19). The church needs to teach both. Many African women struggle with submission, especially when their husbands are domineering and ignore their gifts and abilities. The wife often cannot assert herself without wrecking the marriage. Marriages like this do not bring honour to the church, but instead bring Christ's name into disrespect.

The church must educate both men and women in how to create families in which each person feels fulfilled and appreciated. Husbands should not regard themselves as entitled to demand submission. It must be a gift offered by the wife, not a right demanded by the husband. It is a good idea for churches to hold regular couples seminars at which these truths are taught and Christian husbands and wives learn to live as Christian couples rather than simply following any wrong patterns they experienced while growing up or that they see around them. Sometimes, it may be advisable to hold separate sessions for husbands and wives, so that each group can speak freely and experience the support of their peers. However, in general, couples should attend sessions together, so that each can start listening to their partner's frustrations and joys.

For further discussion of the issue of submission, see the commentary on 2:9–10 (slaves and masters) and 3:1 (civil authorities).

Younger Men

Paul's instructions for young women are followed by similar instructions for young men. However in this case he does not appeal to the older men to set the example but lays that responsibility on Titus himself. The one specific virtue mentioned is self-control: *encourage the young men to be self-controlled* (2:6). However we can assume that they are also expected to show the other virtues that Titus models (2:7).

The need for self-control has already been mentioned in relation to older men and younger women (2:2, 5), and was among the qualifications required for being an elder (1 Tim 3:2; Titus 1:8). It was a virtue that was highly regarded in Greek culture, ranking alongside justice, wisdom and courage[97] – qualities that any young man would crave. But Paul is thinking of more than just Greek ethics. For Christians, self-control derives from the understanding that they are servants of God. Consequently, our emotions and desires must be subordinated to God's will so that we can serve him better. The young men of every generation of Christians must respond to the particular challenges of their times by placing themselves under the discipline of the gospel. This will guard them from being led astray by the promptings of their own sinful natures or by external influences.

The call to be self-controlled cries out to Christian young people today as loudly as it ever did to the Cretans, if not louder because we live in an age that does not value self-control. There are many young men in Africa whose minds are disturbed by drugs and alcohol. There are also many who see themselves as entitled to sleep with anyone they want to. (It is not that women are immune to these temptations, but they are more prevalent among men.) As churches, we need to be asking what we are doing to minister to young people in order to help them develop self-control. We need programmes in the churches. We need people who can be role models for them. In schools where there are chaplains, we need to make sure that those appointed to these positions are committed to the gospel, have a deep love and concern for the young people they serve, and are worthy role models.

Slaves

In the first century, a man would be referred to as "lord" (*kurios*, equivalent to the modern "sir") by his wife and children, but to his slaves he was the "master" (*despotes*) who exercised unrestricted authority over them. Society imposed constraints on his behaviour as a husband and father, but recognized no such restraints when it came to his behaviour towards his slaves.[98] Slaves had no rights. It is within this context that we have to read Paul's instructions to slaves. He is not supporting slavery as an institution, but is asking Christians to maintain harmony in the social and cultural context of the times.

Fortunately the spread of understanding of the implications of Christian beliefs has led to the abolition of slavery, and so it may not always be appropriate to apply Paul's instructions literally in our times. But the principles underlying what he says are still relevant because they address universal issues affecting the relationship between employers and employees. Although employees have much greater freedom than slaves, they are still under their employer's authority and should show the same five good qualities as Christian slaves in Paul's day (2:9). Our goal should be to serve in a way that avoids bringing dishonour to Christ.

A corollary of this point is that we must recognize the social and cultural constraints in our own societies. For example, it would be unwise to assume that we can simply impose Western labour laws or concepts of workers' rights in an African country. The entire cultural context has to taken into account when deciding what laws are appropriate. There is no point in instituting laws that will paralyse a system and destroy a functioning economy.

Be subject to masters

Paul instructs slaves who are believers *to be subject to their masters in everything* (2:9a). It was tempting for slaves to argue that their freedom in Christ meant that they were no longer under any obligation to obey their masters. The slaves in Ephesus seem to have been making a similar argument (see comments on 1 Tim 6:1–2). But our unity and the quality in Christ do not do away with our social responsibilities. Being a Christian means that slaves will be better slaves! (In the same way wives will be better wives, husbands better husbands, and parents better parents.)

In saying that they must be subject "in everything", Paul is not saying that slaves must obey their masters if what they are commanded to do is in clear violation of God's word. God is the ultimate master, and everyone must honour his authority. When a conflict arises between God's will and an earthly master's will, the instruction to be subject to or to obey the earthly master ceases to apply.

Today, employees are still obligated to place themselves under their employer's authority. Doing otherwise confuses the order of command. Of course, employees also have freedom to demand fairness in this relationship, but the way they make these demands should not confuse the order of authority. Wisdom is necessary to know how to balance the need to express oneself as an employee with the employer's need to remain in charge.

Christian employees are called to be good employees. As such, they will contribute to the prosperity of their employer and will also benefit the national economy and the well-being of the entire nation.

Try to please them

Every other time Paul uses the word translated "pleasing", he uses it in relation to God or the Lord Jesus Christ (Rom 12:1, 2; 14:18; 2 Cor 5:9; Eph 5:10; Phil 4:18; Col 3:20). He sees it as an essential element in a relationship that gives satisfaction rather than causing emotional pain.

Once again, Paul assumes that the person to be pleased is operating within God's standards. A slave or employee will be able to discern whether someone is or is not breaking God's standards, but there is also a need for wisdom here. For example, I am sometimes approached by someone who believes that Christians should not drink, asking me what he should do when his employer sends him out to buy alcohol. I usually tell him to do as his employer instructs him, adding: "It is your obedience that will enable you to quietly tell your employer that the errand troubles your conscience". However, when an employer asks for sex or immoral conduct, the request falls into a completely different category. Such situations call for outright disobedience. Our heavenly Master is able to provide if we lose our job because we honour him. But where God's right to be honoured is not being violated, employees' duty is to please their employer.

Do not be disrespectful

Part of pleasing someone in authority is obeying their instructions without opposition. This is what lies behind Paul's statement that slaves should not *talk back* to their masters. Some commentators assert that Greek slaves often answered back or got into arguments with their masters and mistresses.[99] This kind of behaviour is implied by the fact that the Greek legal system included instructions on what to do if this became a problem. But masters of Christian slaves should never have to appeal to the law because their slaves live by the philosophy that their service is rendered to the Lord. This is a much higher standard than society in general would expect. The masters would be impressed by the dignity and quality of service offered by believers.

Paul is not prohibiting dialogue or even debate between employers and employees on issues that are important to them. Rather, he is reminding Christians that when there is disagreement about some aspect of a job or the terms of their employment, they should express their disagreement in a respectful way.

The same principle carries over to the larger issue of strikes and other forms of industrial action. Just as it is important to glorify God and serve others by serving an employer well, so it is also important to consider whether supporting a strike will glorify God and serve others. Teachers, for example, who want to fight some injustice need to remember that a strike during the weeks when students are scheduled to write examinations may cause serious difficulties for the students. It might be better if the teachers were to strike during the school holidays – but then the strike would probably be ineffective because there would be no angry parents pressing the authorities to address the issue being raised. Strikes do need to cause some inconvenience and public unrest if they are to be effective. But do the ends justify the means?

When considering whether to strike, we need to ask questions such as "Why is this strike being called?" "Is a strike the best way to solve the problem? Is there a better option?" "Will people be hurt by the strike?" We cannot say that workers should never strike, but we can say that calling a strike should be a last resort and that the reason for the strike must be right, the motives pure, and the effects must not harm others. It may sometimes be better to suffer and allow God to fight for us rather than fight for selfish motives without consideration of his will.

Be trustworthy

Slaves are *not to steal from their masters* (2:10). The verb Paul uses here literally means "to separate" or "to lay on one side".[100] In other words, slaves are not to pilfer their owner's goods by taking some things for themselves. They may have been tempted to argue that they were only getting what was owed to them in exchange for what they had to put up with. But Paul does not buy this argument. A Christian slave *must show that they can be fully trusted*. They should be dependable in every aspect of their service to their masters, for they are not serving an earthly master but their heavenly Master and Saviour. His reputation will suffer if his servants are not honest and trustworthy.

In today's terms, Christian employees must be honest in carrying out their responsibilities. They must take care of their employer's property, honestly record their work hours, and honestly account for every cent when a supervisor sends them out to make a purchase. Unfortunately, it seems that such honesty and dependability are rare. It can take a long time to find someone to whom you can give the keys of the house or office and go away for a week, knowing that the employee will carry on working diligently. Even in Christian institutions, employers have to keep constant watch over their workers to ensure that they perform their duties honestly.

This lack of dependability is also apparent at the highest levels of institutions and governments. There appears to be truth in the allegations that many African presidents divert large sums of public money into personal bank accounts overseas and that civil servants enrich themselves from the funds under their care. Presidents and civil servants are employed by the taxpayers, and what they are doing is nothing less than stealing. Their example is followed by the rest of society, right down to the farm workers who steal vegetables. Paul's "no stealing" applies to everyone, no matter what their status. To go against his instruction is to be an enemy of what is right. And when stealing is done by a Christian, that person's behaviour is an insult to the Christian faith.

Churches often put effort into cultivating good values among couples, adults and young people, but they sometimes neglect to talk about what it means to be a good employee. Most of us are employees. We should not only chat about our work when we meet at church, we should also spend time reflecting on the ethics of our behaviour at work. It would be good if churches conducted seminars on this topic, too.

Attract others to the gospel

The motive for this extraordinary behaviour by Christian slaves must be *that in every way they will make the teaching about God our Saviour attractive* (2:10b).[101] The verb translated as "make attractive" is the same one used in 1 Timothy 2:9 in relation to the way women should "adorn" themselves (nasb). It is the same verb from which we get the English word "cosmetics". Just as the appropriate use of cosmetics can enhance a woman's beauty, so the exemplary behaviour of the Christian slaves will draw attention and make the gospel attractive to unbelievers.

To Sum Up

The good reputation of God's name, his word and his church is clearly of great importance. Three times in this chapter Paul mentions the need to maintain a good reputation for the sake of the gospel (2:5, 8, 10). Nor is Paul alone in recognizing that what we do affects God's reputation. Peter makes the same point when he encourages women to be submissive to their husbands "so that, if any of them do not believe the word, they may be won over without words by the behaviour of their wives" (1 Pet 3:1). The principle that "actions speak louder than words" is as true in evangelism as it is in life in general. It applies to all aspects of life; we are to make the gospel attractive "in every way".

All believers carry a tremendous responsibility. What we do and what we say affects how other people see Christ. We should ask ourselves, "What do others say about God, Jesus, the gospel and Christianity after they have observed my way of life – in public and in private, at home and at work?"

In Africa, where most people are religious, many more could be drawn to the church if they saw all Christians behaving like Christians. Unfortunately, too often we hear unbelievers say, "Even the Christians are no different" when it comes to corruption, immorality, cover-ups, financial mismanagement, and so on. This is not true of all Christians, but it is true that many of us have not attracted people to the gospel as we should. Our way of life has betrayed the gospel more than it has promoted it.

Questions for Discussion

1. Recently one of the wheels of my car got stuck into a ditch. In less than a minute a group of young men appeared, apparently eager to help me. But their very first words were *"Lete pesa tukutoe"* (Pay us and we'll help you get out). I paid, and they pushed the car out of the ditch. What did their actions tell me about their values? Now think about other incidents that you have experienced. What did you learn about people's values? Has the way anyone behaved ever made you praise God or attracted you to their church? Have you ever behaved in a way that has led someone else to praise God or to accompany you to church?

2. Paul attaches great importance to self-control. He lists it as one of the virtues required of church leaders and older and younger church members. In the commentary, self-control is linked to drugs, alcohol and extramarital sex. Are there other areas in which Christians also need to exercise self-control in order to bring glory to God? In what areas do you struggle with self-control?

3. What is your evaluation of the work ethics in your community? How does it compare to the standards Paul lays down? What changes should you be making? What can your church do to help Christian employees attract their employers to Christ?

4. Most of the members of the church in Crete were either poor or slaves, so Paul did not discuss how masters should behave to attract their slaves to Christ. If you are an employer (whether in a business or in the home) how do you think he would ask you to behave to make Christ attractive to your employees?

UNIT 5
TITUS 2:7–8, 11–15

PROMOTING SOUND DOCTRINE

Every farmer knows that when the rains come, it is not only the carefully planted seeds that will sprout. So will the weeds. These weeds have to be pulled out if the crop is to do well. The growing plants will also need an application of fertilizer to make them grow stronger, and will do even better if given a second application of fertilizer later in the season. Some plants may need to be sprayed to keep destructive pests away. Others will be pruned to increase the yield. All of this work is needed to create an environment that supports the growth of healthy plants that produce an abundant harvest.

When the crop is harvested, it is eaten and strengthens those who consume it. If it is a commercial crop, it is sold for good money, which helps the farmer meet the family's needs. The crop is thus precious, and so the farmer tends it carefully.

In the same way, Titus must tend the seed of the gospel that has been planted on Crete and brings spiritual health to those who remain true to it. He must provide the believers with what they need to grow and flourish and produce an abundant harvest. As part of this job, he may also have to uproot "weeds" that could prevent individuals and the congregation from maturing and bearing fruit.

Titus' Responsibility

The call to teach sound doctrine lays a heavy responsibility on Titus. Paul is adamant that he must not only teach it, he must also live it.

Set an example

The deceitfulness of the false teachers is evident from the fact that although they claim to know God, they deny him with their actions. They are "unfit for doing anything good" (1:16). By contrast, *in everything* Titus must *set them an example by doing what is good* (2:7; see also 1 Tim 4:12). Like Timothy, Titus is to be a model that others can follow. He must take this responsibility seriously at all times.[102]

The tniv translation focuses on how Titus will be an example: "by doing what is good." But the literal translation of the Greek focuses on the content of his example: Titus will be an "example of good works". Paul wants Titus to go beyond just being someone others can follow to being someone who illustrates what good works are. In other words, "if any one asked what a real Christian was, it would be enough to point to Titus and say: "Look at him".[103]

Teach well

The content of the sound doctrine Titus teaches must obviously be the message given by Christ, but Paul is also concerned about how Titus presents this message. In 1:7b–8a he reminds him of three things that must characterize his teaching:

- *Integrity*. Integrity relates not just to the content of Titus' teaching (which must reflect the truth entrusted to him) but also to his motive for ministry. He must have pure motives and not show any of the eagerness for gain that characterizes the false teachers. Instead, he must follow Jesus' example and give himself for others. He must not use his position to show off, get money, exercise power or for any other selfish purpose. Many pastors in Africa have followed Jesus' example for many years, and we praise God for them. But with the coming of the prosperity gospel, things have changed drastically. Preachers of this gospel are speaking the truth when they tell people that if they give to the Lord they will be blessed. But they are less concerned about the Lord's work than they are about building up their own empires. They use the money contributed by poor parishioners to make themselves rich. This is contrary to the way of life Christ modelled. Yes, people must give. However, what they give should be used to provide for everyone's needs, not simply to make the preacher prosperous.

- *Seriousness.* The word translated seriousness could also be translated as "dignity" (nasb). It does not mean that Titus can never laugh or relax, but it does imply that he must never forget that whatever he is doing, he is an ambassador for Christ, or in other words, Christ's representative (2 Cor 5:20).[104] Others will judge Christ by how he behaves. Thus he must not do anything that will bring Christ's name into disrepute. In practical terms, this means that "others may stoop to pettiness; Titus must be above it. Others may bear their grudges; he must have no bitterness. Others may be touchy about their place; he must have a humility which has forgotten that it has a place. Others may grow irritable or blaze into anger in an argument; he must have a serenity which cannot be provoked."[105] It is no easy task to serve in this way but we should all make Paul's claim in Philippians 4:13 our own: "I can do all this through him who gives me strength."

- *Soundness of speech that cannot be condemned.* Sound speech conveys a message of life, wholeness and health (see 1:9; 1 Tim 1:10). What we teach should always bring health to our listeners and must never cause an "infection". It must be in conformity with the goal of the gospel, which is to bring love, enhance the purity of lives and increase zeal to reach the unsaved. Thus preachers and teachers must weigh every word they speak and make sure that their message cannot be interpreted as an attack on someone rather than as the proclamation of Christ. Unfortunately, this is a test we often fail in Africa. Too often preachers deliver sermons that are actually veiled attacks on someone else for personal, political or other reasons. When this happens, the pulpit becomes a place for creating wounds rather than healing them, and the number of the spiritually sick is multiplied. Sometimes tough words do need to be said from the pulpit, but they must spring from love, and love must be evident in the way they are spoken. May the Lord help us speak with pure motives and the right words. We thank God for those ministers who by his grace overcome the temptation to use their pulpit to promote political or personal opinions. They stay on course, nurturing souls to be like Christ. Their congregations often include a mix of races, ethnic groups and social classes, with every member rejoicing in this diversity.

Disarm the opposition

The purpose of modelling this good lifestyle is *so that those who oppose you may be ashamed because they have nothing bad to say about us* (2:8b). To oppose someone is to be on the opposite side to them. These people are against Titus and the gospel he stands for.[106] They may be unbelievers who are eager to find reasons to criticize Christianity, they may be people in the congregation who are looking for something to criticize, or they may be people inside or outside the church who have taken a dislike to Titus and those associated with him.[107] However, it seems that although the group opposing Titus "can, and no doubt does, include pagan critics of Christianity … its primary reference is to ill-disposed individuals in the community itself who … are eagerly waiting for the least opportunity to catch him out."[108]

Because the opponents take pride in criticizing Christianity, Titus can put them to shame by depriving them of any basis for their criticism. They will have nothing to be proud about. Over time the critics will become even more ashamed when their criticism is proved wrong.

Paul begins this sentence talking about the people who oppose "you", but he ends with the same people talking about "us". Titus is not alone. Paul and other believers stand alongside him. As Titus faces criticism, he should remember this. Believers facing opposition today can have the same confidence that they are not alone.

Unfortunately, rather than making their opponents ashamed, some African Christians embolden them and actually place weapons in their hands. This is what happens when church leaders (and ordinary church members) get involved in questionable deals that promise quick riches, fight among themselves, misuse church money or behave immorally. When we forget that we are ambassadors of Christ and act contrary to the faith, we give our opponents an opportunity to attack the church Christ established.

While we cannot win victory on earth in our own power, we should not be the ones to sow the seeds of defeat! Instead, we must determine to accurately represent Christ here on earth and to live as citizens of heaven (Phil 3:20).

Encourage and rebuke others

Paul often mentions the need to *encourage and rebuke* others in his letters to Timothy and Titus (2:15b; see also 1 Tim 1:3; 2:1; 5:1, 20; 6:2; 2 Tim 4:2; Titus 1:9, 13; 2:6). Clearly this is to be a regular part of their ministry.[109]

Paul sees encouragement as more than just patting someone on the back and telling them that they are doing a good job. It involves pointing people in the right direction; a direction that is not arbitrarily chosen by the person doing the pointing but one that is true and important.

For a discussion of what he means by rebuking people, see the commentary on Titus 1:9.

The basis for the encouraging and rebuking is given in 2:15a: *These, then, are the things you should teach.* "These things" certainly include what Paul has been saying in 2:2–14, but may also extend to 1:10–16 or to the entire letter.[110] Given that Paul does not compartmentalize truth, it is likely that he is referring to everything he says in this letter to Titus.

This linking of "teaching", "encouraging" and "rebuking" indicates how we are to minister to others to ensure their spiritual health.[111]

- In teaching we proclaim God's message, which is not negotiable.
- In encouraging, we help people to see that this teaching will help them acquire and maintain spiritual health. The encourager recognizes the specific situation each person is in and reminds them of God's grace, which offers hope in a situation that might otherwise be hopeless.
- In rebuking, we attempt to make those who have chosen the wrong course recognize that what they are doing is sinful.

There is a sense in which all these three tasks are to be done *with all authority*. However, it is also possible that these words apply specifically to the encouragement and rebuking, *or just to the rebuking*.[112] In context, it seems most likely that Paul is speaking of rebuking with authority. Usually it is only people who are deliberately doing something wrong who need to be reminded of the authority with which someone speaks to them.

Titus should not avoid confronting people who are sinning. After all, he is not rebuking them on his own authority.[113] God is the one who sets the standard for right conduct. Although Titus is only a messenger, he is a messenger who has a duty to convey the message entrusted to him. When he does so, his words are backed up by God's authority.

If we see our task from this perspective, we will have the confidence to rebuke anyone who needs rebuking. We will not only rebuke young people or ordinary church members, but we will also rebuke wealthy and powerful church members. More than that, we will be prepared to rebuke the most powerful people in the land: company executives, members of parliament, government ministers, and even the president of the country. Far too few of the African politicians who have misruled nations have been privately rebuked by pastors, as King David was by Nathan (2 Sam 12:1–15). We need to remember that God is the ruler over all kings and authority figures. He sets the standard to which they should be held. But when we speak out to rebuke leaders, our conduct and choice of words must make it very clear that we are God's messengers. As such, we must not speak in a spirit of hatred but with love. We must not shrink from pastoring our African leaders in the full sense of the word.

A key principle to keep in mind is that rebuking is the third of three pastoral activities. It follows teaching and encouraging. Rebuking those we have never taught and encouraged is like punishing children for doing something they have not been taught is wrong. So our ministry to our political leaders must include all three activities. Those who have been taught what is right and encouraged to do it deserve to be rebuked when they ignore what is right. But those who do not know what is right need to be taught and encouraged before being rebuked. By implication, those who are in the church and know the truth deserve to be rebuked sooner than those who are not part of the church.

Paul himself demonstrates encouragement when he tells Titus, *Do not let anyone despise you* (2:15b). He said the same to Timothy, who was inclined to shrink back because he was still a young man (1 Tim 4:12). We do not know what age Titus was, but whatever his age there would be some people who would refuse to recognize his authority and the source of his message. Titus must not let their contempt for him deter him from carrying out his task. In saying this, Paul may also be sending two other messages: he is gently reminding Titus that he must avoid giving others any justification for despising him (see also 2:8), and he is reminding the Cretan believers (with whom Titus will share this letter) that Titus is in charge.

When people have good grounds for despising a Christian worker, the worker must repent before God and set things right with other people. This is the only way to have an effective ministry. But when a Christian worker is despised for faithfully carrying out the responsibilities assigned in God's word, he or she must persevere, trusting that God knows the truth of the situation.

Grace and Sound Doctrine

In these letters Paul has repeatedly stressed that sound doctrine affects not only what we believe but also how we live. It requires us to live holy lives. This is not an impossible ideal. Titus can confidently give the type of teaching set out in 2:2–10 because the way of life described there is achievable through God's grace.

We are often inclined to think about the operation of God's grace only in relation to the start of our Christian journey, when it saves and justifies us. We tend to forget that it is still available to us through the rest of our journey, making it possible for us to live in accordance with sound doctrine and teaching us what sound doctrine is.

So Paul is not just telling Titus, "This is what abiding by sound doctrine demands from you and the congregation." He is also saying, "This is how you are going to be able to do it."

Grace Saves Us

God's grace is "God's free favour, the spontaneous goodness by which he intervenes to help and deliver men".[114] It is a one-word summary of all God has done to save human beings. Paul rejoices that *the grace of God has appeared that offers salvation to all people* (2:11).

This grace can be said to have "appeared" when Christ came. In other words, it was revealed to us though Christ's entire life on earth from his incarnation through his years of living in obedience to the

Father to his death and resurrection.[115] In a narrower sense, grace can also be said to have appeared to the Cretans at the time when Paul and Titus preached the gospel to them and they understood and accepted it (see 1:3 and 3:3–4).[116] However, Paul's reference to its appearing to "all people" seems to call for a wider meaning than just preaching on Crete.

But while this interpretation makes sense, it raises another problem that is evident from the niv's more literal translation of the Greek: "For the grace of God that brings salvation has appeared to all men". If this appearance is linked to the life of Christ, how can it be said to have "appeared to all men" (or "all people")? The Cretans never saw Christ while he was on earth, and nor did most of the rest of humanity. Thus it is preferable to translate this phrase "for all people" rather than "to all people".[117] Other translations get around the problem by adding a verb, which is why the tniv adds the word "offers" and the nasb the word "bringing" to the phrase "salvation to all people".

But no sooner have we have solved that problem, than another one appears: What does Paul mean when he speaks of salvation having appeared "for all people"? This was the same problem we ran into in 1 Timothy 2:4. The answer to the question depends on one's understanding of the theology of salvation. There are three main possibilities:

- Paul is saying that everybody will be saved. This universalist position has the flaw that it implies that there is no real need for anyone to have faith in Christ, whereas the need for faith is clearly taught in John 3:16 and Ephesians 2:8. Those who support this view tend to overemphasize the importance of godly behaviour but deny the central place of faith when it comes to salvation.

- Paul is saying that salvation is open to all groups. Whereas God had once revealed himself only to the Jewish people, now his salvation is freely offered to Jews, Gentiles, free people and slaves.[118] God does not discriminate by race, gender or social class. This interpretation fits the context, for in 2:9–10 Paul has been speaking of the way of life of Christian slaves.

- Paul is saying that salvation is available to everyone who chooses to accept it.[119] In other words, salvation is available to everyone, but is only experienced by those who exercise faith in Christ.

Either of the last two interpretations is possible, but the last one is probably preferable as it is a more natural way of interpreting the word translated "people". This position also avoids the problem of downplaying certain Scriptures while trying to understand others, which is what happens with the "universal salvation" view. We need to weigh all the truths of Scripture if we are to reach accurate conclusions.

But in the midst of all these arguments, it is important to remember the central point that Paul is making: Salvation is available. And salvation makes it possible for us to do everything that sound doctrine requires of us.

Grace Teaches Us

Godliness is the goal of our salvation, for we are saved so that we can become like Christ. Therefore we should be grateful that God's grace also teaches us sound doctrine about how we should live. The Holy Spirit works in us to convict us when we stray from the path of life he desires. He often does this by taking the Scripture we are reading and opening our eyes to see what it means for our own lives. It is in this sense that the grace of God *teaches us* (2:12). This teaching combines education and discipline.[120] It can be summarized under two headings: deny vices and pursue virtues.

To deny vices

Grace *teaches us to say "No" to* certain things, which Paul summarizes under the general headings *ungodliness* and *worldly passions* (2:12). Ungodliness is shorthand for everything that is contrary to God's will (Rom 1:18; 1 Tim 1:9–10). It is the opposite of godliness, which is shorthand for everything that pleases God and conforms to his character. Godliness is a key theme in these letters to Timothy and Titus (see comments on 1 Tim 2:2).

The word translated "passions" is morally neutral – the passions may be either good or bad (see comments on 1 Tim 6:9; 2 Tim 2:22). However the fact that these passions are described as "worldly" means that they are contrasted with heavenly desires and are "limited to the present world and characteristic of it".[121] We must say "No" to any desire that causes us to focus on the world at the expense of focusing on God. Such desires are negative and sinful. They include, but are not limited to, sexual desires.

Saying "No" is not something we do once and are then never tempted again. Rather, it is an ongoing denial of everything that is ungodly and of every desire that is sinful each time they come into our minds.[122] Becoming spiritually mature is a process, not a one-time event.

To pursue virtues

Grace also teaches us *to live self-controlled, upright and godly lives in this present age* (2:12b). We start living in this way when we first come to Christ, but we have to continue living it every day.[123] This life involves active pursuit of the three virtues Paul mentions here: self-control, uprightness and godliness. All three were very highly regarded by the Stoic philosophers of Paul's day.[124] This serves as a reminder that we do not need to reject all the values of our traditional heritage. Many of them are compatible with the requirements of godly living. However, the difference between Paul and the Stoics was that they appealed solely to human reason and will power when it came to practising these virtues, whereas Paul called on Christians to practise them in response to and in the power of God's free grace.

- *Self-control* has been mentioned as a requirement for various groups in the Christian community (Titus 2:2, 5, 6). It involves self-mastery in all matters of life.
- *Uprightness* is characteristic of someone who focuses on giving "both to God and to our neighbours that which is due".[125] In other words, those who live upright lives are righteous in their relationship to God and just and loving in their relationships with other people.
- *Godliness* has been Paul's constant focus in these letters. It involves acknowledging God in all that we do and living "in the awareness that this world is nothing other than the temple of God".[126]

Some commentators see these verses as representing our three fundamental human relationships: "self-control" focuses on how we relate to ourselves; "uprightness" focuses on how we relate to other people; and godliness focuses on our relationship to God.[127] While we cannot be certain that this is what Paul had in mind when writing this list, it would certainly be compatible with Jesus' teaching that we are to love God first, love his people, and control our lives in a manner that is pleasing to him (Matt 22:37–39; Mark 12:30–31; Luke 10:27–28). Our love for God controls all our other relationships, and none of them should be neglected. We have to take care of ourselves because it is when we are strong and healthy that we have the energy to serve God and others. Caring for ourselves involves eating a balanced diet, exercising regularly, sleeping enough, and so on. At the same time, we should not be so overly interested in caring for ourselves that we neglect the needs of people around us. When we truly love God, the love we give to ourselves and to others will be balanced.

To live in anticipation

The fact that we are to live virtuous lives "in this present age" indicates that the present is not all that exists. There is a future we anticipate: *we wait for the blessed hope – the appearing of the glory of our great God and Saviour, Jesus Christ* (2:13). In some translations, the opening of this verse can be read as suggesting that two events are involved: "the blessed hope and glorious appearing" (nkjv). But both refer to the same thing, as the dash in the tniv translation makes clear.[128] The hope and the appearing are both blessed because the one who appears is blessed and he brings blessings to those who are expectantly awaiting his arrival.

When someone "appears", the event is only as great as the one appearing. No one lines up or makes extra-special preparations to see someone they meet everyday, but when someone like a president appears, no effort is spared. This was true in relation to Jesus' first appearing, when he revealed his grace (2:11), but it is even more true at his second appearing, when he will reveal his glory. At his appearance to reveal grace he seemed weak: an infant, a suffering man. But at his appearance to reveal glory, we will see all the power and majesty of the one Paul describes as "our great God and Saviour, Jesus Christ".[129] These words constitute one of the clearest statements in the Bible that Jesus is God.[130]

Besides reminding us of who Jesus is, Paul also tells us what he has done for us: he *gave himself for us* (2:14). "Gave" summarizes all the sacrifices Christ made for us as he moved from heaven to earth and from life to death.[131] He did not simply give us money or some material possessions, he gave us his very self (see comments on 1 Tim 2:6). We find it much easier to give money or possessions than ourselves. But to be like Christ, we must not limit our giving to what we have. We must give our very selves.

Even more amazingly, Jesus gave himself *for us*, for mere human beings! He took our place and died on our behalf![132] Believers enjoy the benefits of his death.

Why did he do this? He did it *to redeem us from all wickedness and to purify for himself a people that are his very own, eager to do what is good* (2:14b). This one statement addresses the great themes of redemption, sanctification and adoption. Christ gave himself as a ransom (1 Tim 2:6) to redeem us "from all wickedness". The focus here is on what we were rescued from: the power of sin. It is not that believers do not sin (we all know this from experience), but they no longer belong in sin. It is no longer their natural condition. Salvation moves believers from the side of "wickedness" to the side of "good". They have been purified and no longer want to live in rebellion against God's will.

While redeeming us means releasing us from what has bound us, purifying us means washing away what pollutes us. We can only stand in the presence of our Holy God after being cleansed in this way by Christ. Then, once we have been redeemed and purified, God adopts us as "a people that are his very own", just as he adopted the Israelites in Exodus 19:5 (see also Deut 7:6; 14:2; 26:18).

Paul's reminder of who Christ is, what he did for us, and why he did it raises our level of anticipation of Christ's coming. It also gives us strong encouragement to be the people Christ wants us to be, "eager to do what is good". And that is why Titus needs to faithfully teach the believers under his care (2:15). If he teaches them sound doctrine, they will know what is good and will act in a way that brings glory and not shame to their great God and Saviour, Jesus Christ.

Questions for Discussion

1. It is tempting to misuse the pulpit for personal agendas. How can ministers guard against this temptation? For example, could trusted people be asked to review sermons before they are preached? Can you think of other options that would be helpful in your context?

2. Is putting a person "to shame" different from humiliating them? How can we put someone to shame and still uphold Christian principles of love, kindness and gentleness?

3. In order to pursue godly activities, like ministry, we must care for ourselves as well as for others. What area of your life are you struggling to keep healthy? What kind of lifestyle changes can you make to improve this area of your health? Who can you ask to support you and keep you accountable for this?

WORKING TOGETHER FOR CHANGE

Mzee Jomo Kenyatta, the first president of the Republic of Kenya, emphasized the philosophy of *harambee*, which means "pulling together" in Kiswahili. This idea is not unique to Kenya but is found in many other countries in Africa.

Historically, people pulled together and fought for independence. Later, they pulled together to build schools, hospitals, church buildings, and many other facilities. But for a long time no one thought about the need for churches to pull together to build the morals of the people. There was competition between denominations rather than interdenominational cooperation.

In one town, however, a model of pulling together to change people's morals has emerged. This small light may yet shine all over Africa.

This particular town had long had only two main denominations. However, over a ten-year period, the number of denominations swelled to about fifteen. Competing with each other for members, pastors began to dedicate a large part of every sermon to attacking other denominations. They criticised their modes of worship and even the character of their pastors. As the preachers fought, the town grew, and with growth came all sorts of vices. Night clubs multiplied while pastors sparred with each other every Sunday.

But God's Spirit was at work. One of the young pastors began to ask, "Why do we have churches at all? Is it only so that we can compete with other churches, or is so that we can turn this town upside down for Christ?" His questioning eventually led the pastors to work together to conduct a nondenominational crusade. Many people came to the Lord, and even more significantly, the preachers began to see each other as fellow labourers sharing a common task.

That town is not the only place to be afflicted with a spirit of competition. It happens at the national level too. Every African nation has great preachers. They all organize large meetings throughout the year. Sadly, it sometimes seems that the motive for holding a meeting somewhere is to put on a bigger and better show than the preceding preacher. It is time for these preachers to demonstrate what harambee means in the church. We talk of Africa being full of the word of God, but see little evidence of it in day-to-day life. Wouldn't the example of great African preachers pulling together across denominations in the humility of Christ filter down and inspire local pastors to do the same, illuminating every town with the light of the gospel?

Just as the spirit of harambee can help erect a medical facility by bringing together politicians, businesspeople, teachers, doctors and others, so it can change the moral condition of our people by bringing together Christians from all denominations. The benefits of this change have no end. Police work will become easier when criminals are turned into law-abiding citizens. Business people will be more relaxed if they do not have to worry about being attacked by gangs of robbers. Teaching will become easier as students receive better parenting and become less rebellious, and so on. Countries would have no reason to regret the investment of time and national resources in a movement for moral change led by pastors.

When Paul wrote to Timothy and Titus, he was eager to bring goodness – godliness – out of everyone who was willing to cooperate. This goodness would not only benefit individuals but the whole church and society at large. Timothy focused on Ephesus; Titus on Crete. Now it is our turn to focus on the towns where we minister, on our nations, on the African continent and beyond to the rest of the world.

UNIT 6
TITUS 3:1–11

OUR PAST, PRESENT AND FUTURE LIVES

In October 2004, Kenyans celebrated signs of success in fighting corruption. Transparency International, a global anti-corruption watchdog, had released their 2004 Corruption Perception Index.[133] Kenya had improved its score from 1.9 to 2.1 on a corruption scale with 0 being "highly corrupt" and 10 being "highly clean". On a comparative scale ranking 130 countries, Kenya had moved up from being in the bottom ten to being in the bottom twenty, for it was now sixteenth from the bottom. It fared better than Bangladesh, Haiti, Nigeria, Uganda and Tanzania. No country got a perfect score. Finland, the least corrupt country, scored 9.7 and New Zealand followed with a score of 9.6. However, the goal for which all countries should be striving is a perfect score of 10. While Kenya had made great improvements, there was still much work left to be done. We needed to keep working hard in order to reach this goal.

Just as the Kenyans had made progress in fighting corruption, so Titus and the Cretans had made progress in godliness. They were no longer what they had been (3:3–4), but they still had a long way to go before they could achieve a "perfect" score. So Paul gives Titus a final charge, that is, authoritative instructions about his ongoing task and what he is to keep on teaching. He encourages him to persevere by reminding him of what God has done for us.

Remind the People

Titus' ongoing task is to *remind the people,* that is, the Cretan believers (3:1). They already know much of what Titus is going to be telling them. However, they need to be reminded of what they have been taught and need to be helped to understand the implications of the principles that have been outlined. For example, in chapter 2 Paul spoke about the need to be respectful, and addressed these instructions primarily to women and slaves. In chapter 3, he shows how the same principle that guided his words there applies to both men and women in the context of the broader community.

Timothy, too, was instructed to remind people (2 Tim 2:14). And reminding people of what they already know is still a regular part of the duty of every preacher. Through our teaching, new believers should be learning things they did not know before, older believers should be reminded of what they have already learned, and all believers should be growing in their knowledge of the grace of God. So Paul mentions seven specific things that Titus should remind the Cretan believers of (3:1–2).

At first glance, much of what Paul says here seems to be little more than a repetition of the call for obedience based on an understanding of God's purpose of redemption that he gave in 2:1–14. But when we look at the passages closely, we discover that Paul now has a different focus here. In chapter 2 he was primarily concerned about the relationships between Cretan believers. Their relationships should attract others to Christianity and not give them any grounds to despise it. In chapter 3:1–2, however, Paul's focus is on the believers' relationships with society at large, beginning with the civil authorities and then extending to everyone.[134] He reminds believers of the duties, attitudes and virtues they should display in all their relationships.[135]

Be subject to rulers and authorities

We do not know why Paul thought it necessary to remind the Cretans to *be subject to rulers and authorities* (3:1a). He may have been afraid that what he said about Christ's coming in 2:12–13 could be misinterpreted as being "anti-emperor" and encouraging civil disobedience. Or maybe the Cretans were generally inclined to be rebellious and resist authority.

Most likely, he is simply repeating a point that he often made to believers (see Rom 13:1–17; see also 1 Pet 2:13–17).[136] He taught that since civil authorities exist by the will of God (either because he appoints them or allows them to be in office), believers are expected to obey them.

The mention of both "rulers" and "authorities" is not unnecessary repetition.[137] Paul is describing different aspects of leadership. The best way to illustrate this may be by means of an example. If I go to my local chief's office with some request, I am appearing before a ruler. That is the task he has been appointed to do, and he may grant or refuse my request. However, if the chief takes the collection in church on Sunday, he is not acting as a ruler, but he still has inherent authority that we should respect. He is still a chief even when he is not acting as a chief. In the same way, a president is always a president, even when he is not meeting with his cabinet.[138]

But what should we do if a ruler fails to carry out his responsibilities? For example a local chief may become corrupt and abuse his authority. Because his authority derives from the president, we would expect the president to remove him from office. But the president may not be aware of the situation (or may have no interest in finding out what is going on). In such situations we have a president who has authority by virtue of his office, but is not acting as a ruler. Yet Paul's instruction is that even such a president is to be honoured for the sake of the office he holds. The corrupt local official should also be treated with respect, even when we disagree with his behaviour – and even when we may have to take him to court or throw him out of office in an election. We should always acknowledge that our leaders have been given authority, even if they choose not to exercise it and even if they abuse it.

Paul issues the same command "to be subject" to wives (2:5) and slaves (2:9). He also speaks of submission in passages addressing church life (1 Tim 2:11) and family life (1 Tim 3:4; Eph 5:21). He is not calling for blind obedience but for people to maintain good human relationships while preserving the right spiritual perspective. People at lower levels of authority can only ignore God's order of command when they are being told to do something that goes against what God has commanded. God is always the ultimate authority, and all human authority is subordinate to him.[139]

When Paul wrote to Titus, Rome was not yet aggressively attacking the church.[140] However, that time would come, and Paul himself would demonstrate by his death that when the state stands in opposition to God, it becomes time to obey God and not human authorities (see also Acts 5:29). In such circumstances, "submission" means being willing to endure the consequences of civil disobedience, even if that means death.[141]

Be obedient

Paul does not say whom the Cretan believers are to *be obedient* to (3:1b). It is likely that it is the "rulers and authorities" he has just mentioned. However, he is also implying that the Cretans need to obey Titus, whom he has just instructed to carry out his duties with authority (2:15). The verb communicates the idea of "rendering obedience to duly constituted authority, an obedience to which a state that commanded idolatry may be said to have forfeited its right".[142] It is not a submission in which "civil authorities have an ascendancy over the church, even in church affairs, and legislate accordingly."[143]

In Kenya, the authorities have normally shown respect for the church. For example, when an important national holiday falls on a Sunday, the politicians arrange for the accompanying political rallies to be held in the afternoon so that they do not clash with the time when worship services are held. However, should some future politician insist that a political rally be held on a Sunday morning, believers should leave the politician to enjoy his own company. Worshipping God should take precedence over any political celebration.

But, some people will argue, is it really such a big deal to skip church one day a year to attend a political rally? Yes, because if we accommodate a politician once, we will be expected to do so again and again. Moreover, once we start compromising our principles on minor issues, we will soon end up willing to compromise on major issues.

The instruction to be obedient is given within a context. This context includes the state acknowledging that it has a responsibility to God, who established it to promote righteousness, mercy and justice for all. When the state stands against God, it ceases to have the right to be obeyed. Thus Rwandan Christians in 1994 and Kenyan Christians in 2007 and 2008 should not have obeyed those authorities who directed them to do things that were contrary to the will of God. In the Ten Commandments, God forbids murder, and in the New Testament Christ commands us to love our enemies. Christians should thus have adamantly refused to kill Tutsis in Rwanda or Luos, Kalenjin or Kikuyu in Kenya. Similarly, Christians should not participate in any form of election fraud, no matter what authority orders them to do so, for fraud violates the command against bearing false witness and steals the vote of fellow citizens.

Understanding God's intention for us to submit to our rulers in this way encourages us to support them when they rule in harmony with God and oppose them when they ignore God's commandments. The situation varies from one African country to another, but in many cases the church has kept silent when it should have supported a government, and also when it should have opposed one.

On the few occasions when the church has spoken out, it has been to oppose the government of the day. This has usually only happened in response to the most extreme situations, such as Idi Amin's misrule of Uganda. But if we only speak out when we oppose the actions of the authorities, we will be seen as supporting the opposition party. To avoid this, we need to make sure that we express our support for leaders of all parties when they do what is right. Instead of simply denouncing corruption, we should also praise the authorities when they do things like planting trees and offering free education. We should acknowledge their actions when they convict and imprison their own supporters who are guilty of corruption. Quiet words of praise may encourage them in their fight against corruption and may open their ears to our shouts of protest when they do wrong.

Be ready to do whatever is good

Paul has already mentioned "good works" in Titus. In 1:16 he described the false teachers as "unfit for doing anything good". In 2:14 he says that Christ's desire for his people is that they should be "eager to do what is good". In the context of 3:1c, the general phrase *whatever is good* would include doing what is right as a citizen and as a member of a community – including things like paying taxes![144] However, it would also extend to any activity that promotes righteousness, justice and mercy. We should not make a distinction between religious and secular good works. All good works are the practical expression of sound doctrine. In doing them we are following the example of our Lord Jesus Christ and are motivated by the love of God, who is the ultimate Master in all things.

Slander no one

The mention of good works in general marks the transition from characteristics focusing on our relationship to authorities to our relationship with everyone. We are told "to slander no one" (3:2a) – that is, not to speak evil of them with bad intentions. Again, this behaviour is in contrast to the false teachers, who were fond of "malicious talk" (1 Tim 6:4). The same word is used of the way unbelievers may talk if our bad behaviour leads them to "malign the word of God" (Titus 2:5).

This does not mean that Christians should never evaluate behaviour or criticize ideas. After all, Titus has been instructed to rebuke some people. The difference between such criticism and slander lies in our motive in making the criticism. Our aim must be to build others up and not to destroy them or humiliate them. Whatever we say about other people must be accurate, without exaggeration or misrepresentation, and must be intended to be helpful.

Be peaceable

Like the elders in 1 Timothy 3:3 and "the Lord's servant" (2 Tim 2:24), believers in Crete need *to be peaceable* (3:2b). The opposite of being "peaceable" is being "a fighter", which carries with it the negative sense of never listening to anyone one disagrees with. However, being peaceable does not mean that we must not stand up for what is right.[145] It simply means that we must not believe that our own opinions are the only possible right opinions. Someone who is peaceable can disagree with someone else without hurting the other person's feelings. Such people make good team members.

Be considerate

Being *considerate* (3:2c) must be characteristic of both ordinary church members and elders (1 Tim 3:3). It is the quality of gentleness that enables someone to be in the right without hurting other people's feelings. A considerate person "is ever ready to avoid the injustice which often lies in being strictly just."[146] This is one of the most difficult qualities to achieve in human relations, yet it is tremendously important for building up the souls of men and women. Without it, the shepherd scatters the flock.

When working in administration, one needs to find right balance between policy and persons. To give an example: an employer's policy may be to fire any employee who is fifteen minutes late. One day, an employee is delayed by a traffic accident on the way to work – should he or she be fired? An employer who is considerate will look at the whole picture before rigidly applying the policy.

Be gentle to everyone

Believers are *always to be gentle to everyone* (3:2d). Gentleness is a fruit of the Spirit (Gal 5:22–23). Those who are gentle always keep their tempers under complete control, knowing when to be angry and when not to be.[147] "This gentle courtesy must be exhibited to the world in general, including those who are most hostile or whom one likes least, and not just to one's fellow-Christians or personal friends."[148]

Courtesy knows no boundaries. While it is easier to practise it with relatives and friends, we should extend it to everyone we meet, whether a fellow passenger in a bus or taxi, a shop assistant or a beggar in the street. When the opportunity presents itself, we must act gently and humbly because this spirit is what attracts others to Christ through us.

The Basis for the Charge

The reason believers can show these qualities is that God's love has transformed them, so that there is an enormous difference between what they were like in the past and what they are like now. The unchangeable nature of the Christian message means that everything Paul says to Titus and the Cretans also applies to us today.

Their past lives

Every believer's pre-Christian life is characterized by vices. Paul reminds his readers of this when he introduces his list of vices with *at one time we too were* (3:3). His "we" is emphatic, and makes the point that he includes himself in the same category as Titus, the Cretan believers and all other Christians. He often does this when speaking of the effect of the gospel (see, for example, 2:11-14; 2 Tim 1:9-10; Gal 1:4).[149] These words are a gentle reminder that just as God worked in his and Titus' lives, so he is also able to work in the lives of those who are still living in sin and rebellion.

There was a time then when Paul and the other believers were very different from what they are now.[150] They used to indulge in "the sins of humanity in general".[151] He mentions seven characteristics that describe their past lives (3:3):

- *Foolish*. Spiritual ignorance and blindness made them *foolish*, unable to understand God and his laws, the redemption he offers and his dealings with humanity in general.[152] Paul also called the Galatian Christians "foolish", because they had forgotten what they had once known about God's way of redemption and were abandoning it (Gal 3:1). Walking in the way of the Lord is the path of wisdom and not to do so is foolishness (Ps 111:10; Jas 1:5).

- *Disobedient*. Before they are converted, all believers are disobedient to God, just like the false teachers in Crete (1:6). Although this is Paul's main point, he may also be thinking of the Cretans tendency to flout authority (3:1). Disobedient people show contempt for God's will. They know what is right but ignore it.[153]

- *Deceived*. Unbelievers are not only disobedient, but are easily led into more disobedience because they have been deceived by someone else (see also 2 Tim 3:13).[154] Paul does not say who duped them, but it was probably Satan (2 Cor 4:4; 1 Tim 4:1-2).[155]

- *Enslaved by all kinds of passions and pleasures*. Being enslaved is a natural consequence of being deceived. The deceiver is in charge and ensures that unbelievers become entangled in "all kinds of passions and pleasures". While the words translated as "passions" and "pleasures" do not necessarily refer to sinful behaviours, in this context they indicate pleasures that show a disregard for God and a desire to please only oneself.[156] When Paul says that they committed "all kinds" of sin, he does not mean that every individual was enslaved to every possible sin. Rather, he is saying that everyone has committed a wide variety of sins. Take Paul as an example. Before his conversion, Paul was a Pharisee who took great pains to obey God's law. He was not guilty of murder or theft. But he was guilty of trying to destroy the church of Christ (Gal 1:13–14).

- *Lived in malice and envy.* The antisocial vices of malice and envy are closely related, with envy being the outward manifestation of inner malice. Malicious people enjoy causing harm.[157] If someone has something that they want, they are envious and seek to bring some harm or evil on them.[158] This is one of the vices stirred up by the false teachers (1 Tim 6:4).

- *Hated.* Being hated is often a consequence of our own envy of others because of their social position or material possessions. When we demonstrate our malice and hatred towards them, the people we hate respond in kind.[159] Hatred is a vicious circle. My hatred for you leads you to hate me, which exacerbates my original hatred. It is only when one of the parties can stop hating that the circle can be broken. Hatred also grows from our self-centredness, which causes us to ignore the feelings of others and the hurt we cause them.[160]

- *Hating one another.*[161] Hatred starts with one person and spreads until there is a full camp of hate-filled people. This is true in the community at large and even in the church. The cancerous nature of hatred calls for us to address it as soon as it appears. If hatred goes unchecked, it can tear the greatest family, church, institution or nation to pieces.

Their present status

What a contrast between the old nature Paul has just described and the Christian lifestyle he described in 3:1! The believers now enjoy a completely new life because they are saved, justified and heirs of eternal life (3:5, 7).

- *Saved.* Only a divine act could change people who are living in bondage to their own desires and hating each other. And God has done this. Yes, *he saved us* (3:5), that is, Paul, the Cretans, and us today, from destroying ourselves and others. We were being led astray when God intervened and caused us to make an about turn in our lives. Instead of following the one who deceived us, we turned to Christ and were converted. At that moment we ceased to be slaves of Satan and became children in the family of God. Of course, we still fall into sin from time to time, but sinning is now an aberration, not our normal state. The Apostle John recognized this when he told his readers that he was writing so that they would not sin, but also reminded them that forgiveness was available through Christ if they did slip into sin (1 John 2:1).[162]

- *Justified.* While we still lived sinful lives, we were lost and under God's condemnation. Now, however, we have *been justified* (3:7), that is, we are no longer under condemnation and instead enjoy fellowship with God. The believer's new status begins at conversion and remains forever. In justifying us, God declares us "not guilty", bringing us into a right standing with himself. Once we have been justified, our lives have to be brought in line with our new status, and that is where sanctification comes in. These two elements are interconnected. Justification changes our legal status, and sanctification changes our nature so that we can live as God's children ought to live.

- *Adopted.* God justifies us for a reason: *so that ... we might become heirs having the hope of eternal life* (3:7; see also Rom 4:14; 8:17; Gal 3:29; Heb 11:7; Jas 2:5).[163] An heir is someone to whom someone else passes on possessions or privileges. This inheritance comes with full rights to what is given. No one can legally deprive the heir of what is due to him. When God makes us his heirs, the possession he gives us is eternal life. We have the right to enjoy his presence for ever, and no one can take this away from us. There is sometimes an argument about whether we are heirs of the "hope of eternal life" or "of eternal life", but theologically the question is irrelevant.[164] Believers will inherit eternal life and eternal life is part and parcel of their hope – a hope that is not merely wishful thinking but a confident assurance of what is to come. The reference to "hope" reminds us of the tension between the "already" and the "not yet" that is part of the Christian life. We are already saved and justified, and we already have eternal life, but we will not fully enjoy our status until Christ returns.[165]

Believers are blessed to have been prevented from destroying themselves in hatred and lust. They are blessed to have been made right before God and even adopted as his heirs. But there are still many people in Africa and around the world who have yet to experience these blessings. They are still living the lives Paul described in 1:3.

Our call is to show unbelievers the way of salvation by faith in Christ. We do this for their own sake, to enable them to enjoy fellowship with God, and also for the sake of our whole society. A society full of disobedience, evil desires, malice, envy and hatred is a miserable one! But when people come into the blessing of a new status in Christ, they and the society they live in will enjoy the benefits of obedience, holiness and love.

God's kindness

The only reason that believers have acquired their new status is God's kindness, love, mercy and grace (3:4, 5, 7). Paul introduces these qualities with the word *but* which highlights the contrast between their earlier state and their present one and stresses what caused that change. What made the difference was the appearance of *the kindness and love of God our Saviour* (3:4).[166] "Kindness" involves more than just a generally warm feeling towards people; it implies generous action on their behalf.[167] This kindness was manifested in everything that Christ did to bring us salvation, from his incarnation to his resurrection.[168]

God's act of kindness was accompanied by love. The Greek work for love that Paul uses here is the same one from which we get the word "philanthropy". It literally means "love of humanity". Jewish and Greek writers mention this attitude as an important characteristic of deities and human rulers.[169] As Paul uses it here, it refers to "a Sovereign Lord who makes an act of unprompted and undeserved favour to his subjects, and does so in a personal appearance."[170]

Again the word "but" emphasizes that what happens is contrary to what we deserve. God saves purely *because of his mercy* (3:5).[171] (See comments on 1 Tim 1:13, 16 for more on mercy). God's mercy is what enables him to change the verdict we face from condemnation to acquittal and to declare us justified in his sight. Paul also describes this as being a result of God's *grace*, his undeserved blessing that justifies us and gives us the status of being heirs of God (3:7).

Paul underlines the point that our salvation is solely the result of God's love, mercy and grace by stressing that it was *not because of righteous things we had done* (3:5).[172] The "we" is emphatic. We cannot take credit for having done anything righteous. Many people like to think that God deposits their good deeds in a sort of heavenly bank account and then totals up the account when they die in order to determine their reward (or punishment, although they prefer not to think about this!). But Paul would use the banking metaphor quite differently. He would say that when we go and look into our spiritual "savings account" to see how much righteousness we have deposited, we are in for a shock. The account is empty! Nothing that we have done or can do qualifies as worth depositing in that account! There is not even one cent in our favour. In fact, the bank would probably turn us away, saying that we do not have enough righteousness to even open an account. And that is where the goodness and grace of God came in. If we ask him, he will open accounts in our names and deposit righteousness in them for us. This is not something we earn. It is his gift, drawn from his own enormous resources of righteousness. All we have to do is to ask him for it.

God's cleansing

The legal condemnation that we deserved was taken care of by our justification, but there is the further problem that we are polluted by sin – the dirt of it clings to us. Thus we are in deep need of the *washing of rebirth and renewal by the Holy Spirit* (3:5) that transforms us into people who can appear before God's holiness and righteousness. The change is accomplished by the Holy Spirit.[173]

That much is clear. However, when we get down to the details, there are disagreements. First, what exactly is this "washing"? Is it related to baptism?[174] Second, is the rebirth brought about by washing or is the washing just another way of referring to the rebirth?[175] Third, is Paul thinking of one or two events? In other words is "washing and renewal" one concept, or are these two different aspects of what happens at conversion?[176] Three main positions have emerged.[177]

- The "washing" is equivalent to water baptism and the "renewal" represents the coming of the Holy Spirit.[178] Those who hold this position would generally hold that baptism and conversion go together. However, they do not agree on when the renewal by the Holy Spirit takes place. The traditional view is that it happens at confirmation. Pentecostals are more likely to say that renewal is equivalent to the baptism of the Holy Spirit, which comes some time after conversion.

- The "washing" is equivalent to water baptism, and the terms "rebirth" and "renewal" are either synonyms or explanations for what happens when a person is baptized. There is thus one event (baptism) and one agent (the Holy Spirit).
- "Washing" does not refer to baptism but is a metaphor for spiritual cleansing. This is the position taken in this commentary. The whole phrase means "the cleansing, regenerative work of the Holy Spirit".[179] Paul's point is that God makes sinners acceptable by paying their debt (justification) and by cleansing them from the pollution of sin. This cleansing happens through two different acts. Rebirth or regeneration is one[180] and the second is renewal by the Holy Spirit. When we are reborn, our old nature is rendered powerless. But like an uprooted plant, this nature may take some time to wither away completely. While it withers, the Holy Spirit is renewing us, implanting a new nature that will blossom and bear fruit as we grow in Christian maturity.

In his next words, Paul brings out the involvement of all three persons of the Trinity in our salvation. He refers to the Holy Spirit as the one *whom he poured out on us generously through Jesus Christ our Saviour* (3:6). God the Father is "he". Paul is saying is that God the Father pours out the Holy Spirit through the Son (see also John 14:16, 26; 15:26).

The fact that the Holy Spirit is "poured out" does not mean that he is not a person. Paul is not speaking about who he is, but about what he does. He actively applies all God's spiritual blessings (note the word "generously") in the lives of believers.[181] His work is not done separately from the work of Christ, but through Christ. God the Father initiates the process that Christ and the Holy Spirit carry out.[182]

The unchangeable message

Paul labels what he has been saying to Titus in 3:4–7 as *a trustworthy saying* (3:8a). This is the fifth time he has used this expression in these letters.[183] It is a label he attaches to statements of timeless truth that represent the unchangeable essence of the Christian message.

Questions for Discussion

1. African Christians commonly include a time for testimonies in their meetings, especially during youth meetings. Many of the testimonies state what the person was like and how the Lord turned the person around. How is Paul's discussion of the past and present similar to or different from the testimonies that you have heard? Who did the people you listened to glorify by placing at the centre of their testimonies? How can we shape our testimonies so that we can be like Paul and keep focused on the grace and mercy of God?

2. In April 2009 some leading women in Kenya called on Kenyan women to join them in a strike to make a political point. They urged women to deny men any sexual rights for seven days. How do you think a Christian wife should have responded to this call? Should she obey her husband or these prominent women? Is there a conflict of values here? What principles should guide a believer in situations like this?

3. Backslidden believers sometimes say that since God has already adopted them and made them heirs, they will enjoy worldly pleasures for a while before starting to live as members of God's family. Is there any contradiction in this position? Since our status as God's heirs is based on our relationship with God, is it possible that such persons were never heirs at all? If yes, why? If no, why?

UNIT 7
TITUS 3:12–15

CONCLUDING MATTERS

In Africa, it is common for someone who is travelling to take greetings to those he will meet. Someone who is about to set off on a journey will ask church members if they have greetings to send to the congregation he or she plans to visit. At times, the church members simply assume that the person will greet the congregation on their behalf because it is such a common practice.

Paul, too, seems to send greetings whenever he has the opportunity to do so, as can be seen in his letters. But in this letter to Titus his closing words include more than just greetings. In fact, he sounds rather like the chairman of a diocese or district church council as he addresses Titus as the one in charge of the church and speaks of those who are to assist him, and those he is to assist. He clearly has a coordinated plan of work that involves the whole community.

He also has some final words of advice to Timothy on what he should stress and what he should avoid.

Stress This

When Paul gives his instructions to Titus he says, *I want you to* (3:8a). This "want" carries the force of a command, for Paul is speaking as an apostle and is not merely stating his personal preferences. But he wants Titus to speak even more strongly when passing on this message to the Cretans. When speaking to them, he is to *stress these things*. The word translated "stress" means "insist emphatically"[184] or speak firmly. The same Greek word is used in only one other place in the New Testament, when Paul says the false teachers are insisting on things they do not understand (1 Tim 1:7). In contrast, Titus is to insist on "these things" because they are sound doctrine. As the nasb puts it, he is to "speak confidently" about the truths of the faith.

What are the "things" Titus is to insist on? Scholars are agreed that Paul is referring to everything he has said in 3:1–7, although some think that he is laying more stress on the great theological statements of 3:4–7, and others think that the stress falls on the ethical matters (good works) mentioned in 3:1–2.[185] Yet given Paul's insistence in Titus 2 that sound teaching embraces both theology and practice, it seems more likely that he would insist that Titus is to teach both what has been said in the verses dealing with theology and those dealing with ethical exhortations. The two are interrelated. Titus must insist that the Cretan believers both believe and live out the sound doctrine he teaches.

Paul gives two reasons why Titus is to stress these things. The first is *so that those who have trusted in God may be careful to devote themselves to doing what is good* (3:8b). His insistence on these things will result in "those who have trusted in God" (that is, believers) living lives that are in conformity with their beliefs.[186] Some translators interpret the phrase translated as "devote themselves to doing what is good" as meaning "engage in honourable occupations" (neb).[187] In other words, believers should do honest work, and not be thieves, drug dealers, prostitutes or any job that was ethically questionable. However, it seems more likely that Paul does not have this restricted meaning in mind and is simply saying that believers should concentrate on doing what is good. He is more concerned about "their behavior in general and not merely one aspect such as a profession."[188] This interpretation is strengthened by the fact that the phrase translated as "doing what is good" occurs many times in this letter to Titus as well as in the letters to Timothy.[189] It is a comprehensive term, touching all areas of ethics. The Cretan believers are to be careful in the sense of taking great care (and not in the sense of being worried or burdened with cares)[190] to ensure that good works characterize all their behaviour. Paul's point is simple: "Right belief must exhibit its fruit in life".[191]

The second reason why Titus is to stress these things is because they *are excellent and profitable for everyone* (3:8c). The adjective "profitable" is the same word translated "value" when Paul contrasted the superior value of godliness to the value of bodily discipline (1 Tim 4:8). The things Titus is to teach have the same function as the Scriptures in 2 Timothy 3:16 (where the same Greek word is used) in that they make a positive contribution to building up individuals and the body of Christ, the church.

When believers practise their beliefs, they confirm that these beliefs are genuine. God will bless their adherence to the truths Paul commended to Titus in verses 3:1–7 and to doing "what is good" (3:8). Their compassion and generosity will benefit the community at large and may draw non-believers towards the Christian faith.

Avoid That

Having told Titus to stress things that are excellent and profitable, Paul continues his charge to him by telling him to avoid things and people that will undermine his ministry.

Unprofitable and useless activities

Just as Titus is to make it his habit to remind the believers of certain things, so he is to make it his habit to *avoid certain things*.[192] This is the same approach Paul commended to Timothy when he told him to "avoid godless chatter" (2 Tim 2:16). In 3:9 Paul mentions four things Titus is to avoid:

- *Foolish controversies* are controversies sparked by people who do not know what they are talking about but insist that their views be accepted. Such people are foolish, and so are the controversies that flare up around them (see also 1 Tim 6:4; 2 Tim 2:23).[193] They do nothing to promote sound doctrine.
- *Genealogies* are probably related to the "Jewish myths" mentioned in Titus 1:14 (see commentary on 1 Tim 1:14).
- *Arguments* frequently qualify as a vice in Paul's writings (the same Greek word is also used in Rom 1:29; 13:13; 1 Cor 3:3; 2 Cor 12:20; Gal 5:20; see commentary on 1 Tim 6:4).
- *Quarrels about the law* are comparable to the "quarrelling about words" that Paul condemned when writing to Timothy (1 Tim 6:4; 2 Tim 2:14). Such quarrels are battles that are fought without physical weapons. They should be avoided by elders and by all Christians (1

Tim 3:3; Titus 3:2). Here, "the law" most likely refers to different interpretations of God's law. Titus' opponents preoccupy themselves with their interpretations and reinterpretations of it rather than with God's revealed word. People still indulge in these sorts of quarrels today. For example, some insist that the command to "remember the Sabbath day by keeping it holy" (Exod 20:8) means that no shops should be open on Sunday, even after worship is finished. Others argue that shops can be open on Sunday, but should sell only the most essential items like water or soft drinks because these refresh people before they head home after worship. Then people get embroiled in arguments about whether it is legitimate to also sell bread on a Sunday. But the principle underlying the command is that we should leave everything else and gather to worship God. What we should be discussing is how we will enrich our time of worship so that we make the day holy – not whether opening little shops and selling water or bread is acceptable.

Titus should avoid these things because they *are unprofitable and useless* (3:9). Paul's standard for evaluating things is whether they contribute to a better understanding of God's way of salvation and the spiritual nurture of men and women. Because the things he has just listed contribute nothing in these areas, he declares them "fruitless, useless, without substance".[194]

Divisive people

Just as there are some arguments that are best avoided, so there are some people who are best avoided. If they refuse to respond to Titus' overtures, he should *have nothing to do with them* (3:10).[195] This action is consistent with Paul's instructions elsewhere on how to deal with false teachers and others who persist in their ways after being corrected (Rom 16:17 and 1 Cor 5:12), but it is not as severe as Paul's treatment of Hymenaeus and Alexander, whom he says he "handed over to Satan" (1 Tim 1:20).

The people Titus is to avoid are described as *divisive*. The Greek word translated "divisive" is translated as "heretic" in the kjv because it was later used to refer to heretics.[196] But that was not the meaning of the word when Paul was writing. Rather, Paul is referring to people who cause splits and divisions among the believers. By implication these people are also insubordinate to authority figures like Titus, who represents Paul.

Titus must not shun these people until he has given them an opportunity to change. He must give them "a first and second warning" (3:10 nasb). The goal is to help them, as becomes clear when we note that the word translated "warning" is also translated as "instruction" in Ephesians 6:4. But there is a limit to how much time ministers should give to unrepentant people. Their main task is not to argue with people unwilling to change but to teach and exhort those who want to grow in the Lord. This is a better use of their time. One way Christian ministers can follow this instruction is to "discern what is heretical, name it as such, and confront it, but not spend time in refutation."[197]

Paul tells Titus why unrepentant divisive people are to be treated this way when he adds, *You may be sure that such people are warped and sinful; they are self-condemned* (3:11). The "you may be sure" can also be translated "since you have come to know".[198] Titus will have learned this as he engaged with them when trying to warn them. He will know that they are set in their ways when they ignore repeated warnings. Such behaviour is evidence of a "warped" or "perverted" (nasb) nature.[199] Their warped nature leads them to sin regularly, and thus means that they are condemned.[200]

Society in general recognizes that some suffering is self-inflicted. Someone who deliberately cuts off his or her own hand has no one else to blame. Similarly, the condemnation here is self-inflicted. These people are not rejected because God or his servants are unwilling to accept them, or because they have hurt someone's feelings, or for any personal reason. Rather, their rejection is an acknowledgement of the logic of the position they have chosen to take. By refusing to repent, they have excluded themselves.[201]

We have to confront false teachings, and also those who spread them. Church leaders should reject the teaching right away, but should take their brothers or sisters through the process of being warned a first and second time in order to establish that they are determined to continue to spread it. Our goal must be to stop false teaching and bring people onto the right path. We should thus exercise patience when dealing with people as long as there is hope that they might be won over to agree with sound doctrine.

Final Instructions

Paul closes his letter with a few detailed instructions about practical matters relating to his travels and those of his associates.

Instructions about Meeting Paul

Paul tells Titus, *Do your best to come to me at Nicopolis* (3:12). Apparently, Paul himself has not yet reached Nicopolis, for he adds, *I have decided to winter there* (3:12) rather than "here", which he would have used if he were already in the city. But which Nicopolis did he mean? The name joins the Greek words *nike* (victory) and *polis* (city) and means "city of victory". It was thus a popular name, and there were at least three cities called Nicopolis. One was in Cilicia (in modern Turkey), another was in Thrace (modern Bulgaria) and a third in Epirus (today part of north-western Greece). Scholars generally agree that Paul was probably in Nicopolis of Epirus, which was a common stopping place for travellers going north or south and the largest city on the western shore of Greece, two hundred miles northwest of Athens.[202] It would be a good location for Paul to continue his ministry in the winter months, when travel came to a standstill, for it was the best centre for work in the Roman province of Dalmatia. If Paul wanted to travel again when the spring came, he was only two hundred miles across the Adriatic Sea from Brindisium in Italy, where he could join the famous road called the Appian Way and go to Rome.

Titus is told to "do your best" to join Paul in Nicopolis. The same phrase was used when Paul asked Timothy to join him in Rome (2 Tim 4:9). It could also be translated as "do everything you can", as in 3:13. The word focuses more on determination than speed. Paul is not telling Titus to "carelessly drop everything you are doing in Crete and come to me". Rather, he wants Titus to come as soon as is possible, and not to waste too much time before setting out.

Paul is planning to send a substitute to take Titus' place while he is away, but he has not yet decided whether the substitute will be *Artemas or Tychicus*. We know a bit about Tychicus from Acts 20:4, where he is said to have been one of Paul's companions on his third missionary journey, and to have been from the province of Asia. In his other letters, Paul describes him as a "dear brother and faithful servant in the Lord" (Eph 6:21; see also Col 4:7). However, given that Paul later sent Tychicus to Ephesus to relieve Timothy of his ministry there (1 Tim 4:12), it seems more likely that Artemas was the one who ended up going to Crete.

This is the only reference to Artemas in the Bible, so we know very little about him. However, there is an ancient tradition that says that he became the first bishop of Lystra (in modern Turkey).[203]

Titus is to leave *as soon as* his replacement arrives, but not before. Allowing for the time it would take for this letter to reach Crete, for Titus to make his preparations while he waits for Artemas (or Tychicus) to arrive, and for him to travel to Nicopolis, it would seem that Paul probably wrote this letter around mid-summer, when he was beginning to look ahead to the coming winter. He probably wrote it from somewhere in Achaia or Macedonia.

Instructions about Zenas and Apollos

Titus is instructed to, *Do everything you can to help Zenas the lawyer and Apollos* (3:13a). These men probably delivered Paul's letter to Titus. We do not know anything about Zenas other than what is told here, though a late tradition says that he became the bishop of Diospolis.[204] Here, Zenas is called a *nomikos* (lawyer), a title that was used for experts in Jewish law (Matt 22:35; Luke 7:30; 10:25; 11:45–46, 52; 14:3) and secular jurists. Given the fact that the name Zenas is Greek, it is more likely that he was a secular jurist than an expert in Jewish law.[205]

Assuming that this Apollos is the same man described in Acts 18:24 as Alexandrian by birth (see also 1 Cor 1:12), he may have had connections with Alexandria in Egypt. He and Zenas may have been travelling to Egypt via Crete when they handed over this letter. Certainly, the Greek implies that Crete was not their final destination.

When these brothers pass through Crete Titus should see to it that their needs are met and that they receive a good send-off "so that nothing is lacking for them" (3:13b nasb).[206] The "help" he must give them is generous hospitality, of the kind that used to characterize Africa.

Instructions about Believers

Paul also gives a final instruction to believers: *Our people must learn to devote themselves to doing what is good* (3:14a). The nasb translates the Greek literally as "our people must also learn", indicating that there is a link between Paul's instruction about caring for Zenas and Apollos and this instruction.[207] Given that the first half of the statement about hospitality for the travellers seems to trigger the second half in Paul's mind, it is fair to say that part of "doing good" is exercising hospitality. The exact words translated "doing what is good" also appear in 3:8 (see commentary on that verse).

"Our people" are the Cretan Christians who do not follow the false teachers but remain faithful to the sound doctrine that Titus and Paul teach.[208] The believers need "to learn", but the type of learning referred to here is not mere head knowledge but the type of learning that is expressed in practice.[209] This lesson is consistent with the very important theme in these letters, namely, that sound doctrine involves living out the truth in everyday life.

The reason the believers must do good is so that they can *provide for urgent needs and not live unproductive lives* (3:14b). Christians should not only work to have enough to meet their own needs, but also to have enough to give to others in need.[210] As noted earlier in 1:12, Cretans may have been inclined to be self-centred rather than generous. So Paul wants Titus to make sure that they view generosity as a necessary quality for Christians, no matter what their cultural background.[211] The core of Christianity is to give rather than to receive. This is what Christ taught by his own example (Matt 20:28; Mark 10:45; Gal 1:4).

There should be no restrictions other than need on who can benefit from the generosity of Christians. As long as resources last, they should be given to fellow believers and then to others, without any discrimination on the basis of whether the recipients are "our people" or "not our people". Our criterion for giving must be the depth of need, not our personal relationship to the one in need.

Greetings and Prayer

In closing, Paul specifies who sends and who receives greetings. As usual, he sends greetings from his companions saying, *Everyone with me sends you greetings* (3:15a; see also Rom 16:21–23; 1 Cor 16:19–20; 2 Cor 13:12–13; Phil 4:22; Col 4:10–14; and Phlm 23–24). He does not mention his associates by name, which is typical of his letters. The lists of names in Romans 16:21–23 and Colossians 4:10–14 are an exception to his normal practice.

These greetings are sent to *those who love us in the faith* (3:15b).[212] These are the Cretan believers who share a bond with Paul and Titus (and definitely not the false teachers).

As he concludes, Paul prays for Titus and the others, *Grace be with you all* (3:15c). Just as he does when writing to Timothy, he ends his letter with a prayer for more than one person. In Timothy, he prays for "you" plural (1 Tim 6:21; 2 Tim 4:22) and in Titus he prays for "you all". This may be a clue that Paul is not writing these letters for Timothy and Titus alone, to be carefully tucked away in a drawer once they had been read. The letters are directly addressed to them, and are personal in that they offer them specific encouragement and support, but they are also intended for public reading.

Paul's prayer is that God will shower his favour on the believers in Crete, and on all who read this letter.[213]

Paul's knows that pastoral work is holistic. While pastors' primary calling is to announce salvation and the effect salvation has on our relationship with God and with others, they must also be alert to things that affect the welfare of his community in which they minister. Therefore pastors should be involved in advocating for justice as well as in announcing salvation for all who believe. This is the type of ministry that Paul asks Titus to model in Crete.

Questions for Discussion

1. Discipline can be one of the most painful aspects of Christian ministry, especially in a community in which the members of the church are all related and will react to something done to another member, especially by an outsider. How can we balance our desire for people to like us with our responsibility as ministers to rebuke and discipline people?

2. Titus is a child of God. He is also a spiritual son to Paul, a pastor to the Cretans and a model to society in general. Reflecting on these relationships (or any others that you have noticed in this letter), what struck you most as you read through Titus?

3. The point has repeatedly been made that sound doctrine includes both what we believe and how we live. When there is true knowledge of sound doctrine, lives and churches should be being transformed. Do you see any evidence of such transformation in the church you attend each week? What can be done to promote even greater transformation?

NOTES

NOTES

1 Timothy

1. Issues of authorship are also important because they affect the dating of these letters, and thus their interpretation.
2. The Pauline authorship of the Pastoral Epistles, and particularly of 1 Timothy, was first questioned by Schleiermacher, a German theologian, in 1807. His objections were based on linguistic and biographical features of the letters.
3. Those who hold this view include Martin Dibelius and Hans Conzelmann. They argue that the Pastoral Epistles are pseudonymous, fictional, spurious or forgeries and have no link to Paul as a person. They regard them as having been written "in the second century as an attempt to make Paul's message relevant or to oppose second-century heresy" (William D. Mounce, *Pastoral Epistles* [Word Biblical Commentary; Nashville: Thomas Nelson, 2000]), cxviii.
4. This fragmentary theory states "that after Paul's death a person collected a few genuine fragments of Paul's writing and wove them into three fabricated letters in an attempt to preserve the fragments and make Paul's message relevant to a later church" (Mounce, cxviii). P. N. Harrison (*The Problem of the Pastoral Epistles* [London: Oxford University Press, 1921]) suggests that these four fragments are Titus 3:12-15; 2 Timothy 4:13-15, 20, 21a; 2 Timothy 4:16-18a and 2 Timothy 4:9-12, 22b.
5. The only mention of Crete in relation to Paul's travels is his stormy sea journey along its coast (Acts 27:7-12). It does not seem likely that he stopped anywhere long enough to establish a church that Titus would be left to organize.
6. According to 1 Timothy 1:3, Paul left Timothy in Ephesus while he himself travelled to Macedonia. These two areas are mentioned at three points in Acts:
    - Acts 16:9-10 – Paul travelled to Macedonia on his second missionary journey. The church in Ephesus was still too young to match the description in 1 Timothy.
    - Acts 18:19 – Paul was in Ephesus, but when he left he did not go to Macedonia but to Caesarea and then Antioch.
    - Acts 19:8–20:31 – Paul spent roughly three years in Ephesus, but there is no mention of his making a trip to Macedonia during those years, especially a trip long enough to warrant a letter like the one written to Timothy.
    - Acts 20:1 – Following Paul's final departure from Ephesus, he went to Macedonia. But he did not leave Timothy behind in Ephesus; he sent him on ahead (Acts 19:22; 20:5). They were setting out for Jerusalem, and there is no indication that he was planning to travel to Ephesus soon, as implied in 1 Timothy 3:14 and 4:13.
7. In 2 Timothy, Paul wants Timothy to come to him, picking up Mark on the way (4:9, 11). But according to Colossians 1:1 and 4:10, and Philemon 24, Timothy and Mark were with him in Rome. Moreover, Paul speaks as if he has recently been in Troas (4:13), Corinth and Miletus (4:20), which are in Asia Minor. But in Acts his journey to Rome starts in Caesarea in Palestine. It must have been at least three years since he had been in Asia Minor. All this makes it unlikely that the imprisonment referred to is that of Acts 28.
   Some suggest that 2 Timothy was written during Paul's two-year imprisonment in Caesarea (Acts 23–26), shortly after he had passed through Corinth, Troas and Miletus. However, Timothy and Trophimus were with Paul in Jerusalem (Acts 20:4; 21:29), whereas 2 Timothy says that Trophimus had recently been left at Miletus (4:20) and Timothy is said to be in Ephesus. It is also difficult to reconcile the information we have about Demas with the Caesarean imprisonment. In Colossians 4:14 and Philemon 24, Demas is said to be one of Paul's helpers in Rome, where Paul was sent from Caesarea, but in 2 Timothy 4:10 he is said to have abandoned Paul. A final

argument against the Caesarean location is the fact that 2 Timothy 1:17 strongly suggests that Paul is a prisoner in Rome.

8 The linguistic argument was put forward strongly by P. N. Harrison in *The Problem of the Pastoral Epistles*. He listed all the 849 words (excluding proper names) used at least once in the Pastoral Epistles. He then compared these words with the words used in the ten epistles he accepted as written by Paul, and with the rest of the New Testament. He identified the following patterns:

- 175 words are used only in the Pastoral Epistles and nowhere else in the New Testament. These words include *theopneustos* (God-breathed), *kalodidaskalos* (teaching what is good) and *agathoergein* (doing good).
- 131 words are used only in the Pastoral Epistles and in New Testament books not written by Paul. They include *eusebeia* (piety) and *epiphanein* (to appear). Combining these 131 words with the previous 175 words gives a total of 306 words out of the 849 in the epistle that are not characteristic of Paul's style as we know it elsewhere.
- Many of the words Paul uses elsewhere are used with a different meaning in the Pastoral Epistles. These words include *pistis* (faith); *didaskalia* (teaching, doctrine); *soter* (Saviour); and *mesites* (mediator).
- A number of key terms in Paul's other ten epistles are not used in the Pastoral Epistles. These include *akrobustia* (uncircumcision – used 19 times in the other epistles); *apothneskein* (to die – 42 times); *eleutheros* (free – 16 times); *ergazesthai* (to work, perform – 18 times); *euangelizesthai* (to preach good news – 21 times); *eucharistein* to give thanks – 24 times); *kauchasthai* (to boast about – 34 times); *ouranos* (heaven – 21 times); *pneumatikos* (spiritual – 24 times); *prassein* (to do, accomplish – 18 times); *sophia* (wisdom – 28 times); *soma* (body – 91 times); *huios* (son – 40 times); *chairein* (to rejoice – 29 times); and *psuche* (soul – 13 times).
- Particles, conjunctions, pronouns and prepositions are often used quite differently in the Pastoral Epistles than they are in the rest of Paul's writings. Harrison identified 72 such differences. Examples include the use of *ara* (interrogative particle indicating anxiety or impatience, introducing only direct questions); *arti* (until now); *dioti* (because); *eite* (if ... if, whether ... or); *epei* (since, then); *idou* (behold); kathaper (just as); *nuni de* (but ... now); *ouchi* (stronger form of *ou* [no] thus, by no means); *hoste* (therefore, so that, for this reason). The preposition *sun* also is not found in the Pastoral Epistles. Arland Hultgren notes: "Paul uses two different Greek prepositions to express 'with'. These are *sun* plus the dative (28 times) and *meta* plus the genitive (37 times). But the writer of the Pastorals never uses the former; he uses only the latter expression (18 times)" (A. Hultgren, *I–II Timothy, Titus* [Minneapolis: Augsburg, 1984], 15).

The linguistic differences between the Pastoral Epistles and Paul's other letters led Harrison to reject Pauline authorship, and thus the early date for these epistles. These linguistic differences are even more striking to those who accept Hultgren's position that only seven of the epistles (Romans, 1 & 2 Corinthians, Galatians, Philippians, 1 Thessalonians and Philemon) were written by Paul.

Having rejected Pauline authorship, Harrison set out to identify when these letters were probably written. He compared the 306 words the Pastorals have and Paul's ten epistles do not with later writings. He found that 121 of these words were used by second-century apostolic fathers and apologists, and thus claimed that these epistles were written in the second century ad.

While all scholars agree that there are differences in the vocabulary in these letters, they disagree about how the differences are to be interpreted. Some point out that more than fifty percent of the words in the Pastoral Epistles are used elsewhere by Paul, meaning that these letters are more like his other writings than they are unlike them. Moreover, because these letters are brief, there may be too few words for a fair comparison. G. Udny Yule (a Cambridge statistician) argued that a minimum sample of 10,000 words is needed for serious application of this approach. His point is still accepted today (see I. H. Marshall, *The Pastoral Epistles*. [International Critical Commentary; London: T&T Clark, 1999], 62 and Mounce, cxv). It may thus be safer to say that the Pastoral Epistles are unlike Paul's other epistles than to say that they are not by Paul.

It has also been pointed out that many of the words identified as "unusual" in the context of the New Testament were used by other Greek writers before ad 50. In fact, eighty percent of them are found in the Septuagint, which Paul knew well.

The difference in vocabulary between these epistles and the rest of Paul's writings can largely be explained by the context and circumstances in which they were written. Mounce (civ–cxii) identifies five categories that accommodate most of the "unusual" vocabulary:
- Words related to the historical situation
- Words Paul appropriated from his opponents
- Words related to church leadership
- Words to do with vices
- Words within quoted or traditional material
- Words influenced by the Latin Paul would have constantly been exposed to in Rome

The differences in the use of the basic words like prepositions may be adequately explained by Paul's use of a different amanuensis for these letters.

Many scholars have been satisfied with such explanations and accept that the Pastoral Epistles were written by Paul.

9 Scholars have identified the following concerns. Each of us will need to decide whether it is reasonable to expect absolute consistency in Paul, or whether he should be permitted some freedom to vary his themes.
- *Some central Pauline theological themes are not mentioned.* Such themes include the Parousia, the conflict between the flesh and the spirit, the Holy Spirit, the fatherhood of God, and the church. (For a full discussion of this issue, see Mounce, lxxxix–xci.)
- *Pauline theological themes are treated differently.* For example, Paul normally speaks of faith as meaning trust in God, Christ or the gospel. However, in the Pastoral Epistles, he refers to it more as a body of belief (e.g. 1 Tim 3:13) or as a Christian virtue (1 Tim 1:5; 4:12). Similarly, in Paul's other epistles, the phrase "in Christ" refers to some kind of mystical union. In the Pastoral Epistles, it refers to the quality of life made available to the believer (e.g. 1 Tim 1:14; 3:13; 2 Tim 1:9, 13). Finally, whereas Paul elsewhere treats righteousness as a gift of God, in the Pastoral Epistles, it is a virtue to be pursued (1 Tim 6:11).
- *New theological themes are introduced.* Such themes include godliness (*eusebeia*), which is mentioned ten times in the Pastoral Epistles, but nowhere else in Paul's writing. Paul also usually speaks of Christ's coming (*parousia*), but the Pastoral Epistles speaks of his appearing or manifestation (*epiphaneia*). The only other place this word is used by Paul is in 2 Thessalonians 2:8, where a literal translation reads, "the appearing of His coming" (*te epiphaneia tes parousias autou*).
- *References to a fixed theological tradition.* In Paul's other writings, he does not seem to refer to a fixed tradition, but in the Pastoral Epistles he speaks of the gospel as a deposit that has been entrusted to him and to Timothy (1 Tim 6:20; 2 Tim 1:12, 14) and that is to be passed on (2 Tim 2:2). He also speaks of "sound teaching", "the faith" and "the truth". There are also signs of what appear to be creeds, for example, in 1 Timothy 3:16 and Titus 2:11–14.

10 In the Pastoral Epistles, the church structure is headed by Timothy and Titus, who as Paul's representatives are responsible for evangelism, preaching and organization. They are to resist error and those who propagate it, and have authority to discipline church members. Under them are overseers or elders, that is, ordained local leaders who receive some stipend for their services. The church at Ephesus also had deacons and possibly deaconesses.

Some have argued that this type of church organization developed only after Paul's death, particularly in the time of Clement (ad 95), and Ignatius (ad 110), who wrote to the churches in Asia Minor.

11 The Dead Sea Scrolls, written before Paul's time, speak of different ranks within the Qumran community, including the priests, the Levites, and the many. The superintendent or moderator of the community received reports about violations of the law and was in charge of training and examining those who applied for membership in the community. This example, in combination

with the established role of the head of a synagogue, means that the type of overseer mentioned in the Pastoral Epistles is not necessarily the same as the second-century monarchical bishop.

12 His parents may have named him Saul in honour of his famous ancestor, King Saul, who was also from the tribe of Benjamin (1 Sam 9:1–2; Phil 3:5). This name represented his ethnicity. Paul may have been his second name, for he was born in Tarsus, an important city that was the capital of the Roman district of Cilicia. It was also, along with Athens and Alexandria, a centre of Greek learning. The name Paul would then have represented the wider world to which he belonged. Alternatively, he may have chosen the name Paul after his encounter with Sergius Paulus during his first missionary journey (Acts 13:7–12). The name may have reminded him of the grace and power that God had displayed on that occasion. His use of this name is a sign of his full identification with Gentiles.

13 Donald Guthrie, *Galatians* (New Century Bible; London: Oliphants, 1969), 56.

14 Andronicus and Junias may also be referred to as apostles in Romans 16:7, although the interpretation of that verse is disputed. Epaphroditus may be termed an apostle on the basis of the Greek used in Philemon 2:25.

15 See also Adama Ouedraogo, "Prophets and Apostles", in *Africa Bible Commentary* (ed. Tokunboh Adeyemo; Nairobi: Word Alive, 2006), 1434.

16 Excluding the references in the Pastoral Epistles, Timothy is mentioned seventeen times in Paul's letters: for example, Rom 16:21 ("Timothy, my co-worker"); 1 Cor 4:17 ("Timothy, my son whom I love, who is faithful"); 16:10 ("Timothy ... carrying on the work of the Lord, just as I am"); 2 Cor 1:1 ("and Timothy our brother"); 1:19 ("Jesus Christ ... preached among you by us – by me and Silas and Timothy"); Phil 1:1 ("Paul and Timothy, servants of Christ Jesus"); 2:19 ("I hope ... to send Timothy to you soon"); Col 1:1 ("and Timothy our brother"); 1 Thess 1:1 ("Paul, Silas and Timothy"), 3:2 ("We sent Timothy, who is our brother and co-worker in God's service in spreading the gospel of Christ"), 3:6 ("But Timothy has just now come to us from you"); 2 Thess 1:1 ("Paul, Silas and Timothy"); and Phlm 1 ("and Timothy our brother").

17 Rom 1:7; 1 Cor 1:3; 2 Cor 1:2; Gal 1:3; Eph 1:2; Phil 1:2; Col 1:2; 1 Thess 1:1; 2 Thess 1:2; Titus 1:4; Phlm 3.

18 George W. Knight *The Pastoral Epistles: A Commentary on the Greek Text* (New International Greek Testament Commentary; Grand Rapids: Eerdmans, 1992), 66.

19 Grand Rapids: Zondervan, 2002.

20 The following passages suggest that the church in Ephesus was founded by or under the guidance of Paul: Acts 18:19–21; 18:24–26; 1 Cor 16:8–9; 2 Cor 1:8–9.

21 In 1 Timothy, the verb "to command" (*parangellein*) is used in 1:3; 4:11; 5:7; 6:13, 17, and the noun "command" in 1:5, 18.

22 The words "to teach false doctrines" are the translation of a compound verb (*heterodidaskalein*, formed from the adjective "other" (*heteros*) and the verb "to teach" (*didaskalein*). In Greek, there were two words that could be translated as "different". *Allos* was used when speaking about something that was different but still of the same kind (e.g. two different kinds of apple). *Heteros*, the word Paul uses here, has the idea of something of a completely different kind (e.g. an apple and a pineapple). In Gal 1:6–7, Paul admits that there may be a gospel that is *eteros* but there cannot be a gospel that is *allos*.

23 The word gnostic comes from the Greek word *gnosis*, which means knowledge. Gnostics believed that salvation was attained by acquiring secret knowledge. They divided human beings into three classes. The *pneumatic* or spiritual were the few who were highest on the ladder of knowledge and came closest to knowing the *pleroma* or fullness of God. Below them were the *psychic* (mental) who had faith but not knowledge. The majority of people were *hylic* (physical), living solely in the material world rather than the spiritual world. This material world was evil because matter itself was evil. Consequently gnostics insisted that the world could not have been created by the Supreme Being. Instead it must have been created by one of the thirty personal beings, referred to as *aeons*, who emanated from the Supreme Being but became less and less like that Being as one aeon "gave birth" to another. They insisted that one of these aeons, acting either in ignorance or in rebellion, was the God of the Old Testament, the creator of heaven and earth.

Dualism (the existence of equal forces of good and evil) was also a key element of the gnostic outlook on life.

Gnosticism as a philosophical system developed slowly over time, borrowing ideas from various sources. It seems to have blossomed in the second century ad, although some of its ideas were probably already around in the first century ad when Paul was writing. However, we must not assume that every time Paul uses a word like *gnosis* or *pleroma*, he is thinking in terms of a fully developed gnostic system.

Gnostic beliefs seem very strange to Africans (unless, perhaps, we think of the ancestors as equivalent to *aeons*). However, it is possible to illustrate the differences between the categories of people they identified in everyday terms. In almost every country in Africa, a limited number of people enjoy the wealth of the nation, a few more are able to make ends meet, while the majority live in hopeless poverty. Just as this economic division is wrong, so is the gnostic idea that knowledge of God is distributed in the same way. The Bible teaches that such knowledge is available to all who turn to Christ.

24 This interpretation is based on reading *en pistei* as an instrumental dative. It could also be read as a dative of sphere, in which case the idea would be that God's administration is within the sphere of faith and is not affected by human wisdom or efforts to keep the law.

25 R. G. Gromacki, *Stand True to the Charge: An Exposition of 1 Timothy* (Grand Rapids: Baker Book House, 1982), 26.

26 He uses the masculine *aner*, rather than *anthropos*, which is the word for people in general.

27 The interpretation reflected in the tniv translation is preferred by many commentators including Mounce, 43; Gordon D. Fee, *1 and 2 Timothy, Titus* (Good News Commentary; San Francisco: Harper & Row, 1984), 12; J. N. D. Kelly, *A Commentary on the Pastoral Epistles: I & II Timothy, Titus* (Black's New Testament Commentaries; London: Adam & Charles Black, 1963), 51; J. H. Bernard, *Pastoral Epistles* (Thornapple Commentaries; Grand Rapids: Baker, 1980 repr.), 29. See also Knight, 90; Marshall, 382–383.

28 In 1:11 Paul uses the emphatic "I", so that the phrase could be translated "which I myself was trusted with".

29 The three Greek verbs are in the aorist tense, with the first and third being participles. Thus the three actions may represent either independent or simultaneous events. In this commentary, I regard them as separate events.

30 Mounce, 49. See also Kelly, 52. Some commentators see the strengthening within the context of Paul's early ministry after his conversion (Bernard, 30). Others relate it to Paul's ministry in general, and see this statement as equivalent to the one in Philippians 4:13 (Walter Liefeld, *1 & 2 Timothy/Titus* [NIV Application Commentary; Grand Rapids: Zondervan, 1999], 70).

31 It is also possible, however, to view being considered trustworthy as the Lord's evaluation of Paul following the strengthening. In this case, the progression would be from the initial strengthening to being considered trustworthy and to being put into service.

32 The Greek is *hoti agnoon epoiesa en apistia*, which can be literally translated as "because, being ignorant, I acted in unbelief".

33 The literal translation of *charin echo* in 1:12a is "I have gratitude" to Christ Jesus. The verb "I have" (*echo*) is in the aorist present, which indicates that Paul is not focusing on his habitual inclination to thank Christ but on the immediate response of his own whole being to what Christ has done for him.

34 *East African Standard*, Nairobi, August 2, 2004.

35 *East African Standard*, Nairobi, August 3, 2004.

36 The verb *elthen* (came) is in the aorist tense, inceptive shade. It focuses on Christ's entrance into existence at a specific time in the past.

37 "Sinners" (*hamartoloi*) derives from *hamartia*, which is the most inclusive term used for sin in the New Testament. Like *chata* in the Old Testament, its basic idea is "to miss the mark". A list of other words used for sin can be found in Charles C. Ryrie, *Basic Theology* (Wheaton: Victor Books, 1986), 210–212.

38. The Greek is *pistos eimi ego*. The personal pronoun "I" (*ego*) is used here for emphasis. Paul is literally saying, "I myself am the worst" of these sinners. The present tense "am" (*eimi*) is a durative present, encompassing both his past and his present.
39. For a discussion of this rule, see Walter Kaiser, Jr., *Toward an Exegetical Theology* (Grand Rapids: Baker Book House, 1981), 53–54, discussed under *Qol wehomer*.
40. Scholars disagree on the number of descriptors in 1:17. Some, like Mounce (60) argue that the key word is "King", and that "eternal" is one of four adjectives describing this king. Others, like Bernard (35) take "King eternal" as one concept, parallel to the three adjectives that follow. This commentary accepts the latter position.
41. John S. Mbiti, *Introduction to African Religion* (2nd ed.; New York: Praeger, 1991), 58.
42. Ibid., 59.
43. "African peoples are agreed that nobody has seen God" (ibid., 54).
44. See, for example, Kelly, 57; Fee, 21; Mounce, 65; Ronald A. Ward, *A Commentary on 1 & II Timothy and Titus* (Waco: Word Books, 1974), 40; Bernard, 35. There are two main problems with this position:
    - There is rather a large gap between the "command" mentioned in 1:3 and 1:5 and the same word used in 1:18. Is there nothing closer to 1:18 which can be interpreted as a command? Bernard suggests that the gap is bridged by the fact that Paul talks of a similar subject in 1:6 and 1:19, but not all scholars are convinced of this.
    - The verb translated "give" is in the present tense. This could indicate that Paul is thinking of all that he is saying in this letter, and could thus refer back to 1:3 and 1:5. Against this, it could be noted that Paul uses the aorist tense in 1:3, when he says that he "urged" Timothy to stay in Ephesus. It is thus sensible to look for something closer to 1:18 that can feasibly be interpreted as a command.
45. Commentators who interpret the command in this way include Arland J. Hultgren, 60, and Martin Dibelius and Hans Conzelmann (*The Pastoral Epistles* [Hermeneia; Philadelphia: Fortress Press, 1972], 32). However, to identify "this command" as the fight of 1:18b ignores the wording of the phrase, "that [*hina*] by them you may fight". This phrase expresses the purpose of the command, not its content.
46. The assumption here is that Paul's meaning can be paraphrased as follows: "Christ Jesus came into the world" is a trustworthy statement, deserving full acceptance, and the maintenance of it ("maintain" or some similar verb being implied, and equal to "this command" of 1:18), I entrust to you. The weakness of this position is that it assumes some verb like "maintain" to explain "this command". Its strength is that it makes good sense, both in its immediate context and in terms of the focus on purity of doctrine throughout the epistle.
47. Ward, 40; Mounce, 65.
48. The phase could also be translated "the prophecies that led me to you".
49. William Barclay, *The Letters of Paul to Timothy, Titus and Philemon*, (3rd ed. Louisville, Ken.: Westminster John Knox Press, 2003), 49; Hultgren, 60.
50. Hultgren (60–61) discusses whether it was Paul or the church who laid hands on Timothy.
51. For other military metaphors, see 1 Cor 9:7; 2 Cor 10:3; Eph 6:11–16; Phil 2:25; 2 Tim 2:3.
52. Some theories about these men are set out in C. K. Barrett, *The Pastoral Epistles* (New Clarendon Bible; Oxford: Clarendon Press, 1963), 48.
53. The debate about whether it is only "a good conscience" that is rejected or whether both faith and conscience are rejected has implications for what is meant by the two references to the "faith" that can be held on to or shipwrecked in 1:19. If it is only a good conscience that is rejected, the faith that is shipwrecked is the same faith mentioned earlier in the verse (literally translated as "the faith"). However, if both faith and a good conscience are rejected, then the second faith must refer to something else. Some argue that what is rejected is personal faith, and what is shipwrecked is "the faith", taken as equivalent to the Christian movement (Mounce, 67; Barrett, 48).

54 Those who say that both faith and a good conscience are rejected include Fee (22) and Mounce (66–67). Those who say that only conscience was rejected include Bernard (35), C. K. Barrett (47) and Hultgren (61).
55 The Greek here is *ina paideuthosin* and the idea behind *paideuein* is to learn by way of discipline.
56 Bernard, 38. According to Mounce (79), the term "describes an actual instance of prayer and not prayer in general".
57 Bernard, 38; C. J. Ellicott, *A Critical and Exegetical Commentary on the Pastoral Epistles* (Andover: Warren F. Draper, 1865), 25; Mounce, 79.
58 Mounce, 80; Ward, 43.
59 Kelly, 60.
60 Kelly, 60: "Paul's object is to insist on the centrality of prayer rather than to provide a systematic analysis of it". Fee, 26: "Paul's point is not to define or distinguish the various kinds of prayer that should mark Christian worship, but to urge that prayers of all kinds be offered to God for all people". Hultgren, 62–63: "The terms need not be distinguished sharply, for they are but different aspects of prayer; the writer speaks of these aspects for fullness and emphasis". Dibelius and Conzelmann, 36: "The different terms for 'prayer' do not invite a systematic differentiation, nor do they offer a complete list – 'supplication' [*hikesia*], for example, is missing."
61 Kelly, 60.
62 The mention of "kings" plural (*huper basileon*) in 2:2 should not be read as implying that two people were sharing power as "kings" when 1 Timothy was written, as F. C. Baur argues (see Mounce, 81).
63 Ward, 43.
64 Ellicott, 20. The Greek words are not used in the New Testament in enough different contexts for any firm conclusions to be drawn. *Eremos* does not occur elsewhere in the New Testament, and *hesuchios* occurs only in 1 Peter 3:4. See also the warning in Bernard, 39.
65 Barclay, 67.
66 The words of the second pair are not common in Paul's other letters. "Godliness" (*eusebeia*) appears ten times in the Pastoral Epistles, but its only other appearances in the New Testament are in Acts and 2 Peter. "Holiness" (*semnotes*) is not used elsewhere in the New Testament, and appears only two more times in the Pastoral Epistles (1 Tim 3:4; Titus 2:7).
67 Barclay, 68.
68 The tniv translation reflects one interpretation of the Greek, which could more literally be translated as "this is good and acceptable in the sight of God our Saviour" (nasb). Scholars debate whether the "good" means that such prayer is good in itself, as well as being acceptable in God's sight, or whether it is both good and acceptable in God's sight. But the distinction is not an important one: the key point is that it is God's will that we pray for everyone. See Bernard, 40; Mounce, 85; Ellicott, 27.
69 God is not described as Saviour in Paul's other writings, although this description of God is found six times in the Pastoral Epistles (1 Tim 1:1; 2:3; 4:10; Titus 1:3; 2:10; 3:4). However, this term was used in the Septuagint (Pss 24:5; 27:1, 9; Hab 3:18; Isa 12:2) and thus Paul was likely to have been familiar with it. Its usage also does not contradict the New Testament's general teaching that God the Father is the ultimate source of salvation.
70 Paul uses *thelo*, not *boulomai*, and *sothenai* (to be saved) is in the passive voice.
71 Bernard (41) comments: "That this Divine intention may be thwarted by man's misuse of his free will is part of the great mystery of evil, unexplained and inexplicable; that its bounty is not confined to particular races or individuals but takes in the whole race of man is the very essence of the Gospel." See also Ward, 45–46; Kelly, 62–63.
72 Bernard (41) regards the phrase, *and to come to a knowledge of the truth* (2:4) as inseparably connected *to be saved* (*sothenai*). Kelly (62) also sees the whole expression as equivalent to "be converted to Christianity". Dibelius and Conzelmann (41) regard "coming to a knowledge of the truth" as a technical way of talking about conversion.
73 See Hultgren, 65: "to know and accept true apostolic teaching". See, also, Fee, 28; Mounce, 86.

74 Here the word *anthropos* (man) is anarthrous. The article is not omitted to indicate some indefiniteness (a man). Rather, the omission of the article emphasizes the nature of the one being spoken of. The mediator is a human being. In saying this, Paul is not denying Christ's deity; he is merely asserting his humanity. The English translations are thus correct when they translate this word as "the man".

75 The word here translated as "ransom" is *antilutron*. This word is not used anywhere else in the New Testament, although the similar word *lutron* is used in Matthew 20:28 and Mark 10:45.

76 The image of a ransom must not be extended to imply that Christ's payment was made to Satan or to sin that held us captive. Rather, the payment was required by God's system of justice, which states that "without the shedding of blood there is no forgiveness" (Heb 9:22). God could not just ignore our sin. It had to be punished. Christ paid the penalty on our behalf.

77 Christ's death is here said to be "for" (*huper*) all, rather than *anti* (instead of) all. Some have used this point to argue against the idea of substitutionary atonement. However, although *huper* commonly means "on behalf of", it had also acquired the meaning "instead of" (Mounce, 89–90). The argument that "substitution" is intended here is strengthened by the use of the preposition *anti* in the compound word *antilutron* (ransom).

78 The Greek dative *kairois idiois* can also mean "in its own time", implying that this happened in the natural course of events. However, the translation used in the tniv is to be preferred. Scholars have also debated whether the one who determines the proper time is God the Father (as in 1 Tim 6:15; Titus 1:3) or Jesus, a possibility that is suggested by the fact that some manuscripts have the Greek word *ou* (whose) before *marturion* (testimony). While the exact answer would not make a difference since God the Father and God the Son work together as one, the idea that it is God the Father seems to fit the context better. See also Dibelius and Conzelmann, 43; Fee, 30; Ward, 48).

79 See Hultgren, 65; Kelly, 64.

80 See Fee, 30.

81 Kelly, 64.

82 These positions are represented by Kelly (64), Barrett (52) and Bernard (42), respectively.

83 Mounce, 91.

84 Fee, 30, takes this position, limiting the witness to the content of 1:5–6a.

85 Bernard, 42; Ward, 48.

86 This testimony (*marturion*) is the subject of Paul's preaching. In *eis ho etethen ego kerux kai apostolos*, the *eis* expresses purpose, and the relative pronoun *ho* refers back to *marturion*. Etethen (I was appointed) is in the passive voice. He uses an emphatic *ego* (I myself).

87 The word *kerux* is found only here and in 2 Timothy 1:11 and 2 Peter 2:5. However, Paul uses its verb cognate *kerussein* (to proclaim) nineteen times in his epistles, including in 1 Timothy 3:16 and 2 Timothy 4:2. It is equivalent to *euangelizesthai* (to preach the good news).

88 Ward, 48.

89 Bernard, 43.

90 Paul here refers to himself as *didaskalos* (a teacher) but he does not seem to be thinking in terms of the office of a teacher within the church, as it is in Acts 13:1; 1 Corinthians 12:28 and Ephesians 4:11. Being a teacher is his mission, not his title.

91 Mounce, 93.

92 The words "faith" and "truth" are datives, which can be interpreted either as datives of sphere or datives of manner. The niv translation is based on the argument that this is an instance of hendiadys (from the Greek *hen dia duoin*, "one through two"). Hendiadys uses "two words connected by a conjunction to express the same idea as a single word with a qualifier". Fee (31) says that Paul's message is "'the true faith', over against the exclusivism of the false teachers". However, on the basis of the way these two words are used elsewhere in 1 Timothy (e.g. in 1 Tim 1:2; 2:4), it seems likely that the focus is on the content of the gospel, and that the niv translation is flawed. Paul viewed his ministry as operating within the sphere of "faith" and "truth", and that is what he proclaimed. See also Mounce, 93; Fee, 31; Kelly, 43; Mounce, 92.

93 Paul uses a very similar technique to emphasize his words in Romans 9:1; 2 Corinthians 11:31 and Galatians 1:20.
94 Kelly, 65. See also Bernard, 43; Mounce, 92; Fee, 31.
95 Mounce, 92.
96 Scholars debate the difference between *boulomai*, the word used here, and *thelo*, the word used in 2:4 (see Bernard, 43; Kelly, 65).
97 Mounce, 107; Bernard, 43; Ward, 49.
98 Fee, 34.
99 Kelly, 66.
100 *Dialogismos* can also mean "doubt", and Barclay (73) argues for this interpretation. However, the translation "dissension" seems more likely in the Ephesian context.
101 Barrett (55) who takes this position, notes that in the Greek the verse lacks a main verb, and he thus supplies the verb "to pray" from 2:8. Against this, it can be argued that the Greek verb *kosmein* (to dress) fits naturally as an expansion to the verb *boulomai*, which is translated "I want" in this verse. Paul is simply giving a second exhortation, separate from the first one addressed to men in 2:8.
102 Barrett 1963, 55. See also Ward, 50; Köstenberger, Schreiner and Baldwin, eds., *Women in the Church: A Fresh Analysis of I Timothy 2:9–15* (Grand Rapids: Baker, 1995), 114 note 39.
103 See Fee, 34.
104 Kelly, 66.
105 Bernard, 44; Mounce, 108.
106 The phrase translated "dress modestly" in the niv and "with proper clothing" in the nasb, is a dative (*katastole kosmio*). This may be a dative of sphere, distinguishing, "those who dress improperly" from "those who dress properly". The sphere of those who dress properly is marked by modesty and discretion. It is, however, probably best to see the dative as instrumental, indicating that the clothing they use to adorn themselves is to be proper.
107 Bernard (45) describes this as the "modesty which shrinks from overstepping the limits of womanly reserve".
108 The word *sophrosune* can also be translated as "discretion". Bernard (45) describes it as referring to "a command over bodily passions, a state of perfect self-mastery in respect of appetite. It marked the attitude towards pleasure of the man with a well-balanced mind, and was equally opposed to asceticism and to over-indulgence."
109 "The accent of the Pastorals lies not in the idea that women should (modestly) adorn themselves, but rather that true ornamentation is not external at all" (Dibelius and Conzelmann, 46).
110 In other words, what is the distinction between *manthaneto* (imperative) in 2:11, *boulomai* in 2:8 and *ouk epitrepo* (indicative) in 2:12?
111 *Hesuchia* occurs only four times in the New Testament (Acts 22:2; 2 Thess 3:12; 1 Tim 2:11–12). Its adjectival form *hesuchios* occurs twice (2 Tim 2:2; 1 Pet 3:4), and its verb form *hesuchazein* five times (Luke 14:4; 23:56; Acts 11:18; 21:14; 1 Thess 4:11).
112 For details, see Mounce, 128; Köstenberger, Schreiner and Baldwin, 65–80.
113 Scholars also debate whether *didaskein* and *authentein* constitute an example of hendiadys. In other words, are these two infinitives linked at the grammatical level, so that it means that women are not to teach men in a domineering manner, or do they constitute two separate instructions (that is, women are not to teach, nor are they to dominate men). At the heart of the debate is the meaning of the conjunction *oude*. It seems to me to be more natural to let *oude* have its common meaning of "not even" (or "also not", "and not"), with the result that these phrases are seen as separate but related instructions.
114 There is discussion about whether the *gar* ("for") at the beginning of 2:13 is illative (introducing the reason for Paul's practice) or illustrative (introducing an example). The illative usage seems the more likely in this context.
115 The result of Eve's being deceived is expressed in the perfect tense *gegonen*, which literally means "has come to be". What she became is *en parabasis* (literally, "in transgression"). The roots of

the Greek word, like those of the English word "transgression", mean "to step across". Thus this word emphasizes that Eve went beyond the limits God had set.

116 This is the ontological argument for male leadership, which identifies leadership as part of the very nature of men.

117 In the Greek, *sothesetai* is a predictive future tense, referring to something that will certainly happen if conditions are right.

118 The word *sozein* encompasses both "saving" and "preserving".

119 *Episkopos* is a singular noun both in 1 Timothy 3:1 and in Titus 1:7, leading some to assume that Paul was talking about an office equivalent to that of the monarchical bishop, who had begun to appear by the time of Ignatius, the third bishop of Antioch (martyred about ad 110). However, the singular here can be taken as generic.

120 The phrase *pistos ho logos* (a trustworthy saying) is used five times in the Pastoral Epistles (1 Tim 1:15; 3:1; 4:9; 2 Tim 2:11; Titus 3:8) to affirm the trustworthiness, reliability, and correctness of a statement. On all occasions except this one, it is used in the context of a statement about salvation. Some commentators thus insist that the statement Paul is affirming here is the one in 2:15 about women being saved through childbearing. However, linking this affirmation to what follows fits the context well. Paul is saying that his statement about the nature of the office of overseer is so important that it should be believed without question. See Mounce (167) for further discussion of this point.

121 "Above reproach" or "without reproach" translates the Greek word *anepilemptos* (used also in 5:7 for widows and in 6:14 for Timothy). Mounce (170) describes it as "the key term", Ward (54) notes that it "dominates the list", and Fee (43) describes it as a "general, covering term for the following list". It is stronger than *amemptos* ("blameless", "faultless" [BAGD see Bauer, Arndt, Gingrich, and Danker]) or *anegletos* ("blameless", "irreproachable" [BAGD]).

122 Barclay, 84.

123 Kelly, 75.

124 For further evaluation of these positions, see Mounce, 170–173; Ed Glasscock, "The Husband of One Wife Requirement in 1 Timothy 3:2." *Bibliotheca Sacra* 140 (1983): 244–258. Online: http://www.galaxie.com/article.php?article_id=2168. Cited 17 March 2009.

125 Barclay (85) and Glasscock (253–254) for example, say it was still common. Bernard (53) and Fee (43) are among those who say polygamy was uncommon at this time, so that an exhortation to avoid it would have been irrelevant.

126 Hultgren (73) supports this position, saying that divorce shows a lack of "lifelong fidelity to one wife".

127 On this interpretation, the genitive *gunaikos* (woman) is qualitative in shade.

128 Ward, 55.

129 Barclay, 89.

130 Quoted in Ward, 55.

131 Barclay, 91.

132 William M. Ramsay, *Historical Commentary on the Pastoral Epistles* (ed. Mark Wilson; Grand Rapids: Kregel Publications, 1996), 70; Barclay, 91–92.

133 See Kelly, 76.

134 Ward, 56.

135 Ramsay, 71.

136 Barclay, 89.

137 Kelly, 77.

138 Kelly, 77. See also Mounce, 176.

139 Kelly (77) translates *epieikesas* as "magnanimous" and says that it refers to "the gracious condescension, or forbearingness, with which the Christian pastor should deal with his charges, however exasperating they may on occasion be".

140 Bernard (54) claims that Aristotle viewed the word as referring to a person who "does not press for the last farthing of his legal rights". Barclay (93) says Aristotle explained it as "that which is

just and better than justice", and "that quality which corrects the law when the law errs because of its generality".

141 As Ward (56) puts it, the gentle overseer does not roughly say, "Now my man, right is right and that is the end of it". He "listens to the other's point and then applies the Christian call to duty on a broader front. He does not insist on his rights but leads the other to yet higher duty". Trench (quoted in Barclay, 93) defines gentleness as, "retreating from the letter of right better to preserve the spirit of right".

142 Charles J. Ellicott, *A Critical and Grammatical Commentary on the Pastoral Epistles* (Andover: Warren F. Draper, 1865), 41. See also Mounce, 176–177.

143 Barclay, 94.

144 The Greek of this verse has three phrases, "managing his own household well", "having children who conduct themselves in submission", and "with all respect". There is no consensus whether the last phrase qualifies the first phrase (making the overseer the one to carry his role with all respect, as in the tniv and nasb) or the second (with the children being the ones to submit with all respect, as in the niv and hcsb). Either interpretation is possible.

145 Mounce, 178; Fee, 45.

146 The age of the church in Ephesus can be estimated on the basis of Acts 19, which describes Paul's extended ministry in Ephesus in the course of his third missionary journey (ad 54–58). Roughly eight years elapsed between this ministry and Paul's first Roman imprisonment (ad 61–63). Assuming that the first letter to Timothy was written after his release, but before his second imprisonment, it must be dated some time between ad 63 and 67. Thus some of those in the church at Ephesus could have been believers for ten years by this stage.

147 Here the genitive, *tou diabolou*, is taken to be objective in shade. This position is reflected in the nasb translation "incurred by the devil".

148 On this reading, *tou diabolou* is taken to be a subjective genitive. The condemnation is then seen as something the devil inflicts upon the recently converted overseer.

149 This position can be combined with the subjective understanding of the genitive *tou diabolou*. For more on the subjective genitive, see Fee, 45; Kelly, 79; Ward, 58; and Bernard, 56. The latter treats the genitive as subjective, but identifies the "devil" as a human being. The New Testament does include other examples of *diabolos* meaning "a person acting for or like Satan" (see Bernard, 56; Mounce, 181).

150 Barclay, 83.

151 *Tou diabolou* is here taken as subjective, indicating that the devil is the one who has set the trap for Christians.

152 Comparison of the lists of requirements for overseers and for deacons identifies the following patterns of similarities and differences:
- Same wording: *mias gunaikos andra* ("faithful to his wife" in 3:2 is identical to *mias gunaikos andres* in 3:13, except for the change from singular to plural).
- Minor change in wording: *tou idiou oikou kalos proistamenon, tekna echonta hupotage* ("manage his own family well, and see that his children obey him" – 3:4) vs. *teknon kalos proistamenoi kai ton idion oikon* ("manage his children and his household well" – 3:12b).
- Synonymous word or thought: *kosmios* ("respectable" – 3:2) vs. *semnos* ("worthy of respect" – 3:8); *me paroinos* ("not given to drunkenness" – 3:3) vs. *me oino pollo prosechontas* ("not indulging in much wine" – 3:8); *me aphilargyros* ("not a lover of money" – 3:3) vs. *me aischrokerdeis* ("not pursuing dishonest gain" – 3:8); and *anepilemptos* ("above reproach" – 3:2) vs. *anengletoi ontes* ("if there is nothing against them" – 3:10).

153 Mounce, 199.

154 Kelly, 81.

155 Kelly, 81.

156 Kelly, 81.

157 Mounce, 199.

158 Barclay, 96.

159. The word *aischrokerdes*, which BAGD translates as "fond of dishonest gain", is a combination of *aischros* and *kerdos*. While *kerdos* means "gain", *aischros* may mean "ugly", "shameful", "base".
160. Kelly, 81–82.
161. Ward, 59.
162. *Musterion* (deep truths) would better be translated as "mystery", as in the kjv. It is used a total of twenty-seven times in the New Testament. Paul uses it twenty times, always with reference to God's redemptive plan in Christ, which was once unknown but has now been revealed. The genitive *tes pisteos* (of faith) may be subjective, giving the meaning "the mystery produced by faith" – which means that we need to figure out what it is), or epexegetical (the mystery, namely, faith), among other possibilities. Since Paul's chief concern in the Pastoral Epistles is purity of faith (belief and practice), it makes good sense to view "mystery" here as referring to faith. The faith defines what the mystery is.
163. *Echontas* (holding) is a durative present tense, indicating that something is part of the normal practice of the person in question.
164. *Kathara suneidesei* represents a dative of manner, with the adjective *katharos* used in a moral sense to mean "pure", "free from sin" (see BAGD, 388). For further comment on "conscience", see commentary on 1:3.
165. A second but less likely view is that the "also" merely serves to link what has been said about deacons in 3:8–9 with what follows in 3:12.
166. Mounce, 202.
167. Bernard, 58.
168. Hultgren, 74; Kelly, 83.
169. See BAGD, 63.
170. Here the nasb translation of 3:13 is closer to the Greek: "for those who have served well as deacons". The "for" connects the list of required qualities in a deacon with what follows.
171. The service is expressed by *diakonesantes* (having served), using an aorist participle, while the main verb of the sentence *peripoiountai* (acquire/obtain) is in the present tense. Thus, the service precedes the reward.
172. See Barclay, 96. For an evaluation of the view, see Kelly, 85, and Mounce, 206.
173. This seems to be the more widely supported view. See, for example, Kelly, 85; Bernard, 60; Ward, 61; Hultgren, 75; Mounce, 205–206; and Fee, 51.
174. Barrett, 69.
175. Mounce, 206. See also Bernard, 60; Hultgren, 76.
176. Kelly, 85.
177. Hultgren, 76.
178. Mounce, 204.
179. Ward, 60; Bernard, 59; Barclay, 96, 80; Fee, 50; Hultgren, 75. For a longer list of scholars supporting one or other of the two positions, see Mounce, 202–203.
180. Kelly, 84.
181. Mounce, 204.
182. See also Mounce, 204; Fee, 50.
183. Kelly, 86; Mounce, 214–215.
184. Bernard, 60.
185. Mounce, 219.
186. Kelly, 86; Fee, 53; Ward, 62.
187. Paul's use of the present tense *grapho* is aoristic, suggesting that he is focusing on what he is writing as a unit, as if he were doing it in one stroke.
188. The participle *elpizon* (I hope) could be taken as modal, circumstantial or concessive. If it is modal, it suggests that Paul is providing Timothy with only the essential information, which will be expanded on when Paul arrives in Ephesus. If taken as circumstantial (with temporal leaning), Paul is telling Timothy to treat this letter as preparation for his coming (i.e., the meaning is, "as I hope to come"). If it is concessive, it implies that Timothy needs to know these things now (in

189 *Eides* (you) is singular, and so must refer to Timothy. However, the subject of *dei ... anastrephesthai* (ought to conduct) is not given. It is unlikely that it is only Timothy who has to know how to conduct himself, and thus some translations supply the word "people", but this may be too wide in its scope. It seems that the indefinite pronoun "one" is the best choice, as used in the nasb translation: "so that you may know how one ought to conduct himself" (3:15).
190 Ward, 62.
191 The genitive *theou* (of God) can be possessive or qualitative or both.
192 Kelly, 86.
193 The lack of an article before *ekklesia* is unlikely to be significant. There is no article with most of the nouns here.
194 The title "the living God" was already in use in the Old Testament. See Deut 5:26: "For what mortal man has ever heard the voice of the living God" (*theou zontos* [LXX]). See also Pss 42:2; 84:2; Isa 37:4, 17; Jer 10:10; 23:36; Dan 6:20, 26; Hos 1:10. It is also used elsewhere in Paul's writings: 2 Cor 3:3 (*pneumati theou zontos* – "Spirit of the living God"); 6:16 (*hemeis gar naos theou esmen zontos* – "For we are the temple of the living God"); 1 Thess 1:9 (*epestrepsate pros ton theon apo ton eidolon douleuein theo zonti* – "you turned to God from idols to serve the living God").
195 See Bernard, 61; Ward, 62.
196 Mounce, 221.
197 The genitive *tes aletheias* (of the truth) is best taken as objective.
198 Barclay, 100.
199 Bernard – "stay", 61, 63; Mounce – "protector", 222; Dibelius and Conzelmann – "fortress", 60.
200 Kelly, 84. Hultgren (77) commenting on the Greek word the nasb translates as "by common confession", states that the phrase "combines ideas of confession and common agreement in matters under dispute".
201 The debate about whether this is a hymn or a creed hinges on the nature of Greek verse. If this were a two-stanza hymn, we would expect the matching lines to have the same number of strokes. But examination of the Greek text shows that line three, *ophthe angelos* (seen by angels) is much shorter than line six, *auelemphthe en doze* (taken up in glory). The same problem, in a slightly milder form, appears when we compare line one *ephanephothe en sarki* (appeared in a body) and line four, *ekernchthe en ethnesin* (preached among the nations). It thus seems that this passage is not a hymn to be sung but a creed to be recited. For further comment on the nature of this passage, see Barclay, 100–101; Ward, 63; Fee, 54; Hultgren, 78–79; Mounce, 224–226.
202 Some manuscripts have "God" in place of "who" (see the notes in the Greek New Testament), but it is still clear that the passage speaks of the Second Person of the Trinity.
203 The verbs are all in the aorist passive, and each is followed by a dative. The implied subject is Christ.
204 Not all commentators agree with the interpretation of the creed given in this commentary. Other possible interpretations of the six lines include:
- Incarnation, exaltation, heavenly reign, proclamation in the world, and the consequent emergence of the believing community (Hultgren, 79).
- Incarnation, resurrection, ascension, preaching, belief, and glorification (Mounce, 225).
- Incarnation, resurrection, ascension, preaching of the gospel, response to the gospel, and final victory of Christ (Barrett, 66).
205 If the aorist verb "was revealed" is taken as constative and the dative "in the flesh" as a dative of manner, the focus is on Christ's entrance into the human sphere. However, if the verb is regarded as inceptive and the dative is seen as a dative of sphere, the revelation covers the whole period Christ was living in the human sphere.
206 BAGD, 196.

207 Kelly, 88. See also Ward, 59, which defines it as the "open secret of God's truth, which is hidden to man's unaided reason but revealed in Christ". *Musterion* (mystery) is used a total of twenty-seven times in the New Testament. Paul uses it twenty times, always with reference to God's redemptive plan in Christ. In 3:9, the tniv translates it as "deep truths".

208 *Eusebeais* is probably a partitive genitive, the genitive of the whole, and means "the mystery which forms part of godliness, or of which godliness is the whole". The genitive may, however, be qualitative, in which case it means "this is the mystery which qualifies as godliness". Bernard (62) regards it as a possessive genitive, and explains it as "the mystery of piety, i.e., the mystery which piety embraces, and on which it feeds". However, this last definition seems a little more removed from the context of the Pastoral Epistles than the other two.

209 Debate about the meaning of *legei* focuses on whether the shade of the present is aoristic (a present revelation), iterative (based on a series of previous revelations) or gnomic (a specific past revelation that still applies at the time of writing and beyond).

210 The word *husteros* is a comparative (literally "later"), but translating it as "last" is correct in view of the fact that "superlative forms in general were in decline in koine and the superlative form hustatos, 'last' does not occur in the NT" (Mounce, 235). See also Kelly, 94; Fee, 60.

211 The genitive *tes pisteos* (of the faith) has been taken as qualitative, referring to "some of the faith". In this case, Paul is saying that some people who belong to the faith will fall away. Other translations like the nasb take it as a genitive of separation, indicating that some people will fall away from the faith. The end result is the same with either interpretation.

212 The genitive *daimonion* (of demons) is here taken as a genitive of source, implying that the source of what the false teachers are teaching is demonic. If the genitive is qualitative, Paul is focusing on the characteristic of the false teachers and saying that they are demonic as opposed to Christian.

213 The preposition *en* in the phrase *en hupokrisei pseudologo* indicates that these teachers are the instrument used to mislead those of the faith.

214 *Kekausteriasmenon* is perfect participle which focuses on the state of existence (intensive perfect) following the branding, that is, on what the false teachers do. The verb is passive. The owner who applies the brand is not mentioned, but there can be no doubt that it is Satan or his agent.

215 See note 23 on Gnosticism. See also Barclay, 105; Kelly, 95.

216 Ward, 68–69.

217 Philip H. Towner, *1–2 Timothy and Titus* (IVP New Testament Commentary; ed. Grant R. Osborne; Downers Grove: InterVarsity Press, 1994), 103–104; Mounce, 238.

218 What we have here is an over-realized eschatology, insisting that the new life of the new age is already here. See Fee, 61 and Mounce, 239, especially the comment on Lane's argument.

219 Ward, 69.

220 Barclay, 107.

221 The "if" in the phrase "if it is received with thanksgiving" (*meta eucharistias lambanomenon*) reflects the translator's decision that the participle *lambanomenon* is conditional. The participle could also be taken as temporal, giving the reading "when it is received". But whichever translation is adopted, there is a condition here, whether emphasized ("if") or implied ("when").

222 Barclay (106) discusses different kinds of prayer at the table.

223 Barclay, 107.

224 Kelly, 96–97. See also Mounce, 240; Ward, 70.

225 Fee, 63; Hultgren, 82; Mounce, 241. Against those who argue that the genitive *theou* is a subjective genitive, focusing on God as the speaker of the word. Bernard argues that the tense of the verb *agiazetai* (is sanctified) indicates a recurring activity. However, there is no problem in seeing the setting apart associated with the word of God as gnomic (remaining true at all times) and the prayer as iterative (recurring each time grace is said). After all, God's sanctification marks the food as sacred intrinsically, and saying grace at the table simply affirms this. Both acts are associated with the same verb (*agiazetai*) but with different subjects (God, and the person who prays).

226 Kelly, 97; Dibelius and Conzelmann, 64; Ward, 70; and Bernard, 67.

227 Mounce, 241; Fee, 63.
228 The translation of the participle *hupotithemenos* as modal ("in pointing out" nrsv) indicates the means by which being a good servant will be achieved. It could also be taken as conditional ("if you point out" niv) but the modal use seems preferable.
229 Barclay, 108.
230 The genitive *Christou Iesou* (of Christ Jesus) is a genitive of possession, or possibly a qualitative genitive.
231 "You will be" (*ese*) is gnomic future. The equation "pointing out" = "good servanthood" is an abiding truth.
232 Mounce, 248; Hultgren, 82.
233 Bernard, 68; Ward, 70; Kelly, 98.
234 Fee, 65.
235 The participle *entrephomenos* (being nourished) is in the present tense, passive voice, and thus represents an action simultaneous with the main verb of the sentence, namely, "you will become". See also Mounce (249) who speaks of Timothy's "training".
236 The kjv reads "truths of faith" rather than "truths of the faith", suggesting that the phrase refers to "personal trust". However, this commentary follows Mounce, 249 and the tniv in preferring to retain the article, so that "words of the faith" refers to "the basic gospel message" from which then comes "the good teaching".
237 The perfect tense, *parekolouthekas* (you have followed) may be extensive or consummative, focusing on the action as something that produces results.
238 The Greek word used here is *bebelos*, which means "worldly", "profane" or "godless".
239 Kelly, 99.
240 Mounce, 251.
241 Kelly, 99; Dibelius and Conzelman, 68.
242 Paul's statement that *he gar somatike gumnasia pros oligon* (for bodily discipline is only of little profit) has been interpreted as offering support for some ascetic practices or physical exercise (Ward, 73). While this interpretation may be correct, we should not forget that Paul's main purpose here is to stress the value of godliness, and that physical exercise is merely introduced for comparison and contrast.
243 The participle *echousa* is probably causal (since it holds) rather than independent (it holds a promise).
244 Ward, 73; Hultgren, 83; Bernard, 69; Fee, 67; Kelly, 101; and Barrett, 70 argue that *pistos ho logos* looks back to either the whole or part of 4:8. Mounce, 254, argues that it looks forward to 4:10. The context seems to favour the majority view that it refers particularly to 4:8b.
245 Ward, 73; BAGD, 444.
246 BAGD, 15.
247 The verb *elpikamen* (we have fixed hope) is in the intensive shade of the perfect tense and focuses on the result of the action.
248 Compare Mounce, 246.
249 Bernard, 70.
250 Ward, 74. See also Kelly, 107.
251 H. P. Liddon, *Explanatory Analysis of St. Paul's First Epistle to Timothy* (London: Longman, Green and Company, 1897), 45; Burton Scott Easton, *The Pastoral Epistles: Introduction, Translation, Commentary and Word Studies* (New York: Charles Scribner's Sons, 1947), 146.
252 Estimates of Timothy's age vary. Simpson (*Pastoral Epistles* [Grand Rapids: Eerdmans, 1954], 69) estimates between thirty and forty; Mounce (258–259) between mid-twenties and mid-thirties; Kelly (104) mid-thirties; Hultgren (85) between thirty and thirty-five years.
253 The translation of the genitive *ton piston* as "of those who believe" is correct here. If Timothy were merely to be an example "to" others, we would expect the dative case, as in 1 Thessalonians 1:7 and 2 Thessalonians 3:9. Although it is possible to treat the genitive here as objective and so take it as "to" or "for", the qualitative interpretation seems to fit the context better.

254 All these words are in the dative case and are preceded by *en* ("in" or "by"). The first two (speech and conduct) are datives of sphere, stating the areas in which the last three (love, faith and purity) should be exercised.
255 Mounce, 259.
256 Kelly, 104.
257 Kelly, 104; Walter Lock, *A Critical and Exegetical Commentary on the Pastoral Epistles* (Edinburgh: T&T Clark, 1924), 52; E. D. Hiebert, *1 Timothy* (Chicago: Moody Press, 1957), 86.
258 Kelly, 104; Lock, 53.
259 Barclay (110–112) makes some valuable comments on this passage.
260 Ellicott, 64.
261 Hultgren, 87.
262 Fee, 70; Mounce, 265. A variant on this view is proposed by Kelly (109), who suggests that Paul means that Timothy will be secure from disqualification (see 1 Cor 9:27) while his hearers will be saved in the sense of being justified.
263 It is true that Paul generally uses *ruesthai* and not *sozein* when he speaks of keeping something safe. However, this interpretation of the word is plausible and fits the context, whereas other interpretations do not. S. Jebb discusses this meaning of being saved in "Short Comment: A Suggested Interpretation of 1 Timothy 2:15," *Expository Times* 81 (1970): 221–222.
264 C. S. Keener, "Family and Household", in *Dictionary of New Testament Background* (ed. Craig A. Evans and Stanley E. Porter; Downers Grove: InterVarsity Press, 2000), 355.
265 Kelly, 110. Note that Paul uses an aorist subjunctive, which can refer to an action not yet started.
266 The verb translated "harshly" in the tniv has the idea of rough treatment (Kelly, 118), striking out at a person (Hultgren, 87) or rebuking severely (Bernard, 78).
267 Bernard, 78.
268 The verb "treat" is added in the tniv, but in the Greek the only verb governing the instructions regarding all these groups is *parakalei* (exhort).
269 Keener, "Family and Household", 356.
270 *Hagneia* means purity or cleanness in general, but in certain contexts it refers to purity from sexual sin (e.g. its cognate, *hagnen*, is used to describe a virgin in 2 Corinthians 11:2).
271 Kelly, 74.
272 Marshall, 576.
273 In the Greek, *tima* (honour) is a present imperative, indicating that Timothy is to make it his habit to honour widows "who are widows indeed" (1 Tim 5:3 nasb).
274 Every interpreter needs to make up their mind on whether the widows mentioned as being "really in need" in 5:3 and 5:5 are the same as those "put on the list of widows" (5:9–10). This commentary argues that they are. However, many commentators hold that the list contains the names of those registered for duties in the church, rather than for material support. For more detailed discussion of these positions, see Mounce, 273–277.
275 The tense of *elpiken* (has fixed) is perfect (probably extensive perfect – with focus on the action as finished product, without losing sight of the results) and tells us what she did and continues to do once all she has on earth to depend on is gone.
276 Craig S. Keener, *The IVP Bible Background Commentary* (Downers Grove: IVP, 1993), 617.
277 The verb *katalegein* is a technical term for registration; see Dibelius and Conzelmann, 75.
278 "The point of the restriction is that for certain duties the church required women who could be counted on to devote themselves wholly to the work. At the age of sixty they would have given up all thought of remarriage; they would have little inclination to take up worldly pleasures and interests" (E. F. Scott, *Pastoral Epistles* [Moffatt New Testament Commentary; New York: Harper, 1936], 60).
279 All of the verbs in this list are constative aorists, summarizing all that has been done in this area.
280 The subject of the verb *manthanetosan* (let them learn) is not entirely clear in the Greek. However, the fact that it is in the present, active, imperative, third-person plural indicates that its subject must also be plural, and is therefore most likely the children and grandchildren, rather

than *chera* (the widow), a single subject. Mounce (280) offers more arguments to support the position that the verb refers to the children and grandchildren.
281 Bernard, 79.
282 *Amoibes*, which can be translated as "return" or "recompense", is a common term used in inscriptions honouring someone. It was probably a standard expression for "giving back to parents" (Mounce, 281).
283 Quoted in Barclay, 120. See also Mounce, 280.
284 Dibelius and Conzelmann (74) speak of "practical disavowal", and Kelly (115) of failure to follow the faith "to all its intents and purposes".
285 Barrett, 75.
286 Ward, 83.
287 The kjv translation, "any man or woman", reflects textual variants of the Greek *tis piste* which apply this instruction to male relatives. However, the weight of the textual evidence leans toward the tniv's translation.
288 This verse presents several difficulties, including why there is such a sudden change from the content of 5:11–15, where Paul is addressing the question of dealing with younger widows. However, 5:16 logically continues Paul's thought in 5:4 and 5:8. On this basis, some commentators have suggested that scribal error resulted in 5:16 being displaced to its current position. But this view, though attractive, is not supported by the text. Kelly (120) suggests that Paul "may well have remembered an important possibility he had overlooked and hastened to include it before passing to the subject of elders".
289 Barrett, 77.
290 Kelly, 121.
291 Kelly, 114. See also Anthony T. Hanson, *The Pastoral Epistles* (The New Century Bible Commentary; Grand Rapids: Eerdmans, 1982), 97. Issues relating to sex are also mentioned in 5:11.
292 The former position is taken by Easton (152) and the latter by Mounce (283). Barrett (74) says, "It is not licentious, but luxurious, living that is meant here". See also Hultgren, 88.
293 *Spatalosa* (living wantonly) is a present active participle, and so is *zosa* ("living", rendered "while she lives" in the tniv). These participles indicate an ongoing habit. The "living" is simultaneous with the action of the main verb *tethneken* (she has died) and is taken as intensive perfect that stresses her state or condition. Thus Paul juxtaposes life and death.
294 Ward, 83.
295 The Greek word is *pistis* and is used in 5:8 to mean faith. However, it can also mean oath or pledge. It is this latter sense that fits the context better here.
296 Fee, 81. See also Mounce, 291–293.
297 Kelly, 117; Bernard, 83; Barrett, 76; Hultgren, 89; Ward, 85.
298 *Perierchomenai* (as they go around) is a telic use of participle, with the meaning that they learn to be idle from being fully supported by the church, leaving them with nothing to do. Then, as a result of their idleness, they start wandering from house to house. The nasb, however, sees this as a temporal use of the participle, implying that they learn as they go from house to house.
299 *Periergoi* (busybodies) may mean "pertaining to magic". Kelly (118) argues that Paul "may therefore be expressing, in discreetly veiled language, the fear that irresponsible young widows, if encouraged to undertake house-to-house visiting, will resort to charms, incantations, and magical formulae in dealing, for example, with sick people". There is, however, little support for this position from the text. And the interpretation of busybodies as people who are interested in things about others that do not involve them, and whose speech is improper, seems most appropriate. See Mounce, 294.
300 Ward, 85.
301 Bernard, 83. See also Dibelius and Conzelmann, 75.
302 Kelly, 119.
303 Mounce, 295, describes it as "a ruling to solve a difficult problem".
304 Mounce, 296.

305 BAGD, 560.
306 Ward, 86.
307 Fee, 83; Kelly, 119; Mounce, 296. In support of this position they argue that Paul uses the article (the enemy), and that Satan is mentioned in the following verse.
308 Dibelius and Conzelmann, 78; Bernard, 84.
309 Fee, 83. Kelly, 119, says, "It is unlikely, however, that Paul drew a sharp distinction in his mind; the men and women who would tear the church's reputation to pieces were the instruments of the devil (cf. 4:1)." Mounce (296) comments, "With either interpretation, Satan is involved, working through people either implicitly or explicitly."
310 Hanson, 99.
311 Fee, 84.
312 Fee, 78; Bernard, 80; Ward, 83; Kelly, 114. In this case, *tauta* (these instructions) refers to 5:5, 6, 11, and 15.
313 In which case *tauta* refers to 5:4, 8, and 16.
314 In which case *tauta* refers to everything said in this passage.
315 Barrett, 77–78.
316 Some identify only three groups: a) those who are elders by virtue of their age; b) those who serve as church officers (equating the ruling well with official duties); c) elders doing preaching and teaching.
317 Advocates of this position often translate *malista* (especially) as "namely".
318 Barrett, 79. See also Mounce, 308; Fee, 88; Bernard, 85; Kelly, 124.
319 Kelly, 125.
320 Barrett, 79.
321 Fee, 89; Ward, 78.
322 See also Barclay, 129–130; Mounce, 310.
323 Paul is unlikely to be quoting from the Gospel of Luke because 1 Timothy was probably written before that gospel. It seems likely that this phrase was a common saying at the time (a variant using the word "food" is quoted in Matt 10:10). This has led some people to wonder why Paul introduces this proverb with the words "for the Scripture says" (5:18), seeing that it was not in Scripture at the time he was writing. The answer may be that he intended these words to apply only to his first quotation from Deuteronomy, with the second quotation simply illustrating the same principle. Hultgren (91) argues that "the author does not concern himself with whether it is a quotation from Scripture (the Old Testament) or from Jesus, but simply appends it as a common proverbial saying which carries its own logical weight ... Its existence in Luke can be taken as evidence of its currency in Christian tradition, as can the similar saying in Matt. 10:10." For further discussion of this, see Dibelius and Conzelmann, 97; Mounce, 311; Ward 88.
324 Hultgren, 91.
325 Mounce, 314.
326 Ibid.
327 Bernard, 87; Kelly, 127.
328 Ward, 89.
329 Bernard, 87; Ward, 89.
330 Barclay, 132.
331 Though strict application of the Granville Sharp theory here would mean treating God and Jesus Christ as the same person (note that in the passage God has the article but Jesus Christ does not), the fact that Jesus Christ is a proper name allows this construction without making God and Jesus Christ the same person.
332 Bernard, 87; Mounce, 316; Kelly, 127; Ward, 89.
333 Kelly, 127; Bernard, 88; Mounce, 316; Hultgren, 92. Some commentators argue from the context that Paul is talking about a ceremony for restoring members who have sinned into the fellowship. However, this position is unlikely because this practice only began in the third century (see Kelly, 127).
334 Fee, 92–93.

335 Mounce, 317.
336 Ward, 90.
337 Barclay, 134.
338 Many commentators treat these words as part of the discussion on elders that Paul begins in 5:17–23 (Mounce, 319; Kelly, 129; Fee, 92; Bernard, 89; Ward, 90–91; Hultgren, 93–94). Others link them to the instruction to Timothy to "keep yourself pure" (Dibelius and Conzelmann, 81). However, I think the words apply not just to elders but also to the wider context of relationships in the church. Barrett (82), although relating them primarily to the elders, also admits that they should possibly be "applied more widely".
339 In 1:9, 15; 5:20, 22, 24, Paul uses the verb *hamartanein* (to sin) or its cognates. In 2:14, he uses *en parabasis* (in transgression), which is translated as "became a sinner" in the tniv.
340 Fee, 95.
341 Hultgren, 94.
342 *Funk and Wagnall's Standard Dictionary of the English Language*, International Edition, 1973.
343 It is unlikely that Paul is here referring only to heathen masters. See Bernard, 91; Ward, 91.
344 The reason why the slaves are to serve their Christian masters is that the masters are believers (*pistoi*) and beloved (*agapetoi*), to which Paul adds, *hoi tes euergesias antilambanomenoi*. This phrase can be translated as "the ones benefiting from the good service", which is the interpretation preferred by the niv and nasb. But it can equally well be translated as "the ones devoting themselves to good service", as in the tniv. The context does not indicate which translation is to be preferred.
345 Hultgren, 95; Kelly, 133.
346 Bernard, 92.
347 Fee, 100.
348 Scholars debate whether the genitive "of our Lord Jesus Christ" (*tou kuriou 'Iesou Christou*) is a subjective genitive referring to specific words taught by our Lord (this seems unlikely); a genitive of origin or source, referring to ideas that had came from our Lord (Bernard, 93); or a genitive of content, referring to words about our Lord (Mounce, 337; Hultgren, 96). The last two options are not mutually exclusive. Kelly (134) rightly says that the instruction's "ultimate source is Christ himself and ... he is its theme." Fee (100) also says that what we have here is the "truth of the gospel, which comes from our Lord Jesus Christ himself, who is the ultimate origin of the faith".
In support of the last two options, it should be noted that *hugiainousin logois* (wholesome words) is an anarthrous dative that focuses more on the nature of what is said than on the actual words. The only other occurrence of this phrase in the New Testament is in 2 Timothy 1:13, where the context indicates that it refers to the gospel in a general sense and not some particular saying. Moreover, the false teachers whom Timothy is to combat are presented as straying from the gospel (1 Tim 1:6) and replacing Jesus with myths and legends (1 Tim 1:4). It is the person of Jesus and the truths concerning his work that are in the forefront, not some specific saying by him.
349 Mounce, 336.
350 The verb *proserchesthai* is used with the negative particle *me*. This is the only occurrence in the New Testament of this particle being used with indicative mood. Elsewhere in the New Testament, *ou* is used with the indicative and *me* with the other moods. The verb has the idea of "occupying oneself" (Mounce, 337) and, therefore, "agree" is a good translation.
351 The perfect *tetuphotai* is intensive in shade, focusing on the teacher's present attitude. The related word, *tuphousthai*, can also mean "foolish" and some commentators prefer this translation (Mounce, 338). However, in 3:6 and here, "conceited" fits the context better.
352 Fee, 101. See also Kelly, 79.
353 The participle *epistamenos* (knowing) is in the middle or passive voice. It is best taken as concessive, with the meaning of "although". The false teacher has been caused (*tetuphotai* is in the passive voice) by their self-evaluation to have an attitude of conceit, although his or her continuing status (note the present tense of *epistamenos*) is that of understanding nothing. As Ward, 95, puts it, we have a "size – huge; content – nil" situation.

354 When *nosein* is followed by *peri* with the accusative, it suggests the idea of "morbid movement round a central point" (Bernard, 93). Mounce (338) says that the false teachers display a "sickly craving" for these things.

355 The word *zetesis* (controversies) is related to *ekzetesis*, which is translated by the same English word in 1:4.

356 *Logomachia* here and *logomachein* in 2 Tim 2:14 are a compound of *logos* (word) and *mache* (fight).

357 *Diaparatribe* is a heightened form of *paratribe* (BAGD, 86). The word includes two prepositions, and its interpretation is governed by the rule that "the first of two prepositions in a composite word governs the meaning, and thus *dia* is emphatic, signifying the persistency and obstinacy of the dispute" (Bernard, 94).

358 There is some debate as to how the genitive in the participle phrase *diephtharmenon anthropon ton noun* (6:5; people of corrupt mind) relates to *diaparatribai* (constant friction). Is it a qualitative genitive, that is, "the constant friction that characterizes people with a corrupt mind"? Is it a genitive of source, referring to "constant friction from people of corrupted minds", or is it genitive of association, meaning "constant friction with/between people of corrupted mind"? The last option seems the most likely, and is the one adopted in the tniv.

359 The participle *diephtharmenon* is a perfect, probably intensive in shade, focusing on their state.

360 Bernard, 94.

361 The genitive "of the truth" in *apesteremenon tes aletheias* gives the content they have been deprived of.

362 Ward, 96.

363 Fee, 102.

364 Barclay, 145.

365 The Greek construction has *hoti* between the statement on what we brought into the world and the statement on what we can take out of it. *Hoti* usually means "because" and introduces a reason for the preceding statement. But it does not make sense to say that "we brought nothing" because "we take nothing". Consequently there have been some scribal attempts to improve on the text by adding *delon* (clear, plain) in some manuscripts. The nasb translation attempts to stay close to the traditional meaning of *hoti* with its translation, "we have brought nothing into the world, so we cannot take anything out of it either." It is treating *hoti* as introducing a consequence, but even this does not make much logical sense. The alternative is to regard Paul's use of the word *hoti* here as unique. Bernard (95) takes it as resumptive, and suggests that it should be translated "I say". Kelly (136) suggests it could be translated "as" or "and". Others who see a weakened sense of *hoti* here include Mounce (343), Ward (97) and Fee (103). The key point is that Paul is making two assertions in support of his argument and treating *hoti* as "and", "even", "consequently" or some similar word that fits the context.

366 Mounce, 344.

367 Ward, 98–99.

368 The temptation may, however, be expressed in "self-confidence, desertion of the fellowship of Christians, and a delight in being dazzled" (Ward, 99).

369 Mounce, 345.

370 Kelly, 137.

371 Commentators debate whether these desires are to be seen as a third stage on the route from temptation to destruction or have been there all along. Ward (100) comments: "These are not a development later than the temptation and the snare but are coincident with them." However, there seems to be, at least, an intensification of these desires, even if they have been there from the very start.

372 Barclay, 148.

373 The present tense may be taken as iterative in shade. The desires repeatedly submerge one person after another in ruin and destruction.

374 Kelly, 137.

375 Mounce, 345.

376 Barclay, 148.
377 Ward, 101.
378 *Oregomenoi* (longing) is a present tense participle, denoting that this longing for money has become a habit. It is also contemporaneous with the action of the main verb, "wandered", which is a constative aorist, summarizing all the wandering done. The preposition *apo* (from) followed by the genitive *tes pisteos* communicates a separation from the realm of faith.
379 Ward, 102.
380 *Periepeiran* (piercing) is in the aorist tense. It is best taken as resultative aorist, with the focus on their present state that results from an earlier action. Paul thinks of these people as already pierced. The verb could, however, also be a constative aorist.
381 The genitive here may either be relational or qualitative, as shown in the discussion that follows.
382 Mounce, 353; Hultgren, 98–99.
383 Ellicott, 93.
384 Barclay, 150.
385 Ibid., 151.
386 Mounce, 354.
387 Barclay, 151.
388 Ward, 107.
389 Ward, 104.
390 Barclay, 152.
391 The genitive *tes pisteos* (of faith) could be either subjective genitive (the struggle faith itself undertakes against error) or qualitative genitive (the kind of struggle against evil that Christians are involved in) (Bernard, 98; Ward, 109). Since the picture is one in which Timothy is the contender, the qualitative genitive is the better choice.
392 *Agon* (noun) is a cognate of *agonizomai* (verb) and carries, in addition to the idea of conflict, the idea of a contest in which the winner gets a prize. It can thus be translated as "play", as in "play your part in the noble contest of faith" (Kelly, 141), or as "run" (Fee, 108).
393 Guthrie, *The Pastoral Epistles* (Tyndale New Testament Commentary; Grand Rapids: Eerdmans, 1957), 115.
394 Ward, 109.
395 Of the four imperatives in 6:11–12, *epilabou*, is the only one that is aorist. Because the aorist tense may be used either of a continuous action or a single act, some argue that Paul's change of tense suggests that he is focusing on a single act. For example, Ellicott (89) says that while the fighting is continuous, "the taking hold is one act in the fight". Kelly (142) says, "The aorist imperative 'possess yourself' suggests that Timothy can lay hold on eternal life immediately, in a single act." (See also Simpson, 88; Ward, 111.) Yet despite these views, it seems best to take the aorist as constative, summarizing all the activities involved in keeping hold of salvation.
396 Ellicott, 89; Simpson, 88.
397 Kelly, 142; Barclay, 152; Ward, 111.
398 The present tense of *zoogonein* is durative, focusing on the continuity of the action. See Mounce, 357; Fee, 110.
399 Ward, 113; Kelly, 143; Bernard, 98.
400 It is difficult to say whether Paul intends to draw any parallels between Jesus' confession and Timothy's confession, which he referred to in 6:12. The same words or synonyms are used in both sections (*homologesas* – Timothy [6:12]; *marturesantos* – Jesus [6:13]; *ten kalen homologian* [both 6:12 and 6:13]; and possibly *enopion* [6:12] and *epi* [6:13], if the spatial meaning is chosen for *epi*). However these similarities do not justify dogmatic conclusions on the matter. Paul could simply have used similar words without any intention of asking the reader to relate Jesus' confession to that of Timothy.
401 The preposition *epi* with the genitive may mean either "in the presence of" or "before", or "in the time of".
402 Bernard, 99; Kelly, 144.

403 "It really summarizes the basic thrust of the letter, that Timothy will best stem the tide of the false teachers as he himself is steadfast in his faith and calling" (Fee, 110).

404 Barrett, 87.

405 "The commandment refers to the whole Christian religion (as at 2 Peter 2:21), not any specific commandment" (Hultgren, 100. See also Kelly, 144; Mounce, 359).

406 Bernard, 99.

407 Guthrie (116) argues: "The context seems to demand the application of the words to Timothy himself". The opposite view is taken by Hendriksen (205), Mounce (359), Bernard (99), Kelly (145) and Dibelius and Conzelmann (89). The disagreement arises because the pronoun *se* (you) and the noun *entolen* (command) are both in the accusative case, and so are the two adjectives, *aspilon* and *anepilempton*. Grammatically, the adjectives could apply to either the noun or the pronoun. Analysis of usage provides no clarity because these adjectives were used of both persons and things. However, although the adjectives are closer to *entole* than to *se* in the sentence, and so may qualify the command directly, they indirectly qualify Timothy as well.

408 The position taken here is that the participle *apothesaurizontas* (storing up) is achieved by way of doing good. It is the product of sharing what the rich person has in this world. The "coming age", or the future, in this verse is parallel to "this present world" in 6:17, and is therefore eschatological.

409 The same verb, *epilambanein*, was used in 6:12 in relationship to Timothy's laying hold of eternal life. Here, too, the shade of the aorist is constative. It summarizes the taking hold of eternal life at the point of their justification, their continuing to take hold of it now, and their taking hold of it in the future.

410 John Stott, *Guard the Truth: The Message of 1 Timothy and Titus* (Downers Grove: InterVarsity Press, 1996), 82.

411 The participle that could be translated as "turning away from" or "avoiding" is taken here to be circumstantial with a focus on manner.

2 Timothy

1. For fuller discussion of issues of dating and authorship, see the introduction to this volume and the accompanying end notes.
2. This translation of *kat' epangelian zoes tes en Christo Iesou* is more accurate than the tniv's "in keeping with the promise of life". *Kata* can be used to express purpose. It is used in this way in Titus 1:1 (*kata pistin eklekton theou*), which the niv and hcsb translate as "for the faith of God's elect"; the nasb as "for the faith of those chosen of God"; and the nrsv as "for the sake of the faith of God's elect". The only exception is the nkjv, which still renders the *kata* in Titus 1:1 as "according to". For further discussion, see Bauer, W., W. F. Arndt, F. W. Gingrich and F. W. Danker, *A Greek-English Lexicon of the New Testament and Other Early Christian Literature* (BAGD see Bauer, Arndt, Gingrich and Danker), (Chicago: University of Chicago Press, 1979), 407; and J. H. Bernard, *The Pastoral Epistles* (Thornapple Commentaries; Grand Rapids: Baker, 1980), 107.
3. In the phrase *epangelian zoes* the genitive *zoes* is a genitive of content.
4. The dative *Christo Iesou* is taken to be a dative of sphere.
5. J. N. D. Kelly, *A Commentary on the Pastoral Epistles: I & II Timothy, Titus* (Black's New Testament Commentaries; London: Adam & Charles Black, 1963), 153.
6. The Greek term that is rendered "son" by the tniv literally means "child". In 1 Timothy 1:2, where Timothy is described as Paul's "true son", the stress is on his legitimacy and the translation "child" is appropriate, as in the nasb. However, in 2 Timothy 1:2 the stress is on how dear Timothy is to Paul, and thus the translation "son" is appropriate.
7. Ronald A. Ward, *A Commentary on I & II Timothy and Titus* (Waco: Word, 1974), 140.
8. The phrase *charin echo* was also used in 1 Timothy 1:12. Literally it means "I have gratitude". *Echo* is in an example of the durative use of the present tense, describing habitual action. It conveys the idea of a continuous attitude.
9. The verb *latreuo* may be taken as a durative present tense, in which case Paul is thinking of the totality of his service.
10. William D. Mounce, *Pastoral Epistles* (Word Biblical Commentary; Nashville: Thomas Nelson, 2000), 469.
11. The Greek phrase *ho latreuo apo progonon en kathara suneidesei* literally means, "whom I serve as my forefathers with a clear conscience". Thus the "clear conscience" could also apply to the way Paul's forefathers served. However, it is better to restrict it to applying only to Paul's conscience. The dative *kathara suneidesei* may be taken as a dative of sphere.
12. The participle *epipothon* (I long) is in present tense and therefore simultaneous with the remembering. It is also circumstantial in function, with the focus on the state accompanying the remembering, namely, a longing to see Timothy.
13. Bernard, 108.
14. Gordon D. Fee, *1 and 2 Timothy, Titus* (Good News Commentary; San Francisco: Harper & Row, 1984), 172; Kelly, 156; Mounce, 470; Ward, 142.
15. Assuming that 2 Timothy was written during Paul's second and final Roman imprisonment.
16. Ward, 143.
17. The participle *labon* may be understood as a circumstantial participle, with the cause as the focus. Taken together with its object, *hupomnesis* (recollection), it expresses the reason for Paul's thankfulness. It is because of the faith in Timothy, which he remembers even now that he is in prison, that Paul is thankful.

18 Sincere faith is said to have "lived" in these women. The verb *enokesen* could also be translated as "dwelt", as in John 1:14. It is a constative aorist that summarizes everything that confirmed to Paul that they were women of faith.
19 *Pepeismai* (I am persuaded) is an intensive perfect that focuses on the present.
20 One other option, put forward by those who deny Pauline authorship, is that this is simply a careless contradiction. For more discussion of the options, see Arland J. Hultgren, *I–II Timothy, Titus* (Augsburg Commentary on the New Testament; Minneapolis: Augsburg, 1984), 60–61.
21 Taking *theou* as a genitive of source.
22 Bernard, 109.
23 The Greek is *me oun epaischunthes*. A prohibition expressed using *me* and the aorist subjunctive usually indicates that what is prohibited is something that has not yet happened.
24 The first interpretation takes the genitive *tou kuriou*, which qualifies testimony (*marturion*), as a subjective genitive and relates it to 1 Timothy 6:13; the second takes it as an objective genitive.
25 Ward, 149.
26 Kelly, 161.
27 *Sunkakopatheson* (join me in suffering) is a compound word that Paul coined from the words *sun* (with), *kakos* (evil), and *paschein* (to suffer) (see Kelly, 161; Mounce, 480). He uses the aorist imperative, probably constative in shade, to suggest that Timothy is to join with him whenever the opportunity presents itself. Although the Greek does not specifically indicate who Timothy is to associate himself with in suffering, the context makes it clear that Paul is referring to himself, and thus the tniv and other translations translate it as "join with me".
28 The tniv takes *to euangelio* to be a dative of advantage or interest, and so translates it "for the gospel". In context, this is a better rendering than the Vulgate's "suffer with the gospel" (which treats *to euangelio* as a dative of association) or the kjv's "be thou partaker of the afflictions of the gospel" (which treats it as a dative of possession).
29 Taking *theou* as a genitive of source.
30 William Barclay, *The Letters of Paul to Timothy, Titus and Philemon* (1975; rev. ed.; Louisville, Ken.: Westminster John Knox Press, 2003), 164.
31 Dibelius and Conzelmann comment: "'To save' (*sozein*) and 'to call' (*kalein*) are perhaps introduced in this order because the event of salvation and its mediation in the proclamation form the entirety of the salvation occurrence 'for us'" (Martin Dibelius and Hans Conzelmann, *The Pastoral Epistles* [trans. Philip Buttolph and Adela Yarbro; ed. Helmet Koester; Philadelphia: Fortress, 1972], 99).
32 The former take the dative *klesei hagia* as a dative of means, and the latter as a dative of advantage.
33 Mounce, 482. See also George W. Knight, *The Pastoral Epistles: A Commentary on the Greek Text* (Grand Rapids: Eerdmans, 1992), 374. Other commentators make the same point: "The sense of the clause is that God, who is himself holy, has called Christians out of the world to a new life of consecration. They are 'called to be saints' (1 Cor 1:2), or 'called to holiness' (1 Thess 4:7)" (Kelly, 162).
34 Mounce, 147.
35 Ibid., 481.
36 C. K. Barrett suggests that this is an example of hendiadys, which would mean that the correct translation would be "gracious purpose", but there is no need to combine the thoughts into one (*Pastoral Epistles* [Oxford: Clarendon, 1963], 95).
37 Barclay, 165.
38 Kelly, 162.
39 The dative *Christo Iesou* can be taken as a dative of sphere, suggesting that Christ is God's way of mediating between himself and humanity.
40 Bernard, 110.
41 The participles *dotheisan* (was given) and *phanerotheisan* (has been revealed) are in the aorist tense. The first is taken to be an inceptive (or constative) aorist, while the second is taken to be a resultative aorist, hence the use of the perfect tense for the second verb in the tniv. The "was given" focuses on the finished act, while the "revealing" focuses on the ongoing results of that

42   act. However, if the second aorist is also assumed to be a constative aorist, the translation could be "was revealed", in which case it refers to "the whole life of Jesus on earth, his hidden years, his public ministry, his death and resurrection and ascension" (Ward, 152).

42 In 1 Timothy 6:14, Paul also spoke of Christ's appearing, but there he was clearly referring to his future return in glory, whereas here he is speaking of his incarnation and life. The same word is used in Titus 2:11–14; 3:4–7.

43 The basic meaning of "revealing" is "to make visible". In this context it goes beyond a "mere apprehension" to the idea of "actually accomplishing something concrete" (Mounce, 484). It is "actualized in historical process" (Kelly, 163).

44 In the Pastoral Epistles, God the Father is described as the Saviour in 1 Timothy 1:1; 2:3; 4:10; Titus 1:4; 2:10 and 3:4. God the Son is described as the Saviour in 2 Timothy 1:10; Titus 2:13 and 3:6. For an extensive discussion of the meaning of *soter* in the first century, see Dibelius and Conzelmann, 100–103.

45 The phrase could be translated literally as "on the one hand, destroying death, but on the other hand, bringing life and immortality through the gospel". Both actions are expressed using aorist participles. The TNIV's translation of the latter as if it is a perfect tense is based on the assumption that it is a resultative aorist.

46 Mounce, 485.
47 Ward, 153.
48 Bernard, 110.
49 Ward, 153.
50 Bernard, 111.
51 "Christ has brought imperishability to light as a consequence of his abolishing death. Prior to that action, perishability leading to death was the known mode of human existence" (Hultgren, 114).
52 There is an emphatic use of *ego* here, thus, literally "I myself".
53 Barclay, 167.
54 The former treats *pasko* as an aoristic present, referring to suffering he is enduring as he writes. This interpretation is reflected in the TNIV and is endorsed by Mounce (486), Bernard (111) and Kelly (165). The latter treats *pasko* as either a durative or iterative present tense.
55 The present tense is gnomic, indicating that the absence of shame is Paul's constant state.
56 The "who" in this passage could refer to either God or Christ. A number of commentators favour God rather than Christ because God is presented as the one who saves in 1:8–9 (Fee, 181; Mounce, 487; Kelly, 165; Barrett, 96).
57 Taking the verb *pepeisthai* as extensive perfect.
58 Barclay, 171.
59 *Pepeisthai* (persuaded or convinced) is also a perfect tense, but is intensive in shade. The focus thus falls not on the past but on the present results of what has happened in the past.
60 For discussion of this interpretation, see Mounce, 487–488; Kelly, 165–166; Bernard, 111.
61 Fee, 181; Mounce, 488.
62 Mounce, 488; Ward, 155; Kelly, 166; Bernard, 111.
63 If Paul is writing 2 Timothy from prison in Rome, the TNIV's translation of *apestraphesan* as a resultative aorist ("has deserted") may be less accurate than treating it as a constative ("deserted"). The desertion may have happened some time earlier when Paul was in Asia. He may have chosen this example because Timothy is serving at Ephesus in Asia.
64 Kelly, 169; Mounce, 494.
65 In Titus 1:14, the same verb is used to describe those who committed apostasy, but that does not seem to be the situation here (see Fee, 186).
66 Kelly, 169; Ward, 157.
67 Ward, 158.
68 Bernard, 113.
69 Barclay (174–175) paints an inspiring picture. See also Ward, 158.
70 Barrett, 99.

71. Fee, 186.
72. Kelly, 170.
73. Mounce, 497.
74. They are all aorist tenses in the Greek, and are all constative in shade.
75. The apocryphal *Acts of Paul and Thecla* suggests that Onesiphorus and his wife, given the name Lectra, offered hospitality to Paul during his first missionary journey. Such legends cannot be relied on but have probably grown up because their names are mentioned in these letters.
76. Those who hold this position include Fee (186), Hultgren (116–117), Bernard (114) and Kelly (171–172). Ward, however, insists that "Onesiphorus must have been alive still as it is hard to think of Paul praying for the dead" (157).
77. See, for example, 2 Maccabees 12:43–45; see also Barclay, 175–176.
78. Kelly, 171, cites the inscriptions in the Roman catacombs.
79. Bernard (114) argues: "It cannot be supposed impossible or even improbable that St. Paul should have shared in the practice, which the Christian Church seems to have taken over from Judaism." See also Kelly, 171; Ward, 157; Barrett, 99.
80. Hultgren, 117. Those who hold this position include Fee (187): "it is an expression of Paul's sentiment toward, or desire for Onesiphorus"; Mounce (497): "verses 16 and 18 are a far cry from any notion of intercessory or petitionary prayer. They are Paul's general wish for Onesiphorus and his family".
81. Kelly, 171.
82. Barclay, 176.
83. Barrett (99–100) argues that he is referring to God twice. However, Kelly (170) argues that "the Lord" (first mention, with article) refers to Christ and that this usage "is in harmony with the usage of the Pastorals (e.g., 2, 8, 16)" whereas "Lord" (second mention, without an article) refers to God, "whom Paul elsewhere (e.g., Rom 2:6; 3:6) represented as exercising judgement, and who in the Pastorals is regularly described as Saviour". Hultgren (117) and Bernard (114) agree with Kelly.
84. Barrett, 99–100.
85. *Ekousas* is a constative aorist.
86. Ward, 156.
87. In the Greek, "pattern" is the first word in the sentence, emphasizing its importance. Ward (156) defines it as, "an outline which is to be regarded as a standard" and Kelly (166) as "a rough draft forming the basis of a fuller exposition".
88. The noun "pattern" is qualified by the genitive "of sound teaching" (literally, "of sound words"), which is a genitive of content. The sound words constitute the standard Timothy is to keep before him as he contextualizes them, creatively making the gospel relevant in different contexts.
89. Ward, 156.
90. Ward, 156.
91. The datives "in faith" (*en pistei*) and "in love" (*agape* – the preposition *en* belongs to both "faith" and "love") are datives of manner.
92. Fee, 182.
93. *En Christo Iesou* is a dative of sphere.
94. The subject "you" is built into the verb *endunamou* – "you, be strong". Paul adds *su* to emphasize that he is talking to Timothy.
95. Barrett (101), sees the whole of 2:1 as expressing "in more general terms the exhortations of 1 Timothy 4:14; 2 Timothy 1:6".
96. *Endunamou* (be strong) is a durative present tense, implying that Timothy will enjoy "an abiding and continual strengthening" (Bernard, 116).
97. "By grace" treats this as an instrumental dative, an interpretation that is supported by Mounce (503), Kelly (172) and Ward (159). Fee (190) prefers to see it as a dative of sphere, as do the tniv, nasb, nrsv, hcsb and nkjv.
98. Contrast with Hultgren (118): "Here the exhortation is that Timothy be strong in the strength grace provides. Grace is itself a power in the Pastorals (1 Tim 1:14; 2 Tim 1:9; Tit 2:11)".

99   This is the only undisputed (see also Col 3:16) occurrence in Paul's writings of the preposition *en* + article + *charis*. Paul's normal construction is anarthrous (no article – see Rom 5:15; 2 Cor 1:12; Gal 1:6; Col 4:6; 2 Thess 2:16). It was common to drop the article in prepositional phrases, which was what Paul normally did. Hence his inclusion of the article here seems to be a deliberate attempt to stress that "the" grace mentioned here is what will enable him to do his work victoriously.
100   Taking "in Christ Jesus" as a dative of sphere.
101   "An outline of the faith" (Kelly, 173).
102   The last two are preferred by scholars: "ordination" (Hultgren, 118); "baptism or (better still) ordination" (Kelly, 173); "ordination or baptism" (Ward, 160); "ordination or (perhaps) baptism" (Barrett, 101).
103   This interpretation treats "have heard' as a constative aorist.
104   The preposition *dia* with the genitives *pollon marturon* would usually be rendered "through". Fee (191) supports this translation and argues, "it probably means not that Timothy himself heard Paul's teachings as they were mediated through many witnesses, but that, as Timothy should well know, what Paul taught is also attested to by many others – a needed emphasis in light of the many defections in Ephesus." Mounce (506) also supports this position. He says, "Paul's concern is to emphasize that the gospel Timothy heard was not heard in secret from Paul alone but rather was heard from many people." He adds, "This is not to say Paul appeals to the authority of others. It is saying that in contrast to the Ephesian opponents with their myths and legends, the gospel is widely and publicly attested, and this is the gospel Timothy is to entrust to faithful Ephesians." He concludes that "in this case *dia* means through in the sense of being attested to, denoting the manner, attendant circumstance, or perhaps occasion of Timothy hearing the gospel repeatedly from Paul." My objection to Fee's and Mounce's position is that they do not adequately identify the recipients of the many witnesses' testimony.
105   Kelly, 172; Ward, 160; Barrett, 101; Hultgren, 118.
106   The verb *parathou*, (entrust) is the aorist imperative of *paratithemai* and is related to *paratheke* of 2 Timothy 1:12 and 1:14 (where it is translated as "deposit").
107   The tniv correctly renders this as "people" because *anthropos* is the generic term for all members of the human race.
108   Barclay, 178.
109   The same verb, *sunkakopatheson*, is used. It is an aorist imperative, taken here as a constative aorist.
110   Taking the genitive *Christou Iesou* as genitive of relationship.
111   Taking the genitive *Christou Iesou* as genitive of possession.
112   Both verbs are in the present tense and indicate a full-time commitment.
113   Theodosius as quoted in Barclay, 159.
114   A more literal translation of 2:5 is "if anyone competes as an athlete" (niv). Paul's "if" introduces a third class condition (a more probable situation – note *ean* + subjunctive [*athle*] in the protasis).
115   Mounce, 510; also Kelly, 176.
116   Kelly, 175. The position is held by Fee (192) and Mounce (510), among others.
117   Barrett, 102.
118   The phrase "does not receive the victor's crown" uses a negative and a gnomic present, *stephanoutai*, to state what is expected or normal.
119   Taking *lego* as an aoristic present.
120   M. Shaw. *The Kingdom of God in Africa: A Short History of African Christianity* (Grand Rapids: Baker, 1996), 192.
121   J. L. Gonzalez, *The Early Church to the Dawn of the Reformation* (vol. 1 of *The Story of Christianity*; San Francisco: Harper, 1984), 44.
122   Barclay (164) calls it, "the greatest appeal of all." Fee (195) refers to it as "the theological basis of Paul's appeal to Timothy."
123   Regardless of the order of the titles, Paul is referring to the same person.

124 This is made clear by Paul's choice of the perfect tense here, *egegermenon* – literally, "having been raised". Its shade is intensive perfect with the focus on the result of the action. Compare Romans 1:3, 4 where we have the two aspects along with the focus on God's power.
125 Fee, 196.
126 Kelly (177), for example, describes these words as a "fragment of semi-stereotyped credal material" and as "irrelevant in the context".
127 Barclay, 164.
128 This position is held mostly by those who date this letter later than Paul's time.
129 Hultgren, 120.
130 The verb *kakopathein* (to suffer) is a simplified form of *sunkakopathein* (to suffer with). Paul uses the former for himself here and the latter in 2:3 where he called upon Timothy to join him in suffering. In 4:5, Paul uses *kakopathein* for Timothy, calling him to endure hardship.
131 The former position, reflected in the nasb, nrsv, hcsb, nkjv translations, "I suffer" takes *kakopatho* as durative present. The latter position, reflected in the tniv translation, "I am suffering", takes *kakopatho* as an aoristic present.
132 Bernard, 119. See also Fee, 196.
133 Taking the genitive *tou theou* as a genitive of source.
134 Taking the perfect *dedetai* as an intensive perfect.
135 Taking the perfect *dedetai* as a gnomic perfect.
136 If *hupomeno* is taken as an aoristic present, the meaning is restricted to the present suffering. However, it seems more likely that it is a durative present, particularly given the fact that Paul relates his suffering to the salvation of the elect in 2:10.
137 Kelly (178) says that the elect are "those whom God's eternal predestination has chosen to receive salvation (Rom 8:33; Col 3:12; Tit 1:13), but who have not yet responded to his call."
138 Hultgren (121) says, "The term elect (as in Titus 1:1) refers to Christians. It is rooted in the Old Testament. Israel as a nation is spoken of there as God's elect people (Deut. 7:6–7; Isa. 43:20; 45:4; 65:9, 15; Pss. 105:43; 106:5), and that understanding also appears in the New Testament (Acts 13:17; Romans 9:11; 11:23)". Fee (197) also supports this position.
139 Bernard observes that in Paul's letters and also in 1 and 2 Peter, the words *kletoi* and *ekletoi* "are continually used of the whole body of believers, 'chosen' and 'called' by God to the privileges of the gospel" (120).
140 Paul's focus was on the eternal position in Christ of all those whom God plans to bring to knowledge of the truth, not just on the current realization of God's plan in history (covering only those who have already believed). The former is determined by the will of God; the latter by the free will of human beings.
141 Taking *Christo Iesou* here as dative of sphere.
142 This phrase indicates that the salvation Paul refers to here is eschatological. The emphasis on future eternal salvation that will come at Christ's return does not deny the present salvation of the elect. Paul's endurance has led to their being saved and justified, it contributes to their current sanctification, and will result in their future glorification.
143 Most commentators, including Bernard (120), Fee (198) and Kelly (179), regard the "trustworthy saying" as 2:11–13. A few, including John Chrysostom, argue that it is actually the preceding statements, either the one about patient endurance or the one about the resurrection and ancestry of Christ (2:8, 10). The main reason they offer is that the saying in 2:11b is introduced by the Greek word *gar*, which is usually translated as "therefore" or "for" (see nasb). This would be an odd word to use to introduce a saying. Against this, it can be pointed out that 2:8 is too far removed from the statement to justify the "for", and that 2:10 does not sound like something that would be remembered as a "saying". It is probably better either to take *gar* as an explanatory word (equivalent to "that is" – Fee, 198) or to regard it as part of the original source that Paul is quoting verbatim (Kelly, 179).
144 Last in terms of the date of writing, for 1 Timothy was written first, then Titus, and then 2 Timothy.

145 Kelly (179) says, "The obvious explanation of "for" is that the extract cited is an incomplete one; Paul begins it at a point relevant to his subject, disregarding the abrupt opening" (see also Ward, 166–167).
146 Bernard (120) says, "there can be little doubt that vv. 12, 13 are a quotation from a Christian hymn or confession". See also Mounce, 515; Hultgren, 121–122; Kelly, 179.
147 Fee, 199; Ward, 169.
148 In academic terms, what was its *Sitz im Leben*?
149 The first position is supported by Hultgren (122), Kelly (179) and Mounce (515). The second is supported by Bernard (120), who describes the hymn as "an incentive to courage and endurance". See also Barclay, 169; Barrett, 104.
150 Kelly, 179.
151 The aorist *sunapethanomen* may be a resultative aorist (focusing on the fact that we are now dead) or an inceptive aorist (focusing on our entrance to the state of being dead).
152 The future, "we will reign" (like the future tenses in lines one and three) is a predictive future. It will come to pass.
153 Mounce (517) argues that the line must refer to Christians because if Paul was speaking of non-Christians he would use the present tense when referring to the denying. However, it could also be argued that these persons are not yet denying Christ as a matter of habit, but they have also not yet fully embraced the Christian faith. They are opening themselves to the possibility of denying becoming a habit, something that will inevitably happen if they do not change their attitude.
154 Bernard, 121; Hultgren, 123. Their argument is based on the fact that the verb *arnesometha* is in the future tense, unlike "endure" (*hupomenomen*) and "being faithless" (*apistoumen*), which are in present tense. They think that the future tense indicates that the action is improbable.
155 In 2:12b, the "if we disown him" is a first class condition, paralleling the construction in the first two lines of the hymn. In Greek, there are four possible ways of interpreting an "if" clause (a conditional clause):
   - *First class condition:* The premise of the "if" clause is taken as a fact, and the conclusion follows naturally. The construction is *ei* + any tense of the indicative mood in the protasis (the "if" clause), and any mood or tense in the apodosis (the "then" clause").
   - *Second class condition:* The premise is not a fact (contrary to fact). In this construction we usually find *ei* in the protasis and *an* in the apodosis.
   - *Third class condition:* The premise is not certain, but is very probable. The subjunctive mood is used in the protasis (introduced by *ean*) and any form of the verb in the apodosis.
   - *Fourth class condition:* The premise is not certain, and is also less likely, though possible. Here a verb in the optative mood (introduced by *ei*) is used in the protasis and another optative (introduced by *an*) in the apodosis.
156 The verb *upomenon* is a progressive present and *arnesometha* is a progressive future.
157 This interpretation is made even more likely by the use of "we" in line four of the hymn.
158 Taking the shade of the future here as predictive.
159 Hultgren, 170.
160 The clause represents another first class condition. The verb in the apodosis is a gnomic present, focusing on Jesus' character in general.
161 This view is supported by most commentators. Kelly (180) states, "The great affirmation of the hymn is that, however wayward and faithless men may be, God's love continues unalterable and he remains true to his promises". See also Barclay (170) – Jesus is "for ever true to the man who, however much he has failed, has tried to be true to him"; Ward (169) – "God is faithful to his covenant with his people in spite of their conduct"; Fee (200–201) –"This can mean that God will override our infidelity with his grace (as most commentators) or that his overall faithfulness to his gracious gift of eschatological salvation for his people is not negated by the faithlessness of some. This latter seems more in keeping with Paul and the immediate context. Some have proved faithless, but God's saving faithfulness has not been diminished thereby". Similar views

are expressed by Hultgren, 124; Bernard, 121; Mounce, 518; Barrett, 102; and Dibelius and Conzelmann, 109.

162 The verb *hupomimneske* is a present imperative.

163 Barrett (122) takes the view that he is to remind "those over whom you are placed"; Fee (204), "your people"; and Mounce (523), "all the Ephesians". However, Hultgren (124) applies it to "the ministers of the word ['faithful persons'] referred to in 2:2."

164 Mounce (523) argues that the "things" refers specifically to "the faithful saying", claiming that this interpretation "fits the contextual needs of vv. 14–26". Barrett (105) agrees and insists that Timothy is to remind his listeners "of the requirement that Christians should be faithful to Christ even at the cost of life, and of the promise that God keeps faith." Ward (170), however, says that it also includes the teaching mentioned in 2:2. Hultgren (124) prefers the position that Paul is talking about "all the teachings which have been given to this point in the letter, such as the doctrinal affirmations of 2:8 and 2:11–13, but also the assertions about Paul's apostleship, suffering, and teaching". Finally, Kelly (182) sees it as embracing all Paul's teaching: "in the first instance the profound gospel truth summarized in 11–13, but also, more generally, the Christian message as he had learned it from the Apostle (2:2)".

165 The participle *diamartyromenos* could be circumstantial, focusing on the manner in which Timothy should remind people (that is, "remind them, by warning them"). However, it is more likely to be an independent participle with the force of an imperative (as in the tniv, nasb and others).

166 Ward, 170.

167 Barrett (122) makes the point that "those who engage in such wrangles do so with a view to gaining the approval of those who listen to them." The noun form of the verb translated "quarrelling" was used in 1 Timothy 6:4.

168 The function of *epi* here is to mark the result of wrangling about words; if Paul were speaking about the intention, he would have used *eis*.

169 Kelly, 182.

170 Barrett, 122.

171 Greek sentences are usually in the following order: predicate, subject, object, complementary participle. When this order is not followed, one should consider the possibility that something is being emphasized. The emphasized word may be moved from its usual position to a position at the beginning or end of a sentence (or even to the middle, if the sentence involves an antithesis). For more information on this, see A. T, Robertson, *A Grammar of the Greek New Testament in the Light of Historical Research* (New York: Hodder & Stoughton, 1923), 417–418.

172 Taking the aorist imperative *spoudason* as constative, embracing Timothy's "doing" as a totality. The aorist infinitive translated as "to present" likewise looks at the presentation of self in its totality.

173 Ward, 180.

174 The present tense participle, *orthotomounta*, is used only in these two verses in the New Testament, but it is also found in the Septuagint translation of Proverbs 3:6 and 11:5.

175 In other words, Timothy must apply sound hermeneutical principles in his exegesis and must not indulge in eisegesis.

176 The first position regards *tes aletheias* as a genitive of quality; the second regards it as an epexegetical genitive; and the third as a genitive of content.

177 The three virtues of righteousness, faith and love are also mentioned in 1 Timothy 6:11, again in the context of fleeing and pursuing. Peace is mentioned in 1 Timothy 1:2 and a pure heart in 1 Timothy 1:5.

178 The *de* is probably best taken as adversative here. Note that Mounce (533) treats it as inferential – "therefore", "so".

179 The reason for the dispute is that in some Greek texts there is a comma between the word translated "peace" and the prepositional phrase, while in others there is no comma. Bernard (126), for example, says that the prepositional phrase relates only to "peace".

180 Barclay, 180.

181	The nasb, niv, nrsv and hcsb have "with those". This translation is also endorsed by Kelly (189). The translation "along with" is supported by Barclay (180–181); Hultgren (128) and Ward (180).
182	"Avoid" translates a present imperative that indicates that this should be a way of life.
183	Taking *prokopsousin* as gnomic future.
184	Mounce, 526.
185	Barclay, 174.
186	Donald Guthrie, *The Pastoral Epistles* (Tyndale New Testament Commentary Series; Grand Rapids: Eerdmans, 1957), 148–149.
187	Taking *exei* is a gnomic future.
188	Bernard, 123. Mounce (527) mentions that this usage of the word can be traced as early as the time of Hippocrates (460 bc to about 370 bc).
189	Kelly, 184.
190	The Greek phrase is *nomen exei*, and the noun *nome* is used of the type of pasture that sheep might graze on (Mounce, 527).
191	As a present imperative, *pheuge* (flee) denotes a continuing practice.
192	Taking *neoterikas* as qualitative genitive.
193	Hultgren, 127; Fee, 214; Kelly, 189.
194	Ward, 179–180.
195	Barclay, 180.
196	Ward, 180.
197	If *pheuge* (flee) is taken to be aoristic present imperative, it indicates an action now in practice but to be left behind; if it is a durative present imperative, it indicates an action to be continued, and if it is a futuristic present it refers to an action to be adopted when the need arises in the future.
198	Bernard, 125.
199	But see William Hendriksen, who comments, "It is in line with Paul's very practical bent of mind to assume that these crisp commandments bear some reference to reality, and were warnings that were actually needed, yes needed by Timothy because of certain character weaknesses, however unpronounced they may have been" (*Exposition of the Pastoral Epistles* [New Testament Commentary; Grand Rapids: Baker, 1957], 273). See also Kelly, 189.
200	The aorist *estochesan* is probably best taken as constative in shade (viewing as a whole all that they have done or believed in to come to their present status). It could also be resultative aorist, as the niv and nasb translations have it, with the focus on their current status.
201	Kelly, 184.
202	Mounce (528) says, "Many suggest that Paul's teaching of spiritual death and rising to life (2 Tim 2:11; Rom 6:1–11; Col 2:20 – 3:4; cf. Eph 2:6; 5:14) had been perverted by replacing the bodily with the spiritual resurrection and hence denying the bodily resurrection". Among these are Fee (206–207), Bernard (123), Ward (174) and Kelly (185).
203	Dibelius and Conzelmann, 112.
204	Barclay, 175.
205	Taking *anatrepousin* as an iterative present. It may also be a durative present or a tendential present – something they can only attempt to do but cannot succeed in.
206	The genitive *tou theou* may be taken as subjective (it is God who established it) or qualitative (it is a foundation established by God).
207	Taking *esteken* as intensive perfect (it now stands), though it can also be gnomic (it always stands).
208	Ward, 175–176; Kelly, 186.
209	Kelly, 186.
210	This view is supported by Bernard (124); Hultgren (126); Barclay (176) and Hanson (*The Pastoral Epistles* [New Century Bible Commentary; Grand Rapids: Eerdmans, 1982], 137).
211	Mounce, 529.
212	The Greek verb *egno*, here translated as "knows", is an aorist that would usually be translated as the simple past "knew". There are cases, however, where it needs to be translated differently because of the context, and this is one of them. Thus the tniv, nasb, nrsv, hcsb and nkjv treat

it as a gnomic aorist and translate it as "knows", communicating that God continually has this knowledge. Mounce (529) would prefer the translation "knew", limiting God's knowledge in this context to his past election of believers. He argues, "It is God's prior knowledge in election that assures Timothy that despite the success of the opponents the elect are safe." However, limiting God's knowledge to election does not mean God did not know who belonged to him at the time the letter was written to Timothy. It thus seems more likely that God's enduring knowledge is in view here, and thus the translation "knows" is the better choice.

213 The Greek is *epeskeptai kai egno ho theos tous ontas autou*.
214 Ward, 176.
215 Mounce, 529.
216 Barclay, 178.
217 Kelly, 186. See also Fee, 208: "Despite the devastating inroads made by the false teachers, Timothy and the church are to be heartened by this sure word."
218 Ward, 177.
219 The two terms, *timen* (honour) and *atimen* (dishonour), are accusatives of termination.
220 Ward, 177.
221 This passage is the only place where Paul "directly expresses the thought of the church embracing evil members as well as good" (Bernard, 124). For this reason, some commentators like Fee and Mounce (530) do not agree with the link to Jesus' parable of the wheat and weeds. Fee (211) says that Paul's point is not related to 1 Corinthians 12:21–24 or Matthew 13:24–30, but rather "it has to do with verse 19, that those who name God's name, Timothy and the believers – those who are known to God – are to turn away from evil, especially in the form of the false teaching of such as Hymenaeus and Philetus." Mounce (530) also says, "Building from the requirements of godly living established in v. 19, Paul begins a new paragraph and urges Timothy to righteous conduct. Verse 20 is the metaphor, v. 21 interprets the metaphor, and vv. 22–26 spell out the specific terms of how Timothy is to behave."
222 Here we have the subjunctive verb *ekkathare* used in a third class condition to show that the behaviour is probable, but not certain.
223 Fee, 211 and Hultgren, 127. Both the nasb and hcsb say "these things" and the nrsv reads, "the things I have mentioned".
224 The masculine pronoun used here in the Greek is inclusive of all members of humankind.
225 The perfects *hegiasmenon* (sanctified) and *hetoimasmenon* (prepared) are intensive in shade. They are probably divine passives.
226 Barclay, 178.
227 National Council of Churches of Kenya. Press statement issued 18th March 2009 at Jumuia Conference and Country Home, Limuru. n.p. [cited 20 April 2009] Online: http://blog.marsgroupkenya.org/?p=644. See also http://www.reuters.com/article/latestCrisis/idUSLJ673407
228 The present tense of the imperative "refuse" indicates that Timothy is to continually refuse to have anything to do with them as a matter of principle.
229 Dibelius and Conzelmann, 113.
230 Ward, 181.
231 Taking *kuriou* as a genitive of possession. If it were a genitive of relationship, it would focus only on service and not on belonging.
232 Bernard, 126.
233 Barclay, 181.
234 BAGD, 64: *anexikakos*.
235 Barclay, 181.
236 Ward, 182.
237 The articular participle, *tous antidiatithemenous* (those who are in opposition) is both middle and passive voice in form. If it is taken as middle voice, it is referring to the false teachers who are opposing Timothy. If taken as passive voice, it refers to those who have been deceived by the

false teachers. Bernard (127) takes the latter view, but most commentators take the middle voice position.

238 The tniv translation is a bit misleading for it dilutes the force of a perfect passive participle *ezogremenoi*. This is an intensive perfect, which focuses on the fact that they are still being held captive. The nasb and nrsv rendering is closer, "having been held captive". See also the hcsb, "having been captured", and the nkjv, "having been taken captive".

239 Ward, 185.

240 The use of both *autou* and *ekeinou* in the clause *ezogremenoi up' autou eis to ekeinou thelema* creates some ambiguity about who exactly is being referred to in 2:26b. The options are as follows:
  - Both pronouns refer to the devil. This is the option chosen by the tniv and preferred by Dibelius and Conzelmann (114); Fee (216); Kelly (192) and Ward (185).
  - Both pronouns refer to God. The thought of God granting repentance in 2:25 is carried through so that he is the one holding the false teachers captive in order to do his will.
  - The first pronoun (*autou*) refers to the devil, while the second (*ekeinou*) refers to God. Bernard (123) says, "The *ezogremenoi up' autou* merely affords the explanation, logically necessary for the sense, as to how these unwary ones got into the devil's snare, viz. they were taken captive by him; and *eis to ekeinou thelema* expresses the purpose which they, when rescued, shall strive to fulfill". See also Barrett, 110; Barclay, 118; Mounce, 538.
  - The first pronoun (*autou*) refers to the servant of the Lord (2:24) and the second (*ekeinou*) to God. That is, the false teacher is freed from the devil's snare and made a captive of the servant of the Lord (that is, a minister of the gospel). This leads the false teachers to do God's will.

  Grammatically speaking, it is most accurate to say that both pronouns refer to the same person. As Kelly (192) points out, "the originally sharp distinction between autos ('he') and ekeinos ('that one') had broken down in the koine". It would, therefore, be in order for the two pronouns to refer to the same person. Contextually the view that either of the pronouns refers to the "servant of God" or "God" is a bit of a stretch. The "devil" is closest to both pronouns, and if there is no significant reason for thinking otherwise, it is quite fitting to see the devil as doing the holding.

241 The same Greek verb (*zogrein*) is used in Luke 5:10 to describe "catching men".

242 The Greek words are *prautes* for "gentleness" and *epios* for "kindness".

243 Kelly, 190.

244 Ward, 182.

245 Mounce, 536; Kelly, 190.

246 Kelly, 190.

247 The verb is in the optative mood ("may grant", nasb). This is one of the four possible moods of a verb (the other three being the indicative, imperative and subjunctive). An author would use the optative mood only when the realization is viewed as possible, but with no guarantee or any indications of it.

248 *Epignosin* (knowledge) is an accusative of termination or goal.

249 Taking *aletheias* as a genitive of content.

250 Barrett, 109.

251 Mounce, 537.

252 The genitive *pagidos* accompanied by *ek* is a genitive of exit (from the trap, *pagis*), and the genitive *tou diabolou* (of the devil) is a genitive of possession.

253 Bernard, 127.

254 Ward, 185. See also Dibelius and Conzelmann, 114; Kelly, 191; Mounce, 537.

255 Taking the future middle indicative verb *enosteson* as a predictive future, stating that this will certainly take place.

256 Paul introduces these concepts using compound words that all include *philos* or its opposite, *aphilos*. The compound words are *philautoi* (lovers of self), *philarguroi* (lovers of money), *aphilagathoi* (haters of good) and *philedonoi* (lovers of pleasure).

257 Barclay, 207.
258 Ward, 187.
259 Ward, 188.
260 Barclay, 211.
261 This is the first of eight vices listed in this verse which are compounds with the alpha privative (negating *a*). Without the alpha, the quality would be a virtue; with it, the quality is a vice. The eight are *apeitheis* (disobedient), *acharistoi* (ungrateful), *anosioi* (unholy), *astorgoi* (unloving), *aspondoi* (irreconcilable), *akrateis* (without self-control), *anemeroi* (brutal) and *aphilagathoi* (haters of good).
262 Kelly, 194.
263 Barclay, 211.
264 Ibid., 213.
265 Ibid.
266 BAGD, 711.
267 Kelly, 194. See also, Bernard, 130; Fee, 220; Mounce, 545.
268 Barclay, 210.
269 Bernard, 130.
270 Barclay, 211–212.
271 The Greek word used here is *astorgos* and its opposite, in noun form, is *storge*.
272 This second option is based on the fact that the opposite of the Greek word for "unforgiving" (*aspondos*) in its noun form (*sponde*) is the word for truce or an agreement (Barclay, 212).
273 Barclay, 212.
274 Fee, 220. Kelly (194) says that it "denotes a man who cannot bring himself to come to terms with other people".
275 Note that the focus is on the person's status. The shade of the perfect participle *tetuphomenoi* (the only participle in the list of vices) is intensive.
276 Barclay, 215.
277 Bernard, 130.
278 Ward, 188.
279 A rebellious attitude would be captured better by the word *akolastos* that Liddell and Scott translate as "undisciplined" (Henry G. Liddell and Robert Scott, *A Greek-English Lexicon* [Oxford: Clarendon, 1968, 52]).
280 Bernard, 130.
281 Ward, 189.
282 Barclay, 213.
283 BAGD, 716.
284 Barclay, 214.
285 Kelly, 194.
286 Ward, 188.
287 Barrett, 111.
288 Kelly, 195. See also Barclay (215), who says that they "go through the correct movements and maintain all the external forms of religion; but they know nothing of Christianity as a dynamic power which changes the lives of men and women."
289 The verb could, of course, also be interpreted as a futuristic present, but the context does not seem to warrant this.
290 Kelly, 195.
291 Kelly, 195.
292 Ward, 189.
293 Ibid.
294 The "because" is justified by the conjunction translated "for" in the nasb, nrsv, hcsb and nkjv, all of which represent the Greek more accurately than the tniv at this point.

295 *Endunontes* and *aichmalotizontes* are both adjectival participles, used substantively, and are governed by the same plural article, *hoi*, thus "those who". A literal translation of the verse would be, "for out of them are those men entering into households and captivating weak women.
296 The genitive *touton* (them) may be taken as a partitive genitive. The nasb uses "among them".
297 Paul uses a definite article before the word translated "homes", making it literally "the homes".
298 Mounce, 548.
299 The Greek word for "woman" is *gune*, but here Paul uses *gunaikarion*, which is pejorative in this context. See Mounce, 548; Fee, 221–222.
300 Kelly, 195.
301 Taking the perfect tense *sesoreumena* (loaded) as intensive in shade. The verb includes a sense of "piling up". *Hamartias* (sins) is taken to be an instrumental dative. See Mounce, 548.
302 Bernard, 131 describes this as seeking "peace in spiritual dissipation".
303 Mounce, 549; Fee, 222.
304 Bernard, 132.
305 Taking the participle *agomena* as an iterative present.
306 Bernard, 132.
307 Mounce, 549. He goes on to say, "It is not that the women would not but that they could not learn the truth".
308 This is a better translation of *epignosin aletheias* than the niv's "acknowledge the truth".
309 Its focus is "the cognitive element in contrast to the theological error of the heresy" (Mounce, 549). The heresy attacked both correct belief and good behaviour. The focus here is on the belief, the statement of faith.
310 Bernard (132) cites the Targum of Jonathan on Exodus 7:11. Fee (222) states that these names were in use by at least 150 bc. See also Dibelius and Conzelmann, 116–117; Barclay, 218; Mounce, 550.
311 The verb here is taken as a constative aorist, summarizing all their efforts.
312 Barclay (218) describes them as "typifying all those who opposed the purposes of God and the work of his true leaders".
313 *Anthistantai* is a present tense, showing that this is their constant practice.
314 The phrase can also be translated "men with depraved minds." The passive participle *katephtharmenoi* (depraved) is adjectival, qualifying "men" and with *ton noun*, the mind as its object.
315 Mounce, 550.
316 Ward, 96.
317 Barrett, 112.
318 The future "they will not get very far" (or "they will not make further progress" – nasb) together with the strong adversative "but" (*alla*) emphasize that these men may have success at the moment but will come to a bad end. *Prokopsousin* is taken as a predictive future.
319 Barclay, 219. See also Bernard, 120: "Truth must prevail in the end, and imposture cannot permanently deceive."
320 Gerald Businge, "Seven Years Since the Kanungu Massacre", www.ugpulse.com. Article published March 17, 2007. Cited 14 March 2009.
321 The fact that Timothy is informed about Paul's life is also evident in other Bible translations: "you have observed" – nrsv; "you have followed" – hcsb; "you have carefully followed" – nkjv. This is why the tniv translates the phrase as "you know".
322 The former position takes *parekolouthesas* (followed) as a constative aorist, and the latter as a resultative aorist.
323 Barclay, 220. See also Kelly, 198.
324 Paul does not exclude how he teaches, but the emphasis here is on what is taught.
325 Barclay, 221.
326 Ibid., 222.
327 Both "happened" and "endured" are in the aorist tense and are best taken as constative, summarizing all he endured as a whole.

328 The aorist *errusato* (rescued/delivered) is constative. Thus, Paul endured (constative aorist idea) and the Lord delivered (constative aorist).
329 The participle *thelontes* (want) is a durative present, indicating that they constantly have this desire. Grammatically the prepositional phrase "in Christ Jesus" could modify "everyone", implying that all Christians will suffer persecution, but this is unlikely. The "in Christ Jesus" is closer to "godly life" and makes more sense if associated with it. Paul is saying that only those Christians who are sincere about their faith and truly desire to live godly lives will experience persecution. See also Mounce, 560; Bernard, 134; Kelly, 200; Barrett, 113.
330 Taking *diochthesontai* (will be persecuted) as a predictive future.
331 Ward, 196.
332 "Deceiving" (*planontes*) and "being deceived" (*planomenoi*) are both present participles. Their action is simultaneous with the action of the main verb, "will go". As adverbial participles of manner, they focus on the manner of the progression.
333 Literally, the translation should be "You, yourself".
334 The imperative verb, "continue" is in the present tense, indicating that this is to be his habitual practice.
335 If the verb *emathes* (learned) is a constative aorist, the focus in on the sum of the many opportunities Timothy has had for learning. If it is resultative, the focus is on what Timothy has become.
336 If the aorist (*epistothes*) is taken as resultative.
337 Mounce, 561.
338 The perfect participle *eidos* is here taken to be a circumstantial participle of manner in usage, qualifying the basis upon which Timothy is convinced. It is intensive perfect in shade.
339 Kelly, 200–201.
340 The verb *oidas* (have known) is in the perfect tense and is intensive, focusing on Timothy's state since childhood.
341 Barclay, 224; Bernard, 135; Mounce, 563.
342 Some scholars like Kelly (201) insist that "the Old Testament was the only canonical Scripture for Christians as well as Jews in the apostolic age and for several generations after". However, the view that the "Holy Scriptures" here could also include parts of the New Testament is supported by the fact that Paul is thinking about "the culmination of the scriptural hope realized through faith in Christ Jesus" (Mounce, 564). This may also explain why the term is anarthrous and not articular (note that *ta* is in brackets in both the *UBS Greek New Testament* and the Nestle-Aland editions). Mounce argues that Paul may have chosen the anarthrous plural construction, *hiera grammata* "to develop his argument in the direction of joining the Hebrew Scriptures and the gospel" (Mounce, 564). Kelly (201), however, argues that the absence of the article merely proves that Paul is using the term "Holy Scriptures" technically, to refer only to the canonical Old Testament.
343 The participle *dunamena* may be either a durative present or a gnomic present. The infinitive "to make wise" is the object of "are able".
344 Taking *soterian* (salvation) as an accusative of goal or termination. See also Bernard, 136; Kelly, 202.
345 Kelly, 202.
346 The phrase *pasa graphe theopneustos* allows for several translations from the standpoint of both grammar and vocabulary. The basic questions are whether *pasa* is to be translated as "all" or "every" and whether the adjective *theopneustos* is to be taken predicatively (as in the niv) or attributively (attributing a quality). The following possible translations have been suggested:
- Every Scripture inspired by God
- All inspired Scripture
- Every Scripture is divinely inspired
- All Scripture is inspired by God

Most commentators choose between the third and fourth choices above, that is, taking the adjective "inspired" as a predicate (asserting something about the Scriptures). This is the more natural reading of the text in that it sees the adjective "God-breathed" as parallel to the next adjective, "useful". However, Barclay (224) and Dibelius and Conzelmann (120) support the reading, "all Scripture inspired by God".

As regards the debate about whether *pasa* is "every" (individual passage) or "all" (Scripture collectively), the absence of an article before the word supports the translation "every" (see Bernard, 137). However, the context lends some support to "all", given that it speaks of the function of Scripture as a whole (Hultgren, 135). For more arguments in support of this position, see Mounce (569). In the end, the choice of "all" or "every" makes very little difference to the meaning.

347 *Theopneustos* occurs only here in the New Testament. It is a compound word combining *theos* (God) and *pnein* ("to breathe", *pneus* being its aorist form). When used as an adjective (by adding the verbal adjectival ending *-tos*), it means "God-breathed". The most common translation is "inspired", coming from the Latin "inspirare" (meaning "to breathe into").

348 Bernard (137) supports this position with his translation, "Every Scripture inspired by God is profitable also ...". He takes *kai* as having ascensive force (also), and not simply as a copulative (and). Hultgren (136) says, "The emphasis of the writer, in any case, is not so much on a doctrine of inspiration, but rather on the use of Scripture." This understanding does not necessarily exclude the position that Paul viewed Scripture as inspired. Most of those who support it simply say that an emphasis on the inspiration of Scripture would be irrelevant when writing to Timothy, who already viewed Scripture as inspired. However, as said above, the more natural reading of the text is to take "God-breathed" and "useful" as parallel predicate adjectives, both making assertions about Scripture.

349 Ward, 200.
350 Barclay, 227.
351 Ibid., 225. See also Kelly, 203.
352 "Righteousness" summarizes all the aspects of a life that is pleasing to God. See the commentary on 1 Tim 6:11.
353 In classical Greek *hina* (so that) normally expressed purpose, but in Koine Greek it often denoted result. Here it may be stating what will come about as a result of the ministry of the word, or the purpose for which God's word is made available. Purpose is the preferable translation here, though in this context the line between "purpose" and "result" is very narrow. The Scripture was given for a purpose and to achieve that result. See also Kelly, 204; Mounce, 570.
354 The perfect tense verb *exertismen* is an intensive focusing on the status of the person.
355 Ward, 201.
356 This second letter to Timothy is probably one of the last letters Paul's wrote. It is certainly the last one included in the Bible. It was written during his second Roman imprisonment, which ended with his death.
357 Barclay, 228.
358 The Greek uses the periphrastic construction *mellontos krinein*.
359 Both *ten epiphaneia autou* and *ten basileian autou* are accusatives of oath.
360 The verb *keruxon*, like the other five verbs in this section of the charge, is an aorist imperative.
361 Kelly, 205.
362 Ward, 205.
363 Kelly, 206. The two descriptions "in season" and "out of season" denote "fitting time" and "not fitting time", respectively. The adverbs *eukairos* and *akairos* are compounds of *eu* (good) and *kairos* (fitting time), and *a* (negating alpha) + *kairos*, respectively.
364 Barrett, 116.
365 Paul does not clarify whether the inconvenience might be felt by Timothy or by his audience. Should Timothy preach whether or not he is prepared (subjective), or should he preach whether or not the listeners are ready to hear him (objective)? Paul may not have thought of these distinctions, and Mounce (573) is probably right when he says that "the distinction may not be necessary."
366 Barclay, 230.
367 Fee, 234.

368 Kelly, 206.
369 Barclay, 232.
370 Kelly, 206; see also Barclay, 232.
371 Barclay, 232.
372 Of the nine instructions, this is the only one expressed using the present imperative (the other eight are all aorist imperatives). It is the first of four instructions listed here as a contrast (note the emphatic *su* and the adversative *de*) to the nature and practice of the false teachers discussed in 4:3.
373 Ward, 208.
374 Taking the genitive *euangelistou* as qualitative. Kelly (207) comments that here "the idea of a special office is quite inappropriate".
375 The Greek term *diakonia* is used as in 1 Tim 1:12, where it is translated "service". Here, too, it is used in a general sense and does not refer to the office of a deacon.
376 Barclay, 234.
377 Nobel Foundation, "Wangari Muta Maathai: The Nobel Peace Prize 2004", Biography, n.p. [cited 12 December 2008]. Online: http://nobelprize.org/nobel_prizes/peace/laureates/2004/. The Peace Prize and the other Nobel prizes were established by the Swedish industrialist Alfred Nobel, the inventor of dynamite. Along with Maathai, 7 Americans, 2 Israelis, 1 Australian and 1 Norwegian were honoured with these prestigious awards in 2004.
378 "Environmentalist Awarded Nobel Peace Prize", [cited 21 April 2009]. Online: www.greenbeltmovement.org.
379 Taking *estai* ("will come") and *ouk anexountai* ("they will not endure") as predictive future tenses, stating what will undoubtedly happen.
380 The verb used here is *knethein*, which means "to scratch", and in the passive, "to be scratched" or "tickled" (Bernard, 141).
381 Fee, 235. See also Bernard, 141.
382 Mounce, 575.
383 Taking *episoreusousin* (they will accumulate), *apostrepsousin* (they will turn away) and *ektrapesontai* (they will turn aside) as predictive future tenses, stating something that will definitely happen.
384 The verb *episoreuein* is a compound from *epi* + *soros* (a mound) and it means "to heap together", one after another.
385 The present tense *spendomai* is a futuristic present in terms of fulfillment.
386 Kelly, 208.
387 Barclay, 235. See also Fee, 238; Ward, 210–211; Kelly, 208.
388 The perfect *ephesteken* ("has come") is intensive and indicates the status of things.
389 The perfect tenses *egonismai*, *teteleka*, and *tetereka* are extensive in shade. Paul is referring to a completed action.
390 Kelly, 208.
391 Fee, 238.
392 Mounce, 579.
393 Mounce (580) and Bernard (143), among others, regard "the faith" here as objective, whereas Fee (238–239), Barclay (236) and Kelly (209) argue that it is subjective.
394 Barclay, 238.
395 The former position regards the genitive *tes dikaiosunes* as epexegetical, the latter as a genitive of possession. The latter position is supported by Bernard (143) and Mounce (582). The main support for the epexegetical interpretation is that in some other places in the New Testament where crown is followed by a genitive, this would be the best way of taking it. The references are given in the text.
396 Kelly, 210.
397 Barclay, 238.
398 Suggested by the perfect verb "have longed for" (Ward, 212).
399 Fee, 250.
400 Kelly, 222; Mounce, 600.

401 Paul uses the aorist tense, which would literally be translated as "I sent", implying that Tychicus set out in the past. But it is likely that Paul is using what is called the epistolary aorist in which the writer puts himself in the shoes of the one receiving the letter. When Tychicus delivers this letter to Timothy, Timothy will say that "Paul sent Tychicus". See also Fee, 244; Mounce, 591; Ward, 213.
402 Hultgren (141–142) comments: "Whether Mark is assumed to be in Ephesus or is to be summoned by Timothy along the way to Rome is not clear; although the latter appears more probable." Bernard (146) puts it this way: "It is probable that at the time of writing 2 Timothy Mark was somewhere on the coast in the Province of Asia Proper, and thus Timothy could pick him up on his way northwards".
403 Commenting on Mark, Barclay (245) says that Jesus can "turn the shame of failure to the joy of triumphant service" and that in Mark, "the quitter has become the man who can turn his hand to anything in the service of Paul and of the gospel". See also Ward, 215.
404 Even some who doubt the Pauline authorship of the Pastoral Epistles regard this as one of the fragments written by Paul himself. (See the Introduction for a fuller discussion of issues of authorship.)
405 Barclay, 247; see also Kelly, 215. The Greek *phailones* describes the type of cloak the Romans called a *paenula*.
406 See Bernard, 147.
407 See Kelly, 216.
408 See Fee, 244.
409 Kelly (217) suggests a specific occasion, but if both *enedexato* (did a great deal of harm) and *anteste* (opposed) are taken as constative, they can be understood as summarizing numerous actions.
410 The present imperative *phulassou* indicates that this is to be his constant attitude.
411 Mounce (594) comments: "Although Alexander has done considerable harm to Paul, it is doubtful that Paul's primary motive in mentioning him is to call down judgement. It seems more likely that Paul's love and concern for Timothy prompt the warning."
412 This is something that will happen, taking *apodosei* as a predictive future tense.
413 Ward, 220.
414 This position was popular among early commentators who believed that Paul wrote the Pastoral Epistles and accepted that there was a second Roman imprisonment view. See Kelly, 217; Mounce, 597.
415 Barclay, 248; Fee, 245; Bernard, 148; Kelly, 218; Mounce, 595.
416 Kelly, 218.
417 Mounce, 595.
418 Ward (220) gives the meaning of *paregeneto* (an aorist form) as "to support either as advocate or as witness". See also Kelly, 218.
419 Mounce, 596.
420 Ward, 220; Kelly, 218.
421 Fee, 246. The word used is *kerygma*.
422 "Fully proclaimed, accomplished, carried out or completed" convey a more accurate idea than the "fully known", used in translations like the kjv.
423 Ward (221), says, "In the crowd which attended the trial we may see the representatives of all the Gentiles. Both at the time and in the subsequent gossip the gospel was made known to men." See also Kelly (219), "By 'all nations' Paul is likely alluding to the cosmopolitan audience assembled in the imperial court before whom he delivered his message."
424 Kelly, 219; Ward, 221. The interpretation that this is a generic saying rather than a specific reference is strengthened by the absence of any article before the word "lion".
425 Taking *errusthen* (delivered) as a constative aorist, summarizing the Lord's handling of each activity and every word that could have resulted in his death at the conclusion of the preliminary examination. The preposition "from" in the expression "from the lion's mouth" would be literally translated "out of", which suggests that he was in imminent danger of death.
426 Barclay, 249.
427 See, for example, Kelly, 220; Bernard, 149; Fee, 247.

[428] Barclay, 249.
[429] Kelly, 220.
[430] For more on Priscilla and Aquila, see Mounce, 599.
[431] Mounce, 600.
[432] Fee, 251; Barrett, 124; Kelly, 222.
[433] The first "you" is singular and is addressed to Timothy; the second is plural and addresses other members of the church.
[434] Mounce, 601.
[435] Kelly, 223.

Titus

1. J. N. D. Kelly, *A Commentary on the Pastoral Epistles: I & II Timothy, Titus* (Black's New Testament Commentaries; London: Adam & Charles Black, 1963), 226. See also William D. Mounce, *The Pastoral Epistles* (Word Biblical Commentary; Nashville: Thomas Nelson, 2000), 378; W. Barclay, *The Letters of Paul to Timothy, Titus and Philemon* (Philadelphia: Westminster, 1975), 227.
2. *Iesou Christou* can be treated as a genitive of relationship or a genitive of possession.
3. The usual translation of the preposition *kata* followed by the accusative case would be "according to". However, the translation "for" is supported by many scholars including J. H. Bernard, *The Pastoral Epistles* (Thornapple Commentaries; Grand Rapids: Baker, 1980), 155; G. D. Fee, *1 and 2 Timothy, Titus* (A Good News Commentary; San Francisco: Harper & Row, 1984), 122; Kelly, 226; Mounce, 379). See also the note on *kat' epangelian zoes* in the commentary on 2 Timothy 1:1b.
4. R. A. Ward, *A Commentary on I & II Timothy and Titus* (Waco: Word Books, 1974), 233.
5. See also commentary on 2 Tim 2:10.
6. Taking *aletheias* as an objective genitive.
7. Arland J. Hultgren, *I–II Timothy, Titus* (Augsburg Commentary on the New Testament; Minneapolis: Augsburg, 1984), 150.
8. Hultgren, 150.
9. The preposition in the phrase *aletheias tes kat' eusebeian* can be interpreted as indicating that the purpose of the truth is to produce godliness (as in the tniv and hcsb). However, it can also be interpreted as indicating that "the truth" is equivalent to godliness. Hence the NRSV translates the phrase as "in accordance with godliness" (see also the nasb and nkjv). Though the two possible functions of the phrase do not need to exclude each other, the latter is preferred here. This view is also supported by Mounce, 379; Bernard, 155; William Barclay, *Letters of Paul to Timothy, Titus and Philemon* (Philadelphia: Westminster, 1975), 229; Kelly, 227.
10. Mounce, 380.
11. In this case, *epi* in 1:2 is taken as parallel to *kata* in 1:1 (translated "for") and as having the same function (that is, introducing a purpose statement). A similar use of *epi* with a dative to express purpose is found in Ephesians 2:10, where *epi ergois* is translated "for good works" (nasb, nrsv, hcsb, nkjv) or "to good works" (niv). Similarly, the *epi akatharsia* of 1 Thessalonians 4:7 is translated as "for the purpose of impurity" (nasb); "to uncleanness" (nkjv); "to impurity" (hcsb, nrsv); "to be impure" (niv). The interpretation of the preposition as expressing purpose in Titus is supported by M. Dibelius and H. Conzelmann (*The Pastoral Epistles* [Hermeneia; trans. P. Buttolph and A. Yarbro; ed. H. Koester; Philadelphia: Fortress Press, 1972], 131), Kelly (227) and Mounce (380).
12. Taking *zoes aioniou* as an epexegetical genitive.
13. Calvin endorsed this view in his commentary on the Epistles to Timothy, Titus and Philemon.
14. Taking *epengeilato* (promised) as a constative aorist.
15. Ward, 235; Hultgren, 151.
16. Barclay, 231.
17. The Greek phrase *ton logon autou en kerugmati* is an example of anacoluthon, a rhetorical form in which the syntax of a sentence does not follow strict grammatical rules and the reader is expected to supply whatever is needed to make sense of it. The problem is that translators disagree about what is needed. The rsv, for example, has supplied "in", to make it read "manifested in his word". The problem with this rendering is that if this were the meaning, "word" would be in the dative

18. case, but here it is in the accusative case. The nasb addresses the problem by inserting the word "even", to give the translation, "manifested, even His word, in the proclamation with which I was entrusted". C. K. Barrett, *The Pastoral Epistles in the New English Bible* (Oxford: Clarendon Press, 1963), 127, argues that it is better to "keep closer to the ... somewhat clumsy Greek and say: he manifested his word." This position is adopted by the niv, nrsv, nkjv, hcsb and nasb.
18. Whichever interpretation one chooses has to recognize that the particle at the beginning of 1:3 establishes a relationship between the two periods Paul refers to, the period when the promise was made and the period when it was brought to light. This point applies regardless of whether the particle is translated as "but" (nasb, nkjv) or "and" (tniv, hcsb). The content of the promise and the manifestation thus need to be viewed as parallel. In other words, what was promised is what was manifested. In both cases, it is "the hope of eternal life". There is no reason why the relative pronoun "which" cannot be the object of both "promised" and "brought to light".
19. In this interpretation, the accusative *ton logon* is taken as an adverbial accusative of manner, translatable as "by way of his word".
20. Ward is not wrong when he says, "The life was manifested in the incarnation of Jesus Christ and in a secondary way is still manifested (in another way) in the sermon." However, his comment extends "word of God" beyond its usage in the Pastoral Epistles.
21. Bernard, 156; Fee, 123; Hultgren, 151; Kelly, 123; Mounce, 381.
22. *Kerygma* can mean the content of the gospel message (Bernard, 156; Kelly, 228) or the act of making the message of the gospel known. Given that Paul has just used the "word" to refer to the content of the gospel, it is likely that here "preaching" should be understood as an action. Those who do interpret "preaching" as referring to the content of the gospel see it as a more specific reference to the heart of Paul's message. However it is doubtful that Paul would distinguish between different parts of the gospel message in this way.
23. The personal pronouns "me" or "I" ("with which I was entrusted" nasb) are emphatic.
24. Barclay, 232.
25. The former position is represented by Kelly (228): "As in 1 Timothy 1:2, Paul is recalling that his disciple is one of his own converts" (see also Barclay, 233). The latter position is taken by Fee (123–124): "He is a legitimate child of Paul in carrying on Paul's ministry" (see also Hultgren, 152). Bernard (156) stresses "that we have no certain proof on the point".
26. Fee, 123–124.
27. Barrett, 129.
28. Ward, 237.
29. See commentary on 1 Timothy 1:2.
30. The Greek has *toutou charin*.
31. W. Bauer, W. F. Arndt, F. W. Gingrich, and F. W. Danker. *Greek-English Lexicon of the New Testament and Other Early Christian Literature*. 2nd ed. Chicago: University of Chicago Press. (From now on referred to as BAGD.)
32. Kelly, 230. See also Barrett, 126.
33. Mounce, 387.
34. This position takes the *kai* before *katasteses* (you may appoint) to mean "including" or "especially" (see Mounce, 387), not "and", as it regularly does.
35. In the Pastoral Epistles Paul often first makes a general point and then highlights a crucial aspect of it. For example, in 1 Timothy 2:1-2 Paul starts with prayer for all men and then singles out kings and others in authority for prayer. Similarly in 2 Timothy 1:15 he says that "everyone deserted me" and then singles out Phygelus and Hermogenes.
36. Mounce, 387.
37. The word *pista*, from *pistos*, could mean "having faith" or "being faithful", depending on the context.
38. Mounce, 388. See also Fee, 127.
39. Dibelius and Conzelmann, 132.
40. Ward, 239.
41. Barclay, 263–264.

42 Barclay, 264.
43 Mounce, 389. Also, Ward, 239.
44 Mounce, 389.
45 Kelly (231) says, "A man who cannot bring up his children to be well behaved must lack the combination of sympathy and firmness called for in an elder." Fee (127) says, "A good look at the man's home life will tell much about his character and his ability to give leadership to the church".
46 Personal choice is implied in verses like John 3:16 and Revelation 3:20.
47 Kelly, 232; Barclay, 236.
48 Barclay, 266. The Greek adjective describing the former is *thumos*, and for the latter it is *orgilos*. Paul uses *orgilos* in this letter.
49 Kelly, 232–233.
50 Ward, 242.
51 Barrett, 130.
52 Barclay, 239.
53 Barrett, 130; Hultgren, 155–156.
54 Fee, 132; Kelly, 234; Mounce, 396.
55 Barclay, 241; Kelly, 234; Mounce, 396; Ward, 243.
56 Fee (132) takes this position.
57 Hultgren's (157) caution that "the question has to be left open whether these persons are recent converts from Judaism who have introduced former Jewish ways into Christian thought and practice, or whether they may be of Gentile origin" would be appropriate except for the fact that "of the circumcision" describes Jews as a people.
58 Ward, 243. The phrase "of the circumcision" is used several times in the New Testament. In Romans 4:12 it refers to Jews in general, and in Acts 10:45; 11:2; Galatians 2:12 and Colossians 4:11 it refers to Jewish Christians. The argument that this is an ethnic rather than a theological faction is strengthened by the fact that the same group are referred to as "Cretans" in 1:12, where the term does not focus on their ethnicity but on their residence. Jews and Gentiles alike could be referred to as Cretans if they lived on Crete.
59 Mounce, 400.
60 Bernard, 161.
61 Stromata I. 59.2; see Barclay, 243.
62 Ward, 245: "first half of the sixth century bc"; Kelly, 235: "sixth century bc".
63 Kelly, 235; Hultgren, 157.
64 Kelly, 131. For discussion of this attribution, see Barrett, 131.
65 Barclay, 243.
66 Dibelius and Conzelmann, 137.
67 Barrett, 151; Fee, 133; Ward, 245. Also, Samuel Ngewa, *The Gospel of John* (Nairobi: Evangel Publishing House, 2003), 220–221.
68 Ward, 245.
69 The imperative verb "rebuke" is in the present tense, showing that this is to be his habit. The same tense is used in 1 Timothy 5:20 (where it relates to instructions for dealing with elders). The aorist imperative form is found in 2 Tim 4:2 (where Paul is instructing Timothy about his ministry at Ephesus) and the present infinitive in Titus 1:9.
70 Ward, 246.
71 *Anastreph* is used in John and *anatrep* in Titus.
72 Mounce, 397.
73 Fee, 133.
74 The participle *didaskontes* may be taken as a participle of manner, stating how the ruining is achieved, or as a causal participle.
75 Fee, 133.
76 Fee, 135.

77 Hultgren (159) speaks of "their commitment to a Jewish-Christian Gnosticism". Barrett (133) also says that the claim that "'they know God' indicates the gnostic tendency of the heretics … It is true, as some commentators point out, that this claim could also be Jewish, but it seems to be a Jewish gnosticism with which we are dealing". For further information about Gnosticism as a philosophy see note 23 of the commentary on 1 Timothy.
78 This position is supported by Fee (136) and Ward (248). The addition of "him" is preferred by Hultgren (159), Kelly (237) and Mounce (403).
79 Ward, 248.
80 Bernard, 163.
81 Barclay, 246.
82 Mounce identifies them as "stories the opponents had created around Old Testament characters, stories that contained their secret knowledge". The midrashic approach to the Old Testament opened the door to endless interpretations of any passage.
83 Taking the genitive *anthropon*, qualifying "commands" as a genitive of source.
84 Barclay, 276.
85 "Corrupted" and "not believing" share one article and so are to be taken as referring to the same group (Granville Sharp's rule).
86 The second person pronoun "you" is emphatic. This together with the adversative "but" draws a sharp contrast between Titus's role and the negative contribution of the false teachers. Similar emphatic constructions are used in 1 Timothy 6:11; 2 Timothy 3:10, 14, and 4:5. In each case, Paul is drawing a contrast between Timothy or Titus and those who are in error.
87 The verb "teach" (literally "speak", nasb) is in the present tense, indicating that this is to be a habit.
88 Ward, 252.
89 Mounce, 411.
90 Donald Guthrie, *The Pastoral Epistles* (Tyndale New Testament Commentary Series; Grand Rapids: Eerdmans, 1957), 193.
91 The type of love referred to here is *phileo* (friendship), not *eros* or *agape* love.
92 Ward, 253.
93 Barclay, 284. The Greek uses the singular "opponent" (nasb).
94 Dibelius and Conzelmann, 140.
95 E. F. Scott, *The Pastoral Epistles* (Moffatt New Testament Commentary; London: Hodder & Stoughton, 1948), 164–165.
96 The word *hupotassein* means "subject oneself, be subjected or subordinated, obey".
97 Scott, 165.
98 R. C. Trench, *Synonyms of the New Testament* (London: 1880; repr., Grand Rapids: Eerdmans, 1963), 96.
99 E. K. Simpson, *The Pastoral Epistles* (Grand Rapids: Eerdmans, 1954), 109.
100 Kelly, 243.
101 For discussion on the use of Saviour for God, see 1 Timothy 2:3.
102 *Parechomenos* (set or show) is an independent imperatival participle and emphasizes that this is a serious matter. As with "teach" in 2:1, the present tense indicates that this is to be a matter of practice.
103 Ward, 255.
104 Kelly (242) defines *semnos* as "moral earnestness, affecting outward demeanour as well as interior intention."
105 Barclay, 284.
106 The Greek uses the singular "opponent" (nasb), but is not referring to a particular individual. It uses the singular to identify a category of people who oppose Titus and the gospel he stands for.
107 Scott, 165.
108 Kelly, 242–243. See, also, Fee, 143.
109 Assuming that these present imperatives are iterative, they are an instruction to keep on encouraging and rebuking whenever it is necessary.

110 Fee (150) argues for the inclusion of 1:10–16; Mounce (432) and Ward (264) argue that "these things" refers to the entire letter.
111 Kelly, 247; Barclay, 289.
112 Bernard (174) takes the wider view, while Mounce restricts its application to just the rebuking (432).
113 See the commentary on *epitage* (command) in 1 Timothy 1:1.
114 Kelly, 244.
115 This is inferred from seeing the verb "has appeared" as a whole, taking *epephane* ("appeared") as a constative aorist. See also Mounce, 422; Kelly, 244; Fee, 147.
116 With that understanding, the focus of the aorist *epephane* would then be resultative. This is what NIV and NASB have, translating it as "has appeared". Fee (147) adds that it was then that "the educative dimension of grace, emphasized in verse 12, took place."
117 Here we have a dative (*tois anthropois*) serving as an indirect object.
118 Bernard, 170; Kelly, 245; Mounce, 422.
119 Mounce, 422.
120 Mounce, 423–424.
121 Ward, 259.
122 This interpretation taking the verb *arnesamenoi* (to say "No") as a constative aorist. However, because the aorist can also be used to represent a single action rather than an ongoing one, some scholars argue that this "saying 'No'" took place on one specific occasion, such as at baptism. Bernard (171) says, "The aorist participle seems to point to a definite act of renunciation, such as is made at baptism, which is everywhere in the nt contemplated as the beginning of the Christian life." Kelly (245) says, "The decisiveness of this rupture with the past is brought out in the original by the word rendered 'renounce', which is in the aorist participle indicating a once-for-all act. It is not far-fetched to see in it a reference to their baptism, when they turned their back on their pagan life and accepted Christ." However, although this reading is possible, there is no suggestion of any link to baptism in the context to support it, and it seems preferable to interpret the aorist as summarizing all the actions involved in changing from a life of vice to a life of virtue.
123 The word *zesomen* (live) is either an inceptive/ingressive aorist, focusing on the start of this life, in which case the preferred translation is "may begin to live" (Mounce, 424) or a constative aorist, referring to our new way of life as a whole, from its beginnings in the past to its continuance in the present. The latter view is preferred here.
124 Mounce, 424.
125 Barclay, 288.
126 Ibid.
127 Kelly, 245; Mounce, 424; Ward, 259. However, Bernard (171) cautions that "anything like a sharp division is not to be pressed".
128 One article is shared by both, indicating that "appearing" is in apposition to "blessed hope".
129 The genitive *tes doxes* (of the glory) could be a qualitative genitive, translated as "glorious appearing". Or it could be subjective genitive, with glory as the subject of the implied verb "appearing". Either translation is possible, but in this commentary and in the tniv it is taken to be a subjective genitive. The glory will appear and is owned by someone (Christ Jesus) who common sense implies will appear at the same time, exhibiting the glory.
130 The Granville Sharp rule applies here, for the construction includes two nouns in the same case (*theou* and *soteros*) connected by kai, and the article *tou* is used only with the first noun. Thus *Iesou Christou* which is an epexegetical genitive/genitive of apposition, is identified as both God and Saviour.
131 Taking the aorist *edoken* here as constative.
132 The preposition *huper* does not exclude the idea of "instead of us" (represented by *anti*), but includes and goes beyond it to include the idea of "as our representative".
133 Scores are based on the annual reports by Transparency International (*Corruption Perception Index*, n.p. [cited 25 February 2009]. Online: http://www.transparency.org/policy_research/surveys_indices/cpi).

134 Fee (153) says, "In 2:1–14 the concern for 'good works' had to do largely with relationship between believers, which when seen by outsiders would keep them from 'speaking evil of the message' [2:5] and perhaps would even attract them to it [2:1–10]. Now the interest centers in the effect of Christian behavior upon outsiders [3:1–2, 8]. Again, as in 2:1–14, Paul offers a theological basis for such behavior [3:3–7], this time in the form of a semicreedal statement about salvation". See also Kelly, 249.
135 These are the secondary objects of the imperative "remind" (3:1). The primary object is "the people".
136 Barclay, 290–291; Mounce, 444.
137 The nasb translation "rulers, authorities" is correct, assuming that the omission of *kai* between *archais* and *exousiais* is correct. What we have here is an asyndeton (leaving out of conjunctions) which is "probably best explained as due to the fact that the verse as a whole can be regarded as a listing which in fact contains in the Greek no 'and' at any point" (Barrett, 139; see also Mounce, 444).
138 The distinction between "ruling" and "having authority" as a leader can be described as the difference between actually functioning as a leader when ruling and inherently having authority because of the position of leadership one holds. See also Ward, 265.
139 Barrett (139) says, "Wives and slaves are not told submissively to obey what is wrong, but to recognize the authority (which God himself has given) of those whose calling is different from their own. ... In the same way the Christian may and must recognize the (God-given) authority of the state, but without being submissive to it in a servile way."
140 Mounce, 444.
141 Fee (154) says, "When the state turns against the church (as in the Revelation), believers will submit – (unto death!), and they do so precisely because they must not obey when it contravenes conscience (see Rev 6:9–11; 12:11; 13–14)."
142 Barrett, 139.
143 Ward, 264.
144 Barrett, 139; Kelly, 249; Ward, 265.
145 Barclay, 291.
146 Barclay, 291. Ward (266) says that the believer "should not be so 'regularly regular' with his bristles perfectly straight, that he ruins his message of love!"
147 Barclay, 292.
148 Kelly, 249–250.
149 Fee, 155.
150 The past continuous "were" (an imperfect tense in Greek) indicates that this used to be their way of life.
151 Mounce, 446.
152 Guthrie, 203; Kelly, 250; Mounce, 446; Ward, 267.
153 Kelly, 250; Bernard, 177; Fee, 155; Kelly, 250; Ward, 267.
154 The words translated "deceived" and "enslaved" are both present passive participles, indicating that the deception and enslavement were done by someone else and were an ongoing condition.
155 Fee, 155.
156 *Epithumia* (desire) is neutral but is used in the negative sense here, and so can rightly be translated as "lusts". *Edone* (pleasure) is only used here in Paul's writings, and is also neutral in itself.
157 The present tense participle denotes that this was their lifestyle at that time.
158 Ward, 267–268.
159 Ward, 268.
160 Fee, 155.
161 The present tense participle translated "hating" indicates that this was their state when they were unbelievers.
162 John uses an aorist subjunctive to indicate that he is speaking of sinning as a sinful act, rather than as a way of life.

163 Taking the aorist *genethomen* as resultative. The focus of the verb is on what we have become (heirs).
164 The genitive *zoes aioniou* (of eternal life) could modify "heirs", in which case it is a qualitative genitive and the meaning is "eternal life which believers will inherit". Alternatively, it could be an epexegetical genitive, specifying the substance of the hope, which is "eternal life". If we take the second position, "heir" is absolute and we still have to debate exactly what is inherited. Bernard (170) says that the inheritance is "all the evangelical promises in Christ."
165 Mounce, 451.
166 For more on the description of God as our Saviour, see commentary on 1 Timothy 1:1 (also Titus 1:3; 2:10; 1 Tim 2:3; 4:10).
167 Barclay, 293.
168 Taking the aorist *epephane* as constative.
169 See, for example 2 Maccabees 14:9.
170 Barrett, 141.
171 The genitive pronoun "his" stands for God.
172 The nasb renders the Greek more literally as, "not on the basis of deeds which we have done in righteousness". The aorist *epoiesamen* (we have done) is constative, summarizing all our deeds before God acted on our behalf; "in righteousness" focuses on the sphere of righteousness.
173 Taking the genitive *pneumatos hagiou* (of the Holy Spirit) as subjective means it is the Holy Spirit who brings the renewal, and thus the translation "by the Holy Spirit".
174 Barrett (141), Bernard (178) and Hultgren (170) all support the link to baptism, but there is no necessity to assume this.
175 The former position takes the genitive *palingenesias* (of rebirth) as objective, and the latter as epexegetical.
176 The Greek word translated "and" may be explanatory, indicating that rebirth is the same as renewal by the Holy Spirit or it may be copulative, linking rebirth and renewal as two different things.
177 Fee, 157.
178 This position takes the genitive "of rebirth" as objective (baptism produces rebirth) and "the Holy Spirit" as subjective (the Holy Spirit's act is "to be coming").
179 Fee, 158. See also Mounce, 448-449.
180 Although there is no indication of who does the regeneration, it is clearly implied that it is one of the Trinity.
181 Taking the aorist *execheen* (poured) as constative, referring to everything God has made available to us, which we realize by faith.
182 Mounce, 451.
183 See also 1 Timothy 1:15; 3:1; 4:9; 2 Timothy 2:11. This occurrence is the last one in the canonical order (1 Tim, 2 Tim, Titus), but the fourth in chronological order (1 Tim, Titus, 2 Tim).
184 Mounce, 452.
185 Fee (152), for example, thinks the focus is on the theological statements. He says that *touton* "refers at least to verses 4-7, but perhaps Paul intends to include all of verses 1-7." He then goes on to say, "As in 2:11-14, and elsewhere in Paul (cf. Romans 12:1-2; Galatians 5:6), the appeal for truly Christian behaviour is predicated on a proper hearing of the gospel." Kelly (254) also says that it refers to "the truth just expounded about God's free grace and our rebirth in baptism through the Spirit". Mounce (452) is an example of those who think the focus is on the ethical exhortations. He says that *touton* "includes all of chapter 3 with the demands it places in lifestyle, specifically the qualities enumerated in vv. 1-2 and perhaps recalling the *tauta*, 'these things' in 2:15." He then adds, "It is essential that they live out the practical implications of their theology as expressed by the creed."
186 The act of believing is presented in the perfect tense as an exercise of faith with results that continue in the present.
187 Kelly (254) comments that this interpretation introduces "a completely fresh and not strictly relevant theme."

188. Mounce, 452. See also Kelly, 254.
189. Titus 1:16; 2:7, 14; 3:1, 8, 14; also 1 Tim 2:10; 3:1; 5:10, 25; 6:18; 2 Tim 2:21; 3:17.
190. Ward, 277.
191. Bernard, 180.
192. The use of the present tense means that avoiding them should be his regular practice.
193. This is a typically Pauline evaluation of the teachings of his opponents.
194. Mounce, 453.
195. Again, the present tense indicates that this is to be Titus's regular practice. The same phrase is used in 1 Timothy 4:7.
196. In the letters of Ignatius of Antioch, one of the earliest church fathers (see Hultgren, 173; Kelly, 256; Mounce, 454).
197. Hultgren, 173.
198. Taking the perfect participle *eidos* is causal.
199. Taking the shade of the perfect *exestraptai* as intensive, to indicate that they have become perverted and have remained that way.
200. The present tense participle *on* is used with "condemned" (thus, "being condemned") to indicate that the condemnation is simultaneous with the sinning. The habit of sinning is the mother of the condemnation.
201. Hultgren, 174. Ward (278) treats *exestraptai* as passive and not as middle and comments that such a person has been turned aside and "is therefore on the wrong road. He is sinful: he goes on sinning by remaining on the wrong road. He is self-condemned in that he has rejected conscience, made shipwreck of his own faith and is willing to overturn the faith of others (cf. 1 Timothy 1:19; 2 Timothy 2:18) without a thought of the church or its members." See also Mounce (454): "The result of a steadfast refusal to repent (v. 10) is perversion and constant sin, and the sin condemns the sinner (hence self-condemned)"; Fee (163–164): "By his very persistence in his sinful behavior he has condemned himself, thus putting himself on the outside, hence to be rejected by Titus and the church".
202. Barclay, 299; Barrett, 147; Bernard, 182; Hultgren, 174; Kelly, 257; Mounce, 457; Ward, 279.
203. Bernard, 182; Kelly, 257.
204. Mounce, 458.
205. Kelly, 258; Barrett, 148.
206. The tniv translation "and see that they have everything they need" loses the power of *ina*, expressing purpose or result. The nasb renders the Greek more accurately.
207. The Greek has the two particles, *de* and *kai*, at the beginning of 3:14.
208. Kelly, 258.
209. Mounce, 459.
210. Barclay, 298.
211. Note the imperative: "our people must learn" (niv); "let our people learn" (esv).
212. This phrase could be translated as "those who love us with loyalty." The fact that *pistis* (faith) does not have an article has led to some discussion of whether it could mean "faithful" or "loyal". This conclusion seems unnecessary. *Pistis* does not need an article to mean "faith". Here, it expresses the sphere within which the bond between Paul, Titus and the believers exists.
213. For more on grace, see the commentary on 1 Tim 1:2.

BIBLIOGRAPHY

Adeyemo, Tokunboh, ed. *Africa Bible Commentary*. Nairobi: WordAlive, 2006.
BAGD. See Bauer, W., W. F. Arndt, F. W. Gingrich and F. W. Danker.
Barclay, William. *The Letters of Paul to Timothy, Titus and Philemon*. 1956. 3rd. rev. ed. Louisville, Ken.: Westminster John Knox, 2003.
Barrett, C. K. *The Pastoral Epistles in the New English Bible with Introduction and Commentary*. Oxford: Clarendon, 1963.
Bauer, W., W. F. Arndt, F. W. Gingrich and F. W. Danker. *Greek-English Lexicon of the New Testament and Other Early Christian Literature*. A translation and adaptation of Walter Bauer's *Griechsch-Deutsches Worterbuch zu den Schriften des Neuen Testaments und der ubrigen urchristlichen Literatur*. 2nd ed. Chicago: University of Chicago Press, 1979.
Bernard, J. H. *The Pastoral Epistles*. Thornapple Commentaries. 1899. Repr., Grand Rapids: Baker, 1980.
Dibelius, Martin and Hans Conzelmann. *The Pastoral Epistles*. Hermeneia Series. Translated by P. Buttolph and A. Yarbro. Edited by Helmet Koester. Philadelphia: Fortress, 1972.
Easton, Burton Scott. *The Pastoral Epistles: Introduction, Translation, Commentary and Word Studies*. New York: Charles Scribner's Sons, 1947.
Ellicott, Charles J. *A Critical and Grammatical Commentary on the Pastoral Epistles*. Andover: Warren F. Draper, 1865.
Evans, Craig A. and Stanley E. Porter, eds. *Dictionary of New Testament Background*. Downers Grove: InterVarsity Press, 2000.
Fee, Gordon D. *1 and 2 Timothy, Titus*. A Good News Commentary. San Francisco: Harper & Row, 1984.
Gonzalez, Justo L. *The Early Church to the Dawn of the Reformation*. Vol. 1 of *The Story of Christianity*. San Francisco: Harper & Row, 1984.
Gromacki, R. G. *Stand True to the Charge: An Exposition of 1 Timothy*. Grand Rapids: Baker, 1982.
Guthrie, Donald. *The Pastoral Epistles: An Introduction and Commentary*. Tyndale New Testament Commentary Series. Grand Rapids: Eerdmans, 1957.
Hanson, A. T. *The Pastoral Epistles*. The New Century Bible Commentary. Grand Rapids: Eerdmans, 1982.
Harrison, P. N. *The Problem of the Pastoral Epistles*. London: Oxford University Press, 1921.
Hendriksen, William. *Exposition of the Pastoral Epistles*. New Testament Commentary. Grand Rapids: Baker, 1957.
Hiebert, D. E. *1 Timothy*. Chicago: Moody, 1957.
Hultgren, Arland J. *I–II Timothy, Titus*. Augsburg Commentary on the New Testament. Minneapolis: Augsburg, 1984.

Kelly, J. N. D. *A Commentary on the Pastoral Epistles: I & II Timothy, Titus*. Black's New Testament Commentaries. London: Adam & Charles Black, 1963.

Knight, George W. *The Pastoral Epistles*. New International Greek Testament Commentary. Grand Rapids: Eerdmans, 1992.

Kostenberger, Andreas J., Thomas R. Schreiner and H. Scott Baldwin, eds. *Women in the Church: A Fresh Analysis of I Timothy 2:9–15*. Grand Rapids: Baker, 1995.

Liddell, Henry G. and Robert Scott. *A Greek-English Lexicon*. Oxford: Clarendon, 1968.

Liddon, H. P. *Explanatory Analysis of St. Paul's First Epistle to Timothy*. London: Longmans, Green and Company, 1897.

Liefeld, Walter. *1 & 2 Timothy, Titus*. NIV Application Commentary. Grand Rapids: Zondervan, 1999.

Lock, Walter. *A Critical and Exegetical Commentary on the Pastoral Epistles*. Edinburgh: T&T Clark, 1924.

Marshall, I. Howard and Philip H. Towner, *The Pastoral Epistles: A Critical and Exegetical Commentary*. International Critical Commentary. London: T&T Clark, 1999.

Mounce, William D. *Pastoral Epistles*. Word Biblical Commentary. Nashville: Thomas Nelson, 2000.

Ramsay, William M. *Historical Commentary on the Pastoral Epistles*. Edited by Mark Wilson. Grand Rapids: Kregel, 1996.

Robertson, A. T. *A Grammar of the Greek New Testament in the Light of Historical Research*. 4th rev. ed. New York: Hodder & Stoughton, 1923.

Scott, E. F. *The Pastoral Epistles*. Moffatt New Testament Commentary. London: Hodder & Stoughton, 1936.

Shaw, Mark. *The Kingdom of God in Africa: A Short History of African Christianity*. Grand Rapids: Baker, 1996.

Simpson, E. K. *The Pastoral Epistles*. Grand Rapids: Eerdmans, 1954.

Stott, John. *Guard the Truth: The Message of I Timothy and Titus*. Downers Grove: InterVarsity Press, 1996.

Towner, Philip H. *1–2 Timothy and Titus*. IVP New Testament Commentary. Edited by Grant R. Osborne. Downers Grove: InterVarsity Press, 1994.

Ward, Ronald A. *A Commentary on I & II Timothy and Titus*. Waco: Word, 1974.

www.ingramcontent.com/pod-product-compliance
Lightning Source LLC
Chambersburg PA
CBHW060910300426
44112CB00011B/1409